AUTOBIOGRAPHY

OF AN ARCHIVE

CULTURES OF HISTORY

CULTURES OF HISTORY

Nicholas Dirks, Series Editor

The death of history, reported at the end of the twentieth century, was clearly premature. It has become a hotly contested battleground in struggles over identity, citizenship, and claims of recognition and rights. Each new national history proclaims itself as ancient and universal, while the contingent character of its focus raises questions about the universality and objectivity of any historical tradition. Globalization and American hegemony have created cultural, social, local, and national backlashes. Cultures of History is a new series of books that investigates the forms, understandings, genres, and histories of history, taking history as the primary text of modern life and the foundational basis for state, society, and nation.

Shail Mayaram, *Against History, Against State:*
Counterperspectives from the Margins

Tapati Guha-Thakurta, *Monuments, Objects, Histories:*
Institutions of Art in Colonial and Postcolonial India

Charles Hirschkind, *The Ethical Soundscape:*
Cassette Sermons and Islamic Counterpublics

Ahmad H. Sa'di and Lila Abu-Lughod, editors, *Nakba:*
Palestine, 1948, and the Claims of Memory

Prachi Deshpande, *Creative Pasts:*
Historical Memory and Identity in Western India, 1700–1960

Todd Presner, *Mobile Modernity: Germans, Jews, Trains*

Laura Bear, *Lines of the Nation: Indian Railway Workers,*
Bureaucracy, and the Intimate Historical Self

Vazira Fazila-Yacoobali Zamindar, *The Long Partition and the*
Making of Modern South Asia: Refugees, Boundaries, Histories

Bernard Bate, *Tamil Oratory and the Dravidian Aesthetic:*
Democratic Practice in South India

AUTOBIOGRAPHY OF AN ARCHIVE

A Scholar's Passage to India

NICHOLAS B. DIRKS

COLUMBIA UNIVERSITY PRESS   NEW YORK

Columbia University Press
Publishers Since 1893
New York   Chichester, West Sussex
cup.columbia.edu
Copyright © 2015 Columbia University Press
All rights reserved

Library of Congress Cataloging-in-Publication Data
Dirks, Nicholas B., 1950–
Autobiography of an archive : a scholar's passage to India /
Nicholas B. Dirks
pages cm. — (Cultures of history)
Includes bibliographical references and index.
ISBN 978-0-231-16966-0 (cloth) — ISBN 978-0-231-16967-7 (pbk.) —
ISBN 978-0-231-53851-0 (e-book)
1. Anthropology and history—India.   2. Anthropological archives—
India.   3. Education, Higher—Philosophy—United
States.   4. Interdisciplinary research—Philosophy.   I. Title.

GN345.2.D57   2015
301.0954—dc23

2014020993

Cover design: Jordan Wannemacher

Contents

Part III. Empire

Part IV. The Politics of Knowledge

Part V. University

Acknowledgments

The essays and lectures that make up this book have been written over many years, beginning with a paper that started life as a "job talk" in 1987 for a tenured position at the University of Michigan. That paper, entitled "Castes of Mind," was expanded and finally revised for publication in the journal *Representations* and is included here because of its centrality to much of the scholarly work I did during the decade I spent in Michigan. I am grateful to my colleagues in the departments of history and anthropology at Michigan not just for hiring me but for offering an extraordinarily stimulating environment in which to think about the history and anthropology of caste in India as well as the larger comparative and interdisciplinary questions that enabled the writing both of numerous essays (many of them published here) and the book I subsequently wrote by the same title. Among many Michigan colleagues, I would like especially to thank Tom Trautmann, Bill Sewell, Sherry Ortner, Geoff Eley, (the late) Fernando Coronil, and Terry McDonald. I was delighted when Val Daniel and Ann Stoler came to Michigan two years after I arrived. Val has always been my advisor in matters anthropological, and both Val and Ann played important roles in helping me launch the interdepartmental program in anthropology and history; I owe Ann special thanks for her role over many years in helping me think through critical issues in the anthropology of empire and the ethnography of archives. I have also been indebted to many other colleagues, most importantly Gyan Prakash and Partha Chatterjee, for intellectual exchange, support, and sustenance over the years. David Ludden has been a friend, critic, and resource. I am also grateful to Arjun Appadurai, Chris Fuller, Sheldon Pollock, and Peter van der Veer for their insights and inspiration over the course of my career.

This book also owes a great deal to colleagues at Columbia University, where I taught from 1997 until 2013. In addition to some names already mentioned, I would like to thank David Cohen and Jonathan Cole, who recruited me to chair the legendary department of anthropology, and, among many valued colleagues, offer special thanks as well to Akeel Bilgrami, Mark Mazower, Martha Howell, Alan Brinkley, Tim Mitchell, Mahmood Mamdani, Gayatri Chakravarty Spivak, Claudio Lomnitz, Jean Howard, Ira Katznelson, and Peter Bearman.

My ethnographic encounters with academic administration would never have been possible without the trust, support, and counsel of Lee Bollinger.

In the end, my closest interlocutor for everything written here since 1994 has been my colleague and wife, Janaki Bakhle. She reads everything I write and always has the wisest, the sharpest, and most generous advice. She has sustained me through each one of these autobiographical experiments, in every possible way, and I will never be able to thank her enough.

I look back on some of my writings—covering as they do a span of twenty-five years—with mixed feelings and responses, including astonishment at some of my early concerns and on occasion dismay at some of my early ways of writing. When I think, however, of the scholarly opportunities I have had, across disciplines, continents, institutions, and friendships, I have only deep gratitude and a sense of enduring good fortune for my life in the academy.

As I note in my introduction, my parents have had enormous influence on my life. I dedicate this book to my mother, Annabelle V. Dirks, who played a critical role in supporting me during many stages of my autobiography of an archive, and for much else as well.

AUTOBIOGRAPHY
OF AN ARCHIVE

Introduction

Passage to India

I set off on my first passage to India when I was twelve years old. My father had a Fulbright grant to teach at Madras Christian College, in Tambaram, southern India, and he decided to take our entire family with him for the year. I remember being told about my family's plans some time during the winter of 1963, imagining in the long Connecticut winter that India would mean seeing tigers, elephants, and jungles, but understanding little else. I had met my father's host, the new (and first Indian) principal of the college, who had stayed with us periodically while he was completing his doctoral studies in the United States, and I knew that his sons had a pet python. I read a large book my parents brought home and placed on the coffee table, called *The Wonder That Was India*, and puzzled about what it would mean to go to a different home and school.[1] I had no way of knowing I was going to miss out on the emergence of the Beatles, though I had the usual concerns about leaving my junior high school friends and the eighth grade. But I was excited by the prospect of adventure, and as it turned out, the year was magical. The college campus did have acres of jungle, and there were peacocks, cobras, and leopard cats, much to my mother's horror. I attended school in a khaki uniform; studied the south Indian drum, the *mridangam*, with a maestro in Mylapore (along with the son of another Fulbright scholar); and learned how to negotiate the extremely efficient bus system of the city of Madras. I slept under a mosquito net, figured out how to take bucket baths (we only had an hour of running water each day), and endured the strangeness of having my (Hindustan) corn flakes mixed with warm milk rather than cold—all things that I remember from the vantage point of an early-sixties American kid. The year left a lasting impression and set in motion an interest that led to a career as a scholar of India and a lifetime of passages to India, personal as well as professional.

I begin with this autobiographical paragraph not just to set the stage for a book with "autobiography" in the title and not merely to introduce the succession of intellectual passages to India that follow. Nor do I mean to call attention to the experience of distinctness surrounding my first passage, as it really did seem at the time, except to note that this idiosyncratic experience was in fact a standard part of postwar American life. My passage began with my father's Fulbright grant. The Fulbright Program was established by Senator J. William Fulbright in 1946, just after the end of World War II, and out of the determination to advance international understanding—by which Fulbright and his colleagues also meant the global centrality of the United States—at a time when the United States knew it could not retreat to its prewar isolationism. The program has operated in fifty countries, providing opportunities for the exchange of scholars, educators, graduate students, and professionals, projecting the image of an enlightened and peaceful United States. When my father went to India on a Fulbright in 1963, he worked closely with the director of the India Fulbright Program, a woman by the name of Olive Reddick. Although my father didn't know it at the time, Reddick had worked as an undercover operative in India during the war, employed by the Office of Strategic Services, spying mostly on the British and their imperial intentions though concerning herself as well with the nature of the nationalist movement and its implications for the American war effort in Asia. Like many members of the OSS who had interests in India, she was sympathetic to the nationalist movement, committed to India, and continued after the war to play a role in the development of Indo-American relations (in her case, through scholarship and diplomacy), working with the Fulbright Program in India from 1950 onward.

Before the war, Americans with real connections to India or other parts of Asia (or Africa) mostly had these connections through missionary activities. The war thrust the United States onto a world stage, strategic and military in the first instance but political, economic, and cultural in important ways soon thereafter. FDR was prescient in his recognition of the significance of the globe not just for the survival of the United States but for any hope that the war, however reluctant the entry into it, and however destructive it would be, would also be the basis for newfound global prosperity and power after a decade of depression, economic decline, and isolationist politics. When FDR commissioned William C. Donovan to put together a proposal for a U.S. intelligence service, he understood, too, that global ambition required new forms of knowledge, knowledge that existed neither in Washington nor in American universities of the time. As Donovan assembled the academics and policy wonks who populated his Research and Analysis Branch, first attached to his role as "Coordinator of Information," and then to his newly minted Office of Strategic Services, he made it clear the United States needed to develop far more knowledge about and much greater interaction with the world well beyond Europe and that Asia was critical both in the war and to U.S. geopolitical interests and concerns beyond and after the war. The OSS was shut down by Truman just months after the cessation of hostilities, and though it soon morphed into the CIA, it developed a very different relationship to the academy almost from the start, both because wartime conditions had sustained a much closer relationship between intelligence and academics and because the CIA had much stricter, and more politically motivated, ideas about what constituted usable knowledge. For these and other reasons, the OSS was far more influential than the CIA in shaping academic interests and predispositions. Perhaps most importantly, the OSS played a critical role in the initial formation and development of what soon came to be known as "area studies," the interdisciplinary study of discrete regions of the world outside the United States (with a special emphasis on regions outside North America and western Europe).

W. Norman Brown, a professor of Sanskrit at the University of Pennsylvania, had headed the India division at the OSS's Research and Analysis Branch in Washington during the war years, and he recruited most of the people who worked with him there to Penn after the war to build the first regional department of South Asian studies in the United States. While the U.S. government established the Fulbright Program and then the National Resource Centers funded by Title VI of the National Defense Education Act of 1958, private foundations, especially Ford, Rockefeller, and Carnegie, began to invest major resources into area studies and projects as well. Many Americans lamented the "loss" of China when Mao's revolutionary army established the PRC in 1949, and while this meant that China had now closed its doors to the United States, at the same time that India had taken up leadership of the "non-aligned" movement of "Third World" nations, it also created greater urgency in determining the relationship between the United States and Asia. The defeat of France in Vietnam in 1956 also led to greater U.S. interest in Southeast Asia, especially given prevailing theories about the escalating threat of global communism. And JFK instituted the Peace Corps in the early sixties.

What all this meant for ordinary Americans—even before the growing involvement of the United States in a long and horrible war in Vietnam—was a much greater likelihood of experiencing some set of "accidents" that would lead to a life and career like mine than ever was the case before. There were in fact a myriad of ways young Americans might spend time in Asia, Africa, or some other part of the world as children, college students, and recent graduates in an age that was not yet global in the way we experience the world today, replete with genuinely new and unique experiences, real adventure, and a sense of a different and vastly enlarged and enriched world. We were captivated by other lands and other peoples, ineluctably pulled away from "normal" careers and ambitions, yet systematically supported and often encouraged by the ample opportunities—and funding—that made it possible to engage in the academic study of things global. When I went to the University of Chicago for graduate work in South Asian history in 1972, I heard many distinctive and compelling stories of how my fellow students came to their interest in South Asia (or other parts of the globe), yet they mostly seemed to converge in a collective story that was part of the new relationship the United States had forged, for better and for worse, in its postwar global emergence. But the story is larger than that, too, and was propelled by the aspirations of many likely and unlikely players, from William C. Donovan to J. William Fulbright, from FDR to JFK, from Olive Reddick to my father, a professor at the Yale Divinity School who had been born on a small farm in central Iowa yet spent the decades after the war traveling around the world multiple times. My own story is unique, and uniquely American, at one and the same time.

The essays in this book were all written well after I did my graduate studies, acquired a tenure track and then tenured position, published my first academic monograph, and began working through my research and teaching, and then increasingly in administrative capacities, to secure and expand the place of global studies in American university life in a different moment than the one that had launched my own career. Yet they all build, in one way or another, on the brief story of my life told here, as well as on the unfolding relationship between the American academy and what was then called the "third" or "developing" world. In including several essays that tell stories about my early experiences in archives and in field situations, and in stringing together a set of essays published for the most part during the last decade of the twentieth and the first decade of the twenty-first century (including several unpublished lectures given in the last few years), I am more than slightly aware of a tendency to think back on my own intellectual and academic life as a possible subject of interest not just for its insights, discoveries, and arguments, but for its passages as well. This book is hardly autobiographical in any usual sense, but by including essays that call attention to some of the particular stories that were part of my own formation as a historian and an anthropologist of South Asia, in returning to some earlier and now doubtless dated debates over method, theory, and discipline, as well as through the inclusion of essays about the history of South Asian studies in the postwar United States, I find myself immersed in reflection that traverses the uncomfortable border regions between the personal and the professional. I apologize in advance for any personal indulgence; the historical truth, however, is that the more time passes, the more one becomes not just a commentator on history but an artifact of history as well.

As an undergraduate at Wesleyan University in central Connecticut (which I attended in part because I could study the south Indian drum there) in the tumultuous years after 1968, I concentrated in Asian and African studies, choosing in the end to write a historical thesis for an advisor who was an Oxford-trained historian, while taking courses and working on subjects ranging from political science and economics to philosophy, religion, and literary studies. I had taken one course in anthropology, but it had turned me off, preoccupied as it was with the question of the "primitive" and relying rather too much on the African work of Colin Turnbull, an anthropologist who had done two ethnographic studies painting stereotypical pictures of utopian idylls, in the one case, and nasty and brutish horrors of savage life, in the other.[2] I took advantage of a program sponsoring research for the required senior thesis, returning to the region where I had spent that first magical year in India. It was not a place that bore a great deal of resemblance to my earlier memories. I lived and studied Tamil in the teeming temple town of Madurai, experienced the fauna of India mostly as I became the host for myriad parasites, encountered the problematic state of historical studies in the local university, and struggled to find a relationship between the work I could do and the demands of my senior thesis. After six months, I learned enough Tamil to make my way around the streets of Madurai and gathered enough material on the way Gandhi had been perceived in southern India, especially through the lens of the emergent non-Brahman movement, to write a creditable thesis. I explored dimensions of Gandhi's life and legacy that were diametrically opposed to the sense I had of Gandhi growing up in 1960s America and consuming him and his thought largely through the political activism of Martin Luther King Jr. And even though I dispensed with my childhood romance with India, I became sufficiently hooked to decide to continue this work and life by going to graduate school to study South Asian history.

College is a time when one challenges the certitudes and shibboleths of one's upbringing, and in finding Gandhi to have come up short on the question of caste in his interactions with members of the non-Brahman movement in Madras in the years of the noncooperation movement (1919–1922), I was all too keen to critique the founding father of modern India. The recognition that Gandhi had been shaken by the fault lines between national unity and social justice has stayed with my work, becoming critical to the way in which I wrote my second book, *Castes of Mind*.[3] Yet I look back now with some chagrin at the way I used the contradictions of Gandhi's engagement with the competing demands of nationalist political life to lose sight of some of what drew me to Gandhi in the first place. History ultimately teaches us not just to recognize the particular contradictions of any major historical character but also to realize that contradiction is a necessary condition of life in the world.

Gandhi's thought and positions can hardly be abstracted from the ways in which he negotiated the complex conditions of late colonial rule and the needs, exigencies, limits, and possibilities of nationalist mobilization. His insistence on nonviolence led to numerous controversial decisions about the tactics and strategies of the nationalist movement (as when he suspended noncooperation after the violence in Chauri Chaura in 1922 or fasted against the proposal for separate electorates advanced by B. R. Ambedkar in 1932); his commitment to social reform issues was either seen as destructive of the social compact necessary for national unity or charged with being too apologetic for tradition (as it was around caste in the south); his entanglement in causes such as spinning and his own brand of asceticism was perhaps no less distracting for others than it was enabling for him and, indeed, for many of his followers. More than forty years after writing my senior thesis, I admire Gandhi no less for his personal foibles and contradictions than I do for his obvious brilliance and courage in sustaining his lifelong political struggle for Indian self-rule.

It was not my interest in Gandhi, however, but rather my encounter with the fascinating history of the non-Brahman movement of southern India that in the end propelled my decision to go on to graduate study in the history of India. Chicago seemed an obvious place to go for this. It had received major funding to develop South Asian studies, establishing a new regional studies department and recruiting extraordinary faculty across a range of departments to anchor an impressive array of programs and research activities related to South Asia, and it was a place where the theoretical interests of my undergraduate days could continue to consume me as well. As befit the area studies model for graduate education at the time, I spent far more time with students and faculty working on South Asia than I did with other students and colleagues in the department of history, imbibing as much anthropology, given its critical role in South Asian studies at the time, as I did a larger sense of my own discipline of history. When I arrived in Chicago there was a great deal of excitement, and not insignificant debate, about a project to reconceptualize the social scientific understanding of caste, the subject of extensive work by Chicago scholars as various as McKim Marriott, Milton Singer, Lloyd and Susanne Rudolph, Bernard Cohn, Ralph Nicholas, and Ronald Inden, and the object of renewed academic attention given the recent visit by the French anthropologist Louis Dumont, whose pathbreaking work, *Homo Hierarchicus*, had only recently been translated into English.[4] The terms of debate were in part about caste and India and in part about the nature of social science itself—whether a comparative social science had not been intrinsically shaped, and thus contaminated, by its Western intellectual history and entailments. By implication, we all engaged the question of whether (and if so how) the sociology and anthropology of caste might better be informed by cultural, textual, and linguistic sources and frameworks than by the inheritance of Montesquieu, Comte, Marx, Weber, and Durkheim. Despite the strong hold of Weberianism among many social scientists at Chicago, the exciting new challenge was the effort to understand India and its social institutions in "its own terms," and as a young graduate student of the time, it was hard not to feel the thrill of taking on the ethnocentrism of Western social science.

The most immediate problem for me, however, was that the critique of ethnocentrism, whether by Louis Dumont, on the one side, or by McKim Marriott and Ronald Inden, on the other, seemed radical in Chicago but not in Madras. Dumont began *Homo Hierarchicus* by critiquing the fundamental commitment to equality that underwrites social science, in general, and studies of systems of social stratification (among them caste), in particular. Although he was more than aware of the use of caste solidarities and resentments in modern politics in Madras, coining the term "substantialization" to refer to the ethnic-group-like effects of caste mobilization for political purposes, he not only wanted to recover a full sense of the cultural logic of caste in its premodern form; he also sought to recover the value of hierarchy itself, a value that entailed both a realistic recognition of the complex distribution of human gifts and a sense of a world that had not lost all its sacred aura. Chicago anthropologists argued with Dumont over his alleged misuse of Indian terms and meanings and even over his nostalgic (and putatively French) desire to find meaning for himself in the Indian caste system (through the recovery of the value of hierarchy as a system that deliberately refused to disavow inequality in the differentiation of roles and took ultimate meaning from principles of purity rather than material advantage or exploitation), but the debate was largely over small differences, jettisoning as it did not just the lessons of modern politics but the manifestly oppressive character of caste hierarchy, especially with reference to the lower castes and, most of all, the "outcastes" or "untouchables"—the groups that have now claimed for themselves the term "Dalit." It also carried with it many of the analytic assumptions of postwar American social science, if not about equality, certainly about the autonomy of culture from other analytic categories such as the social, the political, and the psychological, let alone the historical or the material. Like many American social scientists of the time, Marriott had been deeply influenced by Talcott Parsons, and although he was far from an idealist in his use of culture (thus the vehemence of his debate with Dumont), he accepted a definition of culture as a relatively autonomous domain of human meaning. Marriott was committed as well to a kind of empirical behaviorism that entailed supplementing his sense of stated meanings with his observations of actual behavior, an "interactionist" approach, as he put it.[5] The point of anthropology was not just to find the appropriate "native" terms and meanings for social action but also to ensure that self-description was consistent with lived reality and that cultural analysis took on the totality of this lived reality as observed as well as experienced.

Marriott's empirical and theoretical ambition was captivating, but it also created increasingly self-enclosed and self-referential modes of methodology and analysis. For Marriott, history was a cultural form within a value system, not a mode of description that, however much it might be informed and even inflected by analyses of cultural form, required (in my view at the time and since) a resolute position outside the subject (whether the subject was an individual, a society, a ritual, or a text). While his insistence on culture was influential for me in using historical texts as the fundamental access point for historical self-understanding, and by implication as well the basis for rethinking appropriate frames of historical analysis, I could not accept that history was not also more than that, indeed, that it needed to be far more than that, whether directed within or outside the relevant cultural "system." Even though I had already been influenced by Hayden White's startling new claims about metahistory—how historical forms of analysis and interpretation resembled literary genres, the extent to which even the use of sources was framed and structured by predispositions and modalities of thought—I still believed that the historian's calling required broad if historicist perspective, principled if reflexive critique, and steadfast if eclectic commitment to the recalcitrance of the evidence.[6] Fortunately, my dissertation adviser, Bernard Cohn, shared this general sense of history (trained though he was as an anthropologist) and buffered the theoretical extravagances of the general milieu (and my immediate preoccupation) through his steady insistence on historiography, data, and rigorous critique. Meanwhile, the interdisciplinary mix of these first years of professional scholarship not only built on the interdisciplinary base of my undergraduate days but also launched a lifelong conversation in my own work, teaching, and thought about the relationships among history, anthropology, and critical theory.

The most serious decision I had to make in graduate school was the subject of my dissertation since I would not just spend years in planning, research, and writing but also had to anticipate that the dissertation itself would come to stand for my scholarly identity for years to come. Given the nonexistent state of the job market in South Asian history in the mid-1970s, I was strangely free of significant career angst, though I was intent on finding a subject that would be an appropriate vehicle for my empirical and theoretical interests, a topic that would be as new and innovative as it was doable and relevant to current debates. Pushed by my advisors to look at precolonial India—all the better for stripping away the Western biases that had been sedimented through colonial rule and knowledge systems into much social scientific assumption—I chose initially to work on a set of what Bernard Cohn had labeled "little kingdoms," domains ruled by local *palaiyakkarars* (or chiefs, whom the British called "poligars"), who themselves ruled in the names of (or through relationships with) more powerful potentates based in the local temple towns of southern India, and with the nominal "governor" or *nawab* of the Mughal emperor in Arcot. The local chiefs were especially critical for my study because although they took on all the trappings of kingship and courtly life, they were also deeply embedded in their territories and social formations, often members of midlevel castes known more for their military prowess than their ritual authority. They were, that is, ideally situated both in domains of history and anthropology, historical subjects that occasioned deep inquiry into questions regarding "on the ground" ideas of political and ritual authority, regional formations of caste and social structure, and local textual and folk traditions regarding the families that had arisen over time to occupy pivotal positions of political power and cultural prestige across the southern Tamil countryside.

For the dissertation and ultimately for the monograph that grew out of it, I worked extensively in archives and libraries in London, New Delhi, Madras, and Pudukkottai and did fieldwork, first in a more extensive sense across a number of older royal domains in Tamil Nadu, and then intensively in the old princely state of Pudukkottai, where ultimately I settled on my "case study." I tell some stories of work in these archives and field situations in chapters of this book, especially in "Annals of the Archive," "Autobiography of the Archive," and "Ritual and Resistance." Although these pieces were all written after the publication of my monograph, *The Hollow Crown*, the experiences recounted all took place in the service of that book, at least in the first instance.[7] I also include part of the preface to the second edition of *The Hollow Crown*—published six years after the first edition and with the advantage of a bit of distance from a project that had begun as the dissertation proposal many years before that—not just to provide additional commentary on the relationship of history and anthropology but to introduce the work that directly or indirectly spawned all my subsequent writing, including the two books I wrote well after finishing *The Hollow Crown* (*Castes of Mind* and *Scandal of Empire*).

As I settled on one locality—which happened to be a kingdom—for my study, I became (under the sanction of new preoccupations in social history) an anthropologist, doing extensive ethnography by taking royal genealogies, observing village festivals, surveying dominant castes, and above all participating in local life. I lived between history and anthropology, traversing and often creating new spaces in which disciplinary vocabularies were not only cross-referential but sometimes contradictory. My chief "informant" was a local historian who had been a revenue administrator and a loyal subject of the maharaja. My closest friends were the maharaja's family, who lived precariously between past and present in ways I tried both to use in and to exclude from my study. My growing sense of the centrality of "power" for organizing social meanings and relations seemed uneasily linked to my own manifold affiliations with power. My access to archives became a valued commodity in relation to some of my new acquaintances, complicating ethnographic history just at those moments of connection when I was able to link past and present through court cases and management disputes that had gone on for decades. And my ethnographic encounters seemed most compelling when I made connections to the past that confirmed history even as they seemed to render the historical method—focused as it is on tracking change—most irrelevant. It was all very well to write the history of the present to justify a genealogical method for ethnographic history, but my reliance on ethnography seemed to undermine my growing suspicion that the changes wrought by colonial modernity had worked to make the past unrecognizable in the present.

I sought to use the discomfort of ethnographic history to discover new meanings for the term we used at the time to characterize historical anthropology: ethnohistory. Ethnohistory had a number of different meanings, including the history of places and peoples for whom readily recognizable and useable "historical" records did not exist, the use of anthropological methods and theories in historical inquiry, and the investigation of indigenous or "native" ideas of and about the past. Such definitions seemed to make ethnohistory for the most part unnecessary for India, where historical records abound, though there were widespread assumptions about the existence of local historical texts and traditions. But the domination of colonial historiography obscured the local details and dynamics of social history, particularly for the years just before British conquest, which had been written about as a time of political chaos more to justify colonial rule than to provide adequate historical accounts of precolonial polities. Yet when I first began to analyze the genealogical narrative texts of royal families (*vamcavalis*), I (and various colleagues) were worried that these texts could not be used to do "real" history either, except perhaps to help trace the migration patterns of certain caste and clan groups throughout southern India. Part of the problem was that these texts were never fixed either in place or time: they were always being revised in their performative recitation and were especially vulnerable to political exigency because of the periodic recopying made necessary by the evanescent fragility of palm leaf. Unlike inscriptions, written on stone and copper plate and carefully dated, these texts could not be used to construct chronology, measure dynastic change, or learn about land systems or revenue assessments. There were deeper objections—not only were the genealogies not easily appropriated by historical methods, but they also violated a whole set of presumptions about the meaning and nature of history itself. Nevertheless, I persevered.

I was concerned, however, to do more than simply read texts that had previously been classified as myths as "historical" in any straightforward sense. And I began to explore what would happen if the reading of these texts as histories could be used to reconfigure my sense of how to write a different kind of history. Once again, this interest initially bore the traces of the regnant imperative to take other meanings and categories as foundational for a new kind of social science. Nevertheless, the history of politics, even with this strong cultural preoccupation, seemed invariably to provide openings for the politics of history, in every possible sense. The texts I read made claims that had obvious political implications, claims that were contested in the texts of rival chiefly families and either ignored or transformed into very different kinds of claims in the texts of greater overlords and kings. If representations were about culture, they also embodied, and did some of the work of, politics.

My sense of how to read these texts to challenge historical method was both strengthened and given new substance when I started my sustained ethnographic work in the "little kingdom" of Pudukkottai in the summer of 1981 on a postdoctoral grant. I began my fieldwork by mapping the social organization, symbolic constitution, and spatial distribution of castes, subcastes, clans, and lineages, as well as regions, localities, villages, and hamlets in relationship to the kingdom and, in particular, the royal court. I collected local histories and genealogies; studied temples, forms of worship, and local rituals; and investigated the relations and contests of power in as many different forms and guises as I could. And I invariably asked about relationships with kings, the meaning of kingship, the importance of political relations centering on the court for the articulation of social life throughout the kingdom. I found much to support my earlier contention that kingship was central to social organization and that by implication the domain of politics was of great importance to understanding society and culture. I could now take on Louis Dumont, whose writings about the caste system in India announced the encompassment of the political by the religious, even as I could contrast my own ethnographic work with his, since he had begun his research on India engaged in a wonderful and thick ethnography of a different group of Kallars in a part of Tamil Nadu not far from the kingdom where I was working.[8] India had long and strong religious traditions, but it also had a vital history of political institutions and thought and a dynamic social history that was tied up in political processes more than it was determined by otherworldly priestly concerns. I also increasingly found that the claims of ethnosociology lost their force most intriguingly at the very moment I followed its mandated method: that is, when I was asking about local terms and meanings.[9] My ethnographic queries inevitably elicited the full discordance of history and politics, leading me to attend to disputes and debates as well as to the interests and instrumentalities that were part of every social construction of meaning.

While my project had begun in an effort to capture the world of precolonial India along the lines sketched above, it soon became clear as well that the mediations of colonial history and knowledge were not mere impediments to representation but constitutive in important ways of how one could write, and even imagine, that earlier history. Like all such realizations, the process of taking on board the full force of colonial history, not just for India's modern history but for our understanding of India's premodern history as well, was part of a larger conversation. Colonialism had been largely ignored as a force that shaped fundamental structures and processes in the history of India. My dissertation advisor, Bernard Cohn, was uniquely attentive to the relationship between colonial knowledge and social science, and he saw all cultural categories as not just determinative of history but also determined by history.[10] Cohn's insights about the power of colonial sociology were only reinforced, and deepened, by the writings of Michel Foucault on the power-knowledge axis and his historicist critique of modern institutions and epistemologies.[11] Edward Said's critique of orientalism worked to put into question both colonialism and the anthropological conceit that one could get around the historical power of colonial epistemology by constructing the essential categories and meanings of the "other."[12] And Ranajit Guha's critique of colonial power, and the historical work that was part of his important mobilization of a group associated with the publication series "Subaltern Studies," had the effect of further highlighting the problematic nature of colonial knowledge and power.[13] I came increasingly to realize that colonialism was not just a historical stage and an epistemological problem but a critical crucible in which both Indian culture and tradition had been formed.[14] To paraphrase Geertz's story about turtles and the wisdom of the East, it was colonialism all the way down.[15]

My recognition of the central role of power and colonialism did not, however, make me give up on the possibilities of real ethnographic or historical knowledge. I was convinced that the layered, contestatory — historically contingent — world of Pudukkottai was providing me with the empirical means to make a variety of historical claims, among them that a small Indian "state" could provide an optic for understanding the social and cultural dynamics of history across a much broader swath of India in the early modern period. The constitution of sovereignty in the family histories of the seventeenth and eighteenth centuries evoked a powerful alternative form of historicity. The Pallavaraiyar chairman (a relative of the royal family), who featured as a principal informant in *The Hollow Crown*, was very clear about the way his affiliation to the persons, institutions, and values of kingship constituted his position and his social world. The cultural meanings of terms and categories having to do with the thing we call caste entailed the workings of power and were explained with reference to the dynamics of power. The more I learned about ritual life and religious conviction the more I could see that the order of everyday things and life reflected historical processes in which the political world of kingship was dominant. India was not so "otherworldly" after all.

While finally writing *The Hollow Crown* after my second long stint of field and archival work, I realized that I had to engage not just the questions surrounding sources directly but also the ways in which the fundamental questions concerning India's social, cultural, and political history had been framed by and through two hundred years of colonial rule. The last part of the book was entitled "Colonial Mediations," focused as it was on the colonial role in (and models for) the princely state's efforts to resume entitlements in landholding, "rationalize" (and enhance) land revenue, take direct control over temples, and, finally, manage a crisis in which the maharaja—who decided to marry a European woman who had the tastes that had been cultivated in him by his Cambridge tutor, anxious to educate the young man away from the corruption and intrigue that had characterized his forefathers— was forced to abdicate the throne. Once I finished *The Hollow Crown*, I turned directly to a more systematic study of colonial histories, both to analyze further the sources I used for my early study and to scrutinize how colonial understandings (and classifications) of Indian social, cultural, and religious life affected the history of India in the years from the early nineteenth century on. The first substantive essay I wrote after the book was entitled "Castes of Mind," laying out my basic argument, first proposed in *The Hollow Crown* and finally argued in a book by the same name published more than a decade later, about the extent to which ideas of caste in modern India emerged in large part out of the colonial encounter. I include this essay here because it lays out in clear terms my developing sense of how caste, only because of colonial rule, became a social system seemingly governed by otherworldly conventions in which the principle of purity and the institution of the priesthood (and by implication the social position of Brahmans). I decided to focus in particular on the colonial collector Colin Mackenzie, who had compiled the archive that had been so critical for my use of texts and traditions from the eighteenth century. I studied the role of early colonial writings on Indian history and society. I examined the Census of India documents for southern India in connection with the rise of caste societies and movements in the late nineteenth and early twentieth centuries. And I sought in particular to see how colonial understandings were translated into colonial policy and presumption in ways that had powerful historical effects on Indian institutions, understandings, and social, cultural, and political life. So, for example, in another early essay included here, "The Policing of Tradition," I show how the categories "Brahman" and "non-Brahman," especially in the domain of religion (only recently a distinct arena of ritual activity and belief), were defined not just by a vague colonial interest in the ethnography of India but through the specific kinds of laws, administrative routines, and policing tactics that had been spawned by that peculiar colonial combination of a need for social order and the desire for a civilizing mission. The importance of colonial knowledge is discussed in other essays too, especially "Annals of the Archive" and "Autobiography of an Archive" in part 1, and they provide a background and context for the focus on empire that is the theme of part 3.

I used my writing on colonial knowledge and its political consequences, always based on my fieldwork and archival research, increasingly to intervene in contemporary debates, a process that in turn led me to think more about the politics of knowledge in India as well as in the academic contexts of history, anthropology, and critical theory in the United States. In the first instance, much of the framing of my book *Castes of Mind* was a response to the way caste had been used to think about India, ranging from empire's imagining of caste as the explanation and even legitimation for colonial rule, to its uses in Hindu nationalism and in debates over social discrimination in India, to the more contemporary naturalization of India's postcolonial poverty and apparent lack of entrepreneurial economic activity and energy. Even as India's own Dalit movement and dramatic postliberalization economic transformation have made some of these critical points far better than I could ever have done (while raising other issues for consideration), it seemed necessary to adapt the postcolonial preoccupations of cultural and literary theory to help direct attention to the specific political implications and uses of social scientific representations of India. While the essay entitled "In Near Ruins" surveys the general cultural landscape of the late twentieth century from a postcolonial perspective, it is followed by two essays that demonstrate the rather different contexts in India and the United States when thinking about the framing—and the local politics—of colonial knowledge (a seemingly natural imperative for postcolonial thought that was surprisingly slow in gaining traction).

The two essays, "G. S. Ghurye and the Politics of Sociological Knowledge" and "South Asian Studies: Futures Past," also bring us back to the points I made at the opening of this prefatory essay about the origins of my own Indian passage in the American postwar experience, with particular reference to the emergence of South Asian studies in leading U.S. research universities in the decades after the war. I began this preface by reflecting on my own "origin" story, how I "fell into" an interest in India that led the way to a long academic career preoccupied with a subject that required explanations that went beyond statements such as "because it was there" or "I was always fascinated by the subject" (and, indeed, required even more serious explanations in India than in the United States). Those explanations, as I tried to show, were illustrations both of individual serendipity and institutional contexts that grew out of the postwar political and intellectual environment in the United States. Much of what followed in my own academic work was of a piece with this environment, from the interdisciplinary interests that were spawned and nurtured by area studies to the more immediate concerns about the legacies of empire.

It is in part to contextualize my later passage through the institutional corridors of U.S. academia in the late twentieth and early twenty-first century that I include here a lecture, "Franz Boas and the American University: A Personal Account," that I gave about Boas, the founding father of anthropology at Columbia University and the honorific name on the chair I held while I taught at Columbia. It speaks to the extraordinary public engagement of Boas in the context of critical issues in the United States in the early twentieth century; his disillusionment with America's new imperial ambitions after the outbreak of war with Spain over its imperial possessions in 1898 and with the political justifications and implications of the First World War; his engagement with the question of race as he debunked ideas having to do with the racial determination of social, cultural, and intellectual life; his affiliation with such important public figures as W. E. B. DuBois; and his role in the early years of the NAACP. The lecture also notes Boas's keen participation in the academic politics of the time, both in his challenges to (and occasional differences with) the administrators at his home institution and his extraordinary role in building up anthropology in the United States through his training of foundational figures and his institutional work at Columbia. Boas put his intellectual imprint on some of the founding ideas of anthropology in the United States, but the traditions associated with him are not always the most appropriate legacy for his extraordinarily innovative institutional work. Boas provoked me to reflect on my own work in institution building, and in the spirit of autobiography, I should provide a little more background about that, too.

When I started teaching at the University of Michigan in 1987, I had just finished *The Hollow Crown* and was concerned to find a way to provide graduate students—whom I was now to teach and mentor for the first time—the opportunity to become certified in both history and anthropology, genuinely equipped to engage in the kind of new work that I felt I had had the good fortune to do. This project turned out to be timely and propitious, and it succeeded precisely because it could build on the extraordinary collection of scholars at Michigan committed to new kinds of interdisciplinary collaborations. Although other institutions fostered similar kinds of programs, at Michigan we created the first fully bidisciplinary program for graduate training. The Interdepartmental Ph.D. Program in Anthropology and History recruited excellent students because of the stellar reputation of the two departments and because the program afforded real access to each while also providing a genuinely hybrid form of training. It partnered with other faculty workshops, area studies programs, and departments, and it created the possibilities for genuinely new and innovative kinds of intellectual projects. Nevertheless, it made many uncomfortable, always subject to the skepticism of faculty and students who wondered what the real identity of the students was. Immanuel Wallerstein famously recommended once that all academics should have full appointments in at least two departments so they would never settle into a single disciplinary space.[16] As one who never managed to do this in the first place, I thought that was the right way to go.

For reasons detailed in some of the essays here (as well as in others not included, e.g., "Is Vice Versa? Historical Anthropologies and Anthropological Histories" or "Slouching Towards Ambivalence"), the decades between 1970 and the end of the century were years when the close relationship between the two disciplines of record in my own career, history and anthropology, was especially propitious.[17] History had taken the turn from high politics and formal intellectual history toward concern not just with the social and the cultural but with the lives of those who appeared only fleetingly in the historical record of the past—as populations rather than as people with singular lives that could be recaptured through better understanding of the insights of anthropologists who had worked in villages and small towns—where people's lives were defined by the rhythms and preoccupations of agriculture, kinship, ritual, and poverty. Historians such as Natalie Davis, Carlo Ginsburg, Robert Darnton, Emmanuel Le Roy Ladurie, William Sewell, and Keith Thomas all made not just the cultural turn but the anthropological turn, even as anthropologists such as Marshall Sahlins, Clifford Geertz, and Eric Wolf recognized the need to turn to history in important works of theirs at just about the same time (if for somewhat different reasons). Anthropologists had always felt that their craft afforded access to everyday life and politics, to culture as a way of life rather than as high culture, but they knew they needed to take a longer view to understand both the relationship of the present to the changes wrought by colonialism and modernization as well as the dynamic nature of the social structures and cultural frames they sought to explain, especially as they broadened their compass to include all parts of the globe.

It was because of this historical turn in anthropology (and specifically because of my work in founding the Interdepartmental Ph.D. Program in Anthropology and History at Michigan) that a historian like me—anthropologically trained and oriented though I was—was recruited to chair the oldest department of anthropology in the United States in 1996. Recruiting a mix of scholars from international as well as domestic backgrounds, some with Ph.D.'s in fields outside of anthropology (though with experience and scholarly interests that were poised to move anthropology into the next century), I directed my institution building now within a single department, where there was less awkwardness around issues ranging from undergraduate curricular requirements to Ph.D. recruitment and intellectual certification. Still, I harbored a residual concern that departments were not always the best institutional spaces for promoting a genuinely hybrid approach, and I maintained my own affiliations with history while encouraging all my graduate students to seek interdisciplinary training. In retrospect, the department did extraordinary things, training new kinds of graduate students to formulate projects that were often as fresh as they were innovative for the discipline at large, while borrowing liberally from multiple fields. Yet departments often have a normalizing effect on the intellectual work of the academy even when they are pried as far open as possible. This is why in the sciences there are deliberate efforts to engage this kind of problem by building the laboratories of scientists from different disciplines next to one another and why there have been calls from many commentators on higher education to find new models for interdisciplinarity that might resist the building of new "silos" (a peculiar agricultural metaphor now in vogue in university discourse), even when these silos have been built to combat the effects of old ones.

Looking back, I can say that there were at least two reasons for my own sense of professional discomfort with the disciplinary state of affairs, the first having to do with the relative marginality of South Asia for the disciplinary world of history in the years when I first did my graduate work and sought to find regular professorial employment, the second, the lingering imprint of the broadly interdisciplinary liberal arts education that I never fully shook off. In the first instance, places like India had in fact not had a long history within U.S. history departments. Historians of South Asia (rather than, say, historians of British empire who knew only a bit about India in that context) were not hired by any U.S. university until the early 1950s, and then only a handful of universities did so. In 1963, when the University of Chicago sought to hire a historian who could teach the history of India, they turned to an anthropologist with "hands-on" experience in India who had developed an interest in history in his postdoctoral research. In the years after the war, and in some cases to the present day, it was more common to find historians of Asia or the Middle East in area studies departments than in mainstream departments of history. The turn to anthropology was in part a turn to a professional cohort where places like India did not seem completely on the margins, though India had become of central interest to anthropology as a discipline only when it embraced the idea of "complex societies"—and then fastened onto caste as a social form that attained canonic status in anthropological investigations of social organization and stratification—in the mid-twentieth century. Now all this seems like ancient history: the history of South Asia has been incorporated into most history departments as necessary, and anthropology itself no longer makes distinctions between complex and simple societies (or for that matter, West and East, developed and undeveloped, etc.)

The social and political landscape of South Asian scholarship in the United States has changed significantly now since my own entry into the field. Changed first by the dramatic increase in South Asian immigration to the United States after 1965 and then by increasing academic mobility between South Asia and the rest of the world, it has now been radically transformed by the new global conditions that are part of a resurgent Asian presence in the world at many levels. In South Asia at least, the postcolonial condition seems finally consigned to the past, to historical and epistemological debates rather than contemporary social, political, economic, constitutional, or cultural concerns. And many of the young students who in the past two decades have made the decision I made four decades ago to enter graduate school (in the United States) to study South Asian history (or allied fields such as anthropology, sociology, politics, culture, literature, and religion) have done so from very different paths than mine—more often from their personal South Asian origins and connections than from Fulbright or Peace Corps experiences, and more often with questions—or at least points of departure—about selves rather than others. "Subaltern studies" eclipsed the historical anthropology of my graduate training in the 1980s and 1990s, but now no one school or set of questions can be said to dominate or even broadly configure the range of issues that have proliferated across the disciplinary landscapes of South Asian studies, at this point determined far more by disciplines than by the lingering imperatives of area studies, more vitally represented by work in professional schools than regular academic departments, and more genuinely global in their sponsorship and location than ever before. Inasmuch as this is the sign of the health of the field, it is also about the extent to which the field as a single entity is hardly recognizable any more.

Yet the academy changes slowly. Global issues, opportunities and challenges, threats and solutions, and flows of people, goods, resources, and commodities intrude insistently even as they increasingly define metropolitan realities. In many universities, however, especially in the core disciplines and fields across the humanities and social sciences, the global is still often seen as a necessary but supplemental side dish to the main courses, subjects, and preoccupations of education and research. We are still struggling to decide what global studies will consist of and how global studies will be positioned in relation to our disciplinary structures. Yet it is widely accepted now that the liberal arts must be global in their coverage and in their very constitution.

Even as the liberal arts continually adjust to the changing demands and contexts of the worlds outside (and within) the academy, they continue to sustain the foundational idea of the university. I would, therefore, be remiss if I did not stress this last point above all the others, namely, that the kind of intellectual environment that launched me into my graduate work in the first place—that both made the academy seem the kind of utopia where I wanted to spend my life it at all possible and then sustained me through the changing circumstances and conditions of academic life in the different institutions of higher education with which I have been honored to be affiliated—was, in fact, the liberal arts. It had started in a public high school in suburban Connecticut through a series of classes taught by an intense young man who had graduated from college a few years before and brought with him a passionate interest in having his students read texts as various as Norman O. Brown's *Life Against Death* and Huston Smith's *Religions of Man* to provide perspective for required texts such as Melville's *Moby-Dick*.[18] And it had continued and intensified when, at his suggestion, I went to the same nearby college where I heard prominent philosophers and psychologists debate the merits of arguments concerning free will and biological determinism; listened to lectures by visitors such as George Steiner, Jürgen Habermas, Noam Chomsky, and Shlomo Avineri; and took a range of demanding courses in religion, philosophy, literature, politics, economics, history, and anthropology. All this in retrospect speaks to the multiple justifications for the liberal arts, that peculiar mix of traditional and eclectic texts and forms of learning that engage the full personal and political intensity of the time—the time being generational as much as historical. And this same mix entailed a serious engagement with texts and traditions from "other" places—well before the current tide of globalization—as some of my most memorable intellectual experiences were in classes reading authors such as Tanizaki and Kawabata, Gandhi and Tagore, Kenyatta and Achebe.

At a time when there is growing criticism about the irrelevance and unnecessary indulgence—and expense—of this kind of education, I wish to conclude this introduction by stressing the importance of the liberal arts and the kinds of critical intellectual engagements they engender. The essays in this book may not do much to argue directly for them—I focus instead on interdisciplinary connections between history and anthropology, area studies, and the future of academic knowledge at a time of massive globalization—but it is on the foundational significance of the liberal arts that this book is built. While it is doubtless true that in the current moment we need to reexamine the traditional conventions and justifications that affirm the importance of critical thinking, reading, and writing, the essential traditions of the liberal arts are perhaps the single greatest contribution of American higher education not just to the United States but to the world. It will be no mean task to find new ways to support these traditions under current conditions while bringing them into relentless and productive engagement with the issues of our time. Our future, however, will likely depend on our success in doing so.

Part I

Autobiography

1

Annals of the Archive

Ethnographic Notes on the Sources of History

History is the work expended on material documentation (books, texts, accounts, registers, acts, buildings, institutions, laws, techniques, objects, customs, etc.) that exists, in every time and place, in every society . . . in our time, history is that which transforms *documents* into *monuments* . . . in our time, history aspires to the condition of archaeology, to the intrinsic description of the monument.
> —Michel Foucault, *Archaeology of Knowledge*

It is the state which first presents subject-matter that is not only *adapted* to the prose of History, but involves the production of such history in the very progress of its own being.
> —G. F. W. Hegel, *Lectures on the Philosophy of History*

Ethnography of the Archive

The first time I entered an archive, I panicked. My historical zeal inexplicably vanished as I desperately stemmed a welling desire to exit immediately and search for the nearest pub. I saw before me the thousands of documents I could indent, the books I might read, the files I had to wade through. I tried to imagine which index to consult, what department to decipher, how best to control the chaos of what seemed an infinite chain of documents. My proposal for research, so lucid a minute before, seemed inappropriate, unwise, nigh impossible. I felt embarrassed to expose my ignorance in front of professional archivists, helpful though they were. My interest in the small voices, cultural forms, and contradictory ruptures of history seemed designed neither for easy recognition nor ready access. My proposal to understand the essential relationship between political authority and social relations in early modern South India was vast and suddenly incoherent. It could take me to any fragment, yet I knew that all fragments were not equal, that most documents by themselves were mere reminders of the quotidian tedium of history, that I not only needed to start somewhere, I needed to start somewhere promising. The archive is a glorious monument of history, but the documents within are for the most part endless and banal.

Most historians write history before they enter the archive, beginning their professional apprenticeship by using those secondary sources in libraries that are already contaminated by interpretation and selection. Even then, however, such sources establish their authenticity through referencing an archive that demarcates the partial and secondary nature of all sources from outside. The archive is constituted as the only real space that is free of context, argument, ideology—indeed history itself. Accordingly, historians can only really become historians or write history once they have been to the archive. The originary arrival of the historian in the archive is much like the arrival of the anthropologist in the field—that threshold of disciplinary certification—the magical moment when the scientist-scholar sets down upon a shore that beckons with the promise that one can finally engage in the act of discovery, at last come face to face with truth and the realm of unmediated evidence. But while anthropologists have famously subjected their arrival stories to narrative scrutiny—some would say carried away too much by the reflexive turn—the historian's arrival story is still largely untold, shielded by the fact that while the archive has often seemed mystical, it has never appeared exotic. Travelers' tales and adventurers' yarns have never rendered the archive a major source of memoir, yet the monumentality of the archive is enshrined in a set of assumptions about truth that are fundamental both to the discipline of history and to the national foundations of history. While basic assumptions about truth and history have been critiqued in relation to historical writing (and the use of sources), they have rarely been examined in relation to the institutional reposi- tories for the sources themselves, except inside the very historical foot- notes that summon the greatest respect for the archive as a repository of ultimate value.[1] The archive is simultaneously the outcome of historical process and the very condition for the production of historical knowl- edge. What follows is my own archive arrival story.[2]

My formal acquaintance with the archive was prefaced by several years of working with original documents that themselves preceded the establishment of the modern archive. I began my graduate career as a historian by reading epigraphical series and reports, transcriptions and translations of inscriptions that were for the most part etched into either stone or copper surfaces, many dating from the years between 600 and 1400 AD. Stone inscriptions typically recorded endowments to temples and were inscribed on the stone walls of the shrines where worship was to be conducted or on the walls surrounding the centers of wor- ship. Copper-plate inscriptions were typically held by the descendants of kings, landlords, and various other magnates whose entitlements to land, tribute, office, and honor were itemized, publicly declared, and permanently instantiated by the presentation of the material text. In ad- dition to recording details of landholding rights and relations, political positions and perquisites, ritual emoluments and entailments, these in- scribed surfaces provided occasions for textual performances of various kinds, most significantly when the pedigree of the presenter became the basis for historical narrations of the exploits and exemplariness of cer- tain families and their forebears. Inscriptions thus provided the stuff of history—the details of property and politics, identity and institutions— at the same time that they were themselves historical texts, recording in genealogical form the claims made by history itself for and about authority. History was already monumental, most particularly in the elaborate and sometimes enormous temple complexes that yielded sur- face after surface for textual inscription, but also in the use of precious metals to insure the permanence of the text (though its very precious- ness meant there was always the temptation for textual meltdown). In one sense history in this premodern moment could only be monumen- tal, for the myriad other texts that must have been etched on the evanes- cent surfaces of palmyra palm were consigned to certain obsolescence in ways that meant that if history was to last, it had to be written on, or as, a monument.

If the temple complex was itself an archive, it was an archive of a very different kind than we imagine when we contemplate the contemporary institution. The walls of the temple complex served in one sense as a local record room—the origins of most modern archives; these records, however, were attached to a preexisting monument and functioned in effect to secure the monument as well as the authoritative relations and figures whose own power was symbolized and deployed through the institutional formation of the temple. And despite the ample epigraphical record, the actual record was slight compared to any modern paper archive, the details of administrative procedure few and far between, only rarely cross-referenced in ways that might genuinely anticipate the surveillance and custodianship of a bureaucratic managerial elite that would seem the sine qua non of modern archives and states.

Nevertheless, the temple complex was an archive of sorts. It preserved records necessary for the maintenance of a polity, even as the polity itself relied heavily on the institutional relations of the temple. And it preserved these records for reference use as well as in ways that worked to monumentalize both history and its documents. The inscriptional texts themselves appear emblematic of a particular kind of archival history, combining the most banal of details with the most glorious panegyrics in praise of kingly dynasties, local rulers, and institutional arrangements (ranging from the banking functions of temples or the maintenance of ritual performances to the memorialization of property relations and honorific offices). At the same time, neither historians nor "history" proper was necessary for the transformation of documents into history, as happened later when the myriad record offices of government still had to be monumentalized into archives in order to transit from the realm of bureaucracy to the domain of history. In southern India, documents literally began their careers as monuments.

It was with this privileged experience of premodern history that I set off on my journey to the modern archive. Even though by then I had shifted my own historical interests from the eighth and ninth centuries to the eighteenth and nineteenth, I still had ambivalent feelings about this shift of focus. Given my interest in precolonial state and society—specifically in charting out the nature of kingly authority and caste relations in southern India immediately prior to the onset of British colonial rule and then tracing its transformations over the first colonial century—I was keen to find documents that existed before the modern colonial state and its entire apparatus of documentation. At best, the archive might have admitted documents from an earlier age as an expression of the colonial state's need to know how things really were before the British arrived. But I worried that the archive was at least in part about the contamination of the West, or the modern, or both. At the same time, I walked into the archive with all the trepidation of the academic apprentice, worried that I would never penetrate its carefully kept secrets and, worse, that these secrets were impenetrable not because of the daring originality of my line of research but because I had been too ignorant, or not mindful enough, of the archival realities. I knew that historians should not take archives for granted, but I felt for the first time the palpable tension between the archive and the historian.

The archive that formally inaugurated my experience as a historian was the India Office Library in London. Originally the library and record room of the India Office, the agency of the British government that oversaw Britain's colonial relationship with India until independence in 1947, it had been moved into a separate archive in the early 1970s, placed under the management of the British Library, and, well after I did my initial research, moved to and amalgamated with the archival and library holdings of the new British Library in St. Pancras. Despite the shabby postwar high-rise on "The Cut," in what was then an especially dreary part of south London, midway between Blackfriars and Elephant and Castle, I walked into the archive for the first time in 1975 with all the excitement that my fellow anthropology students had reserved for the moment they arrived in a "field of their own." My excitement soon merged with confusion when I realized that I hadn't a clue about what to do next—whether I should look at the index for the political, public, or home departments, what the mechanisms might be for genealogical research, and how to access either Tamil or English manuscript collections. I remember spending the first day paging through the index of one particular department with a key word that failed to appear for anything more than the most trivial of documents. In frustration, I hand copied one very long letter that seemed vaguely important (only to realize later that I had already photocopied the same passage from a government manual back in the university library at home). I felt a bizarre if momentary envy for the traditional research historian who was assigned a topic on the basis of a specific collection of records or documents their supervisor had preselected for them, at the same time wondering if I should just discard history and go to the field instead, starting my project with anthropological fieldwork, the flip side of my disciplinary training.[3] I realized that to be able to use the archive productively, I would have to do extensive research on the archive itself, learning both about the history of British governmental rule at the concrete levels of yearly bureaucratic organization and interaction and about the history of various kinds of collections and record keeping. All historians learn these lessons in their early archival days, yet we rarely confess openly how disconcerting the experience was.[4]

As time went by, I came to understand considerably more about the nature, classificatory structures, and institutional histories of some of the records and collections that were to become the primary documentation for my thesis. I also began to learn about the complex relationship between archives in Britain and archives in India—what sorts of files, what levels of detail, and what manner of departments could be found to organize materials at the India Office Library in London, the National Archives of India in New Delhi, the Tamil Nadu Record Office in Madras (and eventually the record room of the old Pudukkottai Kingdom in a small district town). As I surveyed the full range of little kingdoms in the southern Tamil countryside, I learned that the one kingdom that became a princely state, Pudukkottai, had many of its imperial records not in Madras but in London and Delhi, where the records concerning the administration of princely states had been housed, while the records concerning the landlords, or *zamindars*—once peers of the princes—had been kept in the local archive in Madras. The landlords were occasionally taken under direct rule of government, a kind of "receivership," for reasons either having to do with charges of corruption or the minority of the zamindar. Years of direct management yielded significant records: confidential memos, reports, and accounts, all confirming first the wisdom and then the folly of administrative intervention. Otherwise, the records were primarily made up of accounts of land settlements that implemented the introduction of new forms of property and new relations between "cultivators" and the state. So daunted was I by the stacks of land records when I first encountered them that I found it difficult to anticipate that I would later come to relish them; as it happened, I spent much of my thesis research period looking at records of settlements concerning land that had been held free of tax for reasons that turned out to reveal a complex political structure of entitlements, providing a nuanced picture of the economy as well as the state. When I came to focus on Pudukkottai, in part because the records seemed to be much better kept, I did not at first know that its settlement records had been kept in the Pudukkottai archive itself, never transferred to Madras, Delhi, or London, still part of an active record room that had been transferred to the local district collector's office, first based in nearby Trichirappalli and later in Pudukkottai town itself. These discoveries, as indeed my sense of the importance of these kinds of records for my research, came much later.

My first experience of the archive had thus been frustrating for several reasons, quite apart from the myriad frustrations that any scholar working in Indian archives in the 1970s took for granted, such as the absence of photocopy machines, the now unimaginable absence of the computer, and the often highly personalized contingencies of archival access, even in state- and national-level record offices. I was frustrated not only because I felt buried under the weight of archival excess but because this excess was distributed in historically contingent ways across states, nations, and continents, with little in the way of indices, guides, or user-friendly catalogues that could help prepare the scholar for the task ahead. Furthermore, both the documentary excess and the archival proliferation of documents seemed to signify the limits on access to some of the most important issues of the past—even leaving aside the difficulties that had to do with political censorship, bureaucratic neglect, and the ravages of time and climate on many of the most important documents. While some of these issues seemed endemic to India, they also seemed to amplify the distortions of a colonial regime, one that either sought to obscure the past or to represent it in ways that seemed at best evidence for tendentious arguments in favor of one or another colonial approach to rule. Even for caches of primary records within single archives that promised greatest access, e.g. land settlement records, it soon became clear that the records could only be read against, and ultimately as, the outcome of arguments among various British colonial officials who had identified landlords, cultivators, village communities, and the like as the primary holders of property for reasons that often had more to do with their own theoretical influences (the physiocrats, the utilitarians, etc.) than with any real empirical evidence on the ground. I was, nevertheless, determined to discover what I could about the nature of state and society in the immediate precolonial period, and the more I looked in colonial archives, the more I felt the impossibility of the project. And so I soon decided to take a break from the archives in Madras and to look instead at textual accounts that had been composed before the British took control of India's past, and I spent increasing numbers of hours away from the archive in a library of "Oriental Manuscripts" that—based as it was over the library of the University of Madras—housed the manuscript collection of Colin Mackenzie.

Colin Mackenzie, an engineer and mathematician by training, went to India as an army man in the late eighteenth century and soon became known for his extraordinary cartographic talents, first designing a military assault on the fort of Tipu Sultan, who until his final defeat in 1799 constituted a major threat to British rule, then devising a complex plan for the surveying and mapping of newly conquered territories. His surveying skills were recognized: he was designated as the surveyor-general of Madras in 1810, only to become the first surveyor-general of India in 1815. Mackenzie, a Scot from the outer Hebrides who, like many other educated Scots of his time, went to India to find a more flourishing career than would have been available in Scotland, was also an avid antiquarian and became vitally committed to the collection of historical materials about peninsular India. As he surveyed newly conquered territories in southern India, he devoted himself on the side to the task of local historian, spending his own resources to hire and deploy a group of local assistants to help him collect local texts, traditions, artifacts, and materials. By the time of his death in 1821, he had amassed a collection of three thousand inscriptions, 1,568 literary manuscripts, 2,070 local tracts, and large portfolios and collections of drawings, plans, images, and antiquities.[5]

The Mackenzie archive promised unmediated access to the historical mentalities and genres of the late precolonial period. As I attempted to understand the nature of the holdings of the archive through a range of indexes and annotations that were compiled as early as 1828 by H. H. Wilson, I became especially interested in quasi-historical texts that were generally called *vamcavali*, or dynastic histories of kingly families.[6] These texts are genealogies of a sort, both in that they list the entire line of the family and in that genealogy is the narrative frame of the text. What chronology is to modern historical narrative, genealogy is to the vamcavali — it provides both sequence and structure. Typically, each episode consists of some action performed by a hero-ancestor, which is then followed by an account of gifts made by a great king to a chiefly ancestor. For example, the hero may kill a tiger that has been plaguing villagers in the king's domain or set off to do battle against some enemy of the king's. The king then calls the chief to court, where he presents him with gifts consisting of titles, emblems, and rights over land. The basic structure of the texts often seems repetitive, albeit conveying little in the way of "social historical" information. Rather, historical events that lead to the establishment or reestablishment of a special relationship between the chief and a king are elevated to narrative significance and serve to herald the accomplishments of each noteworthy ancestor. Further, the royal family is seen to have the accumulated merit of these discrete historical events, inheriting the full measure of royal perquisites and entitlements that reflected the heroic history of the family.[7]

Even as I took these texts as the record not just of particular histories but also of particular kinds of history, I became aware that even they were not positioned fully outside colonial history. Many of the kingly family histories concluded with petitions for recognition, reinstatement, or some other claim for authority and position. Some of the most glorious family histories were of kingly families that had participated in the late eighteenth-century wars against the British (sometimes in collaboration with the French), leaving the contemporary kings in disgrace. Other family histories turned out to be claims on behalf of the branch of the family that had been bested by another in internecine struggles for landlord status and privileges under the new terms of British rule. Even as the old regime cultural system of heroism, gift exchange, and kingship was clearly in evidence in the old histories, these texts also demonstrated their inexorable relationship to a new system of colonial power and command.

In subsequent research, I learned how the Mackenzie collection itself was part of the history of early colonial conquest. Mackenzie collected texts while mapping and surveying newly conquered territories of southern India. Even though he never conducted a revenue survey, scrupulously avoiding direct inquiries about production and revenue, there was no way (and no reason) to promise that knowledge about local lineages or tenures might not be used by an imperial power that was at this very point establishing itself as a state based more on the capacity to collect land revenue than support itself through trade. Indeed, virtually all of the information collected by Mackenzie turned out to concern the rights and privileges of kings, chiefs, headmen, Brahmans, and religious institutions. There was good reason for what one of Mackenzie's assistants characterized as "friendless suspicion." Additionally, the collection of materials was actually conducted by a variety of local assistants, many though not all learned Brahmans, who had multiple agendas, interests, and locations of their own. Mackenzie's assistants were invested in certain kinds of representations of India, and at the same time they sought assiduously to please their "master" and satisfy his apparently endless ambition to collect local histories and texts.

So it was that even when traces of precolonial voices, genres, and forms survived in the Mackenzie archive, they did so in the setting of colonial interest. As we will see in the next chapter, many of the different voices, agencies, and modes of authorization that were implicated in the production of the archive were substantially lost once they became assimilated to the grand purposes of the colonial archive, in this case a process hastened by Mackenzie's death in 1821. Distinctions between types of texts (e.g., texts that derived from ancient authorship or the hastily transcribed remarks from a local source) and concerns about the actual uses of textual knowledge became blurred and increasingly unclear at each stage of collection, transcription, translation, and classification. As the Mackenzie collection was absorbed by the colonial state, the role of Mackenzie's native assistants became relegated to the position of technical mediation, their diaries and letters rarely included with the textual material. Even as the "natives" were made invisible and irrelevant, the distinguished orientalist H. H. Wilson almost abandoned his cataloguing project when he realized the growing lack of interest in Mackenzie's work among other orientalists of the time. The materials in the collection seemed neither historical enough to satisfy any genuine historical interest in the reconstruction of precolonial Indian history nor classical enough to provide a respectable basis for a scholar's reputation or labor. The histories that Mackenzie had collected had already been overtaken by a different kind of history.

And so, despite my textual detour—and the genuinely extraordinary insights that some of the Mackenzie texts afforded—I never fully left the colonial archive behind and soon had to return to its heart. I went back to the Mackenzie archive in later years to learn more about the history of the collection and its subsequent uses, but in the short term—for the purposes of dissertation research—I had to begin reading the very land records that I had at first hoped to avoid and that had become so fundamental to the debates over land tenure and settlement in the initial years of British rule. These documents—used so extensively by historians of agrarian relations—turned out to be far more than, as at first I thought, assessments of different land parcels and their potential (or actual) productivity. Rather, they were interventions in the way the colonial state worked to constitute land relations as the basis of the state's ultimate right of ownership. After it shed its initial formation in the mercantilist origins of the East India Company, the early colonial state was above all an agrarian state that used its capacity to tax landed property to support its elaborate bureaucratic, political, and military presence in India. Building on arguments between those who believed that the East India Company was inheriting the king's right of ownership over all property and those who used a Ricardian theory of rent to claim for the company the right to set revenue rates and collect taxes as fundamental to the custodial project of the state, the British (all the while ceding sovereignty at a formal level to the Mughal rulers) gradually established a state bureaucracy, focusing primarily on land revenue, that assumed its sovereign authority over all of India. Decisions about whether the bureaucracy should accord proprietary rights to landlords (zamindars), village brotherhoods, or principal cultivators (*raiyats*) became critical interventions in the relationship between state and society, at the same time that these decisions both produced, and were produced by, a variety of different histories of India that were important parts of early colonial justifications of rule.

When I first waded through land records, I did so with the hope that I might be able to determine the status of agrarian relations in different parts of southern India and also to assess arguments made by different administrators about the nature of the precolonial village community. The arguments were complex and robustly documented and always assumed that historical forms were necessary predicates for colonial policies. Intellectual histories of some of the key players of the period had revealed how much historical argument was tied to political ambition and European experience. Francis and Cornwallis were influenced by the physiocrats and driven by their ambition to recreate in India the authority and position of the landed gentry in Britain (already under major assault in France); Munro and Elphinstone were captured by a rhetoric of paternal responsibility and a Scottish sense of the folk heroism of the yeoman cultivator. Despite the powerful writings of Ranajit Guha, Eric Stokes, and others about the intellectual genealogies of land policy in India in the early nineteenth century, however, I only realized gradually how much the documentation project of the early colonial state around matters of land and revenue was fundamental to the formation of that very state.[8] Indeed, as the colonial state learned from the mistakes of the permanent settlement of 1793, it became progressively bolder in the way it asserted, developed, and maintained control over classification, assessment, and collection, leading finally to the political conclusion of 1858, namely that the indirect rule both of East India Company monopoly and landlord control was no longer necessary under the emergent political and economic imperatives of empire. As the commercial enterprises of the East India Company yielded steadily in importance to the arguments of free traders who saw in landed wealth the development of a new market for British goods, and as economic activity broadened beyond what was made possible directly through the collection of revenue from control over land, a new idea of empire had to develop to accommodate a vastly different scale of global activity. Along the way, the archive itself kept changing, a reminder of the impossibility of using the archive to reconstruct a single, straightforward, political history of change.

The Archive of Ethnography

With the establishment of direct rule in 1858, the colonial state itself was transformed once again. If land and the revenue and authority that accrued from its relationship with the state were so fundamental to the formation of the early colonial state, the fact that the rebellions of 1857 quickly led to agrarian revolt and the steadily diversifying economic character of imperial power (propelled in part by the building of railways in the 1850s) made it clear that some things had to change. Land tax was still an important source of revenue in the late nineteenth century, but imperial ambition moved to an altogether new level. The steady absorption of new lands through the aggressive policies of Lord Dalhousie, which in the taking of Oudh in 1856 had led directly to the Great Rebellion of 1857, were brought abruptly to a halt, and policies of indirect rule were mobilized to accommodate and ultimately abdicate what was an incomplete project of colonial conquest (one-third of India remained under princely control at the time of the rebellion). Concurrently, the rebellion made it clear that some communities in India could be counted as loyal; others became doomed to perpetual suspicion. Bengalis were no longer to be recruited to the armed forces, which were now to be stocked only by the loyal "martial" races, as Macaulay's rhetorical hyperbole was translated into state policy. In the new economy of colonial rule, political loyalty replaced landed status. And the form of knowledge and argument that seemed most appropriate to assess matters of loyalty rather than histories of land control was knowledge of peoples and cultures. To put the matter in bold relief, after 1857 anthropology supplanted history as the principal colonial modality of knowledge. The colonial state changed from a "revenue state" to an "ethnographic state."[9]

I am not referring here to disciplines of knowledge in the modern sense; anthropology had not yet been formally invented as an academic discipline in any case (though its invention was certainly tied to its rising significance for colonial rule), and Indian history for Europe was not only written outside the academy but usually as an extension of colonial bureaucratic reports. Rather, I am suggesting that the foundational importance of historical evidence and argument for land policy yielded at this point in the history of empire to another overriding concern, the need to identify those populations that were inherently loyal (or disloyal) to the British and to learn the customs of other populations in order to understand and if possible control them in a grand effort to avoid any return of the near-fatal calamity of the rebellion. In place of a history that focused on questions of land, rule, property, and sovereignty, an anthropology of the peoples and cultures of India increasingly became the canonical knowledge of empire. The decennial census, begun in 1871–1872, became the apotheosis of the new ethnographic imperative of the colonial state, manifested increasingly as well through a proliferation of manuals, gazetteers, and reports that contained growing amounts of ethnographic data and interpretation.

At the heart of this new knowledge, caste came to be viewed as the primary institution—and sphere of social relations—that articulated the legacies of tradition, standing in place of the historical-mindedness that was seen as absent from Indian sensibilities. Colonial historiography increasingly conceded to anthropology the study of historical subjects that had not yet entered modernity. Anthropology in this sense grew out of modern history, turning into the history of those without history as well as the prehistory of those now mired in history. By the late nineteenth century, anthropology became quite literally the history of the colonized. In this division of disciplinary labor, anthropology, whether of a physical body or a body politic, was less a complement than an extension of modern history, distributed geographically by the logic of conquest and rule, linked directly to the interests and forms of the colonial state. And in the imperial order of things, history was to the modern metropolitan state what anthropology was to the colonial state, reflecting both the similarities and the differences between state systems at home and in the colonies. History constructed a glorious past for the nation in which the present was the inevitable teleological frame; anthropology assumed histories that necessitated colonial rule. History told the story of the nation; anthropology explained why a nation had not yet emerged.[10]

If the British did not see history as a fundamental attribute of Indian culture, it is no coincidence that they established their rule in large part by obscuring their role in conquest and expansion, building their colonial presence on the ruins of a political (and historical) order that they had aggressively conquered and ruled. Mackenzie had been one of the last colonial savants to exercise himself primarily in the collection of local, indigenous histories. James Mill propounded instead that whatever past India might have could be left in the dustbin of history, arguing with liberal intention that all that was good in India would be imported from Britain.[11] Mill's historicist sense of civilizational progress gave way to a cultural sense of India's fundamental exemption from history. Thus the late nineteenth century witnessed the first experiments in ethnographic surveys, even as the records in the archives increasingly reflected a colonial preoccupation with the customs and social relations of the people of India. I have written elsewhere about the way in which late nineteenth-century arguments about social policy tended increasingly to reflect anthropological sensibilities—as for example in British concerns, mobilized in part by missionary pressure to regulate forms of religious expression that appeared to be particularly backward or barbarous.[12] At the same time, there was an explosion of writing—in books, treatises, and administrative files—about caste. Caste was used to explain and to classify, to predict and contain the potential unruliness and recalcitrance of colonial subjects; indeed caste became an alternative colonial civil society that made other kinds of civic institutions, let alone political rights, seem either unnecessary, or foreign, or both.

Ethnography and the Archive

When I began my historical research on the late nineteenth century, I encountered the voluminous workings of direct British rule both at the central level in New Delhi and at the provincial level in Madras. As I paged through indexes of documents that reflected the quotidian procedures of government, I read files that considered and then ruled on issues ranging from the appointment of a particular individual to a position (say, for example, the new superintendent of ethnography) to the reasons why such a superintendent, with a new organization and mission, might be so important to the colonial state at the time. When, looking for ethnographic observations on the part of the state outside the official manuals, gazetteers, and census materials, I found materials about so-called barbaric practices such as hookswinging, I read through files that responded to widespread pressure from missionaries and others regarding the suppression of an activity that brought no grievous bodily harm and little in the way of significant social unrest to the attention of district administrators, who nevertheless had to worry about the representation of governmental activities both within India and back in Britain itself. When I began to correlate the interest of official ethnography in native bodily practices with the Torture Commission Report of 1855, I had to rely on my own archival experience of working with land and settlement records as early as the late eighteenth century in order to see through official self-congratulation and justification when horror stories around brutality and violence in the South Indian countryside were adduced as evidence of the need for colonial rule. As I began to encounter the cross-referentiality of files and reports, documents and contexts, I could begin to see connections between files that were not at first clear. Archival research itself invariably proceeds genealogically—record by record, decision by decision, trace by trace—not in the straightforward linear way that most basic histories imply. Each record in the archive referenced previous records, both as precedent and as paper trail; although documents are frequently scripted with posterity in mind, history is in part an afterthought, only incidentally related to the sources that are fetishized as so fundamental to the craft of history itself. Yet history is encoded on the surfaces of the very files—the numbering systems, the departmental structures, and classificatory rubrics—as well as in the reports, letters, decisions, and scribbles within that make up the archive. The archive contains primary sources at the same time that it is always a secondary trace of historical discourse. Contexts are both inside and outside the archive.

The archive encodes a great many levels, genres, and expressions of what Foucault has called "governmentality."[13] Commissions of Inquiry have very different histories from routine papers that surface in the government orders of everyday official practice; government manuals and gazetteers have very different uses from occasional notes or office correspondence that move in haphazard circuits of official (and semiofficial) exchange. Historical research can reveal connections that become effaced by the effects of history itself: e.g., the connection between the proliferation of debates over the proper way to introduce a proprietary economy into India and the need of the colonial state for a stable form of revenue, between the anxiety over agrarian and military revolt and the social classifications that became hardened into late colonial views of

caste, between the concerns of the police to apprehend habitual criminals and the general criminalization of colonial populations in the early
development of anthropometry, and between the modern career of anthropology and the legacies of the colonial past. Even as the connections
never completely come full circle—never foreclosing the possibilities of
other connections and frequently displacing others—they move us well
away from the certainties of linear and autonomous textual histories
of anthropology and history, dissolving texts into contexts even as contexts constantly become reabsorbed by other texts and traces. While the
archive has no transparency of its own—its facts can be construed in
any number of ways, and the historical record alone can by no means
explain why we write the way we do—it is nevertheless the field within
which we all conduct our research, pushing us by its recalcitrance, limit-
ing us by its aggravating absences, fascinating us by its own patterns of
intertextuality, seducing us by its appearance of the real.

The colonial archive has a peculiar opacity. While all archives reflect
their particular origins as state records, colonial archives betray the additional contradictions of colonial rule. In the case of India, the early
colonial state was officially answerable to the British Parliament and
Crown through a cumbersome process that required a minimum of six
months for the exchange of correspondence by sea. In fact, the East India Company, a monopoly joint stock firm, ran the day-to-day affairs
of the colony as if it were a duly constituted government until 1858.
Even after the assumption of Crown rule, the subjects of empire were
governed by imperial fiat with none of the reforms concerning public
representation and accountability taken on board by the metropolitan
state, limited though they may now seem in historical retrospect. Revenue records might have debated the high points of Mughal history in
order to find precedents for Ricardian theories of rent, but the question
of legitimation was balanced by threats of disorder rather than by the
checks of dissent and debate. Perhaps even more critically, the accumulation of an ethnographic archive in the late nineteenth century worked
not just to displace colonial sovereignty but to proclaim the colonial
subject as lacking both in fundamental political capabilities and in historical consciousness. As a result, the archive reflects the shift of state
anxiety from the political and juridical to the social and cultural levels.
Caste identity, for example, became not just the object of knowledge

but the end of knowledge, eclipsing political persuasion, class position, or regional interests as the basis for state concerns about control and containment. The ethnographic state produced (or at least it tried to produce) ethnographic subjects, not political ones. The colonial archive thus actively resisted the onset of modern history.

In my own case, I not only escaped the confines of the archive to search for historical texts in the Mackenzie collection; I also journeyed off to the record office in the small town and former kingdom of Pudukkottai, to see what local records might have been considered worthy of survival and maintenance in the record office that had been the documentary hub that had once made up the circulatory lifeblood of administrative life in the princely state. Much of the documentation for my first book came in fact from this local archive, thanks to the large investment of the princely state in administration and history. But even in such a rich and well-kept local archive, I initially searched in vain for local land records that might explain the complex archaeology of landholding, social relations, and the political perquisites and privileges that was barely to be glimpsed through the differentiated schema of tax structures—the desiderata of political life as the old regime gave way to the new during the middle decades of the nineteenth century. After months of searching, I finally came upon a locked record room that contained the handwritten records of each land settlement in the old state, most dating to the years between 1875 and 1885, though providing capsule histories of properties going back to the eighteenth century. This was literally a repository rather than archive, but because of my local residence and my relations of trust with the royal family, I was allowed to borrow these huge revenue volumes in order to make a quantitative survey of all the special land tenures in the state, though the volumes were so large and heavy that I had to arrange to have them transported to my bungalow by bullock cart, an ethnographic image of history if ever there was one. Months of copying, annotation, and quantitative analysis began to reveal the local sedimentation of privilege—special land tenures denoting hereditary claims to reduced or zero tax for temples, trusts, and individuals whose entitlements reflected their role in local worship, social and cultural life, and in many instances the survival of an old feudal political system, in which the retainers, officers, and chiefs of the old kingdom hung on to tax-free privileges and titles long after the demise of the old political regime. It was on the basis of these records that my own anthropological history of the old regime was predicated.

Even these records, however, reflected not just a precolonial past but a colonial present, since the terms of "resumption," "settlement," "rationalization," and "reclassification" were set in relation to the "*Inam Settlement*" of the Madras Presidency in 1865, a comprehensive effort to resume revenue rights over vast tracts of land—originally given to temples, Brahmans, artisans, and village servants—that had been protected from taxation, in part as a courtesy to older political, cultural, and political rights and in part to stifle the discontent that would have brought about much greater resistance to the establishment of British rule across the southern Tamil countryside.[14] Princely states tended to preserve the past much more effectively than areas under direct British rule, despite the extent to which the past changed dramatically under the impact of demilitarization and the effective "freezing" of older forms and processes of political life. Even as these old hand-copied records traversed the streets of Pudukkottai town to be copied and transferred into the historical record of postcolonial India, they represented the full force of colonial ideas, institutions, and initiatives as the local "settlement" of revenues followed the logic and protocol of Madras Presidency at large. Much as I tried to escape the confines of the colonial archive, I kept coming up against its powerful tentacles and pervasive influence.

Even so, my most illuminating encounter with the living nature of the archive came when I discovered files in the Pudukkottai record office that began to connect directly with the ethnographic world outside. I came upon myriad disputes in archives that still were alive in local villages, sometimes in memories, sometimes in law courts and administrative files. On occasion I came upon a requisition for a file that was missing in the archive, having been consulted either by the courts or by the District Collector's Office. On other occasions I found that ethnographic work in a village echoed tensions that continued on in long-running quarrels, contests, or disputes. On still other occasions I received delegations asking me to use my privileged access to the archive to find and document a paper trail to support a particular stake or claim. As I began to encounter contexts and texts in this kind of ethnographic dialogue, I became even more aware of the way the opacity of the archive was itself an artifact of the instrumentalities of government rather than the murky reality of history, that the archival paper trail was as contingent, contested, and contradictory as life outside the archive. So much for the primary sanctity of the inner spaces of historical truth.

Archives and the Modernity of History

At one level, modern history could only develop fully in the metropole, where, to paraphrase Marx, farce trumped tragedy and the protocols of modern bureaucracy and state control developed without the full mediation of colonial rule.[15] At the same time, modern history grew out of encounters and struggles that were as present in colonial contexts as in imperial ones, if in ways that reflected the obvious domination of imperial state power. Even after decolonization, the postcolonial nation had always to refer to the imperial power, despite the reversal of historical narrative. The main story of modern history thus still refers back to its primordial contest with the eschatological conventions that were anchored in theological temporalities and religious institutions, producing its own set of discontinuities, shadows, and contradictions. The history of the archive, however, tells a more complicated tale, one that simultaneously privileges the imperial metropole yet at the same time shows the incapacity of that metropole to take full control over colonial history. This history further shows that the main contest at the level of the state—and for that matter the archive—was between imperial and colonial states; theology did not so much disappear as become appropriated by the hidden political history of modernity. As such, the state of record for modern history was the same imperial state that appropriated both the colonies and, in the end, Enlightenment sensibilities too.

As Koselleck has shown, the modern European state became the measure for nascent temporalities as surely as it provided the boundaries for nationally constructed social spaces.[16] The state also became the instrumentality through which historical documents became meaningful as the primary and authentic record of the past. History served as a principal form of governmentality at the same time that governmentality expressed itself through the categories of historical thought and writing. In more prosaic terms, history was organized in narratives that made the state (and, when not arrested by colonial rule, ultimately the nation) into the subject and the object of temporal consequence; as a result, history itself became a form of state power. History was effectively written by the state to educate and justify political policies and practices, and the conditions of its production and preservation were inseparable from the needs and instrumentalities of the state. The archive, that primary site of state monumentality, was the institution that classified and canonized the knowledge required by the state even as it made this knowledge available for subsequent generations in the cultural form of a neutral repository of the past.[17]

Many commentators, from Hegel to Koselleck, have noted that modern history—or rather the modern idea of history—was born with the French Revolution.[18] It is perhaps even more true to say that the modern archive was born with the French Revolution, and, as befits that tumultuous event, the modern archive was as much about the destruction as it was about the preservation of the past.[19] The Archives Nationales of Paris was created by the Decree of September 12, 1790, and open access to the archives was declared a right of citizenship rather than a perquisite of state power (or, for that matter, scholarly interest).[20] Older archives had been in the possession of kings and courts and were placed only at the disposition of those in power, largely for the preservation of titles to rights, privileges, honors, and land. The modern archive was born in the violence of revolution precisely because of the way documents had supported the privilege of the old regime; according to Philippe Sagnac, in many acts of rural rebellion, the French peasant "took his own Bastille, invaded the chateaux, ran straight to the seigneurial archives, held at last in his hands the charters, monuments of his own servitude, and delivered them to the fire."[21] More centrally, the new government itself initiated the wholesale destruction of records as part of its revolutionary program. State-sponsored bonfires consigned papers of the nobility, orders of knighthood, and other documents of the old regime to ashes in the years between 1789 and 1793, a policy extolled by none other than

Condorcet: "It is today that, in the capital, Reason burns, at the foot of the statue of Louis XIV, 600 folio volumes attesting to the vanity of this class whose titles will at last disappear in smoke."[22]

The new French state did not maintain the full openness of the archive, as the imperatives of the postrevolutionary nation-state had to accommodate new forms of privilege and secrecy.[23] In England, where no revolution produced such a dramatic archival history, the modern archive developed directly out of the records of the Chancery Department, most of which were housed in the Tower of London until the Public Record Office was built in the middle of the nineteenth century.[24] Unlike in France, where the new archives were established as part of a new revolutionary state with the specific purpose of undermining the old regime, in England the archives embodied the rights and privileges that had been appropriated by the British aristocracy over centuries.[25] The establishment of the Public Record Office roughly coincided with the electoral reforms that sought to enlarge the voting public and open the procedures of government to the new, increasingly urban and mercantile bourgeoisie. But colonial records remained in the India Office, tied as they were directly to protocols of governance, until the end of empire itself. Unsurprisingly, the idea of public access for colonial records required the emergence of a postcolonial public (although the principal public for the India Office Record Room is still the descendant of the British colonial searching through ecclesiastical and military records for genealogical information). The contradictions of colonial rule extended both to history and to the archives, exemplifying the limits of representation and accountability that were so fundamental to the colonial relationship.

In reflecting briefly on the history of archives, and in retelling the early history of the archives of my own research career, I have attempted to call attention to some of the ways in which the archive not only contains documents but is itself a primary document of history. At the same time, I have called attention to the particular character of the colonial archive. From the beginning of colonial conquest, long before historical narratives gave way to ethnographic accounts, colonial rule produced a different kind of relationship to the past, and to its collection, preservation, and destruction, than had been the case in the imperial metropole. In many ways, the archive was the literal document that expressed the

rupture between nation and state engendered by colonialism. The colonial archive was not just the record of the colonial state but also the
repository of the sources for an imperial history whose primary public
was in the metropole rather than the colony. Thus it was that anticolonial nationalist movements had to struggle not just to narrate alternative
histories but to find different sources and authorities for the development of new national (and local) historiographies.[26]

Anticolonial nationalist movements have been especially inventive
in the domain of history, not just finding alternative narratives but new
sources and forms for the historical imagination. In a way, the ethnographic imperative described in my own historical pursuits reflects the
contradictions inherent in any postcolonial history: encountering, on
the one hand, the power and reach of imperial control over the past and,
on the other, the conditions and fissures that created spaces both for
the anthropological histories I have tried to write and the subaltern and
minority histories that have been fundamental to all struggles for new
political outcomes. As we historicize the archive, therefore, we must
always be alert to the limits of the archive for any history that seeks to
escape the very state forms that constitute so much of the history of the
archive itself.

The archive is the instantiation of the state's interest in history. It sur-
vives as the remains of the record rooms of everyday governmental business, and it is monumentalized by the state to preserve its own history
in the assumed name of the nation (or colony) rather than the state (or
metropole). The monument preserves much of its sacred legacy—with
its hierarchical structures, its labyrinthine procedures, its professional
protocols—enshrining the secularized state with the full solemnity of
the past. As critics of history and historiography we must therefore chip
away at the history of this monument at the same time that we recognize the monumentality of all historical evidence and by implication
the monumental limits and conditions of all historical writing. Historians may make their own history, but they cannot always make it as
they choose. Historians make history in and on the basis of archives
that already sediment an archaeology of the state—indeed an archaeology of history—that, perhaps necessarily, remains to this day largely
unexamined.

2

Autobiography of an Archive

I have told the story of how I came to use the Mackenzie archive for my first major research work, and I provided some sense not just of its importance but of some of the questions I brought to, and then took away from, this transformative archival encounter. This chapter provides a more detailed look both at the archive and my encounter with it. The first volume of T. V. Mahalingam's new catalog of the Mackenzie Collection was published in 1972, the year I went to begin my graduate studies in Indian history.[1] As I built my own work on some of the questions and preoccupations of the then-regnant "ethnosociology," an effort to engage in sociological analysis using only "native" categories, I came to understand that historical research in India—at least for the periods before British rule—would require a level of inventiveness, and even hubris, that my earlier work on Gandhi in southern India had certainly not anticipated. I would need to expand the usual palette of documents that had attained recognition as proper sources for empirical research and attempt to situate historical understanding within larger cultural frames, including texts that might appear in part fanciful or even mythological to provide a full historical record even for the seventeenth, eighteenth, and nineteenth centuries. I was also urged by my advisors to take the long historical view, in part to gain historical perspective, in part to widen the archive of appropriate historical sources, and in part to counter the dominance of colonial assumption and narrative in the writing of early modern history in India. With little historical fanfare (and, I dare say, philological preparation), I started my first research exercise by studying the ample epigraphical record of South Indian dynasties, inscriptions of the Pallavas, Pandyas, and Cholas, dating from the seventh to the fourteenth centuries. Most of these inscriptions recorded gifts of land and other resources to support permanent endowments for the support of temples and specific forms of worship within them.

I focused on the *prashastis*, the prefatory hymns of praise to the king that often began with a genealogical account of the kingly family, rather than on the details of the grants and endowments that made up the bulk of these inscriptions (and that were then being used by some inventive historians to understand the economic and political functions of temples). I came to see these prefaces through anthropological eyes, reading genealogy as a form of history. Genealogy, following from Malinowski's anthropological proposals about myths as charters, made claims about authority, about the right to rule, and also about the specifically divine character, or antecedents, of particular dynastic families.[2] I published my first article on the changing representation of sovereignty for the Pallava kings, detailing a transformation that took place in the eighth century, revealing—I argued—a vastly expanded claim regarding universal sovereignty as the king's genealogy was connected to the great god Vishnu for the first time.[3] This cultural change neatly correlated with the greater political ambition and reach of the late Pallava dynasty in this period, anticipating both the increasing scale of kingly politics in the south and elsewhere and the greater levels of political connectivity across the subcontinent and the Indian Ocean characteristic of the times.

It was with this background that I started reading Mahalingam's summaries of the local Tamil tracts of the Mackenzie Collection. As I began to formulate my dissertation plans around the local lords (*palaiyakkarars*) of the southern Tamil countryside in what we then called the late precolonial period, I hoped the Mackenzie Collection would provide that treasure trove of archival materials every historian so devoutly desires. And while I looked for a set of textual formulations that would constitute the basis for a cultural account of understandings of history, society, and politics, I also imagined a different kind of archive, one that would reflect more than just a canonic—Sanskritic or Brahmanic—view of history and indeed that would focus on historical struggle and inequality as much as, if not more than, it did on hierarchical order.

The Mackenzie Collection was treasure all right. But the valuable nuggets seemed buried deep, and despite (and in part because of) the long history of cataloguing, it was not at all clear how I was to use this archive. My advisor at Chicago, the historical anthropologist Bernard Cohn, was intrigued by Mackenzie, although he was characteristically less interested in the collection as a set of cultural texts than he was in the circumstances of its collection and use. Burton Stein, a historian at the University of Hawaii who was my advisor for all things South Indian, was resolutely skeptical. An unapologetic dualist, he thought of culture either as an ideological cover for material interests or as a kind of ritual overlay to real structures, as in the way he thought about Chola sovereignty as a kind of fictive ritual that made empire a rhetorical conceit, with all the managerial and political operations of peasant society organized inside the segmentary regional units (*natus*) of medieval Tamil history. He, too, had thumbed through Mahalingam, but he doubted the fundamental historicity of most of the Mackenzie texts; unlike inscriptions, they could not be clearly dated, a necessary feature of analysis if one was to develop a longitudinal understanding of endowment or any other cultural activity. He was incredulous at what he felt to be the idealist preoccupations of cultural anthropology, whether promulgated by Dumont or Marriott, and he was hard at work on his own history of precolonial South Indian history that would demonstrate the core importance of peasant values around collective management and agrarian control.[4] So he developed a theory of the state that accorded it "mere" ritual status, a rhetorical gloss that masked the real agrarian relations and structures of peasant society. He focused on the Chola era because of the rich epigraphical record, and while he conceded that there were few local (and noncolonial) sources available for palaiyakkarar history aside from Mackenzie's texts, he argued for extreme caution in the use of these materials. Pursuing my dream, which at the time was the same as my dissertation topic, I went with considerable uncertainty to the Government Oriental Manuscripts Library (GOML) to see what I could find, soon after arriving in Madras in the summer of 1975 to begin my research.

Armed with H. H. Wilson's early nineteenth-century descriptive catalogue, bought from the miraculous bookseller Jayavelu in teeming Moor

Market, and Mahalingam's updated and recently published catalogue, I found that the GOML itself had an entirely different cataloguing system from either of these two works.[5] I also found that some of the manuscripts were on palmyra palm leaf, inscribed with a special cursive (*kutterrittu*) script, and that others had been recopied on different kinds of paper of varying quality and resistance to the termites and other vermin that had sought to consign the collection to the literal dustbin of history. Eventually I found readable copies of different texts, histories, and chronicles (*carittarum, kaiphiyats, varalaru*) and family histories (*vamcavalis*). It was only later that I discovered that many of these had been translated by Mackenzie's assistants, or by translators who worked for British officials, or (at least by self-attribution) by the Rev. William Taylor, an orientalist missionary of prodigious if questionable scholarship. These translations varied greatly in quality, and, like archaeological sediments, revealed different moments in the history of the archive. They were, however, critical components of the history of the collection since Colin Mackenzie was by his own admission no orientalist and therefore relied entirely on the annotation and translation of others; he himself never managed to learn an Indian language.

I also read Tamil copies of various historical texts with a local scholar (Professor Tirunavakkarasu), who corrected the texts as he explained certain passages, feeling no hermeneutic qualms about crossing off whole portions that I had painstakingly copied while telling me they were corrupt and should have been like something else instead, occasionally citing a quotation from other Tamil texts such as the *Periya Puranam* and other poems principally of sixteenth- and seventeenth-century provenance. I now realize I was witnessing the classic reading practices of a local bard, or *karanam* (*puluvar*), who composed and read the court texts of early modern South Indian history in which the texts were situated in relation to many other texts and then interpreted in traditional philological ways, full of cross-references to the local canon of Tamil (and to some extent Telugu) texts. As it turned out, many of the Mackenzie texts were not only seen as corrupt by H. H. Wilson and his scribes but by my contemporary "karanam" as well, whose reading practices seemed to hearken back both to the work of early generations of karanams and the scholarly standards that had been at that time both codified, and further shaped, by the classical Sanskritic orientalism of

Wilson. This, at least for me, was further confirmation of the importance of the Mackenzie archive, uncontaminated not just by the "West" but by the high literary philological traditions of southern India as well.

I have written elsewhere about some of these texts and the methods I used to read and analyze them. Many years later I was chided for exoticizing the historicity of these texts by calling them ethnohistories rather than histories, but in those early days I was content to use the capaciousness of anthropology (the prefix "ethno-" was only intended to gloss the ways in which history was culturally constructed and shaped) to rescue these histories from the pervasive colonial and postcolonial condescension of the times. British officials from the late eighteenth century onward anticipated (indeed, they provided some of the basis for) Hegel's assertion that there was no Hindu sense of history. They used language like that of Samuel Lushington, the collector of Poligar Peshkash in the Southern Pollams in 1800, who noted that local history, when it existed at all, was "generally involved in dark obscurity or embellished with unintelligible fables."[6] H. H. Wilson initially embraced the Mackenzie project as a way of establishing his credentials as a scholar who could bring to light the historical wealth of Mackenzie's unique and monumental collection, but he seemed to abandon the project as soon as he completed his own catalogue raisonné in 1828. He dismissed the importance of most of the collection's Sanskrit texts, and in addition to his general prejudice against allegedly corrupt texts, he was in any event not trained in the languages of the South. Instead, he focused on the high Tamil and Telugu texts that had attained the status of sacred texts rather than on the more vernacular materials that made up the bulk of the Mackenzie Collection. His strategy was a success, at least for his academic career, as he was selected for the Boden Chair at Oxford in 1832.[7] However, in the years after the publication of his catalogue in 1828, the collection fell into the fault line between the texts that commanded proper scholarly attention and the local traditions and folklore that, by the second half of the nineteenth century at least, became the province of colonial ethnography. In the vacuum created by the East India Company's growing disdain for native scholars and scholarship and Wilson's career aspirations, the Mackenzie Collection was in effect taken over by William Taylor, a missionary who produced voluminous catalogues and translations but indulged in speculations that seemed directed toward finding a common scriptural base to provide collateral confirmation of the events of the first few books of the Old Testament. While there were references to a few of the Mackenzie texts in the official gazetteers and manuals produced by the colonial state in the period from the 1860s through the early twentieth century, the collection itself suffered from basic neglect until Mahalingam's team began to survey the manuscripts in the 1950s. That project proceeded very slowly but ultimately yielded a new two-volume catalogue ready for my use when I began graduate school.

The new catalogue did not succeed in making the GOML collection more accessible; no catalogue seemed up to the task of organizing an archive that had been so dispersed and neglected over this long a period of time. Nevertheless, I copied various texts and found that many of the small kingly (palaiyakkarar) families of the southern Tamil country had histories—or, rather, ballads, bardic tales, and heroic genealogies—interspersed among the palm-leaf manuscripts deteriorating in Madras. What I didn't yet know, however, was that the English-language texts that consisted of translations, diaries, log books, and correspondence had been shipped to England and were still housed in the India Office Library in London. Some of these were in volumes referenced only in the Wilson catalogue (Mahalingam focused instead only on the vernacular materials in the GOML library). I was not sure that they had survived, since some materials had disappeared in a shipwreck off the coast of Ceylon in the early nineteenth century, but was elated when I found, after returning to London from Madras in the summer of 1977, that the listed volumes were all available for scrutiny. I only learned much later, on a return visit to London in 1986, that most of the material had never been bound and had sat instead in uncatalogued boxes beyond the reach of scholars until then. In any event, returning to the summer of 1977, I decided to spend considerable time wading through the unbound translations, with special attention to the Class XII group: the "Letters and Reports, from Native Agents Employed to Collect Books, Traditions, etc., in Various Parts of the Peninsula."

The first volume struck my attention immediately. The report of one Nitala Naina of his trip to "Tritchinopoly" (Tiruchirappalli) in 1803 was especially evocative. Nitala had set out from Madras to points south in May 1804. He visited a number of Europeans on his way and soon made contact with a man by the name of Sivaramaiah, who, it was promised, would be able to "procure all the accounts of the Tondamaun People and the genealogical accounts of the former kings of Pallavaraiyar for the satisfaction of his Master."[8] During my time of dissertation research I had decided to focus on this very kingdom, later called the princely state of Pudukkottai, ruled by the Kallar Tondaiman family. I had spent several months trying to locate authentic accounts, histories, and genealogies among other documents concerning the Tondaimans. I had finally found a formal history of the Tondaiman kings in the GOML, and it was, upon examination, the very text that Nitala had himself procured.

Nitala only managed to collect it, however, with great difficulty. He had at first been frightened to go to Pudukkottai without protection—rumors of the martial prowess of the Kallars having circulated widely—and even when he hired a bodyguard to accompany him to the court he was nervous. When he finally arrived at the court, he was asked to present his diplomatic credentials and found to his great astonishment that his letter of introduction from Mackenzie was of no value. Not wanting to spend either the time or money to return to Madras and secure more official-looking papers, he turned to his local contact, Sivaramaiah, complaining as he wrote, "I asked him you had carried me to Tondamaun Country with the promise of getting me a great deal of books at last you put me to tell by their people to go way from their country." Sivaramaiah answered him by saying, "He is a little Palagar in the crowd of 72 palagars, as he is a inferior man he prevented your business of getting the informations," but promised him he would arrange everything and, since he had no heirs, give him any books of his own that would help him in his researches. After these heartfelt assurances, Nitala was asked to wait, only to find that his growing restlessness had little effect other than making Sivaramaiah reiterate his assurances and plead with him not to turn to other possible sources of information on account of the possible danger it would land him in. In blaming the Tondaiman, Sivaramaiah made what was in fact an interesting claim, namely that the Tondaiman was just one of seventy-two other palaiyakkarars who were uniformly subordinate to the Nayaka of Madurai. In this account, which did in fact circulate widely and was reproduced in a number of Mackenzie texts and elsewhere, the Nayaka of Madurai systematized the mounting chaos of local political rule by appointing the top seventy-two local warriors as, in effect, members of his own political cabinet. Each was given the nominal responsibility to guard one of the seventy-two bastions of the Madurai fort. This metaphor of political incorporation, itself an effort to reconnect a wide array of local chiefs and kings to positions of subordination, was a source of shame for the Tondaimans, who quickly emerged as among the most important of the successor states after the growing weakness of the Nayakas. They were hardly pleased to acknowledge early accounts in which they were merely one among "seventy-two," especially since there were later texts that gave them a vastly inflated status, as in some examples the status of belonging only to the exclusive inner circle (*kumaravarkkam*, literally "group of sons") along with only two others: Maravar rulers of Sivagangai and Ramanathapuram.

The account by Nitala Naina made for riveting reading, given my growing sense of recognition at his difficulty in procuring texts and records and also in encountering the complicated thicket of political status and power. Nitala waited for Sivaramaiah for five months, alternatively flattering him in hopes of quicker results and fending off requests to arrange a job—like his own—working for Mackenzie directly in the collection and transcription of local historical records. As he wrote in his account, "We must encourage him by the sweet words, until we get the informations from him, so, he made me to tell him if you get me the kyfeyatts and other informations in two or three months I shall acquaint this to my Master to get you anyone of the petty service." Nitala frequently lost patience, on one occasion quarreling with Sivaramaiah and complaining publicly about his behavior, only to find that, "On the next day, the Seevaraumiah brought up two books, Mallopooranum, and the book of Tondamaun Genealogy . . . composed in Telenga language." Nitala then "asked him to get the particular account of Tondamaun with the dates." He complained that Sivaramaiah had not produced any complete accounts after five months, only to receive repeated assurances in reply. Nevertheless, despite these apparent results, Nitala began to hear from other acquaintances that Sivaramaiah was indeed untrustworthy, in league with some dangerous fellows, even plotting against him (perhaps to try to replace him in Mackenzie's service), and at one point Nitala wrote that he feared for his life. In the end, Sivaramaiah was no great threat, although Nitala was genuinely worried that his own name had been defamed and that he might neither recover the expenses of his trip nor produce enough books and materials to justify to Mackenzie his own salary. He was fortunate to receive support and reassurance from Lutchmia along the way. But as his journal goes on, a sense of intrigue and mystery envelops his endeavors. He noted that while collecting his information he always worked at night to remain in secret, and he concluded his diary entry (on the way to Madurai, where he went after his time in Trichinopoly and the Tondaiman country) by noting how much distress had been part of this journey: "Having come down safely after avoiding all the troubles and dangers by your favor and depend only on your praise." Although he collected some important materials, the cache of two hundred books never actually appeared, and Nitala's curious diary conveys poignantly and sharply, if not always very clearly, the same chimerical sense I had experienced so often when being promised books and other historical materials, all the while being pulled into relationships of negotiation and intrigue, in which the stakes ranged from employment, either with me or the royal family, to the opportunity to have the historical record reflect different accounts of political standing in times of shifting political loyalties.

When, four years later, having finished my dissertation but still wanting more specificity about the history, culture, and political fortunes of the Tondaiman Kallars, I returned to Pudukkottai for a year's research, there were many times I felt that I was once again reliving Nitala Naina's experience, finding myself in the middle of bizarre political negotiations, approached for employment while also lobbied for favorable mention in a book that might matter in law courts and administrative offices. For me as it had been for Nitala, it was a year full of promises to provide texts, manuscripts, books, and access to information in return for favors, influence, employment, and other modes of access to the royal family or other official connections. There were classic moments when I was treated to oral performances and traditions that turned out to owe their origins to the manuals and gazetteers that had been prepared for the princely state, the texts themselves often being referenced back to the original text that Nitala collected in 1804. More and more, the letters and reports written by Mackenzie's agents, and the sets of questions and distilled historical notes that Mackenzie himself conveyed to them, appeared as uncanny precursors to my own research experience.

Some years later, I was able to persuade the archivist of European manuscripts at the India Office Library, David Blake, to take me into the stacks to show me not just where both the General and the Unbound Collections were shelved but also twelve uncatalogued boxes of materials labeled "Mackenzie Collections, Correspondence and Miscellaneous." Now this was a gold mine, and although these materials have since been catalogued and opened for general scholarly scrutiny, I had the feeling then that I was entering the back room of a metropolitan archive for the first time, a good way to begin a second book project that seemed rather less adventurous than the first. I spent much of a year going through these papers, typing lengthy notes on a clunky first-generation Zenith laptop computer, reading through the General and Unbound Collections, the uncatalogued and unindexed boxes of letters and manuscripts, as well as the myriad catalogues and translations (and papers) of Wilson, Taylor, and other Mackenzie scholars. I examined Mackenzie's drawings as well, along with archival materials concerning John Leydon, Mark Wilks, Thomas Munro, and Francis Ellis, among others.

During my years of research on the Mackenzie Collection, I was consistently impressed by Mackenzie's own reflexive sense of the stakes of knowledge, both for others and for himself. Mackenzie's concern for his "native staff" was as palpable as his modesty about his capacity to do this work on his own. For one thing, Mackenzie was always honest about his lack of linguistic training. He wrote in his autobiographical memoir that his early years gave him little time or opportunity to "assiduously cultivate" a knowledge of "the native languages."[9] He noted that these were years of military duty and preoccupation: "Official encouragements to study the languages of the vast countries that have come under our domination since my arrival in India, were reserved for more happy times." But while this made Mackenzie no orientalist in the standard sense of the term and in many ways an outsider to the group of scholars who assembled in the Madras College, he was as rigorous and even obsessively attentive to detail as any philologist, though in matters relating to history, geography, and sociology rather than texts. He began his serious interest in local history, as well as geography, when posted to survey the Nizam's territories between 1792 and 1799. When he commenced the Mysore Survey in 1799, a time when he was officially commissioned to extend his survey to matters related to a "statistical account of the whole country," he began seriously to collect historical materials. The uncatalogued boxes were full of notes recording each of the reports and translations he received, noting further questions and categories of inquiry as he did so. He asked questions about different dialects and terms, even as he posed impressively detailed questions about different tribes, families, and nations. At one point he proposed a philological map of southern India, observing for example that while a number of texts in his collection concerning Krishnadevarayar of Vijayanagara were in Telugu, he was sure there were others in Kannada as well as other languages, judging from their geographical locations: "It is highly probable that their tributes of adulation and gratitude were poured forth in these languages also." As if anticipating late nineteenth-century assumptions about the significance of anthropometry, he also recommended, "Attention should be paid to the features, complexions, stature, appearance and habits of the natives of these countries. . . . Measurements even should be taken of the height and breadth at the chest."[10]

Most impressive of all was his constant effort to trace different dynastic lineages, their chronology, and their geographical movement in his effort to construct a comprehensive political history of southern India in the years before British conquest. He was uniquely aware of the political stakes of knowledge, both because of his direct experience of collecting and because of his clear familiarity with the travails of his assistants as they engaged in their field research. Writing to Barry Close about the Mysore Survey in December 1800, he noted that despite the Mysore raja's professed desire to be helpful and communicative, he was clearly trying to suppress some documents that did not favor the pretensions of his family. Mackenzie was concerned that his survey not appear overly invasive to the inhabitants of the countries through which he marched, and he sought to protect "the persons and properties of the Inhabitants . . . from all violence of any with me" so as to "conciliate their minds, which was indeed necessary for easier obtaining my object."[11] His assistants reported many instances where their inquiries were frustrated by lack of cooperation and the difficulty in procuring texts. It was in part his experience of the politics of local knowledge that made his historical method so sophisticated, to the point that he noted that some texts used fanciful codes to protect against misreadings (or appropriations) of historical traditions for state purposes. Although he was well aware that many of the texts he collected had little clear historical provenance and that some were written by village *karanams* or court retainers, he wrote that where possible,

> The historical accounts of the populations of governments of the districts were compiled from creditable sources of information on the spot: sometimes traditions from registers and checked by dates and eras, ascertained from grants and inscriptions where they could be referred to: a reciprocal correction was frequently derived from one to the other; and more satisfactory as no communication existed between the different authorities wherever certain internal evidence arises favourable to their accuracy.

He was never inattentive to the possible utility of the material he was collecting for the purposes of British rule. When engaged in the monumental Mysore Survey, for example, he wrote: "Of what importance these may be at all considered in regard to matters of present consideration, connected with Our Interests and the Internal Government of the Country to which every additional knowledge of the peculiar manners, Laws, and prevailing habits of the natives may be conceived of some utility, is with deference submitted."[12]

Nevertheless, Mackenzie's work for the Mysore Survey suggests his enduring anxiety about persuading government officials of the relevance of his historical inquiries. His elevation to surveyor-general, first of Madras and then of India, allowed him to indulge his antiquarian tendencies, even if his financial worries never ceased. It is not that he ever lost his sense of the importance of the knowledge he was collecting for British rule in India or that he ever entertained doubts that British rule was just and enlightened in comparison with earlier regimes, but this never fully drove his collecting instincts, and it became progressively less significant throughout his career. Perhaps this was the reason that as his collection grew and his interests clarified, he had more and more difficulty supporting his elaborate operation. This was in part because of his steadily escalating historical ambitions and because he was right to doubt the interest of most of his contemporaries in many of his endeavors. But it was also because of his Indian assistants, whose needs seemed constantly to grow and whose lives were upended by his move to Calcutta in the last years of his life.

Reading through Mackenzie's papers, the consistent concern he expressed for his Indian assistants is as noteworthy as his acute historical interests. His praise for C. V. Boriah, who he wrote "was the first step of my introduction into the portal of Indian knowledge," has been much cited and widely appreciated.[13] But it is still deeply moving to read his account of Boriah's prodigious talent and significance, even if his first praise was always for Boriah's wide knowledge of languages, on which he was entirely reliant. Boriah's "Report from Mysore of 1802" is an impressive document indeed and conveys a level of sophistication in matters ranging from the system of finance under Vijayanagara rule to anthropological details about castes and tribes in the Mysore country.[14] A note of caution must be introduced about the ultimate authorship of the text: while the original document was signed by Boriah, the copy in the survey records includes a note that it is "a copy from the original corrected MS; delivered in by C.V Boriah as the result of enquiries instituted on the Survey, under several Heads and Instructions, and from time to time added to by C. Mackenzie." But even so, there are claims that clearly seem of Boriah's authorship, many of them having to do with the importance of Brahmans in the cultural and intellectual landscape of South Indian life. Boriah writes that before the rise of the Vijayanagara state, Brahmans were ignored in favor of "illiterate men," and "religious animosities [did not permit] of encouragement to the superior and more learned castes . . . and the useful arts and learning were little cultivated." Happily for Boriah, the

> Beejanagur Sovereigns having attained a great and extensive dominion being zealous followers of the Bramin Religion, by which that state was originally established, they invited and encouraged several families of learned men of that Caste . . . to settle in their kingdom, assigning establishments under the various descriptions of Agraharams, Srootreeyums, Battavrooties, to the most learned and religious.

Boriah was unhappy that Vijayanagara did not maintain its political position but approved of the Nayaka and palaiyakkarar rulers that followed in its wake; he did not, however, think so highly of Tipu Sultan, who appropriated many of the palaiyakkarar estates, did not respect the tenures of earlier regimes, and, perhaps most important of all, did not found his authority on the basis of Brahmans and the "Bramin religion."[15]

When Boriah died in 1803, Mackenzie was bereft. In addition to his many other talents, Boriah had recruited a staff of native assistants for Mackenzie, chief among which were his two brothers, Lutchmia and Ramaswamy, and it was Lutchmia who became chief interpreter and manager of his local staff after Boriah's death. Lutchmia's handiwork is seen throughout the Mackenzie manuscripts, both catalogued and uncatalogued, and he was the usual recipient for the reports and letters sent by Mackenzie's various assistants and collected in the unbound manuscripts (Class XII). Lutchmia labored for years as translator, manager of the "native agents," and primary assistant to Mackenzie, and he earned Mackenzie's complete respect, even as he became totally indispensable for Mackenzie's wide-ranging projects. He did not, however, either have the genius of his older brother or, for that matter, his singleness of purpose in living what became for him, as time went by, an extremely complicated life.

If Lutchmia became critical to the maintenance of Mackenzie's establishment, his relationship to Mackenzie was complicated, and when Mackenzie moved to Calcutta in 1818 it became much more so. Mackenzie arranged for Lutchmia to join him, but despite repeated assurances that he was on his way, Lutchmia kept writing to Mackenzie from Madras saying that he could not yet move because of financial and legal entanglements of an ever more confused nature. Mackenzie sought to intercede on his behalf, first with a Colonel Reddell, then with a Mr. Binney. Mackenzie was befuddled that his every effort to relieve Lutchmia from his difficulties only seemed to produce more; he arranged to grant him the revenue from a village only to see it "swindled" out of his hands. Mackenzie lamented the specious acts that were committed by the natives who viewed Lutchmia's connections with a Britisher as an opportunity to enrich themselves, but throughout the entire, and sometimes opaque, correspondence, Mackenzie never wavered in his steadfast loyalty, accepting each one of his increasingly strained explanations for difficulty and delay while assuming that silence implied only embarrassment about circumstances Lutchmia would have preferred his master to know nothing about. In his correspondence, Mackenzie made clear how dependent he was on his native assistants, but he also stressed the depth of his personal commitment and concern. In this latter regard he seemed very nearly unique among his cohort of British officials.

In addition to his concerns about Lutchmia, he was worried about all of his assistants as he sat in Calcutta, removed from Madras and any direct access to the elaborate organization he had built up over his years in southern India. Writing to Riddell in April 1818, Mackenzie insisted that it was critical to provide in a suitable manner for the natives who assisted him for so many years, even if some of these individuals had not been blameless in their personal money matters: "Individuals may have faults but it is for a wise and liberal government to view things on a more extensive scale."[16]

Mackenzie went on, however, to complain bitterly about the difficulties he encountered in attempting to ensure the efficient liberality of his government. "You know the difficulty and loss of time I have had in arranging so as to provide for them with the least trouble and yet shamefully this has been retarded; the case of these Pensions is in point." Mackenzie noted that many of the Indians who had worked for him had been recommended for other offices and had distinguished themselves in their new roles. And he wrote that he had continued to recommend "these Natives without whose aid I could never have effected what has and at the moment does give considerable satisfaction," only "to observe that of all those gentlemen, excepting one in England, B. Sydenham, and yourself, who had little opportunity of knowing the difficulties I had to surmount," and that "as a consequence he had never yet found that I could be sure of these poor Devils being supported in my absence. In that manner the Native Servants of long service are usually rewarded." Mackenzie went on to write specifically about Lutchmia, his principal concern:

> You will be aware that the principal of these was the Bramen Lechmyah who actually formed the rest to my pursuits of the late transaction I have not yet got to the bottom; but this I know he never deceived me as to money matters; that he acted the part of a careful servant in that capacity with me, and that he was even neglectful of his own interests from his at-

tention to mine was well known to me, so far that I knew he was poor and embarrassed and I believe honest. In this state then it would be reasonable that I should assist even his family and those he reared.

In writing about Lutchmia, we get the sense that he was the Indian in whom Mackenzie had the greatest degree of trust, though he never used the praise he had previously bestowed on the elder brother, Boriah. But even where he found shortcomings, for example, with Lutchmia's younger brother Ramaswamy, he understood that the knowledge project of the early colonial state was completely reliant on its native assistants. Mackenzie noted that "Brother Ramasamy" had his own direct claims on "his patronage, given his long service" and the "ingenious explanations he procured me." Admitting some shortcomings he further opined, "He, nor any of them could ever be called Complete Translators by our own strict rules of orthography but where even is such to be got for 4, 5, 6, 8, and 10 pagodas." Mackenzie was well aware that both the Mysore Survey and the subsequent development of the college in Madras were dependent on these assistants:

Long before the College was dreamed of or some of its managers came to India these people were employed, and explained to me what perhaps some of the managers are not yet aware of (Mr Ellis perhaps excepted) and even to him I introduced that learned Sastri Sankaraia to whom the College lately very justly awarded its first degree; that was in the year 1802 when Mr E was studying the Sanskrit etc. Your friend Mr Cochrane can remember that Lechmyah and late Brother were usefully employed with me at Ballary and in Mysore 1800 and 1801.

Mackenzie was concerned that even with the role that Ellis played in the development of the college there was insufficient recognition of the role of native assistants, and certainly their compensation was inadequate. As he wrote,

You will not be surprised then that I felt some concern when I read that a person I had recommended from those motives was called to the College to be examined as a Translator and for a pay little more than half of what I had allowed in his former situation; it was mortifying to the poor man;

it was not very delicate to me, if they could receive him why employ him in a lower situation when they must know it will by the Natives be considered degrading and that he will probably be placed under persons who formerly would have solicited his good offices to be employed if the rest of his pay is to be carried to the Survey Expense it is not what I proposed if the Department is to be loaded still let it by way of Pension which he has a right to and let the rest be at his own disposal. My own opinion is that he or some of similar description will be still requisite as an Interpreter at least to explain the orthography of names in which all your maps are accused of being deficient.

With his characteristic generosity, Mackenzie noted that he would rather pay decent salaries himself for Ramaswamy and others to work at the college. Indeed, so distressed was Mackenzie that he asked that the manuscripts he wished to give to the college library not be deposited "till I know on what footing these people are to be received." Although he was particularly concerned about Lutchmia and Ramaswamy, he was anxious about all the assistants who had worked for him:

> If the rest of the Circars are to be surveyed or even in Cuttack they may usefully be employed as with the College. The Christian Appoo particularly when he recovers I can strike out employment for, and poor Babu Row might be employed somewhere I shall take it as a favor of your endeavor to get these people retained to complete the reports of their late journeys and that Ramaswamy revise their reports and I could wish you to report to me the cause of the delay in the People's pension that I may represent the case to obtain a remedy.

Lutchmia lost the legal case, but he and his associates lost far more when Mackenzie died in 1821. Mackenzie's death not only meant the end of any real protection and support for Lutchmia and their other Indian assistants; it also meant the inauguration of a kind of official colonial regime, one in which Indians could no longer play leading, even active, roles in the production of new forms of knowledge. Government officials still viewed Mackenzie's monumental collection as potentially valuable but also as undigested, chaotic, crude in places, and only usable after it could be properly edited and annotated. When C. V. Lutchmia applied for a position to do that after Mackenzie's death, his application was summarily rejected, with the following words from James Prinsep, the head of the Asiatic Society of Bengal:

Such an extensive scheme would need the control of a master head, accustomed to generalization, and capable of estimating the value or drift of inscriptional and literary evidence. The qualifications of Cavelly Venkata for such an office, judging of them by his "abstract," or indeed of any native, could hardly be pronounced equal to such a task, however useful they may prove as auxiliaries in such a train of research.[17]

Things had changed, and a new regime of colonial orientalism had been set firmly in place. No revisionist account seeking to accord Lutchmia or any other of Mackenzie's assistants in his project agency or a major role in the production of colonial knowledge can overlook this. Although Indian scholars did play major roles in the collection, translation, and dissemination of early colonial knowledge, Mackenzie was unique in the level of editorial and authorial agency he accorded to his assistants; upon his death these assistants were seen at best as wage laborers in what was now a resolutely colonial enterprise. With Mackenzie's death, all of his noble efforts to prove the worth both of his collection and its collectors, translators, and interpreters fell afoul of the development of official knowledge and the growing sense that official knowledge could only be produced by Europeans.

This is why I have I felt so moved by Mackenzie's distinct role in this history and its historiography, despite my sense of the need to situate Mackenzie within the larger context of the early colonial project of conquest and rule. I have also been impressed by Mackenzie's ambivalent place within that history, his single-minded commitment to a history of the southern peninsula that did not merely provide a blueprint for conquest or rule, his virtual obsession to collect and preserve primary documents, and his deep concern for the men who were his "portals," and means, of knowledge. I set out to write a biography of Mackenzie in order to explore both the origins of a modern historiography of southern India and to provide the basis for a cultural history that would precede, and in part exceed, the constraints of colonial modalities of representation. But I also did this to pay homage to a man who was a direct precursor to my own career as a scholar, a career in which I have been deeply critical of the record of colonial rule and yet aware of the extent to which that rule had provided the basis, the context, and the archive for my own scholarly interests and concerns.

I never wrote—or I should say I have not yet written—that book, though I did write an outline for it and drafts of several chapters, parts of which I published elsewhere. However, I will close this essay with an original draft of two paragraphs, still sitting in my desk drawer, that was to open the projected manuscript, then entitled, "Colin Mackenzie: The Biography of an Archive":

This book is not a biography; perhaps, instead, I should call it an anti-biography. The only biography attempted of Mackenzie, published by an enthusiastic member of his clan in 1952, already suggests the impossibility of such a task.[18] There is little to go on, no private correspondence with his intimates having survived. The familial biographer repeats tributes over and again to Mackenzie's greatness with characterizations of the following kind: "He was the type of man who says least where he feels most: a type not uncommon in Scotland." Mackenzie not only wrote little about anything that might be construed as a private life; he wrote as if he did not have one. The private for Mackenzie is available only through his extensive musings on his body; he was frequently ill and described his bodily maladies with a kind of intimate voice used for nothing else we might deem personal. Indeed, his intimacy to others even in official correspondence was directed principally toward their health as well; Mackenzie was always solicitous and sympathetic about the bodily travails of his friends and associates. But beyond the body, it was all work. From this perspective, it need hardly surprise us that we encounter mostly the silence that grows around routine and hard work. Mackenzie's only biography, in order to extend into a book-length text, must interweave the few primary sources for his life that exist with long quotations and paraphrases of standard histories of the East India Company and of the British in India. Mackenzie's silences become filled by conventional wisdom about early imperial history. This book will fill in the silences differently.

Perhaps silence, however, is an unwitting gift to a biographer. Biographical subjects are invariably more firmly situated in their times than the conceit of a life narrative implies. But here we confront the question of how typical Mackenzie really was, as also the particularity of his role in the history of Indian orientalism. For as much as Mackenzie was clearly an instrument of British imperialism in India, as Mahalingam so succinctly put it, his life and his collection stand at an angle to many aspects of early colonial rule. Mackenzie was not alone in his historical interests; they were certainly shared by Wilks, Malcolm, Elphinstone, Raffles, and myriad other British officials of the late eighteenth and early nineteenth centuries. But unlike these other men, Mackenzie was unable to produce a master historical narrative of his own, and he set up an apparatus of collection that turned up works most colonial historians found difficult to use or esteem, then and now. The collection's most eminent bibliographer, H. H. Wilson, became progressively less interested in Mackenzie's project the more he worked on it, casting doubt on the historical value of many of the texts. The company directors complained about the fact that they had been presented as a fait accompli with the payment of £10,000 to Mackenzie's widow for the entire collection shortly after the colonel's death. And they noted that the portion of materials they had seen, "does not lead us to form any very favourable opinion of the value of the remainder." Serious historians, especially in postcolonial times, both in India and in the Western academy, have begun to take a rather different view: when we analyze the variable responses to Mackenzie's collection later in the book we will realize again that although Mackenzie was firmly situated in his times, he was not completely of them. In my view, there is no better reason for a historical biography than this.

3

Preface to the Second Edition
of *The Hollow Crown*

In writing *The Hollow Crown*, I came to see culture differently than I had in my graduate school days. Culture might be a domain of "meaning," as anthropologists had come to insist, but it could simply not be detached from power or from history; by the time I started drafting the final manuscript in the summer of 1984, it seemed no longer possible to describe culture as unitary, stable, or straightforwardly dominant. As I developed a new sense of cultural form, practice, and meaning, I attempted to incorporate this new "cultural" sensibility in my own writing; at the very least, textual, historical, and ethnographic analysis seemed virtually indistinguishable and mutually sustaining. And so in writing the book I engaged in continuous movement from genre to genre, as well as from an insistent empiricism to a recurring skepticism. I moved from reading an eighteenth-century family history to a colonial document to a contemporary ritual statement, and, through them, I tried to write against the grain of both political history and cultural analysis. I used history against anthropology and textual analysis and anthropology against history, using disciplines and preoccupations to unsettle the others, and perhaps the reader too. I embraced the contradictions of positive knowledge, and I attempted to acknowledge the incompleteness and partiality of every conclusive formulation. I tried to write myself into the text in ways that seemed neither exclusively reflexive nor indulgently narcissistic. As one of my reviewers noted,

> The book is not an easy read for anyone conditioned over years to absorb empirical evidence in rhetorical forms dominated by historical theory, debate, and narrative. It is in its very composition that the book presents a critical statement on stylistic formations of historical prose. . . . Dirks turns our gaze from one piece of the puzzle to another, from one facet of the problem to another, backward and forward in time, keeping our critical eye open for the author in every text and for the historical discourse in which every author is shaped, including Dirks himself.[1]

Frequently my reviewers selected the parts of the book for praise that accorded with their own disciplinary interests and training, in ways that reflected how disciplined our reading and knowledge still is. It is perhaps small wonder that most gestures toward interdisciplinary study, even in so well-traveled a corridor as that between history and anthropology, end up more often than not reproducing disciplinary assumption and autonomy. And it is perhaps also small wonder that when I look back at my book today I see more clearly than I did before my own investment in certain disciplinary moments and practices.

After publishing *The Hollow Crown*, I focused in particular on two principal moments in the accumulation of the kind of knowledge I used in my earlier work. First, I began to do extensive work on the collection and codification of an extraordinary archive of texts, documents, and other historical materials by Colin Mackenzie, about which I have written extensively above. I used these texts in *The Hollow Crown* to predicate my reading of different conceptions of authority and different modalities of historical process. Mackenzie's project was steeped in the kind of hybridity and ambivalence that sustained forms of difference that—however much they might have been prefigured by the prerogatives of early colonial power—make the kinds of interpretation and analysis of the book not just possible but fundamental to the argument about what came before the "colonial."[2]

The second focus for my new work was on the development of a colonial anthropology of southern India, figured in particular in the work of

Edgar Thurston, the first official superintendent of ethnography for the Madras Presidency. Thurston, who was curator of the Madras Museum between 1885 and 1908, made two major contributions to the anthropology of southern India: his seven-volume, encyclopedic *Castes and Tribes of Southern India* (1907) and his two-volume book of essays entitled *Ethnographic Notes in Southern India* (1906). When I first engaged in my ethnohistorical work, it was to these texts I naturally turned, initially with more suspicion about the content than about the form of the writing. Although Thurston formalized many of the procedures and canonized much of the categorical knowledge of social anthropology for peninsular India, his greatest enthusiasm and commitment was to anthropometry, the measurement of man. Thurston's obsession with anthropometry was so marked that before he delivered a lecture to the Royal Society of the Arts in London in 1909, Lord Ampthill introduced him with the following story: "A visit to the Government Museum at Madras was always a very pleasant experience, although at first alarming. Such was the author's zeal for anthropometry, that he seized every man, woman, or child in order to measure them."[3] During the first decade of the twentieth century, Thurston worked systematically on his ethnographic survey along lines that had been set down by H. H. Risley, collecting myriad ethnographic details and extensive archives of measurements, all arranged according to the different castes and tribes in the Madras Presidency. Indian subjects were not only organized by but were also contained in their castes and tribes, which determined the cultural, economic, social, moral, and biological characteristics of their constituent members. It was clear you could know a man by his caste.

Thurston's ethnographic writing derived both from his own survey research and from the archives of colonial knowledge about southern India, much of which emerged from colonial attempts to regulate the moral depravity and cultural excess of caste society. His *Ethnographic Notes* cover such peculiar anthropological subjects as "deformity and mutilation," "torture in bygone days," "slavery," "hookswinging," "infanticide," and "Meriah sacrifice." Most of his information comes from colonial reports and commissions of inquiry, where the effort to describe customs and practices was motivated by British discomfort and the allied concern to proclaim Britain as a moral force in India. At the same time, the government took great care after the violent rebellion of

1857 to follow its own injunction against intervening in "native religious practice." Much early colonial anthropology developed in contexts such as these, as well as in the effort to classify and control caste groups that were declared criminal. Thurston's predecessor in Madras anthropology was F. S. Mullaly, who wrote what might be seen as the first proper anthropological study of Madras, entitled *Notes on Criminal Classes of the Madras Presidency*.[4] Mullaly's book covers a range of castes, including the Kallars and Maravars, both caste groups that were represented by established institutions of kingship and rule in the part of Tamil India that I concentrated on in *The Hollow Crown*. In engaging anthropological assumptions about the social organization of South Indian castes, I found myself drawing empirical information from sources that were designed to "prove of some value to Police officers who are continually brought in contact with the predatory classes, and of some slight interest to much of the public who may wish to know something regarding the doings of their less favoured brethren."[5]

The kings of Pudukkottai were Kallars, members of a caste whose very name signified "thief," and under British rule they became the model of a criminal caste. Criminality was defined in relation to habitual predation, based in customs that were presumed to be deviant no doubt in part because they had caused so much difficulty to the British in the years when they were attempting to establish their authority over southern India. It was this presumption that I wrote against in my ethnohistorical study of the Kallars of Pudukkottai, where the very control over the means of coercion had been the basis for accepted forms of kingship in a precolonial setting. Kallars were kings in Pudukkottai, but they were almost necessarily confined to regions that, as the fourteenth to eighteenth centuries ticked by, became progressively marginalized in relation to a wide range of transformations in the political economy of India in the early colonial period. This process was both hastened and naturalized under the conditions of British rule, which, in part through the history of anthropological knowledge I have been tracing through Thurston and Mullaly, further consigned Kallar kingship to a conspicuous marginality in relation to the key institutions of Hinduism as it has been reinvented and redefined. Had I written this book today, I might have moderated my civilizational claims about kingship in terms of this history of ambivalent marginalization, though perhaps this only reflects the fact that today Ranajit Guha is read more than Louis Dumont.[6] In any case, as I argued throughout the pages of *The Hollow Crown*, these historical questions have to be posed in relentless debate with the categories and assumptions of the present, since the more things change, the more difficult it is to map these changes, particularly with the successful colonial insistence on the essential nature of Indian tradition. To emphasize kingship, in other words, is one way of making a polemical point—a critique at once empirical and theoretical—about the enduring legacy of colonial historiography on the preoccupations of later social and anthropological history.

Even as my current exploration of colonial knowledge reveals ways in which my earlier work was necessarily embedded in certain colonial preoccupations and categories, my critique is predicated on the argument I make here that caste was not the single dominant symbol of, or metonym for, social difference in precolonial India. That is, caste neither marks out the fundamental units of Indian society nor defines the essence of Indian social being. I have shown in elaborate detail the contextual character of social identity, the ways in which the markers of social identity—within villages, within localities and regions, and for the precolonial period within kingdoms—were defined and articulated differently at different times. I have also shown that social relations were defined in terms of political processes and political referents, the ultimate referent of course being the king himself. In studying a place where kingship continued to play out a shadow existence throughout the colonial period, I was able to read ethnographic texts against the grain of history, delineating the effects of the political past even when the nature of politics itself had been fundamentally transformed— hollowed out of real politics, as I argue here.

My argument about politics, however, is always somewhat contradictory. On the one hand, I insist that I am giving priority to the cultural construction of power; on the other, I follow that construction through the referential narratives of a historical field where the political becomes a mobile sign of struggle and change. Nevertheless, it was, and is, my conviction that the strength of this work builds on the recognition of the necessity of contradiction, the relentless transitivity of text and context, of meanings exposed and concealed—in this instance, a sense that politics is neither available as a transparent analytic category nor contained solely within the cultural statements that ground any analysis of meaning. Culture, in other words, is never an autonomous or a stable category of analysis. Culture, as well as the other key terms, politics and history, exist as "supplements"—adding only to replace, or insinuating themselves in place of the original, only then to become the original that in turn becomes written over and replaced again. Supplementarity suggests why structures must remain open, why no synthesis can be anything more than provisional.

It is in this sense that Gyan Prakash suggests that *The Hollow Crown* can be classified as one of a new genre of postfoundational histories of India. Prakash writes that I historicize

> the conventional notion of caste by showing its shifting position in a South Indian kingdom. This unstable and changing position of caste and kingdom is accentuated, in turn, by the repeated interruptions of the narrative and its movement in and out of different historical periods and disciplines. The overall result forces the reader to reflect upon the procedures and rhetoric of academic disciplines in which the book is located.[7]

Such a strategy is meant neither to advocate epistemological relativism nor capitulate to the self-congratulatory limits and partialities of much postmodernist writing but rather to acknowledge that when we write the history of the present we also write within the terms of our present. When I initially set out to do this project, I had not intended to devote a third of the book to colonial history. But, as I note several times, I confronted colonialism at virtually every turn in my research. I thus begin the book with the story of the capture and defeat of the rebel king Kattapomman, structuring my account of kingly society in the narrative conceit of a flashback. I also begin my chapter on the discourse of kingship with the ballad about Kattapomman, an oral text that was initially hidden from British collectors but also sung and written against the British, with its formal panegyrics of kingship composed as expressions of nostalgia and resistance. Ironically, the very text that worked best (better than all the family histories collected by Mackenzie) to depict a stable picture of royal life and culture was based on a vision that could only have been written out of loss. And it is loss that I explore throughout my chapters on colonialism, in a discussion of the institutions of kingship, the redistributive structures of landholding, the referential meanings of titles and honors, and the extensive entailments of devotion and worship.[8]

This book examines the character of colonial change through a somewhat peculiar lens; rather than focusing on the new colonial urban centers and elites—the overwhelming choice of recent writings on coloniality and the postcolonial condition—I look instead at a princely state, one of a myriad number of dominant symbols of old India that simultaneously exemplified tradition yet legitimated British colonial rule. Princely states were those areas of India, constituting roughly one-third of the geographical extent of the subcontinent, that were not "conquered" by the British but rather left aside either because of military exhaustion, political alliance, or colonial embarrassment about its increasingly unpopular policy of expansion and annexation. Princely states were to be ruled indirectly, through the traditional agencies of maharajas and chiefs who were to be incorporated into empire through a political economy of honor (manifested in gun salutes and *darbars*) and isolation (the "foreign" policy of these states was to be managed by the British). Despite the growing uncertainty about the exact nature of the political relationship between the Raj and these states, some things were clear: princely India preserved the old, provided playgrounds for the British civil service, presented marked contrasts between the rapacity of feudalism and the progressivism of colonial rule, and ironically protected the idea of imperial expansion both by symbolizing British liberality and by creating a powerful elite fully committed to British rule rather than nationalist politics.

I argue in my last chapter that the princely states became parodies, stages on which British colonial fantasy could play itself out with neither the checks of precolonial politics nor the full restraint of colonial self-consciousness. The farce of indirect rule was exposed in the extraordinary modern history of Pudukkottai. A state that systematically violated the new conventions of postfeudal frugality and management became most successfully mimetic of its colonial conquerors in the person of Martanda Bhairava Tondaiman, who was forced to abdicate his throne for his unorthodox and (for the British and Brahman alike) distasteful marriage to a white woman, the outcome of a lifelong obsession to marry a European cultivated precisely by British efforts to colonize this unruly family of Kallar kings. The Cambridge-educated tutor gave advice the maharaja took far too literally. Martanda's marriage to the Australian Molly Fink captures the contradictory history of colonialism in India, for the story (of love and intrigue in the princely state) reverts to tragedy (in postcolonial India) in the categories and commitments of caste and community that were allowed to flourish under colonial rule. The princely state became the setting for a drama in which the caste leaders of the kingdom refused to accept the cultural failure to marry a proper Hindu, thus creating in effect a new orthodox order in an older feudal kingdom hardly known for its full commitment to Brahmanic scruple. Meanwhile, the raja, effectively exiled from his state, drained its coffers in the casinos of Monte Carlo and through the purchase of estates in Scotland. And so I argue that the present predicament of post-coloniality is rooted in the hollowing out of power—and of the Indian state more generally—under colonial rule, a process that took on its most powerful image in the figure of the prince, the maharaja who was at once host for British entertainment and parody of oriental despotism. Colonial hegemony succeeded even when it seemed to fail; in this case the failure to conquer all of India provided the means for sustaining the myth of continuity, of the survival of eternal India in the midst of colonial transplantation and transformation. In the princely states of India, British colonialism attained its cultural apotheosis.

In the colonial rewriting of the past, both literally in the context of colonial historiography and more figuratively in the sense of the inventions and reinventions of both "tradition" and "modernity," we confront the ultimate problematic of this history. On the one hand, by saying what precolonial society and state were and what they were not, I am not providing an account that fully preexists or exists somehow outside colonial (not to mention postcolonial) history. On the other hand, by drawing attention to the epistemological and methodological limits of an enterprise that takes as its principal object the precolonial (or the pre-modern), I am seeking to work against the certainties and conventions of present assumption and belief. I try not to succumb to the totalizing propensities of colonial knowledge, resisting the overdetermined compulsion to see only colonial power. At the same time, the past emerges in my account not in spite of colonial and disciplinary distortions but through them or, rather, out of the relentless historicizing of both the present and the sources that exist in the present for our encounter with the past.

In unraveling some of the complexity of the interplay of power, ritual, social organization, and regal observance in the old regime I mean to encounter the precolonial "before" even as I struggle with the impossibility of this kind of historical project. I call attention to difference (cultural and historical) with constant reference to the multiple grounds from which I construct difference—in particular having to do with the curious complicities of colonial Britain's dismissal of the political with anthropology's early attraction to the importance of religion and beliefs concerning purity and pollution for explaining and encompassing India's social history. The writing of Louis Dumont is the most compelling target for this critique, both because of the ambition of his civilizational claims and because he made them in large part on the basis of ethnographic work on a group of Kallars in an area of southern India not far from where I worked. The India Dumont describes so well is one that was ironically created by colonialism, with caste serving as the colonial form of civil society under the determination of religious value, with Kallars identified now only as thieves and never as kings.[9] But Dumont is also a figure for a more encompassing Western imaginary, his intellectual power and influence—and his allure as a critic of the fundamental categories of Western sociology—a reminder that colonialism does not define the only historical or epistemological problematic for understanding India today.

The Hollow Crown argues that in ethnographic fieldwork, in the reading of texts traditionally dismissed as so much myth and fabulous legend, in reconstructing the precolonial history of Indian states and societies, in reading colonial documents, and in charting the contradictory effects of colonial rule, one can find, as I constantly did, that the categories of culture and history rub against each other, opening up supplemental readings of caste that made it seem as much a product of rule as a condition for it, and of the state that made its apparent weakness seem an effect of colonial rule rather than the explanation for it. Such an argument does not accord total power to the British nor suggest that caste was by any means invented anew by them. Rather, the point about caste is that it was refigured as a religious system, organizing society in a context where politics and religion had never before been distinct domains of social action. The religious definition of caste enabled colonial procedures of rule through the characterization of India as essentially about spiritual harmony and liberation; when the state had existed in India, it was despotic and epiphenomenal, extractive but fundamentally irrelevant. British rule could be characterized as enlightened when it denied Indian subjects even the minimal rights that constituted the basis for the development of civil society in Europe. I do not mean to suggest that one culture simply gave way to another nor that the politics and historicity of caste in, say, the seventeenth century were the same as the politics and historicity of caste today. Far from it. Rather, salient cultural forms in India became represented as nonhistorical at the same time that these representations were only made possible under specific historical conditions of early colonialism. Caste became the essence of Indian culture and civilization through a historical process, as a direct consequence of a long colonial history.

But this, again, is only one part of the story, told here through many disciplines, with many voices, in multiple narratives, and in great detail. Readers will therefore find themselves confronting what might have been several different books, meanwhile stumbling over Tamil transliterations of place and clan names, lexical signs of key ideas and terms, and myriad other references to specific places and people that will be unfamiliar to most. My claims in this book—some of them far more grandiose than any amount of detail about the specific place known as Pudukkottai would seem to justify—rest precisely in the thickness and multivocality of the historical ethnography.[10] It is this thickness and detail that produces my sustained doubt about the retrievability of any past; it is what makes me see, in the final sentence of the book, that history is a Promethean enterprise. But it is also what made the project seem worthwhile from start to finish, and what makes it seem worthwhile still.

Part II

History and Anthropology

4

Castes of Mind

The Original Caste

W hen we think of India it is hard not to think of caste. In comparative sociology and in common parlance, caste has become a
central metaphor for India, indexing it as fundamentally different from
other places, expressing its essence. A long history of writing, from the
grand treatise of the Abbé Dubois to the general anthropology of Louis
Dumont, or from the desultory observations of Portuguese adventurers
in the sixteenth century to the eye-catching headlines of the *New York
Times*, has identified caste as the basic form and expression of Indian
society. Caste has been seen as always there in Indian history and as
one of the major reasons why India has no history, or at least no sense
of history. Caste defines the core of Indian tradition, and caste is today
the major threat to Indian modernity, even if we concede that it helped
pave the way for the modern or realize that it has been exacerbated
by modern institutions. If we are to understand India properly, and by
implication if we are to understand India's other principal claim to universal fame—Hinduism—we must understand caste.

The agreement in the West about the centrality of caste has not meant
that there has been agreement about what is meant by the term or about
the moral valuation of it. The Abbé Dubois wrote in 1815 that the institution of caste was the only reason accounting for why Hindus did not fall

into "the same state of barbarism as their neighbors and as almost all nations inhabiting the torrid zone." As he went on to observe:

> We can picture what would become of the Hindus if they were not kept within the bounds of duty by the rules and penalties of caste, by looking at the position of the Pariahs, or outcastes of India, who, checked by no moral restraint, abandon themselves to their natural propensities. . . . For my own part, being perfectly familiar with this class, and acquainted with its natural predilections and sentiments, I am persuaded that a nation of Pariahs left to themselves would speedily become worse than the hordes of cannibals who wander in the vast waste of Africa, and would soon take to devouring each other.[1]

A rather different view was held by John Wilson, a missionary of the Church of Scotland who had also been the onetime president of the Bombay branch of the Royal Asiatic Society, and the author of another canonic text on caste published in 1877:

> It is among the Hindus . . . that the imagination of natural and positive distinctions in humanity has been brought to the most fearful and pernicious development ever exhibited on the face of the globe. The doctrine and practice of what is called caste, as held and observed by this people, has been only dimly shadowed by the worst social arrangements which were of old to be witnessed among the proudest nations and among the proudest orders of men in these nations. . . . It is the offspring of extraordinary exaggeration and mystification, and of all the false speculation and religious scrupulosity of a great country undergoing unwonted processes of degeneration and corruption. It is now the soul as well as the body of Hinduism.[2]

In these two quotes we move from Enlightenment mentality to Victorian morality, from early to late colonialism, as also from France to England. But in both these quotes we read that the soul and the body, not to mention the mind, of India reside in caste.

Theories of caste are not only about society but about politics and history as well. Weber, Marx, Henry Maine, and now Louis Dumont have all held that in India, in marked contrast to China, the state was epiphenomenal. Caste, not the state, held society—with its constituent village republics and communities—together. In a more general sense, caste is seen as the foundation and core of Indian civilization; it is responsible for the transmission and reproduction of society in India. And caste, like India itself, has been seen as based on religious rather than political principles.

With the publication of *Homo Hierarchicus* in 1966, Dumont gave canonic formulation to this view of the caste system, setting many of the terms of discourse and debate about Indian society that continue to the present day.[3] Dumont holds that the political and economic domains of social life in India are encompassed by the religious domain, which is articulated in terms of an opposition between purity and pollution. For Dumont, the Brahman represents the religious principle, inasmuch as the Brahman represents the highest form of purity attainable by Hindus. The king, while important and powerful, represents the political domain and is accordingly inferior to, and encompassed by, the Brahman. The overarching value accorded to the religious domain is the central feature of the ideology of caste, which Dumont characterizes with the single word *hierarchy*. Dumont argues that the sociological significance of hierarchy has been systematically missed by modern writers obsessed with the ideology of equality, and he hopes instead to "distinguish fundamental values and ideas from everything else, the ideological from the non-ideological, or rather the more conscious or more valorized from the less conscious or valorized" with this concept.[4]

Dumont thus identifies the politicoeconomic aspects of caste as relatively secondary and isolated. In assessing recent changes in the caste system, he notes that the British government's policy of "not meddling in the domain of religion and the traditional social order, while introducing the minimum of reforms and novelties on the politico-economic plane," significantly reduced the extent of change and conflict under colonial rule. Only with the introduction of modern democratic politics has caste begun to undergo the major transformation of "substantialization," which for Dumont constitutes an important breakdown of the structural relations of parts to wholes and an essential challenge to the ideology of hierarchy.[5]

Caste not only subordinates the political; it also reduces the individual to a position of relative unimportance. The individual only has ideological significance when placed outside society, becoming in Dumont's terms "the individual-outside-the-world."[6] This is the individual as the renouncer, the *sannyasi* who must leave both society and the mundane world to attain transcendental truth. Dumont's position is stated more forcefully by Jan Heesterman:

> Here we touch the inner springs of Indian civilization. Its heart is not with society and its integrative pressures. It devalorizes society and disregards power. The ideal is not hierarchical interdependence but the individual break with society. The ultimate value is release from the world. And this cannot be realized in a hierarchical way, but only by the abrupt break of renunciation. . . . Above the Indian world, rejecting and at the same time informing it, the renouncer stands out as the exemplar of ultimate value and authority.[7]

The individual as renouncer thus occupies a critical position in what Heesterman calls "the inner conflict of tradition" in a transcendental critique of the possibility of politics, economics, and history in the Indian world.

The prominence of Indologists in the contemporary anthropology on India has served both to secure a specialized discourse on India and to mitigate the charge that anthropology has not taken cognizance of a civilization far more venerable and refined than other objects of anthropological scrutiny. In this anthropology, Indology has been substituted for history, and it has been used to dehistoricize both India and anthropological practice in India. Not only has the state been erased as a major force in the constitution and transformation of Indian society; the colonial history of India also has been rendered invisible, as we have just seen in Dumont's peculiar sense of caste's compatibility with empire. I find this sense of compatibility unsettling, and I see similar, and not unrelated, compatibilities existing between the view that the precolonial state was weak, the assertion that traditional society was organized by social and religious rather than political principles, and the sense that caste is the exemplary traditional form that has resisted the development of modern state and social structures. It is thus even more unsettling to read statements such as those in the introduction to Heesterman's recent book: "The modern state . . . wants to bring the ideal of universal order from its ultramundane haven down to earth. The inner conflict then becomes explosively schismatic, as eventually became clear in the drama of the Partition."[8]

In such views, the essential difference between East and West, between the recent histories of India and Europe, would lie in the "invention" of the modern nation-state in eighteenth-century Europe, which went hand in hand with the construction of a new form of civil society. Civil society was to free "individuals" in new and progressive societies from "traditional" modes of social organization and from the myriad constraints of premodern and/or feudal polities. Civil society had been constituted by and institutionalized in a range of bodies—the church, educational institutions, civic organizations—that represented the interests of a private domain, interests construed to be autonomous from the state (even as they were simultaneously protected by it). The modern state, more powerful than ever before, had legitimated itself in part through its claim to free the social from the politics of the past.

In India caste, so colonial sociology had it, always resisted political intrusion; it was already a kind of civil society in that it regulated and represented the private domain, such as it was. But a society based on caste could not be more different from modern Western society, for caste neither permitted the development of voluntarist or politically malleable social institutions, nor did it work to reinforce the modern state. Indeed, caste actively resisted the modern state even more than it did the old, for the modern state opposed rather than supported dharma.

Of course, under colonialism the modern state was not a viable option, since the development of modern states in Europe depended in large part on the conquest and exploitation of premodern states that fell to the technological, military, and economic power of the ascendant West. But colonialism was predicated on more than simple economic exploitation, and its effects were as various as they are still difficult to untangle from the presumed weight of tradition on colonized societies. It is increasingly clear that colonialism in India produced new forms of society that have been taken to be traditional, and that caste itself as we now know it is not a residual survival of ancient India but a specifically colonial form of civil society. As such it both justifies and maintains the colonial vision of an India where religion transcends politics, society resists change, and the state awaits its virgin birth in the postcolonial era.

In a previous study I have written on the relationship between Indian state and Indian society in the old regime and the transformation of this relationship under British colonialism, when the Indian crown became increasingly hollow.[9] But until the emergence of British colonial rule in southern India, the crown was not so hollow as it has generally been made out to be in Indian history, anthropology, and comparative sociology. Kings were not inferior to Brahmans; the political domain was not encompassed by the religious domain. State forms, while not fully assimilable to Western categories of the state, were powerful components in Indian civilization. Indian society, indeed caste itself, was shaped by political struggles and processes. Both the units of social identity and their respective relations were part of a complex, conjunctural, political world. The referents of social identity were multiple and contextually determined; temple communities, territorial groups, lineage segments, family units, royal retinues, warrior subcastes, occupational reference groups, sectarian networks, even priestly cabals were just some of the significant units of identification, all of them at various times far more significant than any uniform metonymy of endogamous "caste" groupings. Caste was just one category among many others, one way of organizing and representing identity. Moreover, caste was not a single category or even a logic of categorization. Regional, village, or residential communities; kinship groups; factional parties; chiefly retinues; and so on could both supersede caste as a rubric for identity and reconstitute the ways caste was organized. Within localities, or kingdoms, groups could rise or fall (in the process becoming more or less castelike), depending on the fortunes of particular warriors or headmen, even as kings could routinely readjust the social order by royal decree.

Social identity was importantly political, as were the contexts in which different units became formed, represented, and mobilized. And politics took on its shape and meaning in relation to local and regional systems of power in which headmen (of lineages, temples, villages), gurus (leaders of sects and monasteries), warrior leaders, chiefs, and kings were figures of central importance, with authority over constituencies that from certain perspectives could look and act like caste groups. To read and organize social difference and deference—pervasive features of Indian society—solely in terms of caste thus required a striking disregard for ethnographic specificity as well as a systematic denial of the political mechanisms that selected different kinds of social units as most significant at different times. Brahmanic texts, both Vedic origin stories and the much later dharma texts of Hinduism's puranic period, provided transregional and metahistorical modes of understanding Indian society that clearly appealed to British colonial interests and attitudes.

In stressing the political logic of Indian society, I am of course conscious of imposing a modern analytic term onto a situation where ritual and political forms were often fundamentally the same. However, I stress the political both to redress the previous emphasis on "religion" and to underscore the social fact that caste structure, ritual form, and political process were all dependent on relations of power. These relations were constituted in and through history, and these relations were culturally constructed. But most recently this cultural construction took place in the context of British colonial rule, when caste was represented as the essential religious basis of Indian society and as the reason why India had no genuine politics.

Colonialism purposefully preserved many of the forms of the old regime, nowhere more conspicuously than in the indirectly ruled Princely States, of which the little kingdom I studied was the only one in the Tamil country of southern India. But these forms were frozen in time, and only the appearances of the old regime—without its vitally connected political and social processes—were saved. Colonialism changed things both more and less than has commonly been thought. While introducing new forms of civil society and separating these forms from the colonial state, colonialism also arrested some of the immediate disruptions of change by preserving many elements of the old regime. Paradoxically, colonialism seems to have created much of what is now accepted as Indian "tradition," including an autonomous caste structure with the Brahman clearly and unambiguously at the head, village-based systems of exchange, isolated ceremonial residues of the old regime state, and fetishistic competition for ritual goods that no longer played a vital role in the political system.

The transformations of Indian society under British rule, as also the contemporary concerns of comparative sociology, are the products not only of a nineteenth-century orientalism but also of the colonial intervention that actively removed politics from colonial societies. Neither British administrators nor orientalists were able to go to India and invent caste through sheer acts of will and rhetorical fancy, however useful caste was as a social mechanism to assist in the management of an immensely complex society. Ironically, it was the very political permeability of Indian society that allowed caste to become India's modern apparition of its traditional being. Under colonial rule, caste—now disembodied from its former political contexts—lived on. In this dissociated form it was appropriated, and reconstructed, by the British. What orientalism did most successfully in the Indian context was to assert the precolonial authority of a specifically colonial form of power and representation, thereby playing a critical role in disguising the politics of caste.

Early Colonial Knowledge and Indian Society

In the late eighteenth and early nineteenth centuries a great number of British writers—among them Alexander Dow, Montstuart Elphinstone, Mark Wilks, John Malcolm, and Colin Mackenzie—felt compelled to write Indian history. Although they all saw the eighteenth century as a decadent prelude to and justification for British rule, and although they frequently disparaged Indian historical sensibilities and traditions, they nevertheless felt the need to understand India historically. During this period very little was written about caste, in marked contrast to the late nineteenth and early twentieth centuries. What was written about caste reflected the textual work of orientalists, but the paucity of general works and the fact that the only major book of the period on caste was composed by a French Jesuit suggest a very different colonial emphasis than that which developed later.

The early period of colonial rule is of course better known for the work of the orientalists than for that of the "historians," though there was not always a strict separation between the two. Alexander Dow studied Persian while an officer in the East India Company's army, and he published a translation of a standard Persian history in 1768.[10] In his introduction to the translation he wrote about subjects such as the nature of Mughal government and the effects of British rule, but he only wrote seven pages on Hindu customs and manners. Though not a Sanskritist, Dow relied on the tutelage of a Brahman pundit in Benares and adopted a textual and Brahmanic view of Indian society. Many years later, the administrator and historian Montstuart Elphinstone wrote his two-volume work on Indian history without any claim to be a proper orientalist.[11] Indeed, when he published his massive tome in 1841 he suggested that his chief qualification for the task, which he feared might seem redundant so soon after the publication of Mill's eight-volume history, was his experience in India.[12] But in his opening sections, titled "State of the Hindus at the Time of Manu's Code" and "Changes Since Manu, and State of the Hindus in Later Times," he reproduced a textual view of caste and early Indian life based almost entirely on the work of orientalists, most especially Sir William Jones's 1798 translation of the *Manusmriti*, the classic, Brahmanically authored, normative Hindu text on social mores and customs. Elphinstone's historical text goes on for pages about the four *varnas* (Brahmans, Kshatriyas, Vaishyas, Shudras), the complex rules and formulations about the separation and mixing of castes, and the consequent proliferation of the myriad *jatis* that become the recognizable caste groups of contemporary India. So pervasive is the reliance on Manu's text that even 388 pages into his book Elphinstone begins a chapter on the history of the Hindus by noting that "the first information we receive on Hindu history is from a passage in Menu." It is striking that Elphinstone sees no contradiction between an orientalist textualism and an administrative historicism; it is clear that India had not yet been fully anthropologized.

When Elphinstone turned to an inquiry into early Indian history outside the purview of the orientalist canon, in particular in his chapter on the early history of the Deccan, he relied upon the manuscript material collected by Colin Mackenzie, a man who had become, through diligent and prodigious effort, the first surveyor general of India. Throughout a career in southern India stretching from 1786 to 1821 as a cartographer and surveyor, Mackenzie was obsessed with an interest in collecting manuscripts and information to supplement the maps he and his associates made of Hyderabad, Mysore, and other regions of the southern peninsula.[13] On his own initiative and with his own resources he hired and trained a group of Brahman assistants who helped him collect local histories of kingly dynasties, chiefly families, castes, villages, temples, monasteries, as well as other local traditions and religious and philosophical texts in a variety of Indian languages. He also took rubbings of stone and copper-plate inscriptions; collected coins, images, and antiquities; and made extensive plans and drawings wherever he went. By the time of his death in 1821, Mackenzie had amassed a collection that still contains the largest set of sources for the study of the early modern historical anthropology of southern India.

Mackenzie played an important if contradictory role in the rescuing of southern India's precolonial historiography. Throughout his career, he consistently advocated the importance of recovering and documenting the precolonial history of southern India, and in this context he stressed the significance of local texts. Unlike most of his contemporaries he did not disparage or dismiss out of hand Indian historical accounts or sensibilities. And he did not assume that his Brahman assistants were mere informers, acknowledging frequently and generously the extremely important role played by his assistants, such as C. V. Boria, in defining as well as transcribing the sociology of knowledge in precolonial peninsular India. Nevertheless, this sociology of knowledge was clearly early colonial rather than precolonial, as neither Mackenzie nor his assistants were unaware of the strategic and political character of their historiographic project.

In Mackenzie's initial project of collecting representative texts, histories of places, particularly temples, and polities, especially little kingdoms, predominated. The southern Indian landscape was dotted with temples that often served as centers for marketing and defense in addition to worship and that, thanks to the tall *gopuram* towers built over their gateways, were also convenient reference points for trigonometrical surveying and general route maps. Every temple had a history that inscribed the significance of its deity and the ground of the deities' worship with a special past of miracle and power. The South Indian landscape had also been controlled by myriad little kingdoms ranging immensely in size, each with a family history for the chief or king. Thus the set of local tracts collected by Mackenzie contain literally hundreds of accounts of one lineage headman after another who, through a combination of strategies and successes, managed to become a little king.

Mackenzie's preoccupation with local chiefs and kings was in part the result of his clear recognition of the political landscape of late precolonial peninsular India, and in part his response to the land tenure debates of British rulers at the time. When Mackenzie began his survey of Mysore after the defeat of Tipu Sultan in 1799, the general assumption among most East India Company officials was that a revenue "settlement" with the local lords or *zamindars*, along the lines of the 1793 "Permanent Settlement" in Bengal, would be the most suitable form of local governance and revenue collection for the Madras Presidency. Thus Mackenzie's historiographical concern with the political history of the Deccan made a great deal of sense for early colonial administrators because of its emphasis on the pasts and pedigrees of the potential landlords of a zamindari revenue settlement.

From my earlier work, I was aware of the prevalence of texts that concerned kings and temples. However, when I first turned to the Mackenzie collection as a repository for early ethnographic knowledge about southern India, I was surprised to find very few caste histories.[14] There were some general texts about castes and some curious lists of caste groups that resembled Jorge Luis Borges's Chinese encyclopedia more than later ethnographic surveys. But there were only a few specific caste histories.[15] Those that did exist, such as the Kallar and Maravar caste histories I had earlier read and copied from the Tamil, seemed of uncertain textual genre; they appeared to have been hastily put together from the chance concerns and remarks of local subcaste headmen. But in all of Mackenzie's obsessive collection, caste as a rubric for textualization was surprisingly uncommon.

Mackenzie seemed far less interested in caste than I would have expected. Although he occasionally mentioned the need to collect texts with information about caste, I only found systematic material about caste in his statistical and cartographic collections and in some of his drawings. In the statistical tables called *caneeshamaris*, "the population of the districts by castes, families, and villages" was carefully counted and presented by local public officials.[16] Some of these tables were transcribed on his actual maps of Mysore and the Ceded Districts. Here, the compilations of population data under caste headings seemed to have the same indexical function for the map as the delineations of field types and irrigation sources. These lists were highly particularistic and idiosyncratic; though Brahmans were usually at the head, the lists were neither regularized nor easy to compare across districts or regions. At first I felt disappointed that my interest in finding early (and little mediated) texts on caste had turned up so little.

Only when I turned to Mackenzie's drawings did it seem that I had finally struck ethnographic gold.[17] One of Mackenzie's largest portfolios has eighty-two drawings depicting different groups in the northern Deccan drawn during the early years of the nineteenth century. The volume is labeled "Costumes of Balla Ghaut, Carnatick, 1800 & 1801."[18] Costume is thus the key sign and objective focus of ethnographic difference. This emphasis on costume is in part a reflection of the fact that clothes in India (as also in England) were important markers of hierarchy and difference, but it was surely also because of the lack of any clear generic sense of what a pictorial survey of the castes and tribes would be like, as well as perhaps because of the influence of the picturesque cult's preoccupation with the colorful and exotic aspects of the Indian social order.

The castes and groups that found their way into Mackenzie's portfolio reveal a very particular ethnographic sensibility. There are a portrait of the ancient kings of Vijayanagara; a fine picture of a royal *darbar* scene; a collection of drawings of "Boya peons," the court servants and soldiers of the local chiefs; and drawings of other court officials such as Brahman *amildars*, or revenue agents. There are also a number of drawings of gurus and itinerant holy men. In addition, the collection included occupational categories such as barbers, basket makers, and palmists, as well as Brahmans of various descriptions including court Brahmans, physicians, even groups of Brahman women. Both in the absence of any kind of systematic and autonomous sense of a "caste system," and in the concentration of pictorial attention given to characters who reflected the political landscape of the eighteenth-century Deccan—the same characters who figure in most of Mackenzie's local texts—we see major differences between Mackenzie's vision of India's ethnography and the ethnography that became canonized in the late nineteenth century.

One of the first indications of the importance of caste—and of the liabilities of official ignorance about it—came in an official memo of 1816 recommending support for and publication of a revision of Abbé Dubois's *Hindu Manners, Customs, and Ceremonies*, the first edition of which was said to contain a large number of errors and omissions. The Board of Control wrote: "There is nothing perhaps of more importance to the Hindoo community than that their distinctions of caste should be well understood by the civil officers of the government in the interior of the country, yet there is no subject at present on which it is so difficult to procure correct information."[19] Lord Bentinck also gave contemporary testimony to the importance of the Abbé's work. "I am of opinion that," he wrote, "in a political point of view, the information which the work of the Abbé Dubois has to impart might be of the greatest benefit in aiding the servants of the Government in conducting themselves more in unison with the customs and prejudices of the natives."[20] Here Bentinck suggests that ethnographic knowledge will contribute to administrative sensitivity, a very different use of ethnography indeed from what develops later in the century.

Early colonial ethnography was thus both unsystematic and still in the service of a regime that remembered the struggle of conquest and that could not yet afford to dehistoricize and recast Indian society. This ethnography also reflected in part what the silences of Mackenzie's collection illustrate, the lack of local textual and cultural traditions about civil society (separated from its political and institutional moorings) that could be immediately appropriated and represented. The uncertain pedigree and recent genre of colonial ethnography is perhaps nowhere more cogently illustrated than in a book compiled by the youngest brother of the Brahman family that had supplied Mackenzie with his chief informants. In 1847 C. V. Ramaswamy privately published *A Digest of the Different Castes of the Southern Division of Southern India, with Descriptions of Their Habits, Customs, Etc.*[21] The work was dedicated to the "British public of India" and was clearly intended for a European audience ("that they may receive that gratification and instruction which it is my anxious desire to impart"). The treatise began with an account of the four varnas with their dharmic duties, and it then in catalogue fashion listed the castes of the south of India with brief descriptions for each one. The list begins like this: "Butler, Dubash, Cook, Cooks' mate, Ayea, Lamplighter, waterwoman, grasscutter," and then includes such standard castes as the dog boy, the palanquin bearer, and the agriculturalist. As idiosyncratic as this work clearly is, it reflects the lack of clarity and convention regarding caste as a site for textualization.

A Colonial Sociology of India

As British colonial rule became increasingly secure, we begin to encounter growing traces of a new ethnographic sensibility. In mid- and late nineteenth-century collections, I found, caste histories had begun to predominate.[22] Part of the reason for this had to do with the demise of the little kings; those who had survived at all had done so as zamindars or landlords with little particular claim to histories of their own. Temple histories continued to be important, but they were considered to be relevant by the colonial state only insofar as they could be used to decide disputes over temple control, management, and honors. But for a variety of reasons caste histories were considered to be particularly important, and caste became increasingly the only relevant social site for the textualization of Indian identity.

During the nineteenth century, the collection of material about castes and tribes and their customs and the specification of what kinds of customs, kinship behaviors, ritual forms, and so on were appropriate and necessary for ethnographic description became increasingly formalized and canonic. In the first half of the century, the emphasis on caste was consistent with the change from revenue settlements with landlords to settlements with village headmen and individual cultivators, providing a ready means to evaluate the authoritative claims and social positions of the individuals to be granted revenue titles. But gradually the institutional provenance of caste expanded, affecting the recruitment of soldiers into the army (particularly after the great rebellion of 1857), the implementation of legal codes that made the provisions of the law applicable on caste lines, the criminalization of certain entire caste groups for local policing purposes, the curtailment of the freedom of the land market when excessive amounts of land were thought to be sold by "agricultural" to "merchant" groups, and the assessment of the political implications of different colonial policies in the area of local administration in caste terms, to mention only a few examples.[23]

One of the first general compilations of material on caste was assembled by the Rev. M. A. Sherring, who in 1872 published his influential three-volume work *Hindu Tribes and Castes*.[24] The work aims to be encyclopedic in coverage, starting with Brahmans, then moving to Kshatriyas, and so on. But unlike earlier colonial works that relied on textual varna categories as a general guide about Indian society and then turned to historical modes of investigation, Sherring used these categories to frame an empirical study of Indian society. The footnotes refer to District Manuals, writings such as those by James Tod on Rajasthan, even Settlement Reports.[25] Gone is the ubiquitous reliance on

Manu; orientalism has become empiricist rather than textual. Ironically, at the very point that race becomes invoked as the biological referent of caste in British anthropological conjecture, the pervasive references to the "mixing of castes" based on Manu's text cease as well.

The new empiricism not only replaced earlier orientalist emphases on textuality and history; it also eclipsed earlier enthusiasms for things Indian, even if, as in the case of most early orientalists, these enthusiasms were exclusively for ancient Indian civilization. Sherring shares the same general outlook on caste as John Wilson, and in clearly betraying his missionary affiliations he also reveals that missionary disdain for caste is no longer incompatible with the colonial scientific scrutiny of it. In his concluding essay on the "Prospects of Hindu Caste," he begins his opening series of paragraphs with the following assertions (which went uncontested in myriad subsequent uses of this text): "Caste is the sworn enemy of human happiness," "Caste is opposed to intellectual freedom," "Caste sets its face sternly against progress," "Caste makes no compromises," "The ties of caste are stronger than those of religion," and "Caste is intensely selfish."[26] Nevertheless, he is wary of progress when not accompanied by Christian conversion. After noting that "some of the caste-emancipated Bengalees have a character for adopting European usages," he goes on to observe that "in our judgment, it is far better for natives of India to adhere to their own customs than to adopt those of foreigners."

Collection of the kind of empirical information assembled by Sherring, and sharing the increasing formalization of his information, soon became the centerpiece of an official colonial sociology of knowledge. As stated in the announcement of the ethnographic survey of India published in the first issue of *Man* in 1901:

It is unnecessary to dwell at length upon the obvious advantages to many branches of the administration in this country of an accurate and well-arranged record of the customs and the domestic and social relations of the various castes and tribes. The entire framework of native life in India is made up of groups of this kind, and the status and conduct of individuals are largely determined by the rules of the group to which they belong. For the purposes of legislation, of judicial procedure, of famine relief, of sanitation and dealings with epidemic disease, and of almost every form of executive action, an ethnographic survey of India, and a record of the customs of the people is as necessary an incident of good administration as a cadastral survey of the land and a record of the rights of its tenants. The census provides the necessary statistics; it remains to bring out and interpret the facts which lie behind the statistics.[27]

And so the political relevance of caste was announced. Caste was the site for detailing a record of the customs of the people, the locus of all important information about Indian society. This information, which the colonial state felt increasingly compelled to collect, organize, and disseminate, would thus become available for a wide variety of governmental initiatives and activities—relating to "almost every form of executive action."

If the ethnographic survey announced the preeminence of caste for colonial sociology, it was the decennial census that played the most important institutional role not only in providing the "facts" but in installing caste as the fundamental unit of India's social structure. There was general agreement among most of the administrators of the census, which began on an all-India basis in 1871, that caste should be the basic category used to organize the population counts. But there was far less agreement about what caste really was. For example, various commissioners debated whether a caste with fewer than one hundred thousand persons should be included, or how to organize the "vague and indefinite" entries that in 1891 exceeded 2.3 million names. There were also debates about whether, and if so how, to list the castes on the basis of "social precedence." When H. H. Risley adopted a procedure to establish precedence in the 1901 Census, caste became politicized all over again. Caste associations sprang up to contest their assigned position in the official hierarchy, holding meetings, writing petitions, and organizing protests. By 1931 some caste groups were distributing handbills to their fellow caste members to tell them how to answer questions about their religious and sectarian affiliations and about their race, language, and caste status. After 1931 the British could no longer ignore the political effects of the census, and they abandoned the use of caste for census counting altogether.[28]

The rise of caste as the single most important symbol of colonial Indian society, and the role of Indian anthropology in the project of colonial state formation, is documented in a great many texts, perhaps nowhere more fully, though complexly, than in Risley's classic work *The People of India*.[29] Risley, who was the census commissioner of India for the 1901 Census (the regulations of which greatly influenced the 1911 Census as well), had earlier produced the multivolume work *The Tribes and Castes of Bengal*.[30] *The People of India* resulted directly from Risley's work as census commissioner, and it is an expanded version of the commissioner's report on the 1901 Census (written with the assistance of E. A. Gait) that, among other things, summarized his views on the origin and classification of the Indian races based on his historical speculations and anthropometric research.

Risley has been much criticized by contemporary as well as subsequent writers for overemphasizing the racial basis of caste and stressing anthropometry. William Crooke argued against Risley with particular vehemence, suggesting that occupational criteria provided much more comprehensive and accurate indices for understanding caste as a system than race.[31] And the anthropometric researches of subsequent scholars steadily eroded the confidence of the anthropological establishment that racial types in India were anywhere near as pure or clear as Risley had assumed. But Risley's general views of caste as a social system and force in India were little challenged. Risley seemed to speak for many in both colonial and academic establishments when he wrote that caste

> forms the cement that holds together the myriad units of Indian society. . . . Were its cohesive power withdrawn or its essential ties relaxed, it is difficult to form any idea of the probable consequences. Such a change would be more than a revolution; it would resemble the withdrawal of some elemental force like gravitation or molecular attraction. Order would vanish and chaos would supervene.[32]

At the dawn of the twentieth century, it would be difficult to put the case much more strongly than that.

When in 1901 the government of India resolved its support for a scheme to carry out an ethnographical survey of India, one of Risley's first acts, as the new director of ethnography for India, was to appoint Edgar Thurston, director of the Madras Museum between 1885 and 1908, as the superintendent of ethnography for the Madras Presidency. Risley was particularly delighted with Thurston's availability because of their common enthusiasm about anthropometry as the principal means for the collection of physical data about the castes and tribes of India.[33]

In the proposal for the ethnographical survey of India, the secretary to the Government of India wrote that

> it has often been observed that anthropometry yields peculiarly good re-sults in India by reason of the caste system which prevails among Hindus, and of the divisions, often closely resembling castes, which are recognized by Muhammadans. Marriage takes place only within a limited circle; the disturbing element of crossing is to a great extent excluded; and the dif-ferences of physical type, which measurement is intended to establish, are more marked and more persistent than anywhere else in the world.[34]

Thus the government justified its project, and its choice of Risley and Thurston, for a survey that was specifically directed "to collect the phys-ical measurements of selected castes and tribes."[35] Risley's advocacy of anthropometry and his theories about the relation of race and caste were clearly fundamental to the definition of the ethnographic project in turn-of-the-century colonial India. The scientific claim about caste re-flects Risley's assumption that he could actually test in India the various theories about race and the human species that had been merely pro-posed on speculative grounds in Europe. At the same time, these claims concealed the continuity between the assumption that castes were bi-ologically discrete and the belief that in cultural as well as biological terms castes in India were like individuals in the West.

During the first decade of the twentieth century, Thurston worked systematically on his ethnographic survey along the lines set down by Risley, collecting myriad ethnographic details and extensive archives of measurements, all arranged according to the different castes and tribes in the presidency. Indian subjects were not only organized by but contained in their castes or tribes, which determined the cultural, eco-nomic, social, moral, and biological characteristics of their constituent members. Individuals only existed as representative types or, rather, as bodies.

Thurston wrote two major ethnographic works. The first was published in 1906 while he was in the middle of his labors for the ethnographic survey. Titled *Ethnographic Notes in Southern India*, it consisted of a series of essays on a variety of subjects that Thurston thought held intrinsic interest.[36] His ethnographic survey ended in Madras with the completion of his seven-volume work, *Castes and Tribes of Southern India*, which had entries on more than three hundred caste groups listed in alphabetical order.[37] The entries on each caste range in length from one sentence to seventy-five pages, and they include such salient ethnographic facts as origin stories, occupational profiles, descriptions of kinship structure, marriage and funerary rituals, manner of dress and decoration, as well as assorted stories, observations, and accounts about each group. Naturally, Thurston also included the results of his anthropometric researches. The text was obviously designed as an easy reference work for colonial administrators, for the police as well as revenue agents, district magistrates, and army recruiters. It was clear that you could know a man by his caste.

The ethnographic survey resulted in a series of similar volumes for the different regions of India, and while not all the surveyors shared Risley's anthropological views to Thurston's extent, all of the volumes nevertheless reflect Risley's general sense of what the survey should entail. Risley's characterization of caste deploys with particular clarity what I have characterized as the standard late colonial conception of Indian society, in which caste is the source of all order and the fundamental basis of the social. It is perhaps not ironic that the surveys were conducted during the early years of Indian nationalism, for the new ethnographic knowledge was to be used to curtail popular agitation as well as to justify the colonial assumption that Indian nationalist aspirations were essentially futile.

Although colonial ethnographers rarely addressed directly the political implications of their scientific projects, Risley did precisely that in his *The People of India*, where he confronts the question of nationalism. In one of the two new chapters written for the 1909 publication of the book, Risley assesses the role caste might play in the future of India's political development. And he quotes with approval the words of Sir Henry Cotton, who surmised that "the problem of the future is not to destroy caste, but to modify it, to preserve its distinctive conceptions, and to gradually place them upon a social instead of a supernatural basis."[38] Here Cotton, and Risley, advocate precisely what I have suggested colonialism in India encouraged: the constitution of caste as a necessary complement to social order and governmental authority, a new kind of civil society for the colonial state.

In Risley's view, caste has an ambivalent status. It is both a religious institution and a social or civil one. It is anarchic, yet it encourages the development of monarchy. It is particularistic, even though it is the necessary and inevitable basis for any unity in the Indian context. On the one hand Risley noted, basing his conclusions largely on the lectures of Sir John Seeley, that "the facts are beyond dispute, and they point to the inevitable conclusion that national sentiment in India can derive no encouragement from the study of Indian history."[39] On the other hand, Risley also wrote that

> the caste system itself, with its singularly perfect communal organization, is a machinery admirably fitted for the diffusion of new ideas; that castes may in course of time group themselves into classes representing the different strata of society; and that India may thus attain, by the agency of these indigenous corporations, the results which have been arrived at elsewhere through the fusion of individual types.[40]

These contradictions are interestingly resolved in (and by) the colonial situation. And here we confront the colonial mind in its most liberal guise. For Risley writes that "the factors of nationality in India are two—the common use of the English language for certain purposes and the common employment of Indians in English administration."[41]

Risley thus holds out a kind of limited but realistic hope for national development in India, measured by his sense that caste ideas and institutions will stand in the way, though he is optimistic that a steady (and English) pragmatism on the part of Indian leaders can sow the seeds of a new mentality. But Risley's liberalism is complicit in the general project of British colonialism, as it supports the notion that caste is simultaneously a barrier to national development and an inevitable reality for Indian society in the foreseeable future. Risley suggests that caste, as he has interpreted it, can be made into a virtue out of its necessity. It can accommodate and shape a gradually developing class society, perhaps even softening its potential conflicts and antagonisms, and it can provide a model (in its idealized varna version) for the articulation of an all-embracing ideology that might work at a general level to confound and even counteract the fissiparous tendencies of caste as a specific social institution. Caste in this sense is the key to the great transition from feudalism to capitalism/democracy—except that in the colonial situation that transition can never be fully made. The teleology of self-rule is here, as always, couched in a future that has absolutely no temporal reality.

Toward a Nationalist Sociology of India

It is usual in analyses such as this to attend only to the British side of colonial discourse and to assume that there were no resistant readings of Risley's anthropological politics. In fact, a number of Indian scholars joined in the growing chorus of critical commentary on Risley's emphasis on the racial basis of caste, extending their criticisms as well to some of the fundamental premises of colonial anthropology.

Shridhar Venkatesh Ketkar, a Maharashtrian who came to Cornell in the early years of the twentieth century to study for a Ph.D. in political science, published his influential *History of Caste in India* in 1909.[42] He began his work by noting that "it is quite natural that no other feeling than that of amusement should occur to the English mind. He can afford to laugh at the absurdities and contradictions in such an antiquated and complicated institution." Writing from America, he did not restrict his concerns to the English: "An American missionary finds the subject very useful to induce his countrymen to subscribe money to save the souls of two hundred millions of people from heathenism."[43] Ketkar does not go on to apologize for caste but rather to suggest that, as a Hindu who cannot remain unmoved and uninvolved in the face of such a momentous topic, he is well placed to propose the methodological guidelines for its scientific study.

One of Ketkar's major complaints was the suspicion about Brahmans held by his contemporary colonial commentators on caste. Indeed, whereas early colonial writers had relied on Brahmans and on their texts, later writers had not only replaced a textual with an empirical

approach; they often accused Brahmans of writing texts—and organizing the caste system—in order to maintain their superior position. Ketkar writes,

> The thankless task of guiding the people and of preventing them from
> doing wrong fell, to a large extent, on spiritual authority, as the political
> authority was unfit for their share of the burden. . . . But with such a huge
> task before the Brahmanas what power did they have? All that they had to
> rely on was their knowledge of the sacred literature, for which all people
> had high respect.[44]

In countering the disregard for India's sacred traditions, Ketkar bought
directly into colonial disregard for India's political past.

Although Ketkar raised a number of critical questions about Risley's
anthropology, disputing his seven-fold classification and blaming the
British for introducing an obsession with race to India, the eminent
sociologist Govind Sadashiv Ghurye moved the critique of Risley, and
of colonial anthropology, to another level altogether.[45] In his *Caste and
Race in India*, Ghurye took up Risley's theory of race as well as his use
of anthropometric methods and data.[46] Ghurye was very critical of both
the data and its uses, and he ultimately determined that only in the Punjab and parts of the United Provinces was there a correlation between
race and caste, in which Brahmans betrayed physiognomic indications
of their hereditary connection to the Aryan invaders of the subcontinent. Everywhere else, and for all other groups, general miscegenation
had eroded any racial distinctness to caste. Ghurye emphasized the mixing of castes particularly in Maharashtra and Madras, where he also felt
caste, in the form of anti-Brahman movements, had become dangerously politicized and erroneously justified by racial categories.

Ghurye was also directly critical of Risley's role in politicizing caste,
particularly in relation to the census. Although Risley was not the first
to use the decennial census for collecting and presenting material about
caste, Ghurye noted that "this procedure reached its culmination in
the Census of 1901 under the guidance of Sir Herbert Risley of ethnographic fame." Risley had assumed that the only intelligible picture of
social groupings in India could be gained by using a classification of
"social precedence as recognized by the native public opinion." Ghurye

complained that Risley adopted this procedure despite "his own clear admission that even in this caste-ridden society a person, when questioned about his caste, may offer a bewildering variety of replies" according to whether he chooses to emphasize his sect, subcaste, exogamous section, titular designation, occupation, or region.[47] Ghurye lamented the growth of caste *sabhas* organized expressly around the attempt to press forward claims of higher status in the census. He quoted with approval the remarks of a Mr. Middleton, one of the two census superintendents in 1921, to the effect that the so-called occupational castes "have been largely manufactured and almost entirely preserved as separate castes by the British Government" and that "Government's passion for labels and pigeon-holes has led to a crystallization of the caste system, which, except amongst the aristocratic castes, was really very fluid under indigenous rule."[48]

Ghurye also felt that various decisions of the government had encouraged the anti-Brahman movement, and he criticized in particular the use of quotas to restrict government employment for Brahmans in Maharashtra and Madras. Ghurye saw this as part of a general strategy on the part of the British to use caste for the purposes of "divide and rule." Indeed, he quoted as evidence of this the 1865 statement of James Kerr, the principal of the Hindu College at Calcutta, that "it may be doubted if the existence of caste is on the whole unfavourable to the permanence of our rule. It may even be considered favourable to it, provided we act with prudence and forbearance. Its spirit is opposed to national union."[49] Not that Ghurye apologized for all aspects of the caste system, and even though he lamented the decline of the "priesthood" and was particularly worried about the rise of prejudice against Brahmans, he clearly supported Gandhi's attempts to ameliorate the conditions of the untouchables (even as he disapproved of Ambedkar's attempt to politicize caste around an untouchable movement). However, Ghurye's sense was that the British were largely responsible for caste's alleged antipathy to nationalist ideals.

While Ketkar and Ghurye accepted many more colonial assumptions in their anthropology than they rejected, and while as active exponents of the Brahmanical cause they were clearly situated in a sociology of knowledge of their own, their readings both anticipate some of my own criticisms and demonstrate the possibility of nationalist resistance within professional discourses. If this resistance does not seem as successful or complete as perhaps it should in retrospect, it is because, as Partha Chatterjee has noted in a slightly different context, colonized discourses were necessarily predicated on colonial ones.[50]

Recasting India

The assumption that the colonial state could manipulate and invent Indian tradition at will, creating a new form of caste and reconstituting the social, and that a study of its own writings and discourse is sufficient to argue such a case is clearly inadequate and largely wrong. Long after I began to study the complex dynamics of colonial intervention in India, the study of what is now called colonial discourse has become the site for a compelling range of theoretical projects in literary and cultural studies.[51] This is in large part because of the impact of Edward Said's work and the ease with which colonialism falls subject to a poststructuralist critique.[52] But in spite of Said's insistence on a reading of Michel Foucault that situates discursive formations in historical processes of institutional domination and hegemony, much recent critical theory has merely gestured toward history—no sooner completing the gesture than appropriating history to support ahistorical—and even antihistorical— readings of texts. The ease with which critical readings of colonial texts and "Third World" referents are made in certain literary circles today may indicate the ironic birth of a new orientalism.[53]

Any study of colonial discourse that fails to examine the historical character and contradictory nature of colonial intervention and the institutional bases of colonial impact must be rejected even if we accept, as I do, Foucault's emphasis on the fields of power created by discursive practices. The power of colonial discourse was not that it created whole new fields of meaning instantaneously but that it shifted old meanings slowly, sometimes imperceptibly, through the colonial control of a range of new institutions, including those for which the study of caste was judged necessary, as in the earlier note from the ethnographic survey. Although an emphasis on ideas and discourses reveals that institutional hegemony is not based solely, or even principally, on brute force, discourse does not do it alone. Institutions activate ideological changes most often and most effectively when they do so subtly, masking seduction as mutuality, resistance as complicity, and change as continuity. Transformations occurred because of the ways colonial discourse inscribed its peculiar, often masterful combination of old and new meanings in institutional theaters with major consequences for the colonial subjects. As I have argued elsewhere, this process often involved the paradoxical preservation of old regime forms, creating a shadow theater in which continuities and changes seemed always to mimic each other.[54]

In the case of caste, we have only begun to examine the complex and contradictory character of colonial change. I do not have the space here to detail the mechanisms by which radically new forms and meanings became inscribed around the trope of caste in the late colonial project of British state formation in India. Suffice it for the moment to say that they included, as anticipated in my discussion of Ghurye, the politicization of invented forms of caste in the census as well as in the communally based franchises of early electoral reform, in the development and implementation of legal codes, in the introduction and elaboration of revenue systems and policies predicated on a colonial sociology of India, and in the textualization and professional appropriation and reinterpretation of Indian traditions and social forms. And all of these historical processes themselves rest on a thick historical base, for caste achieved its critical colonial position only because the British state was successful in separating caste as a social form from its dependence on precolonial political processes.

The history of discourses on caste cannot be separated from the full institutional history of British colonialism. But if colonial discourse and the documentation apparatus that provided the evidence and the ground for the colonial caste of mind was not totally and autonomously constitutive, neither was it epiphenomenal. Orientalist versions of India's essence and anthropological representations of the centrality of caste have conspired to deny Indians their history and their historicity simultaneously; their failure to have history was all their own fault. History belonged to the colonizers, not the colonized. The potential subjectivity of Indian subjects was not suppressed outright but shifted into the cultural logic of reproduction implied by terms such as custom and tradition, which in India meant "caste."[55] At the same time, under colonialism caste became a specifically Indian form of civil society, the most critical site for the textualization of social identity as well as for the specification of public and private domains, the rights and responsibilities of the colonial state, the legitimating conceits of social freedom and societal control, and the development of the documentation and certification regimes of the bureaucratic state.

It seems clear in the Indian case that the forms of casteism and communalism that continue to work against the imagined community of the nascent nation-state have been imagined as well.[56] However, they have been imagined precisely through and within the same historical mechanisms that in the colonizing nations of Europe and America were far more securely harnessed to the project of state formation. And they have been imagined with such success that when we think of India, we must now insistently be reminded that India's postcolonial condition is not its precolonial fault.

5

Ritual and Resistance

Subversion as a Social Fact

There is subversion, no end of subversion, only not for us.
—Stephen Greenblatt, *Shakespearean Negotiations* (1988)

The social history of modern India has developed side by side with anthropology. Often, social history has simply received its fundamental understandings of what constitutes "society" in India from an anthropology that itself betrays all too clearly the traces of colonial forms of knowledge about India. While social historians of areas outside of South Asia (or other Third World areas of special interest to anthropology) have worked in greater autonomy from anthropology, they have recently turned to anthropology to enable them to understand many aspects of social life that had not been addressed by political or intellectual history and that later proved equally intractable to the quantitative methods of early social history. In both cases, social historians have consumed anthropological theories and rubrics too uncritically, little realizing the possibility that interdisciplinary collaboration should leave neither of the constituent disciplines untouched. In this chapter, I focus on everyday forms of resistance, to criticize both anthropological assumptions about ritual and historical reifications of these assumptions. In taking "ritual" as my subject, I argue that too often the combination of the key terms "everyday" and "resistance" leads us to look for new arenas where resistance takes place rather than realizing that there are many old arenas also brimming with resistance. Finally, I suggest that our old theories of either "resistance" or "the political" are not all that are at risk in this enterprise, but also the underlying presuppositions of order itself.

Ritual is a term that sanctifies and marks off a space and a time of special significance. Ritual may be part of everyday life, but it is fundamentally opposed to "the everyday." Anthropologists have typically identified ritual as a moment and an arena in which meaning is crystallized, in which social experience is distilled and displayed. As summarized by Geertz, Durkheim and Robertson-Smith set the terms of anthropological discourse on ritual by emphasizing the manner in which ritual "reinforce[s] the traditional social ties between individuals . . . the social structure of a group is strengthened and perpetuated through the ritualistic or mythic symbolization of the underlying social values upon which it rests."[1] Rituals are thus seen as embodying the essence of culture, "as dramatizing the basic myths and visions of reality, the basic values and moral truths, upon which . . . [the] world rests."[2] This is not to say that anthropologists have always treated ritual as static. In her first book, Sherry Ortner (showing Geertz's influence) clarifies that while she says that rituals "dramatize basic assumptions of fact and value in the culture" she in fact is coding a more complex assertion, namely that "such 'fundamental assumptions' are actually constructed, or reconstructed, and their fundamentality re-established, in the course of the rituals themselves."[3] Nonetheless, as her more current work indicates, this earlier clarification reflected a particular moment in anthropology when Durkheimian assumptions about meaning and ritual were being reevaluated but left basically unchallenged.[4] Ritual might have been viewed as a process that was profoundly integrated into the complex and shifting social worlds of anthropological subjects, but it was still the principal site of cultural construction, and culture was fundamentally about shared meanings and social values.

Interestingly, some years later, when summarizing theoretical developments in anthropology since the sixties, Ortner noted that ritual had been shifted from center stage by new concerns in anthropology with practice and everyday life.[5] This new call to practice has been part of a general move away from traditional subjects such as kinship and ritual, or at least away from traditional approaches to these subjects. And history, viewed more as process than as chronology, is fundamental to this new concern with practice. The movement toward history and practice is not motivated, as the movement toward anthropology was for a time among historians, by a concern about a paucity of meaning and culture, but rather just the opposite; there has been a sense that studies of meaning had become too aestheticized, too abstracted from the everyday contexts in which meanings are produced, reproduced, and manipulated. Nonetheless, even calls for practice-oriented anthropologies from such theorists as Bourdieu confirm the residual centrality of the cultural: in Bourdieu's theoretical work, capital is now modified by the adjective "symbolic."[6]

In recent years, as social history has become increasingly anthropologized, historians have appropriated ritual as a subject and employed anthropological perspectives on ritual. William Sewell invoked a Geertzian conception of ritual to demonstrate that ritual performances—in his particular case, story rituals that employed old-regime forms in post-revolutionary contexts—were used symbolically to mark and socially to solidify the emerging communities of labor in late eighteenth- and early nineteenth-century France.[7] More commonly, the names of Turner, Van Gennep, and Gluckman rather than Geertz have been cited when historians have attempted to grasp ritual. Geertz has been used by historians principally for his semiotic theory of culture, not for his critique of functionalist analyses of ritual.[8] Following from these anthropological authors, historians have typically been interested in rituals such as the carnival or the charivari, in rites of inversion or status reversal. Some historians have accepted the functionalist undergirding of anthropological writing about these rituals, concurring at least to some extent that rituals in Gluckman's terms "obviously include a protest against the established order" but "are intended to preserve and strengthen the established order."[9] As Natalie Davis puts it,

> Rituals are ultimately sources of order and stability in a hierarchical society. They can clarify the structure by the process of reversing it. They

can provide an expression of, and a safety valve for, conflicts within the system. They can correct and relieve the system when it has become authoritarian. But, so it is argued, they do not question the basic order of the society itself. They can renew the system, but they cannot change it.[10]

From a textual perspective, Stephen Greenblatt has recognized that the anxiety about royal authority induced by Shakespeare in such plays as *Richard II* and *Henry V* serves only in the end to enhance the power of authority; as he says, "actions that should have the effect of radically undermining authority turn out to be the props of that authority."[11]

Returning to the carnival, many historians have recognized in it something more than this, seizing on the prepolitical elements of class struggle, concentrating on the disorderly aspects of the periodic inversion. However, in so doing they have had to suspend the teleological framing they might perhaps have rather recorded as critics of the social order; rituals rarely became highly politicized and often did lapse back into the social orders that produced them, whether or not that social order was reinforced or slightly shaken as a result. Subversion was either contained or transformed into order. Indeed, in literary studies, which since the translation of Bakhtin's extraordinary book on Rabelais in 1968 has become even more carnivalesque than social history, the relation between periodic disorder and subversion on the one hand and order and containment on the other has been widely debated.[12] Terry Eagleton is one of many critics of Bakhtin who holds that Bakhtin's celebration of the political potential and meaning of the carnival is misguided:

> Indeed carnival is so vivaciously celebrated that the necessary political criticism is almost too obvious to make. Carnival, after all, is a *licensed* affair in every sense, a permissible rupture of hegemony, a contained popular blow-off as disturbing and relatively ineffectual as a revolutionary work of art. As Shakespeare's Olivia remarks, there is no slander in an allowed fool.[13]

Be this as it may, it is in fact striking how frequently violent social clashes apparently coincided with carnival. And while carnival was always licensed, not all that happened in carnival was similarly licensed. Carnival was socially dangerous, semiotically demystifying, and culturally disrespectful, even though it often confirmed authority, renewed social relations, and was rarely either political or progressive.[14]

In all these debates the question of whether ritual can occasion, or serve as the occasion for, resistance is explored in relation to one specific form of ritual and one particular kind of resistance. We hear only about the carnival or the charivari, about rituals that involve reversal and inversion, not about rituals that involve power and authority of both secular and sacred kinds. And we evaluate the politics of ritual only in terms of a discourse on resistance that seeks out contestatory and confrontational upsurges by the lower classes. It is perhaps no accident that Natalie Davis was less affected by these discursive blinkers than many of her contemporaries since her most critical discussion of the carnival concerns the status of women, who could not participate in public and politicized moments of confrontation, consigned as they were to the private, the domestic, and the particular. A concern with gender issues has led some writers to criticize the virile assumptions underlying most writings on resistance.[15]

Meanwhile, the move among anthropologists from symbolic analysis to practice theory has led to increasing focus on both the everyday and the nonritual. Jean Comaroff, an anthropologist who has worked among the Tshidi of southern Africa and who was clearly deeply influenced by the practice theory of Bourdieu, turned to the everyday for a sense of the repressed and oppressed tensions characteristic of a system of violently established and maintained hegemony such as exists in southern Africa. She found that,

> while awareness of oppression obviously runs deep, reaction may appear erratic, diffuse, and difficult to characterize. It is here that we must look beyond the conventionally explicit domains of "political action" and "consciousness"; for, when expressions of dissent are prevented from attaining the level of open discourse, a subtle but systematic breach of authoritative cultural codes might make a statement of protest which, by virtue of being rooted in a shared structural predicament and experience of dispossession, conveys an unambiguous message.[16]

But the message *is* ambiguous, and anthropologists are still struggling to open up new spaces of inquiry for old subjects of interest.

Among historians, a concern with the social has also led to a concern with the everyday, and social historians interested in a social history of confrontation have redefined their categories of the political and the confrontational. Alf Lüdtke exemplifies this trend in his writing on workers' movements and protests in imperial Germany. As he writes in an important essay:

> My focus will be on the total spectrum of expressions and daily assertions by individuals as well as by different groups and classes. I will emphasize not simply the ways in which people tried to raise demands or resist the demands of others, but also those modes of self-reliance whereby [in theoretical terms] people reappropriated these constraints and pressures—the specific, even peculiar, practices whereby individuals handled their anxieties and desires. I wish to transgress and then blur the usual boundaries between political and private.[17]

Elsewhere Lüdtke writes that protests should be "regarded as occasional manifestations of a wide complex of structured processes and situations" and that "research into traces of suppressed needs should not be confined to manifest expressions of dissatisfaction, opposition, and resistance."[18] In this turn to the "everyday," ritual has too often been left out of the picture. However, ritual is not just a dramatic event but a vital component of everyday experience.[19]

As we increasingly and from differing perspectives examine ordinary life, the fixtures of ordinariness give way to fractures, and we see that struggle is everywhere, even where it is least dramatic and least visible.[20] Struggle emerges where previously we could not see it, a constant marker of critique. Consensus is no longer assumed unless proven otherwise, but even more unsettling for social science, rebellion and resistance are no longer identified through traditional indices of the extraordinary. The ordinary and the extraordinary trade places. In the study of rural India, anthropology has provided most of our social scientific terms of reference. And in anthropology "order" has always been the chief ordering principle of discourse. When anthropology puts particular emphasis on order, it sanctifies it with the adjective "ritual." Ritual is not only principally about order; it is often the domain in which our sociological conception of society is properly realized. We have already noted that anthropologists have often viewed rituals in terms of religious or cultural meanings. They have interpreted the social significance rituals have either directly in terms of these meanings, or—in what is just a slight transformation of this view—as productive of social solidarity. In this view, social relations are displayed and renewed and the hierarchical forms underlying social relations confirmed and strengthened by ritual.

Perhaps, therefore, it comes as no surprise that a writer like James Scott, who has made an important and eloquent plea for the study of everyday forms of peasant resistance, ignores the possibility that ritual could constitute an important site of resistance.[21] Partly, this reveals his understandable economistic emphases, but it is also because he is suspicious of ritual. In a long and rich book he makes only two brief references to rituals of status reversal and several other references to ritual as something that is constitutive of community. Scott is therefore exemplary of how writers concerned with resistance themselves accept with little modification the Durkheimian foundations of social scientific conceptions of ritual.

Jean Comaroff, among others, has argued that ritual need not be about order and domination alone. She has found, at least in her work on southern Africa, that

> ritual provides an appropriate medium through which the values and structures of a contradictory world may be addressed and manipulated. . . . The widespread syncretistic movements that have accompanied capitalist penetration into the Third World are frequently also subversive bricolages; that is, they are motivated by an opposition to the dominant system. While they have generally lacked the degree of self-consciousness of some religious or aesthetic movements, or of the marginal youth cultures of the modern West, they are nevertheless a purposive attempt to defy the authority of the hegemonic order. . . . Such exercises do more than just express revolt, they are also more than mere acts of self-representation. Rather, they are at once both expressive and pragmatic, for they aim to change the real world by inducing transformations in the world of symbol and rite.[22]

Representation, in this view, is one of the most contested resources. But I start with a more basic premise. I do not evaluate ritual practice on the basis of whether or not it aims to change the real world, however much it may lack self-consciousness. Rather, I look at traditional village rituals in India that at face value have the effect of restoring social relations and upholding relations of authority both within the village and between it and the larger political unit of the kingdom or, later, state. And I seek to determine if the way in which order and disorder have been narrativized as basic components of ritual practice is, in fact, adequate to the multiple foci and forms of disorder as I encountered them. For anthropologists have viewed ritual not only as a sociological mechanism for the production of order but also as a cosmological and symbolic site for the containment of chaos and the regeneration of the world (as we, or they, know it).

Elsewhere I have argued that current anthropological writing on ritual underplays, both at the level of large political units and at the level of village festivals, the social fact that ritual constitutes a tremendously important arena for the cultural construction of authority and the dramatic display of the social lineaments of power.[23] However, although I presented examples of conflict, I saw them largely as products of the breakdown of authority under colonialism. Here I argue that precisely because of the centrality of authority to the ritual process, ritual has always been a crucial site of struggle, involving both claims about authority and struggles against (and within) it. By historicizing the study of ritual, we see that while rituals provide critical moments for the definition of collectivities and the articulation of rank and power, they often occasion more conflict than consensus: each consensus is provisional, as much a social moment of liminality in which all relations of power (and powerlessness) are up for grabs as it is a time for the reconstitution and celebration of a highly political (and thus disorderly) ritual order. Resistance to authority can be seen to occur precisely when and where it is least expected.

The ritual I focus on is crucial here because although it is only one of several village rituals it is the one that inaugurates all other village rituals, often setting the calendrical and cosmological agenda for the yearly ritual cycle. The Aiyanar festival, called the *kutirai etuppu*, was critical also in that it vividly reflected and displayed the hierarchical relations

within the village, with the village headman, or *ampalam*, as the osten-
sive center of these relations. The priests for this ritual, who also acted
as the potters who made the clay horses that were consecrated in the
central ritual action, had to obtain permission from the village headman in order to begin making the horses for the festival. The ampalam
was the host for the festival that began and ended at his house and his
emblems were as importantly involved in the procession as were the
clay horses themselves; the ampalam received the first honors, which he
then distributed to the other members of the village at the conclusion of
the ritual. In short, the ampalam represented the totality of the village
in a rite that was seen to celebrate and regenerate the village itself.

When I was in the field, it took little time to realize that Aiyanar was a
critical deity, and the yearly festival in his honor a crucial festival, in the
ritual life of the social formations constituting the focus of my general
ethnohistorical research. Village elders and headmen would regularly
take me to their own Aiyanar shrine as the most important stop on the
village tour. They would tell me all about their village festival, how it
was famous for miles around, how I would be able to observe and recognize the political centrality of the headman, and that I should definitely
plan to return to their village on the occasion of the festival. Clearly
ritual was important, and clearly this was the social ritual par excellence. During the course of my fieldwork, I attended and took extensive
notes on about twelve of these festivals in different villages throughout
the state. Because of my interest in local social relations and structures
of authority, I was drawn into this festival, which became, quite by surprise, a chief focus of my ethnographic research.

There was one festival in particular that I looked forward to attend-
ing. The village headman had been an especially rewarding informant,
or guide, and spent many hours telling me about the complex details of
social organization in his village and his *natu*, the territorial unit that
was coterminous with the settlement zone of his subcaste group (also
called natu) of Kallars, the royal caste in Pudukkottai. He was a patri-
arch of classic proportions. He told me about the Aiyanar festival with
the care and comprehension of a radio cricket commentator, and as the
festival neared he even visited my house in town on two occasions to
submit to further questions and my tape recorder. I was told exactly
when the festival would begin, and we agreed that I would arrive soon

after dusk, to participate in the final preparations, which would culminate in the commencement of the festival around midnight (like many of these rituals, it was to take place through the night). When the festival was still a week away, I expected a formal visit from the headman to invite me as an honored outside guest, but when he failed to turn up I assumed he was unable to come because he was enmeshed in the myriad preparations for the festival. So on the appointed evening I drove my motorcycle the requisite thirty-five miles across potholed tarmac and dusty bullock cart tracks, only to arrive in a village that was virtually dark, with no visible evidence of any approaching festivities. The village headman looked dismayed and surprised as I rolled up on my Enfield, though less dismayed than me since I heard, as I switched off my engine, the unmistakable hiss of a rapidly deflating tire, the devastating effect of a large acacia thorn's penetration of my nonradial Dunlop. The headman told me that the festival had been called off and that he had hoped I would have guessed this since he had not come with the formal invitation. In any case, he said, he could not have come to tell me that there would be no festival since this would have been inauspicious, a bad omen for the village. It had simply been impossible to organize the festival; a long-standing factional dispute in the village was not in the end resolved, and the festival became yet another casualty of this dispute. My immediate concern, apart from the fact that my tire was flat and I was not carrying a spare, was that I had lost a brilliant opportunity to match theory, narrative, and practice, to follow up the story of a festival that I had been tracking industriously over the preceding weeks and months. But as my host instructed his son and assorted relatives to hitch the bullock cart to arrange for my long and bumpy transport back to town, my disappointment yielded to bewilderment. For I learned that the festival on which I had compiled such exquisite notes had not taken place for seven years—and that no one in the village had any genuine expectation that it would take place this year.

Most fieldwork stories have predictable structures. We begin with calm self-confidence, our initial assumptions and convictions yet unchecked by the chaotic realities and serendipities of the field. We then find ourselves in some disastrous predicament that, in unsettling us (and sometimes "them"), enables us to cross the fault line of cultural difference, to familiarize ourselves with the concerns and logics of new social terrains, to achieve new forms of communion with our anthropological subjects, to achieve some fundamental insights. In fact, at the time I was seriously annoyed. Yet, although I had been aware of the extent to which Aiyanar festivals gave rise to conflict and dispute at the time, it was only then, and increasingly over the years since, that I came to realize the extent to which this story illustrates the flip side of my concern with how village rituals reflected and displayed political authority and political relations. I had begun thinking about Aiyanar by using the festival in his honor to critique Dumont's notion (which he developed in a number of places but not insignificantly in an important article on the Aiyanar festival in Tamil Nadu) that religion/ritual always encompasses politics/power.[24] Having established this, it was still difficult to come to terms with the fact that Aiyanar festivals were always sites for struggle and contestation, that speech about the festivals reflected concerns about ritual order and auspiciousness that were part of a different ritual order than the ritual event itself, that even when the ritual event did not happen it was as significant as when it did. The nonevent of the called-off ritual was not, in fact, a nonevent after all.

During the rest of my fieldwork I learned that many of the other great events of ritual calendars were similar nonevents, that Aiyanar festivals did not happen almost as often as they did, and that when they happened they did not always include everyone in the village or result in the village communal harmony that I had previously assumed, and indeed that this communal harmony was disturbed not only along the so-called traditional lines of caste or faction but along developing class lines as well. I also learned that while at one level the festival was about the reestablishment of control over the disorder of a threatening nature, it was also about the range of possibilities that existed precisely at the moment of maximal contact between order and disorder. But it is now time to backtrack to the festival itself, before we allow it, as it did that night for me, to deconstruct itself.

In Pudukkottai, Aiyanar was often the principal village deity, though there are villages which include Aiyanar temples in which the village deity was said to be a goddess. According to most of my informants, the most significant feature of Aiyanar was his role as the protector. He was more specifically called the protection deity, the protector of boundaries, and the one who protected those who took refuge with him.

The kutirai etuppu festival—or the installation of the horses—began a month before the main festival day. The head of the potters (Velars), the community that made the terracotta offerings and often acted as principal priests for Aiyanar, would take a handful of clay (*pitiman*) from the village tank. The pitiman was placed in a brass plate and handed to the village ampalam, who then returned it to the Velars, along with the ritual dues. The ampalam had to make this gift, signifying his permission for the festival to begin, to entitle the Velars to proceed with the preparation of the offerings. The gift was made in part in the form of *puja*, as the blessed return of a gift that was first offered to the superior being. The central position of the ampalam was thus enunciated and displayed at the moment of the festival's inauguration.

Throughout the festival itself, though each one varied in details, the role of the ampalam was particularly conspicuous, as important in many ways as the deity. The festival began and ended at his house, the central locus of all village gatherings. There the first ritual action of the festival had taken place a month earlier, when the ampalam returned the pitiman to the head of the Velars. Similarly, the first ritual action of the festival day was often the puja performed to the ampalam's family deity, adorned with the emblems that represented and encapsulated the family's heritage. Granted by the raja and passed from generation to generation within the family, these emblems now symbolized that this festival was sponsored by the village ampalam, a festival at once personal and public, the private puja of the ampalam's family and the public performance of the entire village.

In Dumont's well-known analysis of this festival he places considerable importance both on the opposition between purity and impurity (deducing from diet that Aiyanar is principally modeled on the Brahman, even though in behavior and legend Aiyanar is far more like the king) and on his contention that Aiyanar's relation to other village deities reflects the subordination of the political to the religious. The kingly aspects of the deity and the critical role of the ampalam are either ignored or accorded only secondary importance. Dumont's inability to provide a fully satisfactory analysis of Aiyanar and his festival is part of his larger inability to grant that a king can, in certain contexts, encompass and incorporate the divine, the Brahmanic, as well as the social and political constituents of caste solidarity and warrior strength. In the village, where the king was represented by the ampalam, the festival at once elevated him and his political authority, displayed his relation to the king, effected an identity between the latter and the village, and produced, through the celebration of a festival on behalf of a god who so dramatically exemplified the royal function, the conditions under which the village could be victorious against the forces of evil.

But this is not the whole story. For it is precisely the political permeability of ritual that makes possible a succession of contested performances, readings, and tellings. In India kingship had been the dominant trope for the political, but far from the only one. As I stated at the beginning, the Aiyanar festival frequently did not happen, or it occasioned everything from violent dispute to multiple celebration, as in one village where three separate village festivals took place under the leadership of three rival castes and their factional affiliates.

For example, in the early 1920s in Tiruvappur, a village close to Pudukkottai town and made up mostly of Kallars, weavers, and service castes, the Velars petitioned that they were under no compulsion to give or receive the pitiman from the village headman. With appropriate bureaucratic justification, they insisted that since the headman's *inam* lands did not specify that he should give the pitiman, there was no other authoritative basis for the claim that pitiman be given only by the headman. The headman in turn petitioned the government that the performance of the festival without his permission, granted through the pitiman, was an infringement of his hereditary right, as proved by the fact that his family had been granted inam lands with the specific injunction to conduct the ordinary pujas and other festivals in the Aiyanar temples of Tiruvappur. Both petitions employed the same colonial logic, giving inams (and the authority of local headmen) a rational legal basis they had not possessed in precolonial times.

For the Diwan's assistant, the Diwan Peishkar, the resolution of the case rested first on the proper interpretation of the significance of the grant of pitiman. His inquiries led him to decide quite correctly that the grant of pitiman signified far more than the intended cooperation of the headmen or Nattars.

If it signifies mere cooperation without the slightest tinge of authority or idea of special privilege the villagers would not have objected to the continuance of the system. On the other hand, the grant of *pitiman* is considered to be a grant of permission by the nattars to conduct the *kutirai etuppu*. Both the nattars and the artisans view it in this light, and it is why the former are unwilling to lose the privilege and the latter anxious to discontinue the system.[25]

He then had to decide whether this privilege could be sustained under the bureaucratic terms of service implied by the wording of the inam grant, which was vague enough to accommodate both interpretations put forward in the petition and counterpetition. The Diwan Peishkar investigated customs in other Aiyanar temples to determine precedent only to find that each case differed, hardly the stuff of precedent. To further complicate matters, the Diwan Peishkar felt that he had to determine whether the dispute concerned the hereditary privileges of the headmen as traditional caste headmen or, in a deliberately alienating bureaucratic move, as state functionaries.

The Diwan Peishkar—like the Diwan a Brahman by caste—was also troubled by his belief that religion was an individual concern and that all devotees should be able to commission the Velars to make horses for them without the intervention of the Nattars. Such control over the individual vows of others seemed to him "revolting to a devotee's sense of honor and reason." He recommended that the Nattars be allowed to commission the installation of horses on their own behalf but not on behalf of others. The separation of the individual rights of Nattars from their right to commission horses on behalf of the entire village only made sense, however, in terms of a newly formulated bureaucratic conception of religion, since the individual vows of devotees would have been encompassed by the social fact that the festival, even when contested, was a village festival. The Diwan Peishkar's recommendation struck at the core of the headman's objections, since he saw his privilege as an enactment of his authoritative position in the village temple and indeed in the village at large. But in the crafting of an autonomous domain and logic of religion, the underlying social issues were ignored. The struggle between the service and dominant groups was a struggle over authority and had its most visible and important expression in the Aiyanar ritual, which itself resisted bureaucratic appropriation by a new

Brahman-British religious sensibility that reflected concerns of Brahmans and the British alike.

As it turned out, the Diwan was less zealous than the Diwan Peishkar to upset the local structure of authoritative relations in Tiruvappur. He recommended that the Nattars continue to be vested with the right to give the pitiman. He did, however, insist that the Nattars had to signify their permission by giving back the pitiman immediately and routinely, thus heading off the mischievous possibility that they might abuse their right, a sacred trust. "Authority" was defended in name but was undermined by the efforts of the bureaucratic establishment to make religion an individual and private rather than a social and public affair. Although this did not allay all the concerns of the petitioners, they had at least been able to use the language of government to lodge an important formal complaint.

Tiruvappur had been the scene of many similar disputes at least as early as 1885. At one point the local Paraiyars asserted themselves against the ampalam by refusing to beat drums outside the temple. At another time, the Velars again resisted the authoritative claims of the Kallar headman, denying his privilege to carry the scythe used for the ritual slaughter and present it to the Velars who actually did the cutting. On one occasion they even refused, in their role as priests, to make *pracatam* (offerings) from Aiyanar to the ampalam. Again the Diwan upheld the rights of the ampalams at the same time that he tried to rationalize the exercise of these rights.

Many similar disputes took place, but only a few of them leaked into official view, usually because the disputes were dealt with in summary (and often brutal) fashion by the local dominant groups. So although these files alerted me to a record of contention, it was only in towns close to the court, and also in bigger towns and temples, that ritual was a clearly contentious affair in the historical record.[26] Many of these disputes concerned the distribution of honors and pracatam in temples and locked dominant lineages and their headmen in fervent dispute with each other; otherwise the disputes were usually buried by the dominant group (which had to seek no higher authority). Thus when Appadurai and Breckenridge proposed that ritual in southern India involved conflict, they were mainly referring to one form of conflict, that

which anthropologists working on India had until then recognized and
accepted: factionalism. Indebted though I am to their analysis, I only
realized the full range of dispute and contestation through a mix of ethnographic accidents and historical investigations.

I found many other instances in which ritual turned out to be a core
arena for resistance, particularly for groups such as artisans and "untouchables" (Dalits) who could resist by simply withholding their services. The closest thing to a municipal strike in the history of Pudukkottai town took place in the early 1930s when the untouchables protested
the establishment of a municipal crematorium by withholding their ritual funeral services for all their patron groups. The municipality backed
down in short order because of the consternation of one high-caste family after another who felt they were dishonoring their dead. Kathleen
Gough has vividly documented the breakdown of village ritual in rural
Tanjavur where untouchable groups, fired in part by the growth of a
local communist movement, increasingly withheld their ritual services
from village festivals.[27] Nonetheless, Gough's assertion that village rituals would not recover from the effects of recent change and growing
class consciousness has not been sustained by the experience of the last
thirty years. In fact, village rituals continue to be important precisely
because of their association with conflict.

Although village rituals were clearly sites for struggle between elite
groups and their factions over who was in charge, this was only part of
the story.[28] Rituals were sites for struggle of all kinds, including—as my
earlier story suggests—the struggle between discourse and event. Ritual
was a discursive and practical field in which a great deal was at stake
and a great deal was up for grabs. But when conflict developed in ritual
it always made the ritual a site for appropriation as well as for struggle.
The headman of the darkened quiet village appropriated the interpretive function of a ritual that he doubtless always knew would not take
place, and he was embarrassed only when I pressed my curiosity and
showed up without the proper invitation. The Brahman administrators
of Pudukkottai appropriated the dispute for their own purposes of undermining the religious authority of rural Kallar elites and implement-
ing new colonial standards for the evaluation of religious activity and
the establishment of religion within a newly created domain of civil
society. Anthropologists have appropriated ritual to advocate the religious dimensions and the character and force of the social, which in

the case of Dumont's transformation of Durkheim is located in a world
of religiously validated hierarchy. Appadurai and Breckenridge found
struggle at the top level of ritual and argued that temples provided political arenas of dispute.[29] These appropriations—including my own—are
examples of the way ritual has become central to the analysis of power
relations in southern India. Yet these appropriations have never fully
succeeded in containing the power of ritual, checked as they were by the
profoundly subversive character of traditional ritual practice. Not only
did ritual discourse and ritual practice operate at angles to each other,
but both discourse and practice were open to a multiplicity of contesting
and resisting agencies.

I have so far completely ignored one of the most important but also
complex sources of agency and action in the Aiyanar festival. I do not
mean the lord Aiyanar himself but rather his incarnation in the form
of the *camiyatis*, the people in the village who during the course of the
festival were routinely possessed by the lord Aiyanar. Possession was an
absolutely critical part of this and other village festivals in the south.
Apart from the goat sacrifice and the feast it was the most charged event
in village ritual practice. Once again I must recount the festival, which
I do with reference to the Aiyanar festival celebrated in the predomi-
nantly Kallar village of Puvaracakuti, in Vallanatu, about eight miles
southeast of Pudukkottai town, in early July 1982.

This particular festival began at the house of the ampalam. When
I arrived the ampalam was bathing, and a number of village folk and
members of the ampalam's family were busy decorating his house, fes-
tooning it with mango and coconut leaves. The Paraiyars who had assembled some distance from the house built small fires to tune their
drums. Flowers, coconuts, and other items for the puja were brought to
the front porch of the house. There were five red ribbons to tie on the
horns of the horses and bulls and towels for the possessed camiyatis as
well as for the service castes such as the dhobi, barber, and Paraiyars.
The ampalam came to the front porch after his bath and worshipped the
images of gods and goddesses hung on the interior walls of the porch.

The emblems of the ampalam were brought out from the vacant house
next door called the big house, unoccupied because of a quarrel within
the ampalam's family between collateral contestants for the position of
ampalam. These emblems consisted of a spear, a sword, a cane, and a
club. The emblems symbolized the office and authority of the ampalam

and were said to have been presented many generations before by the raja. Under a small tiled-roof *mandapam* (pavilion) about twenty yards to the west of the ampalam's house, they were placed next to the *pattavan*, a sword representing an ancestor of the ampalam's family who was worshipped as the family deity. The emblems and the pattavan were shown the flame, camphor was burned, and coconuts were broken, the three most common elements of any performance of puja. After this, the emblems were carried by other Kallars in the village, and the ampalam was summoned. The first procession of the day was ready to begin.

The emblems were carried by Kallars. The entire procession was led by Paraiyars beating their drums. Though the ampalam was the central character, attention was increasingly focused on the camiyatis, five Kallars who were to be possessed by the god. Initially chosen for possessing special spiritual powers, they were the hereditary camiyatis who participated in the festival each year. They walked immediately behind the drum-beating Paraiyars. Not yet in full trance, the camiyatis began to show signs of possession as they walked on to the beat of the drums, their bodies sporadically quivering at the touch of Aiyanar, who was shortly to enter into them. The procession walked straight to the small structural temple to Aiyanar. A puja was performed for Aiyanar, and sacred ash was distributed to all those present. The camiyatis then picked up bags of ash and began walking back to the village, accompanied by the Paraiyars. As they walked through the village, the women of each house came toward them and poured water over their feet to cool them. The camiyatis blessed the women with the ash they carried. We walked through the Kallar section of town, past the ampalam's house, to the Velar settlement on the eastern side of the village. There the procession was welcomed by the playing of the *mela telam* (drum) by the Melakkarars (the pipers) of a nearby temple and by exploding firecrackers. Six terracotta figures, each about four feet high, were lined up on the Velar street—one elephant, three horses, and two bulls in the final stages of decoration. They had been whitewashed, painted with colored stripes, and crowned with stalks of flowering paddy and the ribbons from the ampalam's house. The five Kallar camiyatis stood in front of the terracotta figures. A Paraiyar from a nearby village came forward and carefully dressed the camiyatis in special clothes. The Paraiyar wore a garland made of silver balls, his head was wrapped with a red cloth, his chest was draped with multicolored strands of cloth, a new towel was tied around his waist, and garlands of bells were wrapped around him. His face was painted with vermilion and sandal paste. This Paraiyar was called the *munnoti*, the leader (or the one who went first). In a few minutes he became possessed, to the music of the drums and *nadaswaram* played by the Melakkarars. He began to jump wildly when the incense and camphor smoke were offered to him as he stared fixedly at the sky. He suddenly leapt into the crowd, snatched the ampalam's spear, and began to beat the ground with it. He jumped and ran through the crowd, all the while circumambulating the six figures. The ampalam then came up to him, garlanded him, and smeared sacred ash on his forehead. After, this, the munnoti led the other camiyatis into states of possession. Someone whispered in my ear that the munnoti was the burning lamp that lights other lamps. Each attained full possession as the munnoti held the camphor up to their faces.

The procession was now ready to commence. The Paraiyars went first, followed at some distance by the Melakkarars, then by the munnoti and the five camiyatis, then the terracotta offerings, with the elephant in the lead, followed by the smaller offerings of individual villagers. Behind them walked the ampalam, surrounded by many of his kinsmen. As the procession moved around the village, on its way back to the Aiyanar temple, villagers came up to the camiyatis to be blessed, often asking them questions about the future. When we reached the temple, the eyes of the terracotta figures were opened by the application of blood from a cock, sacrificed by the munnoti (who was then given the cock). The terracotta animals were then placed in front of the temple. A grand puja was held to Aiyanar. The Velar priests made offerings of tamarind rice, broke coconuts, and then displayed the light, after which they offered ash to the worshippers. Then the priests left the Aiyanar shrine, shutting its doors. Aiyanar was said to be vegetarian, and thus he ought not to see the sacrifice to Karuppar, the fierce black god whose shrine is always next to Aiyanar's.

Moving to Karuppar, the priests performed puja again. The villagers surged forward en masse to obtain some ash. One of the priests laid a stone a few yards in front of the Karuppar temple. The villagers assembled in a circle; finally a goat was brought forward and judged ready. The fifth camiyati came forward bearing a large sword taken from the

Karuppar shrine. With one swift slice he cut off the goat's head. As they watched the final convulsions of the goat's body, the crowd became increasingly excited and jubilant. The carcass of the goat, originally donated by the ampalam's family, was now handed over to the Velar priests.

A cloth was laid on the ground for the ampalam to sit. The Velars brought him the huge bowl of tamarind rice and all the pracatam from the puja: flowers, coconuts, and plantains. Sitting there the ampalam distributed the honors, first to the Kallar lineage heads, then to the Valaiyars and the artisans. Again, the village elders took up the ampalam's emblems and beckoned to him to lead the procession back to the village. They then returned to his house, where the emblems had been returned to their accustomed place. The village Paraiyars were then given their pracatam in the village square in front of the ampalam's house, along with sufficient rice and a chicken for a feast of their own.

The final distribution of honors both confirmed the authority of the ampalam and displayed the hierarchical relations of all the caste groups in the village. Or so it seemed. This harmonious village festival began to deconstruct itself when I came to realize shortly after I attended the festival that a rival group of Konars, traditionally herders but now an increasingly powerful agricultural caste, had seceded from the ritual performance and instead held their own Aiyanar festival some weeks later. The appearance of harmony that presented itself so forcefully began to unravel as soon as I began to poke into the affairs of the village. After what I have already argued in this paper, this is hardly surprising. I was, however, still struck by the powerful role of possession.

Most of the literature on possession deals with the nasty kind, when it is the devil rather than the lord who has taken up residence within our mortal coil. Here, rather than the exorcist we have its opposite—a man whose skill and power is precisely to induce possession rather than rid us of it. But this too is an extraordinary form of power, and one that has many dangers. It is significant that for this role a Paraiyar was chosen; while all the other camiyatis were of the dominant Kallar caste, the one person who made their possession possible could never be invited into their houses nor be allowed to dine with them. And his power was not completely contained by hierarchy, for there were moments of real fear when he seized the ampalam's spear and began dancing wildly about.

The fear of Aiyanar was clearly enhanced by his choice of this unruly Paraiyar as his principal vehicle and agent. When I went to visit him later he was completely drunk, and he combined in his person an exaggerated deference and a smoldering bitterness. While he acted as if he was deeply honored that I should visit him, he was the one who told me that there was a rival festival in the village hosted by Konars or shepherds, and as he told me this he almost laughed at the hollow claims of the Kallar headmen who could no longer control an inferior caste group.

Possession was not the only moment of danger nor the only reason why containment was a live issue throughout the festival. Aiyanar was clearly hard to handle, and his agents in possession had to negotiate a delicate balance between playacting and overacting. I was repeatedly told that the possession was real, that it took many years to learn how to accept the visitation of the lord, that it required the supervision of a man of special powers both to learn and to do, and that after a spell of possession it would take days and sometimes weeks for the possessed person, exhausted and shaken by the experience, to return fully to normal. And I was told that if a camiyati turned out not to be really possessed, simply playacting, he would be ridiculed and excluded from any subsequent festival for life.

After all, the festival was critical for the well-being of the village, and if Aiyanar was misrepresented by an impostor, the festival might fail, and the advice handed down by Aiyanar to the anxious and enquiring villagers would be spurious. But there were also times when possession could prove too much. The camiyati was called the vessel, and when this vessel could not contain the concentrated power of the lord, it might crack. In such instances the camiyati would not recover from possession, stay deranged and disturbed, and an exorcist would have to be summoned.

It is possible to account for all of this with a traditional view of ritual. Van Gennep was keenly aware of the danger and disorder that was part of ritual, and he built this into his explanation of liminality and ritual transformation.[30] But his theory contains danger too easily, assuming that any disorder is epiphenomenal rather than fundamental. Possession was in fact another example of how ritual practice was genuinely dangerous and subversive. Part of the subversiveness had to do with the constant possibility of conflict and paralysis. But the subversiveness had also to do with the politics of representation and misrepresentation inherent in both the role of the headman and that of the camiyatis.

The festival was a powerful spectacle precisely because of the role of the possessed camiyatis. To me, it seemed at times like theater. Victor Turner has explained this correlation, using the term "ritual drama," by which he meant that ritual could be analyzed as if it was an unfolding drama with the participants as actors who engaged in the unseen forces through the vicarious agencies of ritualistic enactment.[31] But if what I witnessed was theater to the participants, it was very different from what has come to be accepted as theater in the West. Stephen Greenblatt writes that "the theatre elicits from us complicity rather than belief."[32] But in rural southern India there were elements of both complicity and belief; there were roles and masquerades that depended on far more than skillful artifice and conceit. This was "theatre lived" not "theatre played," as Greenblatt observed when citing an ethnographic example.[33] But even this does not capture the power of this ritual experience. For there was the possibility that something could go wrong, an urgency and unpredictability that rendered a theatrical metaphor too dramatic and even sacrilegious. One of the inescapable implications of the camiyati's predicament—the risk that possession could be inauthentic—was that all agency and all representation in the ritual was at risk as well. Identity was most fragile at the moment of its transformation. The risk that the possessed might be faking it no doubt raised the possibility that the headman, whose authority and connections with the king were both celebrated and renewed in the festival, might also be an imposter. After all, everyone knew (though at the time I did not) that the headman claimed a sovereignty over the entire village that was not granted by the rival shepherds. Participation in the festival was highly politicized. Even the role of the lord was politicized. The dangers were real. The spectators did not simply gaze; they vied with one another to participate more actively and more centrally in the festival, to question the camiyatis, to witness the sacrifice of the goat, and to collect and eat the pracatam—the transubstantiated return of the lord. They also vied with one another to celebrate, to control, and to interpret the ritual.

I have given just a few illustrations to suggest what I mean by the subversive nature of ritual practice and discourse. I close with one last observation. Each ritual event is patterned activity to be sure, but it is also invented anew as it happens. When I witnessed one festival, there was frequent confusion about what was to be done. At one point a participant in the festival leaned over to me, realizing that I had seen many similar festivals, and asked me what I thought they should do next. At the time I thought that I was already intruding too much on the authenticity of the ritual event and that to offer an opinion would be to go across the fragile threshold of legitimate participation implied in the oxymoronic motto of anthropology: participant observation. But I was wrong, for the authenticity of the event was inscribed in its performance, not in some time- and custom-sanctioned version of the ritual. And the authenticity of the Aiyanar festival was in particular inscribed in its uncertainty and its contestability, even when it did not actually take place.

6

The Policing of Tradition

Colonialism and Anthropology in Southern India

Colonial Subjects and Indian Traditions

In late October 1891, the *Madras Mail* brought dramatic attention to the fact that "the barbarous and cruel custom of hookswinging to propitiate the Goddess of Rain, which has been obsolete for some time, has been revived at Sholavandan near Madura."[1] The newspaper describes this event with scandalized disapproval.

> The manner in which this horrible custom is carried out consists in passing iron hooks through the deep muscles of the back, attaching a rope to the hooks, and (after the method of a well sweep) swinging the victim to a height several feet above the heads of the people. The car on which the pole is placed is then drawn along by large ropes in willing hands. . . . Full details of this hookswinging affair are too revolting for publication.

The person swung from the hooks was selected by lot from a larger group that represented a number of the villages sponsoring the festival. Throughout the article, he (for it was always a man) was referred to as "the victim." The newspaper explains its choice of language: "Victim he may well be called, because, though he enters upon this ordeal voluntarily, the chief reason which drives him to it is the sentiment of doing good to his village."

The questions of agency that became fundamental to the moral valuation of the custom of hookswinging were much like those raised during the debate over the abolition of *sati* in the early years of the century. Before the outright suppression of sati, British officials were often required to attend the "rite," to assure that the "victim" was not forced either by the compulsion of family or the mind-altering effect of drugs to jump on the burning funeral pyre of her husband. Worried commentators often wondered whether this kind of monitoring could be anything more than a periodic check on a practice so inscribed in custom and tradition that the voluntary participation of the widow could never be properly ascertained. Besides, the condition of widowhood was itself so deplorable that the decision to jump on the pyre could, in a perverse sense, be seen as rational. Nevertheless, voluntarism as a possibility made little sense in a context where no British official could countenance, let alone approve, such a "barbarous" custom. Sati became a symbol of the backwardness of Indian civilization for the British, even as it became an issue fraught with consequence, given the general British concern not to interfere in traditional practices and customs. As Lata Mani has demonstrated, sati also provided an extraordinary occasion for the rearticulation of the tradition around the designation of, and subsequent debate over, the scriptural sanction for religious practice in early colonial Hinduism.[2] But as Mani and others have shown, the agency of women was only the pretext for other political and cultural concerns.[3] Similarly, while hookswinging became a symbol of British commitment to civilizational reform as well as that of the crisis of enlightened colonial rule, the alleged concern about the victimization of colonial subjects worked to obscure far more salient concerns around the representation of rule and the reorganization of colonial subjectivities.

Colonial subjects, in cases such as those concerning sati and hookswinging, were constructed as victims when they were subjected to some form of custom that either threatened British rule or appeared to violate its moral foundations. Only then did their subjectivity in relation to the possibility of freedom become an issue in colonial discourse. Subjectivity presented itself as an absence; it was only there when it was totally suppressed. Many of the accounts about hookswinging suggested—against the evidence—that the victim was drugged, thus dispensing with the need to worry the issue of agency. But the newspaper account about the hookswinging episode made a far more general assertion: "It might be said that this being a voluntary act, the man submitting himself of his own free will to the torture, it does not come within the letter, and scarcely within the spirit of the law [prohibiting torture]. But it is a case parallel exactly with suttee—the victim in each case being forced to a sacrifice which the press of public opinion fixes on him or her as a duty." Even the possibility that the victim himself believes that his sacrifice is for the good of the village—specifically that it will help bring rain and prosperity—is ignored and obscured in the discursive move that subordinates his agency to the dictates of duty. Custom is enforced by the will of the mob, what is referred to here as public opinion. And it was the public component that was particularly problematic: individual vows that involved similar forms of self-mutilation were not at issue.[4]

Even as "public opinion" seemed to the British a quality of civil society that in India was vastly underdeveloped, the public domain existed only in the most tenuous of ways, for the most part as a site of immense danger. At the very least, colonial officials worried about the maintenance of public order in public spaces: From the beginning of colonial rule, official sources betrayed a consistent concern about the adjudication of competing claims among groups over the right to use public space.[5] Frequently, colonial sources suggest that conflict developed when different religious or caste communities transgressed space, usually in some kind of ritual/religious procession, that was either claimed by another community or came too close to some other group for comfort. Indeed, much early colonial social classification emerged in such adjudicative contexts, and attempts to sort out the relations of "untouchable" and "caste" Hindus, Hindus and Muslims, as well as the congeries of castes such as those labeled "right-hand" and "left-hand," were frequently made in relation to spatial classification and use.[6] For colonial sociology, there could be no uncomplicated designation of a public outside of its own communal categories, though in the last years of the nineteenth century, with the steady development of nationalist thought and activity, the notion of public space loomed dangerously, and was repressed seriously, for other reasons as well. It must have been a comforting thought for colonial rulers that there might be no real Indian public, a notion that, here as in other contexts, was the result of the relentless anthropologizing of India, which served to misrecognize the social and historical possibilities for the nationalist awakening even as it worked to reify categories of social classification.

If the public domain was a contradiction in terms, public space nevertheless preoccupied colonial governance. And even when public space did not occasion the immediate threat of violence or conflict, it required colonial ordering. It seems clear that colonial concern was immensely heightened when an event was by some definition public, and so religious functions that took place outside of the provenance of the temple or home became objects of regulation. Hookswinging was a particular problem not just because of its alleged barbarity but because this barbarity took place in public space with apparent governmental sanction. Missionaries viewed hookswinging both as a major distraction from their own proselytizing efforts and as a public profanation of space that colonial rule should have reserved for civilized purposes. Officials were not only horrified by the event itself but also by the public character of the spectacle, which was disturbing both to their self-representations and to public order. Additionally, the fact that hookswinging appealed to the baser passions of the lower groups in society—who assembled in far greater numbers for village festivals whenever rumors circulated that hookswinging might take place—seemed every bit as troubling as the barbarism of the rite itself. Indeed, civilization itself, in every possible sense, seemed up for grabs.[7]

Colonial power constantly sought to uncover the ways in which Indian tradition worked as a form of power, asserting its hold on the agency of women, protecting other forms of power and patriarchy, and provoking Britain's own disinterested commitment to a civilizing mission even when it claimed a policy of noninterference. However, colonial power never turned its assumptions about power back onto itself, absolving itself implicitly, even as it progressively found new arenas in Indian life in which to press forward its campaign of denunciation and reform. Given colonial reliance on forms of knowledge, it should come as no surprise that the anthropological knowledge of India finds some of its first bearings in the files of administrators, soldiers, policemen, and magistrates who sought to control and order Indian life according to the demands of imperial rule and what these agents of empire considered to be basic and universal standards of civilization. It is impossible to date anthropology in India: the need to understand custom and tradition began with the formation of the state from the beginning and developed with renewed intensity under the British from the early days of their rule. Since notions of custom were fundamental to the establishment of revenue systems and legal codes, much early anthropology can be read in early settlement reports and other colonial records. But in the late nineteenth century the efforts to understand custom and to rule Indian society better became linked to the development of official anthropology in new and important ways. Although this story has many genealogies, I will begin here with the controversies that were generated over whether or not, and if so how, to suppress hookswinging. In these controversies we can discern many of the underlying assumptions of official anthropology about structure and agency, custom and tradition, religion and ritual practice, as well as about the objective provenance of anthropological inquiry. In addition, we will discover some of the footnotes of colonial ethnography, along with a clearer sense of the institutional links between anthropological knowledge and the apparatuses of colonial state power.

The Hookswinging Controversies

I came across the newspaper account with which I opened this chapter because it was enclosed in a file that initiated a series of governmental investigations and reports on the festival.[8] The government was clearly embarrassed by the newspaper's charge, motivated at least in part by missionary pressure, that even though it had been apprised of the event, it took no steps to prevent it. The subject had come up several times before, most recently in the 1850s, but those officials who looked into it had assumed that the festival was dying out on its own and that delicate issues such as the government's declared intention not to interfere in any aspect of native religious practice would be raised.[9] As investigations both in the 1850s and the 1890s soon revealed, however, there was no clear legal mechanism to suppress the ritual on the neutral ground of physical (as opposed to moral or religious) danger. Not only did the victims voluntarily submit to the ordeal (indeed, they often appeared extremely anxious to do so), but they seemed to escape the hookswinging with no grievous bodily harm. As one British official noted early on in the debate, "The fact is that the objection to the hook swinging festival is of a moral, not a physical nature, and Section 144 C.C.P. can only be made applicable to it by distorting it from its original intention."[10] The stated legislation was only designed to prohibit any activity that endangered the life, health, or safety of an individual.

The intention to mount the hookswinging at Sholavandan had in fact been brought to the attention of the government before it took place. The superintendent of police, the divisional officer, and an American doctor from the Madura Mission had all been asked to attend and observe the event. The most that the superintendent of police could legally do to discourage the festival, beyond expressing the moral disapproval of government, was to warn the headmen of the village that they would be held responsible for anything untoward that happened during the festival. If the victim were to die from injuries sustained or cause injuries by falling on top of people in the crowd, the headmen could be booked under the provisions of Section 144. This warning did not have the intended effect, and the festival took place without the dire effects feared (or desired) by some officials.

The district magistrate reported that

there was a crowd of about 5,000 persons. Two hooks were passed through the muscles below the shoulder blades of a Kallan. This was not done in public, but it is believed that the muscles were first kneaded or pounded to induce insensibility and prevent hemorrhage. The man himself says there was no pain. He was swung to a height of twenty feet by the hooks to a pole fixed in the center of a car which was then dragged round the town. He was hung for an hour and a quarter. He was then lowered and given some arrack but says he had none previously. His voice was then full and his pulse strong. There was little or no bleeding. The hooks remained in their place, and he walked about among the crowd. The holes were then large enough to admit the little finger.[11]

This account's tone, clinical rather than condemnatory, is different from that in the newspaper. Whereas the newspaper constantly referred to the victim, we read here that the person who underwent the ordeal was a Kallan and a man who was also allowed to speak for himself.[12] The newspaper had observed that "there can be no doubt that the victim of these proceedings has been heavily drugged before the hooks are passed." But the magistrate's account claims that the hooks were inserted with surgical skill and that the man claimed to have felt no pain and had drunk no liquor before the event.

The account becomes even more clinical when we read the inserted report of Frank Van Allen, MD, the medical man from the Madurai American Mission who had been requested to attend and describe events at the festival:

> [There] were two iron hooks inserted into the skin and subcutaneous tissues, one on each side of the back bone and brought together back to back. Some blood was running down his back. I couldn't learn just how the hooks had been inserted but had heard before that a curved gouge was to be plunged into the tissues cutting down in, and then up and out and in the path thus formed the hooks were to be passed.[13]

The doctor was careful to report what he had actually seen, what he had been able to surmise, and what he had only heard. Whereas the district magistrate had made the painlessness of the insertion seem irrefutable, the doctor only noted that "it is said that the parts were made somewhat insensible by slapping and pounding before the hooks were put in." The doctor reported that the man was "a splendid specimen of brute strength, though not of large frame. He was of medium or under size, stockily built and muscles markedly firm." He also observed that although the man was "evidently under strong excitement," he was "self-controlled." After describing the events of the hookswinging in terms that were clearly the basis for the district magistrate's account, he concluded by saying that "as a physician I am much surprised . . . that the ill effects on the man were so small. No ordinary man could pass through such an ordeal without serious danger to his life."

Colonial sources seemed preoccupied with the question of pain. As we have just seen, the man swung in the Sholavandan hookswinging claimed that he felt no pain and that he was given liquor only after the ordeal. Many colonial observers mistook the signs of possession for intoxication and insisted that the swingers were either drugged or drunk. These observers sought evidence that the obvious pain such an experience would afford was obliterated by unnatural, even immoral, means and assumed all the while that the infliction of pain was both the appeal of the spectacle and the underlying basis for the horror of the rite. Occasionally, men who had been swung complained that the pain had been intense (though most often, it would seem, when an official investigation would have encouraged such a response), but the issue of possession or trance, as well as the very stark images of what was represented as "self-torture," made colonial officials and missionaries extremely uncomfortable, particularly given the overwhelming disavowal of pain as a fundamental ingredient of the experience. Pain became an index of the barbarity of the rite, even as colonial ethnography recognized (with its uneasy Christian religious sensibility) that the acceptance of pain could also be reckoned an index of devotion. Colonial ethnography also saw links between hookswinging and blood sacrifice, conjuring the horror of human sacrifice itself.[14] The determination of agency was of course inextricably mixed in with the question of pain; it seemed unlikely that any agent would willingly subject himself to extreme pain (even if now stripped away from the demand for death), thus suggesting that there were forms of coercion to be unmasked.

This issue of coercion seemed of preeminent importance. The fact that many swingers came from the lower castes suggested that the caste system itself performed the act of coercion, but in Sholavandan as elsewhere the swingers also came from higher, locally dominant caste groups. Although many swingers seemed to have been paid for their service, thus suggesting financial coercion, in other cases swingers actually paid to swing. In Sholavandan men actually competed for the privilege of swinging, as evidenced by the casting of lots. Although there were reports that some swingers backed out at the last minute, there were many more suggesting that swingers not only vied for the right to perform but even collaborated with local authorities to escape the surveillance of British officials intent on persuading the "victims" to desist.

Although there was a range of opinion and commentary, no British official was pleased that such customs survived—indeed, flourished—under

British rule. Nevertheless, the district magistrate of Madurai thought that the only sensible solution would be to downplay the festival. As he put it,

> The festival has been held for years in different places and no proof or reasonable ground for belief that the operation of swinging is dangerous to the life, health, or safety of the person swung or of any one else has so far as known ever been adduced. It is no more dangerous if as much so as taking part in a polo match or an ascent in a balloon or walking on a tight or slack rope. In all these instances, the person or persons concerned voluntarily do an act in which a very considerable risk of limb and life is there.[15]

The comparisons are telling. Had the hookswinging been done purely for entertainment and profit, I suspect there would have been no serious official concern. What clearly horrified the British (and, in particular, missionary opinion) was not just the act itself but that it was done in the name of religion. In spite of a commitment to avoid interference in "native religion," a commitment that had been strengthened after the Great Rebellion of 1857, such clear examples of barbarity in religious practice made the British uncomfortable. And one official even wondered whether the presence of officials and doctors at the hookswinging festivals might not be seen as sanctioning rather than discouraging the events, an echo once again of the concerns that had been raised earlier in the century around the performance of sati.

The government ignored the district magistrate's recommendation to let the festival off the hook. In fact, a number of people were worried that hookswinging would spread throughout the country once it became clear that government did not intend to prevent it.[16] During the next several years, a series of investigations was conducted to determine whether there was sufficient cause to abolish the practice. Each district collector was requested to forward his views on the subject of suppressing the practice by legislation and to base his remarks on the opinions of local officials and citizens.[17] Although there was no specific directive, the inquiries uniformly pursued two complementary aims: to establish, first, that hookswinging did not have the proper sanction of religion at all and, second, that in any case it was performed in the name of religion only to mislead the public and subvert religion itself—that hookswinging was done for the private profit not just of the swinger but, more critically, the corrupt and self-serving temple priests. If these points could be established, there would be no need to confess disbelief and horror as the reasons for wishing to suppress the swinging, no embarrassment about selecting one religious truth over another.

The inquiries turned up a wide range of opinion and concern, much of it anticipated by the earlier investigations of the 1850s. In the first investigation, missionaries were particularly active in condemning the festival. For example, one G. E. Morris, the chaplain of Palavaram (a village near Madras) wrote to the local magistrate that he

> disclaims all intention of wishing to interfere with the religious rites and ceremonies of the Hindoos, but he asks the permission of the Government in this instance on the grounds: 1) that this particular festival forms no part of their religious system, 2) that it involves unnecessary cruelty, 3) that it militates against public order and decency, 4) that it is an infringement of the common laws of humanity, and 5) that in this particular case it disturbed the residents in the quiet and orderly observance of the Lord's Day.[18]

A subsequent letter from Morris to the bishop of Madras went further:

> But, my Lord, I cannot rest satisfied with a humble effort to protect only the Lord's Day from such horrible profanation, or to prevent a repetition of the inhuman ceremony only at this particular station; I feel ashamed of my own country, when I reflect that we have been for so many years Rulers of this Land, and have not yet caused such abominations to cease entirely in every corner of it.[19]

Here, as elsewhere in missionary commentary, it seems clear that hookswinging was a particular problem: Not only did the rite frequently profane the Lord's Day, but it seems to have done so especially because it drew such an intense crowd and did so around a rite that must have been seen to have horrifying resonance with the central event of Christianity, the crucifixion of Christ. A body suspended by iron hooks must have conjured another vision for European missionaries, even as it provided significant competition for proselytizing efforts among the very groups that constituted the most successful target group for conversion, the lower castes.[20] Recall the painstaking descriptions of the penetration of human flesh by the insertion of iron hooks, the repetition of the civilizational horror of the hammering of nails into Christ's hands and feet, and the affixing of Christ's body to the cross. These are the sorts of stories that were used to collect funds for missionary endeavors to combat heathenism, generating as they did collective gasps, sympathy, and contributions in church halls and cathedrals across Great Britain.

Ironically, missionary pressure worked to legitimize upper-caste Hindu opinion, which ultimately sustained colonial efforts to denounce the barbarous rite and find justifications to discount its religiosity. But missionaries were horrified for distinctly Christian reasons. Not only did it raise the specter of the crucifixion and invoke the sacrilege of mistaking Christ's final sacrifice, but hookswinging symbolized the sins against which Jesus struggled so valiantly. The Rev. J. E. Sharkey discounted the religious character of the event in the following terms:

> There are thousands around the pagoda we visited but not one professes to have come to have his sins pardoned and removed. Many have come to vend their wares, about a hundred to petition the idol for children, about seventy to offer thank-offerings for mercies received such as restoration from some illness or success in any important undertaking, and about two-thirds for amusement and for the uncontrolled commission of wickedness.[21]

The denunciation of popular religion here went far beyond the particular spectacle of hookswinging and provided the basis both for a generalized dismissal of all of Hindu religious practice and for the collaboration of high-caste Hindus who for reasons of their own subordinated popular practice to the more spiritual preoccupations of Brahmanic philosophy. Brahmans, many of whom had direct ritual affiliations with shrines and cults that were manifestly part of the mixture that Sharkey condemned, were frequently eager to enunciate their own civilizational genealogy of philosophical purity, thus becoming unwitting partners of missionary discourse, at least to some extent. But in the context of the official enquiry, both missionary horror and high-caste disdain came up against

British colonial concern not to agitate the natives. Although it refused to prohibit the festival outright, the government expressed its strong hope that the festival would gradually die out on its own.

The inquiries of the 1890s followed the same general pattern as earlier investigations, though the range of responses revealed greater differences of opinion. At the same time certain anthropological assumptions about ritual practice at the village level, as well as the provenance of Hinduism as a religion, seemed to have taken deeper root in official circles. As before, some officials echoed missionary opinion by noting their sense of scandal at the continued allowance of such a barbaric spectacle. And those opinions that justified intervention took the view that the festival had no religious sanction whatsoever. Despite these opinions, most officials took the government's point of view that the law would not support intervention, which would be counterproductive at the very least. In 1854, before the Great Rebellion, the government had encouraged local magistrates to take an active role in discouraging the holding of the festival:

> The best method of discouraging this objectionable practice must be left to the discretion of the different Magistrates, but the right Honorable . . . Governor in Council feels confident that if it be properly explained that the object of Government is not to interfere with any religious observance of its subjects but to abolish a cruel and revolting practice, the efforts of the Magistracy will be willingly seconded by the influence of the great mass of the community, and, more particularly, of the wealthy and intelligent classes who do not seem, even now, to countenance or support the Swinging ceremony.[22]

Even years after the Great Rebellion of 1857, the government took a much more narrow view of interference. It sought anthropological justification for prohibition and persevered in making a sharp distinction between religious freedom and ritual excess but repeatedly stopped well short of definitive action.

Some of those consulted by the government in 1893 did in fact admit that there might be some religious basis to hookswinging. R. Fisher, a private citizen in Madurai, wrote that "the festival or practice is a religious one, and closely connected with religious ideas . . . to bring rain, and appease the goddess from bringing smallpox."[23] But British officials mention this explanation with surprising infrequency, even though a number of other files in the Judicial Department suggest that local villagers had expressed genuine anxiety about the consequences of not performing the festival properly. For example, in 1858 the temple headmen of Abisekapuram had signed a written promise that they would discontinue the hookswinging festival.[24] However, in the intervening years they had noticed that the festival had been held in other places and reported that "the goddess was angry, their cattle constantly got sick and died, they had no proper rains or crops for years and that they had their taxes to pay."[25] Indeed, there seems to have been a marked correlation between the performance of the festival and the outbreak of drought. Nevertheless, such concerns found little sympathy and almost no notice in the official inquiry, except in so far as there was a tacit acknowledgment that outright prohibition might engender serious opposition.

Perhaps the most theologically speculative suggestion came from the collector of Nellore: "Fear of the unknown and timidity are almost universal conditions of thought among ordinary Dravidian natives, and consequently their first impulse to meet any difficulty is to offer a sacrifice. This is the basis of the whole of their natural religion."[26] This view seems to summarize a general nineteenth-century European view of primitive religion.[27] Some other officials tried a bit harder to understand the ritual basis and meaning of hookswinging. One reported a mythological basis, citing a story about Viswamitra and Vasishta in which hookswinging took the place of human sacrifice. Another official recognized that forms of penance were regularly used in religious vows. As evidence for this view, P. Sivaramma Ayyar, a Smartha Brahman and the deputy collector of Tinnevelly, opined that

> the practice of hookswinging, no doubt, originally had its origin in that branch of the Hindu yoga philosophy named hatha yogum which was resorted to by certain Hindus with a view to acquire control over the mind by practising certain physical positions and observances causing bodily pain. . . . But like so many Hindu customs, what was once a practice of bodily torture performed in private for a certain purpose has degenerated into a public exhibition of a cruel and barbarous description.[28]

Having thus provided a textual gloss for the very acts of penance that elsewhere were described so disparagingly, he then dismisses the enactment of what had once been a genuine religious impulse as a degraded event now subverted by publicity stunts and profiteering.

Even if the victims of hookswinging were on occasion seen to have been motivated by the purest of religious motives, for the most part the rite was seen as barbarous and the reasons for its enactment predicated in tyranny and profit. Whatever disparate voices were collected in the investigation, it is clear that the official inquiry could not accord religious legitimacy to the ritual act. As stated by the collector of Chingleput:

> It is, in my opinion, unnecessary at the end of the nineteenth century and, having regard to the level to which civilization in India has attained, to consider the motives by which the performers themselves are actuated when taking part in hook swinging, walking though fire, and other barbarities. From their own moral standpoint, their motives may be good or they may be bad; they may indulge in self-torture in satisfaction of pious vows fervently made in all sincerity and for the most disinterested reasons; or they may indulge in it from the lowest motives of personal aggrandizement, whether for the alms they might receive or for the personal distinction and local *eclat* that it may bring them; but the question is whether public opinion in this country is not opposed to the *external acts* of the performers, as being in fact repugnant to the dictates of humanity and demoralizing to themselves and to all who may witness their performances. I am of opinion that the voice of India most entitled to be listened to with respect, that is to say, not only the voice of the advanced school that has received some of the advantages of western education and has been permeated with non-Oriental ideas, but also the voice of those whose views of life and propriety of conduct have been mainly derived from Asiatic philosophy, would gladly proclaim that the time had arrived for Government in the interests of its people to effectively put down all degrading exhibitions of self-torture.[29]

This statement expressed the conviction that civilization in the nineteenth century had reached such an elevated point that the moral relativism of an earlier and indiscriminate kind could no longer be tolerated. Though he dismissed the motives of those involved with ceremonies such as hookswinging, the collector also appealed to enlightened Indian opinion. These are the voices to which the collector would listen; all others would be suppressed. While on the one hand it is easy to place this belief in the ascendency of Enlightenment values in the self-confidence of late Victorian England, it is clear that neither these views nor this kind of predicament have vanished a century later—an issue to which we will return in the final section of this chapter.

For the most part, the Indian voices sought and heard by the British agreed totally with them in their condemnation of ritual practices such as hookswinging, if for somewhat different reasons. The Indian voices were mostly those of Brahmans and upper-caste Hindus who had, with the British, redefined a proper and autonomous domain of religion while actively participating in governmental actions that permitted this autonomy. P. C. Ananthacharlu, a prominent citizen of Bellary, directly subscribed to official opinion when he wrote to the collector to say that "as observed in para 8 of the letter of the Secretary to the Government of India, Home Department, the practice has no religious sanction or obligation among Hindus, and has almost died out in this Presidency." A. Sabapathy Moodeliar, a leading merchant in Bellary, wrote to the collector, Robert Sewell, that

> the individuals who promote such practices do generally belong to the backward classes and to the less-educated portion of the community. The advanced and more intelligent classes have no sympathy with such movements. . . . The intentions of Government in really religious matters are well understood,—and any active steps which Government may take in such matters will be rightly appreciated by the community generally.

The government is here also seen as expressing the wishes and even representing the sympathies of the upper classes. And P. Rajaratna Mudaliar, deputy collector and magistrate of South Arcot, wrote that "education has made rapid strides and even the common people have come to look upon anything that is not countenanced by Government as something which they should not take a pleasure in doing." Informed opinion reads rather like institutionalized sycophancy, since the government is now accorded the legitimacy and moral example of a proper Hindu state. The acting subcollector of South Arcot, Mr. Harding, was certainly correct when he wrote that "the leaders of Hindu society being the educated men would welcome the repressions of these survivals of pre-Arian savagery." After all, these leaders had provided the textual bases and moral support for these very repressions.[30]

Some officials were aware of the partial nature of the inquiry. The district magistrate of Tanjore conceded that

> it is a fact that the men whom we consult, and whom alone we can con-
> sult in a formal manner, have as little sympathy with the practice as we
> have ourselves, and the frequent remark that the practice has no religious
> sanction is only true in so far as the Hindu religion is concerned . . . the
> people who attach importance to it, and the men who allow themselves to
> be swung, are not Hindus save in name, and as their sole idea of religion is
> propitiation it is idle to suppose that in absolutely prohibiting the practice
> we would be doing no violence to religion or, if the term be considered
> more applicable, superstitious feelings.

But this insightful analysis—with its sense of Hinduism as a clearly identifiable set of religious practices and precepts—was only a preface for his condemnation of the temple priests who exploited primitive su-perstitions for their own gain. The district magistrate of Kurnool noted that "although such an observance is not enjoined in the Hindu shastras, yet its resuscitation appears to me to be a species of religious revival, and intended to attract large crowds and create religious enthusiasm. The victims may be drawn from the ignorant and degraded but they are not the originators of the movement." Here, the generous attribution of religious meaning to the festival is again followed by an attack on the priests who took advantage of these popular religious sensibilities.

The judgments about popular religious practices were thus made both by the British and upper-caste Hindus who shared a distaste for far more than the barbarous examples of self-torture under discussion here.[31] These judgments often emerged from extensive descriptions and analyses of Indian religion, part of a developing anthropology of Indian tradition that one reads in the files of the judicial and other depart-ments. E. Turner, the district magistrate of Madura, claimed that

> as far as I have been able to ascertain, the practice [of hookswinging]
> has no special religious significance. It is, however, part of the Tamasha
> [spectacle or hubbub] at certain festivals held at certain localities at cer-

tain seasons. At these festivals it is customary for the lower classes and especially the Kallers to worship the Goddess Mariyammal. The great idea is to put the Goddess into a good humour and get her to interfere in cases of outbreaks of smallpox, scarcity of rain, etc. The Goddess, it is thought, likes to have as much tamasha as possible during these festivals and as hookswinging brings together a large crowd of worshippers the Goddess is pleased with the practice and is likely to be angry if the custom is discontinued. . . . The practice has nothing to do with the Hindu religion. The higher castes look at it with abhorrence as a barbarous custom. But the masses in this district are Hindus only in name. What may be called Devil worship pure and simple is the real religion of the crowd.[32]

Hinduism itself is being defined as a religious system that should properly be consistent with Brahmanic beliefs and practices. While these remarks have clearly not yet been scientized by the purer descriptive efforts of later ethnographers, they represent the mixture of anthropological and official knowledge that oriented perceptions and judgments in the myriad of governmental interactions with Indian society.

Most of the speculations about the actual ritual basis and justification of the hookswinging festival were made within the context of predicting how much trouble would be provoked if the practice were suppressed. Aside from the pragmatics of suppressing the practice, the central justification for it—and about this official British and Indian elites were in agreement—was the assertion that the priests were manipulating the whole affair. The bias against priests was powerful and consistent, aligning British and Brahman sentiment even as it provided an ironic basis for the antipriest arguments that the anti-Brahman movement appropriated only twenty years later (and which were used then against Brahmans as representative of the priestly class). Virtually every negative statement about hookswinging contains a criticism of priests. P. Rajaratna Mudaliar of South Arcot wrote that "the only classes of people who attach any importance to this mode of worship are those that are called Poojaries in the Chingleput and South Arcot District. These generally are fond of reviving the practice because of the income they derive therefrom there being a larger gathering on such occasions than when the worship is carried on in an ordinary manner." E. Turner added, "On ordinary occasions hookswinging merely adds to the gains for the priests and the managers of the festival." P. C. Ananthacharlu of Bellary attributed the recurrence of the festival solely to the large annual income derived by the managers of Durga temples. And J. Sturrock, the deputy magistrate of Tanjore, wrote that "the priests and managers of Hindu temples . . . encourage the practice for the sake of gain."[33] All these statements, as well as some of the statements quoted earlier, are clear in ascribing the motive of profit to the priests. The attribution of the profit motive worked to discredit the priests but also to disparage local religion. Superstition, unlike genuine (or scripturally mandated) belief, was both the product of, and the occasion for, manipulation. The priests were seen first and foremost as manipulators and were accorded absolutely no legitimacy. When limited attempts were made to hold certain people responsible in the event of injury, it was the priests and village headmen who were to be monitored and not the unwitting victims who were swung high on hooks. Victims were victimized not only by custom and tradition but by the men in the middle who simply made money off of the naïve religious sensibilities of the masses. And the linking of custom to the self-interest of priests and others who made money out of custom worked both to desanctify custom and to justify paternalistic intervention and investigation on behalf of the masses.

For the most part, British officials and Indian notables agreed that, however desirable the suppression of hookswinging might be, it would be unwise to legislate its abolition, relying instead on moral persuasion and official disapproval. Nevertheless, the Madras Missionary Conference strongly advocated outright abolition. In a memorial dated November 13, 1893, it recorded that "this practice is barbarous and revolting; and that its public exhibition must inevitably tend to degrade and brutalize the community among which it takes place."[34] The missionaries particularly cited the festivals conducted in Sholavandan and written up in great detail in Madurai and Madras newspapers. Although the government refused to abolish hookswinging and essentially concluded that section 144 of the Indian Penal Code could not be applied to do so, individual magistrates did occasionally use their power to prevent hookswinging from taking place, perhaps as a response to the pressure mounted by the missionary conference. In June 1894, L. C. Miller, the acting district magistrate of Madurai, decided on his own authority to prohibit the annual hookswinging in Sholavandan.[35]

The Meanings of Hookswinging

Miller's intervention in Sholavandan occasioned a great deal of protest from local residents. A petition with close to one thousand signatures was presented to the government, in which it was argued that the villagers should have been allowed to conduct their normal ritual festivities.[36] Interestingly, the signatories included representatives of a great many castes including Brahmans (Aiyars), upper-caste non-Brahmans (Mudaliars and Pillais), as well as Kallars, Maravars, Valaiyars, Paraiyars, and Pallars. The petition was well written and argued, and it appealed clearly and cogently to the concerns and assumptions of governmental officials. For example, the hookswinging festival was glossed as a proper ritual to make it look as if it had a Sanskritic genealogy and high religious justification. The petitioners went on to argue that no physical harm had come to any of the men who had been swung, "even though in the natural course of events it is impossible that the man should not be grievously hurt." Instead of asserting that the concerns about the physical welfare of the swinger were misplaced, the petitioners used the lack of injury to the participants as a way of supporting the religious merits of the penance. "Your humble Memorialists attribute this most remarkable state of things in the selected man coming down from the pole in full consciousness and without any serious injury whatever, to the act of the Almighty, in whom full belief is placed not only by the selected man, but by the whole mass of worshippers who attend the festival." The petitioners further reversed the arguments of the missionaries that the exhibition served only to "degrade and brutalize" the community by suggesting that "this act is calculated to inculcate in the minds of the ignorant masses in a practical manner that firm faith in God and God alone, and full belief in his Divine Revelations, cannot but bring home to the believer the greatest amount of happiness and prosperity." The petitioners were clearly writing with full knowledge of the dominant missionary and colonial discourse, though they also invoked the more standard argument—with all of its internal contradictions—that the swinging was performed to promote the prosperity of the community at large, noting that, since they had begun to celebrate this festival in 1890, "the seasons were more favourable, the crops more abundant, the mortality less appalling, and the dire diseases less virulent."

The petition then objected to the brutal suppression of the hook-swinging festival. In telling this story, the petition made a number of interesting claims. Some claims directly echoed fragments of official British opinion. For example, the petitioners noted that the government permitted far more dangerous events, such as "balloon ascents, para-chute descents, circus feats, horse racing, etc." Other claims seemed to subvert this very point, by including fire walking and "the compulsory shaving of a young Hindu widow's head under which other circum-stances would amount to grievous hurt, being a permanent disfiguration of the face according to the I.G. code."

Perhaps the most interesting claims relate to our earlier discussion of the agency of the swinger. The petition stated that

> the said Malayandi who had been worshipping in the temple having been inspired by the Goddess Mariyamman to have the hookswinging festival, and being in a state of "Aveesam" (in a state of unconsciousness of his real self got therefrom), besmearing himself with ashes and carrying a copper plate in his hands containing bits of lighted camphor, and went round the temple to make the holy Pradakshanam, saying that Goddess has come to him and inspired him to have the hookswinging festival performed.

The petition then specified that Malayandi was in an "unconscious and uncontrollable state of mind, for which he was not responsible." While he was in this vulnerable state the police arrived and carted him off to jail. What the petition had thus established was the religious character of the hookswinging; the swinger was said to be in a state resembling posses-sion, which both absolves him from responsibility and sacralizes his per-son. Indeed, the petition implied that when a worshipper is possessed, his agency becomes that of the deity itself, clearly invoking a different discourse of victimage, agency, and responsibility than would normally be considered relevant in colonial debates. The discourse of the petition appeals both to the transvalued nature of religious action during hook-swinging and the potential culpability of the swinger to police action. In more general terms, the petition intended to invoke a sense of legitimate religious practice, and, in the colonial context, it correctly represented hookswinging as a legitimate extension of Sanskritic religion through the use of terms such as "ootchavam," "pradakshanam," and "aveesam."

The logic of the petition was thus multiple because it employed arguments that both appealed to and no doubt mystified the British, made
legitimating claims that involved a large range of religious understandings and forms, and demonstrated the strategic character of subaltern
agency in the colonial situation. Far from being paralyzed by their lack
of choice under the weight of custom, these subaltern petitioners could
not only speak but write. In the face of colonial efforts to anthropolo-
gize the meanings of custom, the petitioners deployed tactical appeals
to colonial reason while making strong, polyvocal claims for their own.

The government did not intervene on behalf of the petitioners,
though in the end, for reasons that had nothing to do with the arguments in this particular petition, governmental officials did decide that
section 144 provided a rather flimsy basis for the outright prohibition
of hookswinging. So although in an indirect sense they might be seen
to have won their argument, though for only the very short term, the
petitioners began to lose control over the meaning of the event in their
very engagement with the official apparatuses of governmental regulation. What might be called the petition wars of the nineteenth century
ranged widely in subject matter, concerning such matters as land and
irrigation rights, customary law, local taxes, and management rights in
temples, to mention only a few. But all these controversies worked to
secure colonial discursive hegemony over the taxonomies, legitimacies,
and meanings of local social action.[37] Although they did not actually use
all the correct forms and idioms and clearly resisted others, the petitioners for the most part attempted to appeal to the legitimating conceits of
official colonial discourse.

It is difficult to recognize some of the shifts that took place because we
assume that colonial categories had always been in place. For example,
the categories of, and more particularly the rigid separation between,
low popular and high classical religion were produced in colonial contexts such as the one described above. Indeed, the petition does not represent a more accurate or authentic understanding of popular religious
practice than the colonial version because the petition was necessarily
steeped in colonial discourse, but it can still be read as a measure of subaltern agency. After all, the petition was written specifically to persuade
colonial officials to allow the hookswinging to continue. But the uncritical belief that colonial sources can shed light on precolonial meanings

when read through conventional interpretive lenses is as problematic as the faith in anthropological intuition that confers the ring of truth to standard approaches.[38] Colonial sources constituted a basic register both for official knowledge and, as I will go on to demonstrate, the conventional wisdom of early professional anthropology as well.

Nevertheless, the petition reveals that certain elements of the ethnographic location of hookswinging in southern Indian society raise questions about colonial views and provide the basis for critical and oppositional readings of colonial sources. First, the issue of agency that was so fundamental to colonial discourse turned out to be conceptualized in terms that related to the ritual logic of divine possession and the instrumental effects of ritual action, in part because of the specific salience of possession and trance to any event such as hookswinging and in part because of the need to argue against the criminal culpability of either the swingers or their impresarios, as the priests and temple managers were regarded. The colonial obsession with agency was no doubt seen as peculiar, but the petition clearly reveals that it was also significantly connected to official attempts to find fault, round up the culprits, and assess criminality (the significance of which we will come to later) as well as barbarism. Second, the clear separation between Brahmanic and non-Brahmanic domains of religious life is challenged by the fact that the petition was signed by many upper-caste members of the village and that it was distinctly possible (even if not fully plausible) to construct a Brahmanic gloss on and justification for hookswinging. Nevertheless, the clear assumption in the governmental files was that Brahmans and other members of the upper castes would have had nothing to do with such barbaric rites. The upper-caste consultants and informants for the British were, at least officially, complicit in the reading of hookswinging as non-Hindu and barbaric, even though many of these same consultants probably had multiple ritual connections to "popular" ritual practices. Indeed, as I have demonstrated elsewhere, Brahmans who still lived in rural areas in the Tamil country in the late nineteenth and early twentieth centuries often had village deities considered to be "low," such as Aiyanar and Mariyamman, for their tutelary deities.[39] Although many Brahmans would have kept some distance between their own ritual practices and popular events such as hookswinging, it was also the case that most Brahmans worshipped in temples in which hookswinging was performed and in which animal sacrifices and other "low" ritual forms were regularly practiced.

The heavy recruitment of Brahmans into colonial administration and the not unrelated alienation of many Brahmans from their local rural roots had facilitated a high level of tolerance for and participation in "non-Brahmanic" religious activities and created the basis for increasing collaboration between certain Brahmanic precepts and Victorian morals during the nineteenth century. Upper-caste notions of respectability and religious scruples became increasingly Anglicized, as Brahmans and other high castes were clearly incited by circumstance and conventions of colonial acceptability to define more strictly and exclusively the provenance of "Sanskritic" and "Brahmanic" domains. Less ironically than in the instance in which Brahmans helped fuel the criticism of priests, it was this very privilege that helped create the basis for the generalized antipathy against Brahmans that fed into the anti-Brahman movements of the twentieth century.

The meanings of hookswinging were thus transformed in rather complex ways during the nineteenth century. The debate over hookswinging played an important role in constituting certain notions of agency and free will as fundamental to the evaluation of local ritual practices and in redefining the relations between Brahmans and peasants and between Sanskritic and popular religion. And it was precisely because upper- and lower-caste Hindus were encouraged to participate in these debates that both were drafted into a colonial discourse that touched far more than the attitudes of a number of British administrators. In the past, these acts of public devotion had on occasion been supported by kings through tax-free *inam* land grants; increasingly in the nineteenth century, the swingers were paid either by the festival organizers or were encouraged to believe that private vows would most efficaciously be fulfilled by participating in these more public events. Whereas kings had once sanctioned and supported these events, colonial rulers now disapproved of them. Whereas agency had once been multiply constructed around notions of kingly sovereignty, collective interdependence, social forms of (often oppressive) power, and complex technologies—and social relations—of trance and possession, agency was now the index of individual criminal culpability. And whereas religious customs had been shaped by historical forces in which local power had been so closely associated with institutions of local ritual, custom now became the object of new forms of knowledge, control, and classification. Even if the meanings of such intimate experiences such as fear, pain, and belief may never be fully understood, we can be sure that they, and certainly the contexts in which they took place, could not have been totally exempt from the transformations we have surveyed here.

In the end, the governmental reversal of L. C. Miller's action to suppress hookswinging was temporary. Finally, in August 1894, a hookswinging performance in the village of "Bheemanaickenpolien" on the outskirts of Trichinopoly led, it seemed, to a fatality. It was alleged that a fever that killed one of the swingers was the result of the suppuration of his back wounds. A report circulated in late September of the same year proclaimed that sufficient evidence had been garnered to prove that hookswinging could in fact be abolished on the basis of section 144, given the lethal consequences demonstrated in the above-mentioned episode. The hookswinging debate was over.[40]

Custom and Coercion

When it became clear that the hookswinging victims were victimized less by corrupt managers and greedy priests than by their own belief, British officials believed in turn that tyranny resided as much in the dictates of custom as in those who manipulated it for their own ends. As we have seen, this is not to say that the British ever conceded very much to the world of custom—indeed, they continued to seek evidence of manipulation and oppression and sought to defend the gullibility of all who had been designated victim—but custom was the unsettling ground on which the alterity of the colonized resided. Custom also worked to resolve the issue of agency oppositionally by creating a world in which agency and individuals did not exist, thus simultaneously disparaging the traditional world as uncivilized and heralding European modernity as the only haven within which agency was possible and individuals could achieve proper autonomy. Agency can thus be seen as a profoundly problematic category precisely because it disavows the possibility of consent—or anything resembling purposive individual action—outside of particular cultural worlds while using this condemnation as the pretext for dismissal, surveillance, and control. Even when consent was monitored and debated, it was never really thought that sufficient evidence could exist to document it in the contexts in question: sati, hookswinging, firewalking, and so forth. But the focus on consent and agency worked to mask the coercion of colonial power itself, its capacity to define what was acceptable and what was not, what was civilized and what was not, and why it was that the extraordinary burden of knowledge and responsibility was arrogated by the colonizer. Colonial forms of knowledge continuously disavowed their own interests while compelling the knowledge of custom as if it were a neutral mechanism to protect the colonized. Within a world dictated by custom, agency was held out to be a tantalizing promise of freedom, but it was held out by a colonial state that used the term to adjudicate the difference between criminality and barbarism, certainly not to open up any genuine opportunities for freedom of choice.

Even as custom became the site on which the British displaced their own regulative power, custom also became something that was changed and transformed most when it was held to be both totalizing and invariant. And in the case of the ritual forms and socioreligious categories that surrounded the hookswinging controversies, we can detect significant change that was a direct result of colonial intervention. What the eminent contemporary anthropologist M. N. Srinivas has characterized as "sanskritization," a natural social process in India that involved the emulation of Brahmans and Brahmanic social customs by upwardly mobile groups, was in fact officially legislated over and over again in the nineteenth and twentieth centuries.[41] This legislation was the result of British officials using Brahmans as informants and regarding Brahmans as the carriers of high culture. Not only were practices such as hookswinging not voluntarily dropped; they were actually constituted as examples of low ritual practice that should be prohibited if possible and at the very least officially discouraged. In certain temples in southern India, the customary practice of widow remarriage within certain castes was discontinued after the government took over the management of temples and outlawed the use of these temples for rituals not deemed to have support from the *shastras*.[42] In countless other examples, governmental officials—British and Indian alike—used government agencies that were meant simply to manage and protect instead to legislate newly defined codes of conduct that were part of the colonial construction of appropriate Hindu practice. The great debates over the agency of victims in such arenas as hookswinging served not only to miss but to obscure a far more fundamental result of colonial intervention in India—the continual reinvention of the subjectivity of the colonized by and through the technologies of colonial rule.

Regulation and knowledge always went together in the history of British colonialism in India. Forms of knowledge were produced by regulative contexts and concerns even as the parameters of intervention and regulation were constituted by the kinds of knowledge that colonialism produced. Regulation and knowledge thus collaborated in the fixing of tradition, by which I mean both the stabilizing and the repairing of a canonic sense of what had always been done. The effort to fix tradition in the context of hookswinging was certainly not a new activity. From the years during which it first began to collect information about India, the colonial government was concerned to determine how custom dictated the lives of ordinary Indians in regard to the rights to land, labor, and agricultural resources; practices related to marriage, kinship, and caste; and the whole array of social facts that became part of the codification of customary and criminal law. Even though custom could vary radically from place to place, even occasionally from time to time, the essence of custom as it was constructed was that it was fixed, that it reproduced itself through its own inertia. Although it seemed to refer to a single set of social practices and principles, custom steadily became a trope for a society that was outside of history and devoid of individuals.

The specification of Indian custom was never a neutral activity, whether it was related to the allocation of land rights or the management of a temple or charity. Under the conceit of simply following custom, the British both changed it and reified it. With a little help from British rule, custom could now be reproduced through the force of law, with consequences that were as extensive as they were deep. Generally, if custom proved troublesome in the context of British rule, it was only because the British thought they had not gotten it quite right or because discrete customary practices competed against one another in new colonial contexts such as that created by the commercialized land market. But when custom appeared to challenge British rule or, less dramatically, when custom violated the general principles of civilized morality, the British then believed they had to modify the usual practice. The decisions about the authenticity of various customs were administrative judgments that had the appearance of anthropological debates.

Missionaries, whose proselytizing success was confined almost entirely to the lower castes, collaborated in the reformist impulse by providing detailed accounts of local popular customs in terms consistent with their own desire to combat the residual hold of culture over the epistemic terrain of their conversion efforts. The agnostic position of many of those who held positions of governmental authority ironically served to legitimate certain forms of intervention, since the government was adamant in representing itself as committed to a policy of noninterference. Traditions could be legitimately reformed if they were demonstrated to be inauthentic. The measures for authenticity were usually based on a set of Brahmanically defined norms, which were articulated within the context of British administrative judgments that tended to exacerbate the opposition and fixity of what subsequent generations of anthropologists have labeled as great and little traditions. British rule came upon the death of Indian kings, and the ascendency of Brahmans was predicated both on the displacement of kingly authority by the British and on the strategic alliances forged between colonizing and colonized elites.

Governmental debates about activities such as hookswinging thus sought to identify the proper place of tradition in popular social and religious life at the same time that these debates reconstituted the terms by which tradition was identified and evaluated. It was not so much that tradition was invented as that a new definition of tradition was installed. This new sense of tradition created a hierarchialized relation between folk and classical tradition and accorded primacy to the classical tradition in certain contexts of discomfort or dispute.

Although they made arbitrary decisions about what was properly traditional or customary and what was not, the British in India ironically shared with Eric Hobsbawm a comfortable sense of the need to differentiate between authenticity and inauthenticity, between genuine and invented tradition.[43] They even shared a sense of the moral implications of debating the relative plausibility of different specific customs or traditions. The nineteenth-century colonial writers whose arguments have been analyzed here debunked the priests who defined hookswinging as proper tradition in much the same way that Hobsbawm debunks states and elites. The arguments are made differently: most colonial writers used measures of universal moral sensibility as well as Brahmanic notions of how to delineate proper Hindu traditions, but they shared with Hobsbawm an outrage against the pursuit of private interests under the banner of ritual and ceremony.

My aim in making this point here is to suggest, against much of the spirit of the "invention of tradition" literature, that the effort to historicize tradition and custom is not necessarily the same as finding particular histories for traditions that we then presume to authenticate or deauthenticate, for that was precisely the kind of move that colonialism enabled. When it debated Indian tradition, colonial discourse installed certain versions of custom over others, sustained certain forms of discourse that became increasingly hegemonic (as for example in the petition wars), and displaced Indian subjectivity and agency in relation to everything but its own enlightened presence. Colonial discourse also concealed its construction of categories—such as those concerning low and high religion, or Brahmans and non-Brahmans—that in the end survived much longer and with much more important consequences for Indian social life than, as one example, the specific issue of whether or not hookswinging should be suppressed. In the colonial situation, moral discourse and reformist ideology thus concealed the forms (and effects) of the hegemonic power that the colonial state itself exercised.

The British displaced their own politics into such domains as custom and tradition, simultaneously endowing them with new meanings and applications and absolving themselves from the recognition that power was being deployed by them rather than by the fixity of the hold of the past, seen as custom or tradition rather than history. But increasingly, the norms of custom were established by official anthropologists who claimed scientificity and neutrality for their discipline even as they worked directly for the state apparatus of colonial rule. By the late nineteenth century, anthropology became the discourse in which the policing of tradition was transformed into the knowledge of tradition.

Anthropology and the Police

Anthropology in southern India emerged directly out of official projects that collected and interpreted information about Indian social life. Most of these official projects—like those concerning hookswinging, sati, or even subjects such as torture—were directed toward the possibility of reform, and it is illuminating to look back and discover that the footnotes for anthropological writing at the turn of the century refer to the same official reports we have just been reading, reports about practices that many in government wished to suppress.

Ethnography in Madras began formally with concerns about criminality.[44] In 1893 Frederick S. Mullaly, a senior official in the Madras police, was appointed the first honorary superintendent of ethnography for the Madras Presidency.[45] Mullaly's principal qualification for the job was his publication in the previous year of a book entitled *Notes on Criminal Classes of the Madras Presidency.*[46] He wrote his book at the suggestion of the inspector general of police in the hope that it "may prove of some value to Police Officers who are continually brought into contact with the Predatory classes."[47] The construction of entire castes by the British in colonial India as "criminal castes" was part of a larger discourse in which caste determined the occupational and social character of all its constituent members, but what is noteworthy here is that the concern with criminality continued, directly as well as indirectly, to be central to the development of anthropology in Madras for many years.

In 1901 the government of India resolved to support a scheme to carry out an ethnographical survey of India. At that time H. H. Risley was appointed director of ethnography for India, and Edgar Thurston, superintendent of the Madras Museum between 1885 and 1908, was appointed as the superintendent of ethnography for the Madras Presidency.[48] Risley himself, who had previously been the census commissioner for India, saw anthropology as having two central aims: first, to construct a catalogue of customs and, second, to make a meticulous record of physical characteristics. He amply shared Thurston's enthusiasm for anthropometry. Risley's advocacy of anthropometry, along with his theories about the relation of race and caste, were clearly fundamental to the definition of the ethnographic project in turn-of-the-century colonial India. If custom was a preoccupying concern in early Indian anthropology that directed attention toward the social body, anthropometry sought to locate the scientific study of man in the biological body. In the Indian context this was particularly fruitful both because the caste system had an endogamous character and because notions of individuality were thought to be undeveloped: bodies within a certain group all shared, and produced, a fundamental unity. Thurston also noted the importance of anthropometry for criminal identification, which is why he was frequently called upon to deliver anthropological lectures to the Madras Police.[49] In the last years of the decade, anthropometry began to yield other means of criminal identification, such as fingerprinting, which was initially developed in Bengal.[50] Fingerprinting quickly established itself as the universal system of criminal identification. In the technologies of policing, as in many other areas, the empire served as an important laboratory for the metropole.

The replacement of anthropometry by fingerprinting did not lessen Thurston's commitment to collecting the physical measurements of Indian subjects. During the first decade of the twentieth century, Thurston worked systematically to structure his ethnographic survey along the lines set down by Risley, collecting a myriad of ethnographic details and extensive archives of measurements, all arranged according to the different castes and tribes in the presidency. As suggested throughout this article, Indian subjects were not only organized by but also contained in their castes or tribes, which determined the cultural, economic, social, and moral characteristics of their constituent members. Individuals only existed as empirical objects and exemplary subjects. The ethnographic survey ended in Madras when Thurston completed his seven-volume work, *The Castes and Tribes of Southern India*, which had entries on more than three hundred caste groups listed in alphabetical order.[51]

I comment here instead on a long ethnographic work that Thurston published in 1906 while he was in the middle of his labors for the survey. This work, entitled *Ethnographic Notes in Southern India*, consisted of a series of essays, some previously published in the *Government Museum Bulletin*, on a variety of subjects that Thurston thought held intrinsic interest. This work is an example of how ethnographic subjects were constituted when caste was not the organizing category for anthropological inquiry. The book begins with two long essays, the first on marriage customs, the second on death ceremonies, that look like compilations of material that had been collected on a caste-by-caste basis. Caste seems slightly less important in the third essay, on "omens, evil eye, charms, animal superstitions, sorcery, etc.," since the ethnographic material is presented as instances of a general set of beliefs and practices. But in the subsequent chapters the organizing principle is no longer the conventional frame of caste, and the subjects no longer seem to be standard anthropological fare.[52]

The essays can be seen as the critical link in the genealogy between official anthropology and the kinds of investigative enquiries and reports that this essay analyzed earlier. The chapters are, in large part, encyclopedic collections of official material generated by the colonial interest in suppressing practices such as hookswinging, slavery, and torture. In his introduction to his volumes on the castes and tribes, Thurston wrote that he had followed the scheme recommended for completing the ethnographic survey, in which he was instructed to "supplement the information obtained from representative men and by their own enquiries by 'researches into the considerable mass of information which lies buried in official reports, in the journals of learned Societies, and in various books.' Of this injunction full advantage has been taken, as will be evident from the abundant crop of references in foot-notes."[53] But it is in the *Ethnographic Notes* that we can see the extraordinary extent of the connection between official colonial reports and official colonial ethnography.

The essay on hookswinging, like most of the other essays in the volume, is in fact little more than a compilation of the kinds of writings on the custom examined above. The hookswinging essay begins by quoting the Government Report of 1854 and notes that in 1852 two men had been killed during the celebration of the festival in Salem district because the pole from which they were suspended had snapped. Thurston does not always moderate his language, for he refers to the ritual as a "barbarous ceremony" and quotes indiscriminately from commentators as various (and as contemptuous of Indian customs) as Abbé Dubois and Pierre Sonnerat.[54] Aside from the general narrative style and the lack of any specific argument about suppression, there is little to distinguish this ethnographic chapter from the accounts that governmental officials themselves produced. What is different, of course, is that, although there is no moral or legal argument about the suppression of hookswinging, virtually all of the material was generated, as we saw, out of the context of governmental debate. The absence of argument in Thurston's account has the effect of representing the account as scientific (as do all of Thurston's credentials, and the entire framework of the book), despite the fact that it can be seen that this representation works to conceal the nature of the genealogical connection between the work and its sources. In ethnography, the once-compelling stakes of official debate seem to disappear altogether.

Thurston didn't attempt to conceal his sources; in fact, he is far better than many colonial authors in providing footnotes and references. Furthermore, he is in total agreement with Risley that one of the tasks of the ethnographer is to digest the massive accumulation of material in governmental reports and then to present it in clear and systematic form. Thurston was himself a government servant and saw no contradiction between science and government in the task of accumulating anthropological knowledge about India. The relation of knowledge and rule is not simply a colonial fact but one that was actively celebrated in such colonial projects as the ethnographic survey. However, it is easy in retrospect to lose sight of the genealogies of the relations between knowledge and rule, and those who read Thurston's treatise on hookswinging may never know the historical context in which his footnotes were produced. And for contemporary students of Indian society who still consult Thurston for information on practices such as hookswinging, as I did when I began this research, there is little to signal the colonial character of what is still considered to be canonic anthropological knowledge.

Indian anthropology was in fact born directly out of the colonial project of ruling India. On the basis of the writings of Mullaly and Thurston, the latter author undoubtedly the most important official ethnographer in Madras during colonial times, we can see that the key texts of early anthropology were not simply being produced in the context of colonial projects but were the culmination of what had been a long series of colonial projects to rule and reform India. Far from conveying cultural relativism and epistemic neutrality, in other words, anthropology began its career in India as colonial judgment. The ethnographic survey itself was born directly out of the census, an important early apparatus of colonial rule. There, as well as in the above example, we can see how anthropology, in its genealogical connections to colonial governance and policing and also in its development as a separate and scientific discipline, conferred new forms of legitimacy to the administrative texts that we examined above and played a significant role in the history of colonization.

Barbarism and Civilization

In demonstrating that "caste," "religion," or other similar categories were refigured by colonial rule, my project here and elsewhere has been to uncover and underscore British investment in the representation of those aspects of Indian tradition that in postcolonial times have been seen as the principal impediments to genuine progress, if not full-scale modernity.[55]

Whether or not hookswinging constituted grievous harm of a sort that can be usefully compared to sati, we can hear the echoes of the debate about sati in the contestations and interpretations presented above. In some ways, hookswinging is "good to think" precisely because it is less unambiguously horrible than sati or, to shift to another colonial scandal, clitoridectomy. We can chart the construction and development of a reformist colonial discourse that seems clearly in the service of missionary and more general Victorian values that only rarely evidenced convincing concern about other similar practices, except when concerns of state or mission intervened. Even as we unravel the discursive web around the rituals and the inscribed meanings of the events referred to in the hookswinging debates, we also must be aware that when we do shift to other contexts, where the stakes concern, for example, women's lives and bodies in far more pernicious respects, we could easily chart similar critical readings. Ashis Nandy and Veena Das have been severely critical of the liberal critique of sati, suggesting that these arguments, which became mobilized against the so-called ritual renaissance of sati in Rajasthan during the late 1980s (even though they hasten to point out that they are very much against these murderous events), were strictly colonial in character.[56] In pointing out colonial genealogies for the moral denunciation of certain practices that seek the legitimation of cultural authenticity, are we condemned to forsake or licensed to evade the issues and the responsibility of moral judgment—to choose, in other words, between the positions of the colonizers and those of the colonized?

Although there is no particular need at the end of the twentieth century to deliver any resounding judgment on the practice of hookswinging, it is worth commenting on some parallels between the late nineteenth-century debates over hookswinging and the more recent debate that continues to attract attention across the globe, in this case, the debate over clitoridectomy in Africa. That debate effectively began when missionaries denounced the practice and attempted to seek official suppression on the one hand and native support, particularly among converts, for renunciation on the other. But, as in many other missionary initiatives, the discursive use of clitoridectomy generated a good deal of local resistance and produced an enhanced cultural and nationalist value for the practice, a development that Jomo Kenyatta acknowledged when he devoted a large portion of his anthropological monograph on Kenya to a description of the cultural salience of the clitoridectomy initiation rite. The right to perform clitoridectomy also became mixed in with the rise of nationalist resistance, in particular with the Mau Mau revolt.[57] Susan Pederson has recently pointed out that European liberals found themselves in the awkward (though in some ways predictable) position of defending clitoridectomy if they were to be seen in support of Kenyan nationalism.[58] Far more recently, activists such as Alice Walker have, doubtless unintentionally, resurrected missionary and colonial discourses in the moral campaign against the horror of clitoridectomy.[59] One has only to think of editorials by Anthony Lewis in the *New York Times* to accept that nineteenth-century arguments about the unacceptability of certain forms of moral relativism in the face of fundamental Enlightenment values, such as that put forward above by the collector of Chingleput, have by no means disappeared and can be mobilized in the service of causes that have far larger constituencies than the particular forms of moral rhetoric employed.

Horror has the uncanny capacity to obliterate the quotidian. It seems to many of us that it is not simply easy but even necessary to become passionately committed to causes such as the abolition of sati and clitoridectomy. Unfortunately, such causes have both problematic historical genealogies and contemporary uses. While they address universal issues of violence and human rights, the very horror of these events also works to obscure other forms of violence, both those closer to "home" and those embedded in colonial and postcolonial relations more generally. Without succumbing to a position of loose moral relativism, it is worthwhile to note that debates do not simply arise because horrible events take place; hundreds of atrocities escape being reported, let alone receiving sustained international attention, each day, from dramatic cases of genocide to the everyday forms of violence against women, children, and other subaltern groups. It would seem necessary at the very least to examine how certain kinds of events become the basis for grand civilizational debates. Sati was no less horrible because it served colonial claims for a civilizing mission in India, but it was used for purposes that had nothing to do with the actual practice.

When critics point out the colonial genealogies of some moral debates, they do so to point out the ways in which cultural issues still carry the weight of history, even if they may then differ radically about the meanings of that genealogical burden.[60] As a historian of colonialism and of anthropology, I have been particularly concerned, both in this chapter and in other work, to suggest a variety of connections between then and now—between the origins of anthropology and its current concepts, between the discursive formations of colonial thought and the way in which discourses about East and West continue to mobilize images of alterity, exoticism, even barbarism. This means neither that there are no major differences between then and now nor that historical critique should abjure the difficult and complex contemporary realities of moral predicaments. When giving this text orally as a paper I have frequently been asked to take a stand on hookswinging, as if somehow I have evaded my moral responsibility by raising an issue that I have then left unresolved. My reply is that this is a colonial question that cannot be answered as if we confronted an abstract universal puzzle. Instead, I believe that we need to ask why such questions are asked at particular times by particular people. I would insist that, from our present historical and intellectual location, it may be more important to engage in reflexive and contemporary disciplinary critique than in forming a moral evaluation of ritual practices in India in the nineteenth century.

If I have suggested connections between colonial debates and current conundrums, it is not just because the language of moral judgment so frequently carries with it the historical baggage of an unsavory past. We must identify the obligations as well as the limits of judgment. Politics, along with the moral judgments that animate political action, change when they move from place to place as well as from period to period. To accept the logic of the politics of location is not to abandon morality altogether but to suggest that even universal judgments have particularistic histories, contexts, and implications. The same is true for the forms of knowledge that we inherit and transact; they are necessarily shaped by the very forces of the past that we seek now to change and to transcend. Hookswinging may no longer be the pressing issue it once was, but its effects live on. They live on in India around the reconstituted categories of popular and elite religion, proper Hinduism, the priesthood, and in forms of civilizational defensiveness and pride, and the hookswinging debates have resonance not only for contemporary debates over sati but also in relation to the recent rise of communalism and fundamentalism more generally. The effects also live on in anthropology (and history), where the collision of cultural relativism and universal values, as well as the uneasy relationship between beliefs in objective knowledge and concerns about historicist critique, continue in many ways to occupy the forefront of disciplinary debate. Hookswinging may no longer seem a scandal, but we still have scandal enough, wherever we choose to look.

Part III

Empire

7

Imperial Sovereignty

There is a secret veil to be drawn over the beginnings of all governments.
They had their origin, as the beginning of all such things have had, in
some matters that had as good be covered by obscurity. Time in the origin
of most governments has thrown this mysterious veil over them. Prudence
and discretion make it necessary to throw something of that veil over a
business in which otherwise the fortune, the genius, the talents and military virtue of this Nation never shone more conspicuously.
    —Edmund Burke, "Speech on the Opening of the Impeachment,"
                        February 16, 1788

In the last decades of the eighteenth century Britain abandoned its
experiment in American colonization and Asian trade in favor of a
different kind of imperial ambition. Along with this ambition came a developing crisis concerning ideas of sovereignty. This chapter is directed
to examining some of the tensions produced by empire in the developing eighteenth-century consensus about sovereignty. Empire might
have been brought to its ultimate test by colonial nationalism in the
twentieth century, but it had already endured a major crisis when the
European nation-state itself was formed two centuries earlier. During
this formation, an uneasy break was made with earlier imperial forms,
which, while they were often used to justify the new, were well known
to have an association with decline and fall, an association that was seen

by some as of particular relevance to Britain's developing relationship with India.

British Sovereignty

As Hobbes, Locke, and other theorists of the seventeenth century in Britain attempted to find ways to justify and anchor the rapidly changing claims of political leaders and institutions, they assumed that the people who would trade sovereignty for order and property rights would be members of a familiar, distinct, and shared political community. Although there was considerable debate, and ubiquitous uncertainty, about who could legitimately be part of this community, there were always unspoken limits. The limits and conditions of nationality were formed by the same histories of European states that gave rise to modern ideas of sovereignty, providing the ideological stakes for the formation of nations and empires alike. But for theorists as various as Locke, Hobbes, and Burke, there were also limits that attended emergent ideas of community, nationality, and race. As Anderson has argued in his now classic formulation, nations were not only imagined; they were imagined in relation to notions of specific communities that were believed to be natural and primordial (however much they changed and grew over time). National imaginations were stretched as well as formed by print capitalism, state forms of governmentality, and the growing sense that only the nation could both realize and protect linguistic, social, cultural, religious, and political identities.[1] However, these same imaginations were produced as much by the encountering of difference as by consolidation and expansion.[2]

From the late sixteenth century at least, English preoccupations with nationhood were largely reactive, responses to travel in and experience of other worlds beyond Europe.[3] The racial and sectarian conditions of British nationality only became fixed once imperial expansion brought the English up against the terrifying perils of racial and cultural alterity.[4] If the American Revolution played out one contradiction of British sovereignty, it did so by using territory to distract attention from the far more significant contradictions of race, language, religion, and history. The fact that the British recognized their Britishness only when they were in danger of being mistaken for Native Americans or African slaves alerts us to the fundamental exclusions that are part of the history of Western sovereignty. Even when these same British settlers claimed full political rights for themselves, the most enlightened seemed uninterested in extending these rights to other communities.

For many political theorists in eighteenth-century Britain, the foundational crises of sovereignty were thought to have disappeared after the revolution and restoration of the seventeenth century. Debates over sovereignty after 1688 continued to focus on the relationship between the Crown and Parliament, but Filmer's famous defense of monarchy steadily lost any real authority.[5] More importantly, debates about sovereignty became caught up in arguments over political imperatives and civic obligations, private interests and public good, national loyalty and religious belief, and the increasing importance of trade and mercantilism in politics and social life. Trade itself could be used to justify sovereignty even as sovereignty was used to protect and further trade, but convictions about national identity collided with sovereignty only in imperial domains. As a result, concerns about sovereignty came to crisis again in the eighteenth century because of empire. In colonial America, British settlers raised questions around representation, taxation, and local authority in ways that challenged the unquestioned reach of sovereignty at the same time that they began to clarify some of the conditions of that sovereignty. Britain had claimed sovereignty over its own subjects wherever they traveled, but while it had to accept other national sovereignties in Europe, it assumed a virtual extension of its territorial claims in all imperial ventures. The flip side of this extensive extraterritoriality was the unbreakable connection between British settlers in the Americas and the British nation, a connection that was indeed broken, leading Britain to discourage settler colonization in its other imperial domains for the next hundred years. But if the American Revolution raised the question of the relationship of sovereignty and territory with a new sharpness, it also raised the stakes for imperial interests and acquisitions in other parts of the world.

Britain and India

The East India Company began its career in 1600 but conducted its first century in India in relatively desultory fashion, establishing coastal forts; engaging in trade; forming alliances; contesting the Portuguese, the Dutch, and the French; and on occasion attempting to take on the Mughals themselves. Late in the century, the company tried to develop an imperial foothold, without success. The Mughal Empire was at its peak in the seventeenth century, a century that also saw the rise of Maratha power across western and southern India in the wake of the withdrawal of Vijayanagara rule. Fortunes were made, battles were fought, trade was expanded, and territories were claimed, but the seeds of empire were slow in germinating; the British imperial presence did not take on major significance until the long eighteenth century commenced in 1688. The Glorious Revolution might have been designed principally to alleviate the political turmoil of the previous century, but it also had important economic effects, not least in the establishment of the English stock market. And the most prominent stocks traded on Exchange Alley were shares of East India Company stock. Empire and capitalism were born hand in hand, and they both worked to spawn the modern British state.[6]

Scandal, however, was a significant crucible in which both imperial and capitalist expansion was forged. When the East India Company's charter was technically forfeited in 1693, company shares were heavily used to influence parliamentary support for charter renewal. In 1695 the report of a parliamentary investigation into the developing scandal over quick fortunes made through bribery and insider trading led to the dismissal of the speaker of the Commons, the impeachment of the lord president of the council, and the imprisonment of the governor of the East India Company. If the company did, in the end, secure its renewal, it left a bad taste, suggesting to many that there was little to choose from between a licensed monopoly and a free-for-all in which pirate vessels could vie with East Indiamen for control over a new global marketplace, not to mention other possibilities of imperial acquisition. Nevertheless, the company not only survived into the new century; it soon became an engine that provided a steady source of wealth for parliamentarian and investor alike. The company also took much of the credit for—and the profit of—the new trade in tea. In the last years of the seventeenth and the first of the eighteenth century, China tea, laced with sugar from the West Indies, became the staple that it has remained in the English diet. Spices, silk, cotton, and an increasing array of other Asian commodities

established Britain's dependence on the global economy even as it secured growing legitimacy for the role of the East India Company.

But scandal, and its deep association with mercantile trade and imperial venture, hardly disappeared. In fact, the eighteenth century could be
said to be the long century of imperial scandal, a time when trade and
empire led to successive crises around the fundaments of English politics,
culture, and society. By 1788, when Edmund Burke delivered his impassioned denunciations of imperial excess in Parliament at the commencement of the spectacular impeachment trial of India's governor-general
Warren Hastings, it was generally recognized throughout England that
India had been pillaged by a growing succession of increasingly unscrupulous *nabobs*. "Nabob" was the term used for Englishmen who returned
from the East with huge fortunes that allowed them to live like princes;
nabob itself is an English corruption of *nawab*, the term used for the
highest-ranking figures in the Mughal Empire who ruled the provinces of
Bengal, Awadh, and Madras. Imperial corruption had reached its highest point well before the time of Hastings, cresting during Robert Clive's
years of greatest influence—from the 1750s through the 1770s. Clive,
dubbed by many as the "founder of the British empire," used his imperial
winnings to rise from his lowly origins as the son of a Shropshire grocer
to become the richest man in England. Despite his own unsavory record,
major concern about corruption in India came only later, finally preoccupying the metropolitan conscience in the 1780s, a new era of reform
both at home and abroad. Nevertheless, before the India Act of 1784 and
Burke's subsequent assault on Hastings, there had been two major and
several minor parliamentary inquiries into Eastern scandal and a successful—if somewhat limited—attempt at regulatory legislation in 1773,
amid many other efforts to stem the rising tide of corruption.

It is thus small wonder that the growing number of company servants
who returned to England with fortunes to invest in estates, titles, and
seats in Parliament were denominated nabobs and roundly condemned
and scorned by both older gentry and rising mercantile elites alike.[7] But
if the servants of the company brought anxieties about both the place of
commerce and the influence of Asia to a head, they also created a set of
local political crises that made India central to debates over the nature
of corruption, the need for public virtue, the character of the state, and
the justifications as well as constituencies for claims of sovereignty.[8] The

company and its political activities in India represented a scandal of an even higher order. What once was a trading company with an Eastern monopoly vested by Parliament had become a virtual state: waging war, administering justice, minting coin, and collecting revenue over Indian territory.[9] Company servants not only accumulated massive private fortunes; they also engaged the British state in actions and commitments that occasioned considerable skepticism, disapproval, and on occasion outrage at home. The company waged almost constant warfare, both against the French and against a growing array of Indian armies.

Even the much-heralded assumption of administrative and revenue rights (*diwani*) in Bengal in 1765—which led to a negotiated commitment to pay Parliament a subvention of £400,000 a year—hardly compensated for company deficits, the result as well of the spectacular profiteering of company "servants." The subvention was in part a massive bribe to sustain the company monopoly, but it was also part of a compromise to stem the force of the assault on the company from the Chatham Ministry, concerned as it was with the state-like character of the company. Indeed, acceptance of the subvention effectively conceded sovereign rights over conquered territories to the company.[10] But it also increased financial pressure on the company, especially when it turned out that Clive's exuberant estimates were vastly exaggerated. Military victories had come at great cost to the company and the British state, and speculation in company shares after the assumption of the Diwani put unsustainable pressure on profits. Financial crises exerted pressure on company support at home; at the same time they often led to greater exploitation in India, where new methods of revenue collection by the company led to the outbreak of grievous famine conditions throughout Bengal in 1770. An exploding bull market in company shares also developed, only for the bubble to burst by the end of the decade. Company shares lost much of their value after news of company military setbacks.[11] By 1772, the company had not only brought about a world credit crash; it had also come close to bankruptcy, in both financial and political terms.

Sovereignty in India

Despite the critical importance of empire to Burke's concern that British sovereignty itself was being undermined by the company's mischievous duplicity, it has been for the most part forgotten that empire came to constitute a crisis for modern theories of sovereignty. The reforms of 1773 and 1784, while they bailed the company out of debt, attempted to resolve questions of its illicit sovereignty by appropriating as much of it as possible on behalf of the Crown as well as Parliament. In whatever way contemporaries defined the sovereignty of the Mughal emperor or the charter of the company, it was a necessary conceit of early colonial rule that the East India Company held its various rights and privileges in full acknowledgment of its dependence both on the Mughals and on Parliament. In the first instance, the company consistently ceded ultimate sovereignty in India to the Mughals, even after the assumption of full management over Bengal in 1765. That this concession was increasingly seen as a lie, a necessary fiction more than a political reality, first after the company's victory in Plassey in 1757 and certainly after 1765, was another matter. In the second instance, neither Clive nor Hastings had labored under any direct control by Parliament, let alone by the Board of Proprietors, and not only because it frequently took a year for correspondence to go back and forth between India and England. In both respects, the company frequently behaved as if it were an independent entity, a fully functioning state that acted as if it were sovereign and autonomous, for all practical purposes and even some symbolic ones too. In retrospect, it is not so surprising that the rumor spread quickly in 1784 that Hastings was about to declare formal independence for the company-state. Far more widespread was the conviction that even the Mughal emperor ruled by the will of the company, under a rhetorical arrangement that ceded to the company increasing political and economic power.

Most imperial historians had argued that the East India Company was drawn reluctantly into political and military conflicts in India, only taking an interest in territorial power and revenue as a last-ditch effort to protect its trading activities.[12] In fact, however, from the mid-seventeenth century, the company had the legal right and the military will to wage war in aggressive ways, securing greater and greater territorial and political claims within the subcontinent. Through intermittent negotiations with the Mughal state, as well as by a host of "subsidiary alliances" with regional powers, the company increasingly asserted its own sovereign position. As early as 1686, Josiah Childs, the company chairman who waged war against Emperor Aurangzeb in 1688, wrote that "[without territorial revenue] it is impossible to make the English nation's station sure and firm in India upon a sound political basis, and without which we shall always continue in the state of mere merchants subject to be turned out at the pleasure of the Dutch and abused at the discretion of the natives."[13] From 1668, the company in Bombay saw itself as sovereign, at least on behalf of the Crown. The company minted coins in Bombay in the name of the British Crown, even though its own coinage acquired limited currency outside the British settlement. It also established courts of judicature over both European and Indian subjects, a practice that in other parts of India usually had to await the formal grant of *nizamat,* or the right to administer criminal justice.

Dominant official views asserted from the late seventeenth century that Mughal sovereignty, where it applied, was absolute and that oriental despots owned all land, making the right to collect revenue into an entitlement to the land itself. But this official discourse came up against two other trajectories in company ideology concerning British status in India. In the first instance, the British were loath to concede any sovereignty to others, either to the Mughals or to other European powers. As C. A. Bayly notes, "the presumption in the Laws of England that 'Turkes and other infidels were not only excluded from being witnesses against Christians, but are deemed also to be perpetual enemies and capable of no property' was toned down but never entirely forgotten."[14] Indeed, the British systematically (and far more frequently than other European groups) refused to pay forced levies to Indian powers wherever they could get away with it, despite their formal rhetoric of subservience to Mughal sovereignty. In the second instance, the British construed every privilege they received from Indian powers, whether rights to territory, to revenue collection, or to the use of certain honorary titles, as the transfer of full sovereign rights. Perhaps the first major example of this came in 1717, when the emperor Farrukhsiyar granted the right to trade freely within Bengal and its dependencies, providing the company with various tax exemptions as well.[15] When the British claimed sovereignty over the myriad chiefs and poligars of the southern countryside, many of whom had never either ceded sovereign rights or made tributary payments to the Mughals, they used a formal interpretation of Mughal sovereignty to give themselves the right of general conquest. Time after time, the British refused to accept that rights in India—and sovereignty itself—were not conceived in terms of simple, uniform, or exclusive proprietary dominion.[16]

This refusal, however, was far less about cultural misunderstanding than it was about the strategic use of cultural forms to explain and legitimate a relentless pattern of political and territorial conquest. The contradictions in company discourse were manifold. When the company exercised the right of landlord (*zamindar*) or local lord (*jagirdar*), it took upon itself powers that were hardly conceded to any of the other zamindars or jagirdars whose revenues it regularly assumed, lands it appropriated, or rights it absorbed. Even as the British saw fiscal dependency, taxation, and judicial rights of territoriality as incidents of sovereignty, they in fact adjudicated all questions of right in relation to a straightforward calculus of self-interest. Through the use of subsidiary alliances, the British were able to expand their territorial power in a variety of ways, taxing the lands of allies, requiring these allies to support garrisons of their own troops, and ultimately—as we have seen in the case of Hastings—forcing them to bail the company out of debt for unrelated military engagements or financial encumbrances of their own. When, for example, the company in Madras encouraged the nawab of Arcot to wage war against the raja of Tanjore in the early 1770s, in large part to gain lucrative revenue assignments for company servants who had lent large sums of money at usurious interest rates to the nawab for his own obligations to support company military engagements, it argued that the raja was a mere zamindar who was entirely dependent on a Mughal grant. Mughal sovereignty thus applied for the raja of Tanjore in ways that had been entirely circumvented for the nawab, let alone the company itself.

Sovereignty and the British Empire

It was within this larger context that Clive believed he was finally bringing some real political clarity to the unwieldy and often contradictory character of the company's political position as well as its self-representation. The Battle of Plassey was in fact the outcome of company assurance that it had been granted rights over Calcutta and its environs that made it independent of the governor (*nizam*) of Bengal,

Siraj ud-Daulah. From the perspective of the nizam, however, the company's refusal to acknowledge his accession by the gifting of customary presents and its growing fortifications of its settlements no doubt seemed like open acts of rebellion.[17] Although subsequently justified by the largely mythological atrocity of the Black Hole (the alleged event in which 123 of 146 Englishmen and -women crammed in a tiny Calcutta cell died in 1756, the eighteenth-century version of "weapons of mass destruction" or the Gulf of Tonkin), British hostilities in 1756 and 1757 were crude and often opportunistic efforts to gain greater power in Bengal. Some years later, when justifying his policies before the House of Commons in 1772, Clive spoke in what thereafter became the standard disavowal of imperial history. He observed that

> ever since the year 1757 when we were roused to an offensive by the unprovoked injuries of the Tyrant Nabob Serajah Dowlah, an almost uninterrupted series of success has attended us. Perhaps it was not so much our choice as necessity that drove us progressively into the possessions we presently enjoy. One thing however is certain, that aggrandized as we are, we can never be less without ceasing to be at all.[18]

But in the immediate aftermath of Plassey, he had advocated a far less cautious, or for that matter defensive, approach to empire. He observed that

> so large a sovereignty may possibly be an object too extensive for a mercantile company; and it is to be feared they are not of themselves able, without the nation's assistance, to maintain so wide a dominion. . . . [But] I flatter myself I have made it pretty clear to you that there will be little or no difficulty in obtaining the absolute possession of these rich kingdoms; and that with the Moghul's own consent, on condition of paying him less than a fifth of the revenues thereof.[19]

Six years later, when he finally accepted the Diwani, Clive in effect bribed Parliament into accepting his territorial ambitions with extravagant promises of endless riches.

After the decisive Battle of Buxar in 1765, Clive declared that "we have at last arrived at that critical Conjuncture, which I have long foreseen, I mean that Conjuncture which renders it necessary for us to determine, whether we can, or shall take the whole to ourselves." With the defeat of Shuja ud-Daula, the company had taken possession of his dominions, "and it is scarcely a Hyperbole to say that the whole Mogul Empire is in our hands."[20] He asserted that the "Princes of Indostan must conclude our Views to be boundless. . . . We must indeed become the Nabobs ourselves in Fact, if not in Name, perhaps totally without Disguise, but on this subject I cannot be positive until my arrival in Bengal."[21] In August 1765, having promised a huge financial windfall for the company, Clive negotiated the grant of Diwani rights from the Mughal emperor Shah Alam. The agreement formally recognized the emperor's authority over Bengal in the acceptance of a provision entitling the Mughals to an annual tribute of £325,000. Clive did not pursue his ambition to become the nabob in name, preferring instead to inaugurate what came to be known as his "dual system."[22] But the dual system was not merely the split between Mughal imperial authority and British administrative control, as contemporaries understood it, for Clive himself saw it as the resolution of the sham of dual sovereignty. As he wrote to the Court of Directors of the East India Company when he informed them of the assumption of the Diwani, the company "now became the Sovereigns of a rich and potent kingdom," not only the "collectors but the proprietors of the nawab's revenues."[23] Clive spelled this out in straightforward terms in his opening speech to the House of Commons in 1769 when he referred to "the great Mogul (de jure Mogul, de facto nobody at all) [and] the Nabob (de jure Nabob, de facto the East India Company's most obedient humble servant)."[24]

If the grant of the Diwani changed the nature of the relationship between the company and the Mughal empire, it also changed the company's relations with the British state. It could hardly do otherwise. As Clive said in his speech to the House of Commons in 1769,

> I was in India when the Company was established for the purposes of trade only, when their fortifications scarce deserved that name, when their possessions were within very narrow bounds. . . . The East India Company are at this time sovereigns of a rich, populous, fruitful country in extent beyond France and Spain united; they are in possession of the labour, industry, and manufactures of twenty million of subjects; they are in actual

receipt of between five and six millions a year. They have an army of fifty thousand men.[25]

In a dispatch of January 1767, the Select Committee declared that "the armies they maintained, the alliances they formed and the revenues they possessed procured them consideration as a sovereign and politic, as well as a commercial body."[26] Thomas Pownall put it bluntly when he analyzed Indian affairs in 1773: "the merchant is become the sovereign."[27] This transformation was viewed sympathetically, at least at first, because of Clive's estimates as to what the Diwani would be worth. Clive promised that the Diwani would yield close to £4 million a year, suggesting initially that the amount would increase dramatically once under company supervision. After the assumption of the Diwani, company servants certainly thought differently about the company's priorities and mandate. The Bengal Council noted to the directors in 1769 that "your trade from hence may be considered more as a channel for conveying your revenues to Britain than as only a mercantile system."[28] The only problem was that company debts kept mounting, and Clive's optimistic picture was not in fact borne out by subsequent events.

Clive's exuberance—and in turn that of many investors in company stock—ran aground against a steadily worsening financial picture, both for the company and for Bengal. The government quickly became aware that the company seemed to be a growing liability, however sovereignty was defined. Not only did tax collections plunge precipitously, Bengal underwent a serious famine in 1769 and 1770, bringing collections in some areas to a virtual halt. When the ruthless means of collection were not judged to be at fault, the predatory character of British private trade provided a powerful explanation. Speculation in company stock, leading to substantial increases in dividend payments, further eroded the company's financial situation. Worst of all, increasing military expenditures put escalating pressure on company revenues, continuing the crisis that had, in effect, begun with the ascendancy of Clive a decade before. Parliament constituted a Select Committee in April 1772 to inquire into the "nature, state, and condition of the East India Company and of British affairs in India." The inquiries of the Select Committee were followed by those of a Secret Committee, empowered in part to investigate issues around corruption, private trade, and in particular Clive's own personal enrichment through the treaties he negotiated in India.

Clive was soon exonerated of all criminal behavior and instead praised by Parliament for having rendered "great and meritorious service to this country."[29] He was also allowed to keep a personal estate in Bengal that had been granted him at the time of the conferral of Diwani rights. What did emerge out of the parliamentary fracas was the 1773 Regulating Act. If the Regulating Act was limited in its effects, it nevertheless set in place the principle, however abstract, that the company was to be under the ultimate control of Crown and Parliament. As Burke and others had recognized, this change entailed an important structural shift for a trading company that acted under a parliamentary charter as a monopoly firm. Empire had become a matter of official state interest.

Contradictions of Empire

The company continued in many respects as a rogue state in its relations both to the Mughal empire and the British Crown. It was the fate of Warren Hastings to be governor-general during the tumultuous decade that saw these contradictions come to a head. In fact, Hastings was far more attentive to the contradictions of early British conquest and occupation than his predecessors, especially Clive, for whom sovereignty was to be seized along with treasure. Nevertheless, empire's contradictions seemed much more powerfully evidenced by the life and career of Warren Hastings than by others, in large part because Hastings sought both to systematize the company's relations with India and to embed his own rule within a subcontinental context. For this reason, Hastings was a more unlikely target than Clive might have been for Burke. Far more scrupulous than other nabobs, Hastings had greater political than financial ambition, and he made clear his deep frustration with the limits and obfuscations of company authority in India.

His specific mandate in 1772 was to end Clive's system of dual rule, taking direct charge for the collection of the Diwani revenue. Hastings was ordered to "render the accounts of the revenue simple and intelligible, to establish fixed rules for collection, to make the mode of them

uniform in all parts of the province, and to provide for an equal administration of justice."[30] However, in so elevating the company to the
status of a state, Hastings was aware that he would eventually have to
declare British sovereignty over all the company's possessions and that
"the British sovereignty, through whatever channels it may pass into
these provinces, should be all in all."[31] While Hastings achieved some
success in the arena of law, he felt deeply frustrated in his larger ambition to reform company governance and to rationalize company sovereignty. When Hastings pursued aggressive military policies—whether
they failed or succeeded—he ran into the limits of company financial
policy. When Hastings declared that an Indian ruler was dependent on
the company, a mere landlord or bureaucratic functionary, he collided
with the rhetorical sham of company political theory, which was duplicitous both in sketching a formal feudal picture of Indian politics and
in treating the Mughal emperor simultaneously as puppet and sovereign. Moreover, when Hastings argued that the company should buttress
its own authority through establishing clearer ties with the Crown, he
alienated both the Whig faction in Parliament and the company directors, who feared he was willing to give up company rights of territorial
possession over the company's growing conquests.

Hastings's interest in clarifying company sovereignty was a direct expression of his political ambitions. In early 1773, he advocated that the
"sovereignty of this country [be] wholly and absolutely vested in the
Company" and that he be the sole "instrument" of this sovereignty. However, neither the regulating acts of 1773 or 1784 nor the steadily growing
state apparatus changed the company's formal mandate. The Pitt Act of
1784 did clarify the Crown's formal control over the company's political
policies, in particular its power to wage war. A Board of Control was set
up to supervise both the directors at home and the governor-general in
India, and the board was specifically put under royal direction. However,
Parliament not only maintained its supervisory role, soon to be amply
displayed in the Hastings trial; the governor-general was also given far
greater powers than Hastings had previously had. And despite the recognition that the company would be steadily involved in revenue collection
and local administration, it was told that its servants should concentrate
more on the trading aspects of its operation. Pitt went so far as to in-
sert a clause in the act stating "that to pursue schemes of conquest and

extension of dominion in India, are measures repugnant to the wish, the honour, and the policy of this nation."[32] Cornwallis, who went to India as governor-general in 1786, did honor this stricture in formal terms, though his use of a political alliance with the Travancore raja to justify his war against Tipu Sultan in 1792 echoed Hastings's own manipulations of treaties and feudal theories to cover his own aggressive actions. But in fulfilling the other mandates of the Pitt Act, Cornwallis by no means followed his instructions to return to trade.

On the one hand, he raised company salaries to make it easier for him to impose full restrictions on private trade, regularizing the bureaucratic character of company service. On the other, he introduced the permanent revenue settlement on Bengal. Cornwallis got away with all this not just because of his upright image in Britain but because he arranged for £500,000 to be sent annually to the Exchequer in London, not just finally regularizing but increasing the earlier arrangement that had been made after the assumption of the Diwani. As significantly, Cornwallis set himself up as an imperial monarch of sorts, allowing himself to be represented with classical references as part of his own self-image of adhering to Roman civic virtue. Wellesley, when he became governor-general in 1798, not only abandoned the policy of nonexpansion but used the renewed warfare against France to justify his new policy of imperial aggression. In any case, by the 1790s there was an outpouring of patriotic and royal fervor and nationalist pride that was well suited to imperial expansion. Nevertheless, like all of his predecessors, Wellesley felt constrained to justify his conquests and politics in the complicated language of dual sovereignty. The sham of sovereignty—once again both in regard to the company's relationship to the Crown and its relationship to the Mughal—continued unabated.

The Ancient Constitution

As a productive fiction, dual sovereignty served multiple purposes, from disguising the extent and nature of imperial conquest to deferring British responsibility for imperial excesses. Burke's great anxiety was that the fiction of empire would potentially undermine the fiction of the ancient constitution in Britain itself. When Burke challenged his listeners to suspend their ideas of distance and difference in favor of sympathy for their fellow citizens of India, he implored them to realize that the crisis of legitimacy in India could lead to a crisis of legitimacy in Britain. In his speech on the Fox India Bill, he said, "I am certain that every means effectual to preserve India from oppression is a guard to preserve the British Constitution from its worst corruption."[33] Thus it was that the French Revolution only heightened Burke's concern to press for Hastings's conviction. The upending of tradition and order in France was deeply threatening, taking place as it did just across a narrow channel of water. But the relentless duplicity, venality, and corruption of India were in some ways even worse, as these problems implicated the British imperial idea, and as a consequence British sovereignty itself, more centrally. Perhaps most troubling of all, the actions of Hastings, as governor-general and the sole representative of British authority in India (however the sovereignty of company or Mughal was conceived), threatened to draw back the veil over the beginning of imperial government. Hastings's support for the vicious attack on the Rohillas paid no heed to the need for prudence and discretion. Hastings's lack of concern for the maintenance of treaties with either the raja of Benares or the nawab of Awadh could undo the shining fortune, genius, talent, and military virtue of Britain in India. What Hastings defended as necessary for the maintenance of company rule in India was seen by Burke as likely to topple that very rule if not cleansed of scandal. In an age of metropolitan crisis—one that was exacerbated by domestic political scandals, growing popular unrest, and the rapid influx of new money from imperial ventures—it seemed unwise to shine too penetrating a light on the beginnings of empire. In that context, Hastings's indiscretions threatened to call far too much attention to the scandal of imperial conquest.

Burke was perhaps correct to worry that Hastings's immediate legacy would be destabilizing for the expansion of empire, with the increased scrutiny concerning political as well as personal corruption in the years between the loss of America and the fall of old France. But in calling attention to Hastings's contradictions—his missteps as well as his achievements—Burke sought explicitly to separate the person of Hastings from the project of empire. The personalization of imperial excess was a deliberate effort to exorcise the evil from the imperial idea. When Burke made his first great speech in the impeachment trial of Warren Hastings, he made it clear that he was not condemning the idea of empire. In demonizing Hastings, Burke unwittingly paved the way for the nationalist heroes who would follow Hastings. In fact, both Cornwallis and Wellesley continued Hastings's policies and inconsistencies, though they were better placed in Britain to maintain their domestic reputations, even as they rode the wave of a rising nationalist tide that, in the wake of the trial, increasingly took empire as a badge of Britain's honor. But by this time, the contradictions of sovereignty had ceased to cause much concern. On the one side, the sovereignty of the Mughal was seen as a mere rhetorical convenience. On the other, the company was now seen as performing the work of both Crown and Parliament (even if it still did so at great financial cost). Formally speaking, it was not until the great rebellion of 1857 and the final deposing of the Mughal king in 1858 that sovereignty in India was clarified. In one fell swoop, both the Mughal and the company were dethroned, and the British Crown became paramount.[34] But by then, Burke would have hardly been proud. Although he had made possible the apotheosis of British imperial sovereignty in India when the veil was finally drawn for good over the origins of empire in India, he had a very different kind of imperial ideal in mind. Burke's role in imperial justification was, ironically, forgotten along with Hastings's early ignominy, for by 1858 there were none in Britain concerned that empire would compromise British sovereignty and the ancient constitution on which it rested, despite the general sigh of relief when Queen Victoria assumed Crown rule over India.

In drawing back his veil, Burke had been most deeply concerned with the ancient constitution of Britain. His anxious desire to cleanse the imperial idea was not primarily related to his worries about India, preoccupied though he became in the last decade of his life. For Burke, imperial and metropolitan claims to sovereignty were inseparable, making the trial of Warren Hastings a test not only of the ideal of empire but of state sovereignty at home as well. Empire could work to enhance the glory of, even as it could cruelly undermine, the ancient constitution. The story of sovereignty has always been told as a universal tale with origins (and frames of reference) in Europe. The modern idea of sovereignty emerged, so we are told, in the debates of European political theorists and activists—around the historical swirl of kings, revolutionaries, counterrevolutionaries, and demagogues, among others—in the seventeenth, eighteenth, and nineteenth centuries. Modern ideas of empire required a slight modification of the fundamental premise of sovereignty, but empire was always justified by the absence of sovereign forms—identities as well as institutions—in colonized territories and the ultimate export of these forms to them from the imperial metropole. Indeed, Third World nationalism has been seen as the great testimony to the universal value of this European idea, ultimate proof of the foundational originality of Europe and the intrinsic power of the nation-state. Successful entry to the world of nations has always reiterated what appears as a Western triumph, the birth of sovereignty out of the crucible of colonialism. Imperialism has justified itself over and again, in its heyday as well as in its shameful moments of demise, through the great narrative of sovereignty. Of course, empire was most egregious precisely in its denial of sovereignty to colonized populations. But to understand how empire was in fact of fundamental importance to the emergence of both modernity and sovereignty, at least in the English case, we need to return to Burke's prosecution of Hastings, for it was precisely this concern that led Burke to use all his hard-earned political capital—and the last nine years of his political career—on a trial that failed in the end to impeach his enemy.

In 1782, Burke wrote a speech in connection with a parliamentary inquiry into the "State of the Representation of the Commons in Parliament." In this speech, he made one of his clearest statements about the nature of the nation, the meaning of sovereignty, and the relationship of both to the ancient constitution. Following Locke, Burke noted that government was chartered to protect property. Departing from Locke and other seventeenth-century theorists, he stressed even more the importance of the need to preserve a prescriptive constitution. Prescription is the claim sovereignty has to the future, or what he termed presumption: "It is a presumption in favour of any settled scheme of government against any untried project, that a nation has long existed and flourished under it. It is a better presumption even of the choice of a nation, far better than any sudden and temporary arrangement by actual election."[35] The nation itself was not merely an idea but the congealed effect of long historical experience. As he explained, "because a nation is not an idea only of local extent, and individual momentary aggregation; but it is an idea of continuity, which extends in time as well as in numbers and in space." For Burke, national sovereignty was a contract only in an abstract sense since it can hardly be based on a set of discrete, knowable choices.

> And this is a choice, not of one day, or one set of people, not a tumultuary and giddy choice; it is a deliberate election of ages and generations; it is a constitution made by what is ten thousand times better than choice, it is made by the peculiar circumstances, occasions, tempers, dispositions, and moral, civil and social habitudes of the people, which disclose themselves only in a long space of time. It is a vestment which accommodates itself to the body.[36]

Sovereignty, or the ancient constitution itself, has thus become naturalized as the necessary cover for the body politic, accustomed to its specific shapes and changing character. The principle of sovereignty is universal, but the specific form of sovereignty—and by implication any national constitution—is highly particular, the outcome of a specific if ancient history. Sovereignty may be the outcome of choice, but it reflects the agencies and agreements of a community forged through a long and established history.

Burke's views in 1782 had in fact changed greatly from those he held in younger years. In his first writings on law, he had been much more concerned to trace the contextual histories of legal development, arguing as he did against the opinions of Sir Matthew Hale, the great historian of the common law who held that the history of law was necessarily an inscrutable, "immemorial custom in perpetual adaptation." Now Burke seemed to agree with Hale, conceding that history's silences had foundational status for the idea of law.[37] Common wisdom has it that Burke had become more conservative as he aged and was giving vent here to the full traditionalism of his older reactionary years. But it cannot be accidental that in 1782 Burke was spending most of his time thinking about company abuses in India and wondering whether Warren Hastings was undermining universal principles and national reputations in his actions as chief of the East India Company. And in his opening speech on Hastings, he seemed preoccupied with matters concerning law and sovereignty, as if the conduct of Hastings was calling into question fundamental understandings of both. He praised Clive for arranging the transfer of Diwani rights:

> For the Mogul, the head of the Mussulman religion there and likewise of the Empire, a head honoured and esteemed even in its ruins, he obtained recognition by all the persons that were concerned. He got from him the Dewanee, which is the great grand period of the constitutional entrance of the Company into the affairs of India. He quieted the minds of the people. He gave to the settlement of Bengal a constitutional form, and a legal right, acknowledged and recognized now for the first time by all the Princes of the Country, because given by the Charter of the Sovereign.[38]

In Burke's view, dual sovereignty was necessary to accommodate difference, which for him had to be named as the ancient constitution of India. Clive's duplicity is rewritten as morality because of its apparent respect for sovereignty and the constitution of India, though the narrative of morality in conquest would not have borne the weight of Burke's critical scrutiny had he chosen that path.

Sovereignty on Trial

Hastings, however, was a different matter. He was brought to trial under English law on the grounds that he had been a British governor.

> My Lords, we contend that Mr. Hastings, as a British Governor, ought to govern upon British principles, not by British forms, God forbid. For if ever there was a case in which the letter kills and the spirit gives life, it would be an attempt to introduce British forms and the substance of despotic principles together into any Country. No. We call for that spirit of equity, that spirit of justice, that spirit of safety, that spirit of protection, that spirit of lenity, which ought to characterise every British subject in power; and upon these and these principles only, he will be tried.[39]

The trial was thus an epic test of the ancient constitution of Britain, both because Hastings would be brought before justice in London and because he had been the agent of British justice in India. This is why Burke had railed against what he called a "geographical morality." In his oration, he said, "we are to let your Lordships know that these Gentlemen have formed a plan of Geographic morality, by which the duties of men in public and in private situations are not to be governed by their relations to the Great Governor of the Universe, or by their relations to men, but by climates, degrees of longitude and latitude, parallels not of life but of latitudes."[40] Burke was alarmed that relativism of this kind could be used in India to justify unparalleled corruption and abuse. Worse, however, this relativism cast the great law itself into doubt. Cultural relativism would in fact work to give an idea of choice, compact, or contract far too much importance, for the law had to rest on a more transcendental foundation. As he said in his speech on Hastings:

> this great law does not arise from our conventions or compacts; on the contrary, it gives to our conventions and compacts all the force and sanction they can have; it does not arise from our vain institutions. Every good gift is of God; all power is of God; and He who has given the power and from whom it alone originates, will never suffer the exercise of it to be practised upon any less solid foundation than the power itself. Therefore, will it be imagined, if this be true, that He will suffer this great gift of Government, the greatest, the best that was ever given by God to mankind, to be the plaything and the sport of the feeble will of a man, who, by a blasphemous, absurd, and petulant usurpation, would place his own feeble, contemptible, ridiculous will in the place of Divine wisdom and justice?[41]

By cheapening the idea of sovereignty by the use of arbitrary power and despotic action and then justifying this by his account of India's history and culture, Hastings undermined the ancient constitutions of Britain and India alike.

Burke's commitment to a universal understanding of law was no less than an article of faith in the sacrality of the constitution itself. Only a divine principle could provide the force and the sanction for law and sovereignty, at home and abroad. History, in the form of "tradition," would shape specific understandings and institutions of law, but the history of violent conquest had to be hidden behind a veil. Conquest was for Burke the "state of exception," the term Carl Schmitt later coined to characterize the sovereign who was outside or above the very law he was charged to protect.[42] Burke argued against Lockean commitments for a variety of reasons. He was worried that philosophical resort to contract would license popular revolution, as indeed it had in the context of seventeenth-century England. This worry became the source of particular anxiety around the events in France after 1789, but it was not a new concern for Burke, either in the English or the Indian context. Burke also argued against an emphasis on contract because he wanted to ground sovereignty in something other than natural right, a form of universal reason he soundly rejected in favor of history, law, and God. Burke's genius was to invoke the general culture of belief around English common law, especially its combination of ancient wisdom and contemporary custom, to construct his own theory of sovereignty. In this sense, the mandate of the divine was simultaneously to justify and transcend the historical actions of men, to cleanse the law from the tarnish of its historical origins. Clive was a hero because he acted out the charade of dual sovereignty, and indeed because the level of his own corruption was best forgotten if Britain was to maintain its imperial mission. Yet Hastings was to be held accountable to Britain's own ancient constitution. At the very point that Burke came to hold that a prescriptive constitution had to be "immemorial," Hastings was to be judged wanting so that both England and empire might survive.[43]

Burke's condemnation of Hastings's invocation of cultural difference was thus in the service of an absolute idea of truth that slid, however uneasily, from the particularity of England's historical formation to the universality of an idea of law. But he did not leave his case at that, for he also argued that Hastings had misunderstood and viciously violated India's own ancient constitution. It was ironic that Hastings's own commitments to a rule of law—one that was in truth framed much like Burke's—would get him into such trouble, since it was widely believed that he had done himself particular harm when he used Nathaniel Halhed's defense of his record.[44] Halhed had used his understanding of Sanskrit legal texts—the basis of Hastings's major contribution in the area of codifying Hindu law—and his reckoning of Indian understandings of kingly authority to suggest that Hastings had to assume an oriental mantle of despotic authority. Clive had simply acted as the despot, whereas Hastings, who at his worst was more considerate and more reasoned than Clive could ever be, sought to justify despotism under Indian conditions. When Hastings, quoting Halhed, had said in his defense that "the whole history of Asia is nothing more than precedents to prove the invariable exercise of arbitrary power," he had invoked a larger historical context. He had spoken about the great variety of "tenures, rights, and claims, in all cases of landed property and feudal jurisdiction in India from the informality, invalidity, and instability of all engagements in so divided and unsettled a state of society . . . as Hindoostan has been constantly exposed to . . . ever since the Mohomedan conquests."[45] Indeed, when he said that "rebellion itself is the parent and the promoter of despotism," he meant to imply, echoing Burke's own earlier critique of "Mahometan" government in a tract he wrote with his cousin William, that Hindus rebelled for justifiable reasons.[46] But when he went on to say that "sovereignty in India implies nothing else [than despotism]," he fell straight into the trap that Burke had set.[47]

At the time of the great impeachment trial, Burke would hardly concede either the illegitimacy of Mughal rule or the essential rebelliousness of Hindus in the face of foreign rule. The stakes here had shifted far away from Tanjore and Arcot, let alone Bengal, and pertained to matters far more important than merely the future of imperial acquisitions in India. Burke's sense of the particularity of each historical formation of a prescriptive constitution could not countenance either arbitrary power or the language of despotism. The "mean and depraved state" said by Hastings to have been the fault of the Mughals was now turned to Hastings's own account. For Burke, the mandate of history was to transform necessarily iniquitous beginnings into something "better than choice," what he called "the peculiar circumstances . . . and . . . habitudes of the people."[48] History, in short, was about tradition and, by implication, about the sanctification of past contingency. When contrasting Britain and India, Burke used this idea of history to create the space for a difference that did not compromise morality. In the case of Britain's role in India, conquest was not about the original formation of the law but rather its appropriation of India's own law, an appropriation that transferred responsibility for the maintenance of another law rather than Britain's own: "For by conquest which is a more immediate designation of the hand of God, the conqueror only succeeds to all the painful duties and subordination to the power of God which belonged to the Sovereign that held the country before."[49] But even here, cultural relativity labored under the burden of Burke's universalism.

It was in this context that Burke provided his extensive analysis of Islamic political and legal theory, demonstrating the extent to which law in India had been seen as transcendent in much the way it was in Britain. But he was ambivalent about the need for empirical demonstration, his ambivalence suggested as much by his awkwardness in this formulation as by his careless scholarship. He asserted simply that "in Asia as well as in Europe the same Law of Nations prevails, the same principles are continually resorted to, and the same maxims sacredly held and strenuously maintained."[50] Historical analysis thus confirms the universality of the legal ideal, but it cannot capture the force of it. Tamerlane was a better man than Hastings, but in the end, "all power is of God." This was the primary puzzle of sovereignty, the war between the universal and the particular in the formation of Burke's sense of sovereign right and civic virtue. Burke attempted to use Mohammedan legal and theological texts to sustain an idea of an ancient constitution that was formed not only out of the specific historical experience of the British nation but in relation to a decidedly Christian idea of God's generative relationship to the law. Burke's call for sympathy for the fellow citizens of India was predicated both on sameness—the universal province and claim of law—and on difference, the distance as well as the distinctness of place.

The Universal Claim of Sovereignty

In a recent analysis, Uday Mehta has emphasized Burke's commitment to the importance of place, or territory. Mehta shows how Burke was always careful to set up the mise-en-scène by emphasizing territorial and geographical markers as a way to frame his call to respect India's historical and political integrity. He reads Burke's treatment of Mohammedan law as a belief in Indian equivalence. Thus he sees Burke's defense of Indian sovereignty as a tacit acceptance of Indian nationality. And he suggests that Burke's emphasis on location or territory, combined with his use of territory to provide the experiential basis for collective or political identity, anticipates the anti-imperial nationalism of the next century.[51] He goes on to suggest that "Burke's defense of Indian history vindicates a social order in which freedom would not be 'solitary, unconnected, individual, selfish liberty, as if every man was to regulate the whole of his conduct by his own will.' It vindicates what subsequent nationalists might have called the conditions appropriate for the right of self-determination."[52] But in making this argument, Mehta underplays both the complementary emphasis Burke put on the theistic universality of the law and the degree to which Burke was not a critic of empire itself. Far from seeing in India an incipient nationhood that could compromise Britain's own nationhood, Burke saw in British conduct in India a challenge to two different but allied forms of sovereignty that put at risk the sacrality of sovereignty itself.[53] India's sovereignty did not constitute the basis of a claim for liberty so much as a second argument against the "absolute power," or despotism, of Hastings. And the French Revolution only brought more urgency, and proximity, to the danger.

In muting the defensiveness, as well as the reflexive character, of Burke's rhetoric about India, Mehta still makes a compelling argument that English political theory was significantly shaped by imperial connections.[54] But Burke's anglocentrism was hardly moderated by his concern for India. Burke believed that the ancient constitution was both primordial and shaped by shared history even as he was committed to the idea that the law was universal in its principle if singular in its form. His paradoxical formulations were in the end clearly made in the service both of Britain and the idea of empire, rooted as they were in his sense that British justice was the most developed and enlightened in the world. His sympathy for India was the sympathy of a paternalist who believed his charge could only benefit from the relationship of dependency. His sense of Indian sovereignty and nationhood was itself always dependent on his greater concern for the past and future of Britain itself. If he could draw the veil on Clive's duplicitous conquest of India, he set the stage for the ultimate drawing of the veil on Hastings as well. In doing so, he played a vital if unwitting role in the legitimization of the British imperial mission at a time of resurgent British nationalism. Burke's attentiveness to place worked in the end to make one place sovereign and another place colonized. This was a contradiction that would require a different kind of political vision to undo.

Still, Burke's contradictory insistence on universality and specific-ity in the context of India did make clear the extent to which his own sense of sovereignty was both brought into crisis yet unchallenged by difference. On the one hand, he resisted the cultural relativism that both justified company despotism in India and called into question the ab-solute truth and universal provenance of England's own traditions. On the other hand, he formulated a sense of history that was rooted in an ancient but still historical past that could provide the basis for a national claim to the ancient constitution. In this respect, India's alterity had to be simultaneously affirmed and disavowed. Ironically, imperial ideology made it possible for Burke to do this, though the thinly veiled fiction of dual sovereignty compromised the force of this complementary idea. For Burke, the contradictions of English, or British, sovereignty were highlighted by resort to empire, even if the greatest role of empire was to test the very transcendence of his commitment to the ancient consti-tution. Mehta is right to congratulate Burke for his acknowledgment of the role of empire—both its general significance and the excess of its corruption—as a necessary component of a national theory of sover-eignty. Before Burke, most other English political theorists had system-atically denied or ignored the presence of empire in their understanding of sovereignty, despite the obvious fact that modern sovereignty was born in an age of empire. Yet his genius lay less in the recognition of difference than in his use of the imperial context to critique his idea of the social contract.

For Britain, empire as an idea was examined only retrospectively, once the national character of claims about sovereignty made empire appear to be a problem. Empire began as an accidental extension of sov-ereign ambitions that survived largely by dissembling. The conceptual relations between empire and sovereignty could be left vague until they ran up against the anxieties that grew around the expansionist activities of the East India Company on the one hand and the recognition of racial and cultural difference on the other. The underlying national consensus required to make the claims of sovereignty carry weight only gradually became clear. Empire was fundamental to the history of British sover-eignty, but not only in relation to the triumphal connection between English empire and American independence.[55] Instead, empire worked to crystallize the convictions of national sovereignty even as it helped garner the resources to make it possible. Empire also exposed the serious contradictions that emerged when economic interest, military might, and political expansion failed to secure cultural legitimation, whether at home or abroad. In either case, empire ultimately came to be of signal importance to the expanding cult of nationality in England during this same period. Linda Colley shows how an idea of Britishness was in the end triumphant in large part because of the growing collective sense of opposition to France (and the continent more generally). She also demonstrates that imperial ventures were especially useful for folding some Scots and Irish into the mix of Britishness by recruiting them to a project that highlighted differences between East and West.[56] While in some respects the loss of America only made the crisis of empire more pressing, posing a new set of national exclusions as fundamental to the problem of sovereignty, it also made the idea of empire all the more compelling. By the time Cornwallis had moved from the scene of his American failure to his Indian triumph, the contradictions of sovereignty were to be resolved by a new set of commitments around the importance of empire for Britain itself. The problems posed by imperial sovereignty became increasingly erased by the ambitions of national sovereignty.

Burke's role in the trial of Warren Hastings highlights the contradictions that were part of late eighteenth-century ideas of sovereignty. Yet it is sad that Burke's own interrogation of sovereignty—given his commitment to the ancient constitution rather than the idea of contract—made empire ultimately less of a problem than it became for liberal theory, where contradictions outlived the trial.[57] Even for Burke's detractors, the trial brought closure to the crisis over sovereignty that empire in India had posed.[58] In bringing Hastings to scrutiny before the combined houses of Parliament, Burke had allowed British imperial sovereignty to appear to be far more constrained and beneficent than it had been before. For the long nineteenth century, both for liberals and conservatives, empire ceased to threaten the foundations of political sovereignty until, in the end, nationalism appropriated the arguments of contract and ancient constitutions to make a different kind of territorial claim for self-rule, though only with the serious political pressures exerted by anticolonial nationalist movements. The absence of the role of empire in the history of sovereignty continues to obscure the extent to which Burke's challenge to imperial sovereignty was critical to the modern history of national sovereignty itself. It is thus all the more necessary for political theory, historical analysis, and critical thought to join together to write empire back into the history of the West, where it has played such a foundational and constitutive role.

8

Bringing the Company Back In

The Scandal of Early Global Capitalism

It is no small irony that, only a short time after the most spectacular illustration of corporate greed and irresponsibility in recent history, the state has become so much the subject of attack that it seems hard to remember any of the real lessons of the 2008 economic crash. Massive cuts in federal funding are justified by a rhetoric of total faith in the free market. As the short-lived political will behind regulation and enforcement has evaporated, the state itself has been targeted as the agent of our current discontent.

The focus I put on corruption and scandal as fundamental to the history of the East India Company in my recent book has now once again been echoed by current events, reminders of the extent to which modern institutions such as markets, banks, and states, and modern ideas such as commerce, investment, and sovereignty have been associated with scandals.[1] While scandals may be "good to think" for us academics and are more central than ever given the role of the media today, they seem to have an increasingly short shelf life. The larger the scandal, the more urgent the need to restitute normalcy through reform and forgetting.

As Edmund Burke, perhaps the most energetic scandalmonger of them all, well knew, the problem with the East India Company was neither the clear fact of imperial expansion nor the free circulation of capital and goods but the admixture of commerce and rule that was fundamental to the very formation of the company-state in India in the seventeenth and eighteenth centuries. Like his contemporary Adam Smith, he was deeply concerned about how markets could be corrupted by state interests and political interference, but his famous conservatism lay in his deep suspicion of the way economic forces could control human values and in his more abiding concern with the question of sovereignty and the ancient constitution. It is hardly surprising that he had major worries about the status of the company-state in India, both in respect to its relationship to Crown and Parliament in Great Britain and to the duly constituted sovereign powers of the Indian subcontinent. What is surprising in retrospect is how long it took him to see the company-state as a threat to the ancient constitution. In my view it was this early failure to grasp the problem, a failure not unrelated to his own political affiliations and ambitions—nor perhaps as well his own familial relations and economic circumstances—that was in large part the cause of the obsessive zeal with which he later pursued his case against Warren Hastings and the East India Company itself. Nothing like the taint of scandal to clarify the mind, especially when you are talking about the mind of Edmund Burke.

It was, of course, the monumental greed (rather than the "astonishing moderation") of Robert Clive, combined with the great stock market crash of 1769, that led to the parliamentary hearings of 1772 concerning the conduct of the East India Company in India.[2] Clive had gone to India a grocer's son and lowly clerk only to become credited with the founding of the British Empire in India—and to become as well the richest man in England. Although Clive was ultimately vindicated by Parliament (Burke wrote that Clive came "out of the fiery trial much brighter than when he went into it"), Lord North's Regulating Act of 1773 was passed as a response to concerns about Clive's corruption and excess.[3] The act, however, was far more attenuated than many had initially wished, and it was accompanied by a massive bailout for the company, the grant of a loan of £1.4 million to keep the company from collapse. The act prohibited "presents"—or bribes—and put some important restrictions on private trade. But it did not prosecute company agents for their crimes, perhaps most egregious of which had been the excesses of the company merchants of Madras who had profited mightily from a network of debt issuing from and around the figure of the nawab of Arcot.

The scandals around the debts of the nawab of Arcot were not of the same financial scale as the events in Bengal that led directly to the stock market crash and the parliamentary inquiries that followed thereupon. It was the grant of Diwani from the Mughal emperor to the company in 1765 and the extraordinary claims by Clive and others about the riches that would flow to company investors that were most directly responsible for the crash and the financial crisis of both the company and its investors. The stories that circulated from Madras throughout the preceding decade, however, had contributed to the sense of panic and illustrated most graphically the speculative and expropriating logics of imperial trade as practiced under the auspices of company rule that led to a general sense in Britain of the need for reform and regulation. Beginning with the accession of the nawab, Muhammad Ali, in 1755, corruption associated with the European presence in Madras grew at a dizzying pace. By 1763, when George Pigot left the post of governor with a fortune of at least £300,000, the level of generalized corruption was staggering. Pigot left Madras rich and returned to London as a salaried lobbyist on behalf of the nawab, a form of employment that turned routine: the nawab used his money to buy parliamentary seats for supporters (known as the "Arcot interest") who lobbied in London on behalf of the nawab and his creditors. In Madras, company servants soon discovered that the best investment in town was in the debts of the nawab, as these same officials vied with one another for the privilege of lending money to the nawab at usurious rates of interest.

Becoming a creditor afforded the further privilege of receiving lavish presents to substitute for regular payments. These presents, ceremonial commissions for the loan transaction itself rather than direct repayments, often consisted of diamonds and gold and other jewels, but the debt itself was often commuted into the right to collect revenue—under the system of tax farming—from villages or regions nominally under nawabi control. The market in tax farming was thus a bit like an early version of securitized mortgages—rights to collect revenue were transferred from hand to hand, for progressively higher rates, with nothing to erode profits as long as the mortgages changed hands, demand for their generation kept rising, interest was paid, and the mortgages themselves were guaranteed by the court of the nawab. In order to afford the regular supply of presents, the nawab continued to borrow money while also pressuring the company to allow him to wage war on neighbors. The Board of Directors was alarmed that the company had at great expense engaged in hostilities against Hyder Ali of Mysore as a result of the nawab's need for revenue to discharge his personal debt. Given the illustrious list of creditors, the nawab was properly convinced that no matter how indebted he became, the company would never force him into total bankruptcy, even as they would never set about to regularize his administration or his finances. Part indigenous Ponzi scheme and part pure imperial greed, the company-state in Madras became a parody of an oriental fantasy, or nightmare, a riot of opulent consumption, predatory warfare, and rack-renting. The nawab was an Oriental despot par excellence, since he seemed immune from control or regulation, and there were no penalties or risks for the creditors, who not only secured extraordinary profits but also garnered immense political influence at the same time, both in Madras and back home in England.

If there was a single name that became associated with company depredations in Madras, it was Paul Benfield, a spectacularly successful civil architect, engineer, and contractor who earned his initial fortune in a building boom in Madras in the 1760s, only to use his wealth to become a key player in local political intrigue. While loaning money to the nawab, he also loaned cash to his enemy the raja of Tanjore, ultimately encouraging (and bankrolling) the nawab to attack Tanjore to recover his fortune (with ample interest) and depose the raja. Benfield's success (predicated partly on his capacity to bet on both sides and collect from both as well) brought him to the attention of the Board of Directors in London, who sent the former governor George Pigot back to Madras in 1775, with the mandate to restore the sovereignty of Tanjore and to stem the influence of the nawab's chief creditors (in the years since leaving Madras, Pigot had exhausted his own fortune and ceased receiving the promised presents from the nawab). Pigot traveled to Tanjore to restore the throne but upon his return to Madras found himself the victim of a coup. He was accosted and thrown into prison, while the rebellious Madras Council installed one of their number as the new governor. The grateful nawab opened his treasury and distributed what was left in his coffers along with new letters of credit, increasing his total debts to an estimated £2 million. Before the company directors were able to respond, Pigot died in prison, and the company-state in Madras devolved into unmitigated mutiny. Subsequent efforts to regain control over the situation were nominally successful, but corruption around the debts of the nawab continued well into the next century.

Edmund Burke was drawn into the crisis in Madras through his close relative and confidant William Burke, who had gone to India as part of a delegation to reinstate Pigot and subsequently worked for a number of years as an agent for the raja of Tanjore. Edmund had been involved in debates over India for the previous decade, but he had been a supporter of both the company and Clive, and he worried during the parliamentary hearings of 1772 only that the state would take too much control over the company as a result. As Peter Marshall has put it, "Burke believed that state intervention in the affairs of the Company would prove a major constitutional danger, since it would greatly enhance the power and influence of the executive government." In 1779, Edmund coauthored with William an important political and historical tract entitled "Policy of Making Conquests for the Mahometans."⁴ This tract, motivated chiefly by an effort by John and James Macpherson to support the nawab and overturn the restoration of Tanjore, argued strongly for the sovereign claims of the raja of Tanjore, and this began to reflect a change of attitude toward the East India Company. A nuanced intervention into matters concerning Indian sovereignty, the Burke text both defended the local sovereign claims of Tanjore along with those of other princes and principalities (including the *palaiyakkarars* of southern India) and disparaged the excessive sovereign ambition of "Mahometan" rulers, in part because as Muslims they could not establish the same level of sympathy between ruler and people as Hindus such as the Tanjore ruler could. Burke's severest critique of company power was accordingly that it had been used to buttress the "ambition, pride, and tyranny" of Muhammad Ali, "this potentate on sufferance."⁵

Just two years later, however, Burke turned his attention to the perfidious role of Paul Benfield, in what seems in retrospect almost a trial run, as it were, for his monumental attack on Hastings. In January 1781 he drafted charges against the man he regarded as responsible for Pigot's imprisonment and the debacle in Madras. Using rhetoric that became associated with Burke in the halls of Parliament over the next fifteen years, he held that Benfield was "a destroyer of countries," that he had driven "thirty or forty millions of distressed people into absolute despair," and that he should be charged guilty of treachery against both India and Parliament. These charges, however, went nowhere, since Benfield had many friends and allies and was easily able to command sufficient votes to keep the inquiry from proceeding. While succumbing unhappily to the local power of the Arcot interest, Burke was asked to join a Select Committee in the House of Commons to investigate the administration of justice in Bengal, and after this he preoccupied himself almost exclusively with that part of India. The one major exception to this, however, was a rousing speech he gave four years later, in 1785, concerning the debts of the nawab of Arcot. The new Board of Control, the governing body of the company that had been set up as a consequence of the 1784 Pitt India Act, revised a decision earlier made by the Court of Directors to launch a major inquiry into the origins of the debts that had been ordered repaid to the creditors by the revenues of the Carnatic. One of the first acts of the new Board of Control, established precisely to regulate the corruption and scandal of company servants in India, was to squash any effort to inquire into the legitimacy of the transactions that had led to the massive indebtedness of the nawab and to speed the diversion of major portions of the southern revenues to the further private enrichment of the Arcot group and their various supporters and beneficiaries, whatever the actual status of the promissory paper they still held. Burke was understandably outraged and made his famous speech in response.

Burke argued that the first set of debts to the nawab, those that had been made before 1767 and in that year had received the attention of Parliament, had been genuine. But he believed that the new set of claims (amounting, as he said, to "two million four hundred thousand pounds") constituted a "gigantic phantom of debt." He proclaimed that

> the nawab of Arcot and his creditors are not adversaries, but collusive parties, and . . . the whole transaction is under a false color and false names. The litigation is not, nor ever has been, between their rapacity and his hoarded riches. No: it is between him and them combining and confeder-

ating, on one side, and the public revenues, and the miserable inhabitants of a ruined country.[6]

As he continued, Burke exclaimed, "It is therefore not from treasuries and mines, but from the food of your unpaid armies, from the blood withheld from the veins, and whipt out of the backs of the most miserable of men, that we are to pamper extortion, usury, and peculation, under the false names of debtors and creditors of state."[7] Burke targeted the beneficiaries as the "Arcot interest" and singled out Paul Benfield once again as the "chief proprietor, as well as the chief agent, director, and controller of this system of debt."[8] Benfield's claims had been said to range between £500,000 and £800,000, and meanwhile he also had a regular income of around £150,000 solely from interest and commissions from a wide range of transactions on behalf of other parties. And he had used his fortune well, securing, Burke charged, the support of both Dundas and Pitt in his parliamentary bid of 1780. "Every trust, every honour, every distinction, was to be heaped upon him, Benfield. He was at once made a director of the India Company; made an alderman of London; and to be made, if ministry could prevail (and I am sorry to say how near, how very near they were prevailing) representative of the capital of this kingdom."[9] In the end, Benfield was only able to buy the Cricklade seat—though that was enough to incense Burke. He believed that Benfield had not only secured this seat by purchase but that he had funded seats of up to eight others. This was a perversion of the very political process Burke had earlier sought to protect the company against. But now he had seen how this process could be perverted and defiled. As he put it in his speech, "a single Benfield outweighs them all: a criminal, who long ago ought to have fattened the region kites with his offal, is by his Majesty's ministers enthroned in the government of a great kingdom, and enfeoffed with an estate which in the comparison effaces the splendor of all the nobility of Europe."[10]

Burke was going straight after the new Pitt ministry, as he attacked it for being "a standing auxiliary to the oppression, usury, and peculation of multitudes, in order to obtain a corrupt support to their power."[11] Despite his strenuous efforts, Parliament once again ignored his plea. It is perhaps not too far-fetched to argue that Burke turned to Hastings—a man who was far more like him and hardly a scoundrel in any way to be compared to Benfield—solely because Benfield himself was, at least at the time, invulnerable, and out of frustration over his inability to move Parliament to go after the real crooks and excesses of company rule. Although I hinted at this in my book, I don't think I fully grasped the extent to which Burke's ire might be seen in retrospect as most properly being directed at Madras, at the unholy alliance between the Arcot nawab and the British. For the debts of the nawab were indeed paid, while the nawab continued to make loans and incur new debts even after 1785, occasioning the need to establish another commission of inquiry in the early years of the nineteenth century. If Burke ended his career, and life, as the great regulator of the late eighteenth century, it was surely not least because he saw the financial crises associated with the company as rooted in the corrupt appropriation of sovereignty by the interests of commerce under the auspices of the company-state, a horrific betrayal of his earlier conviction that the state would reach too far if it sought to regulate commerce. This betrayal was in fact far more vivid and fundamental than those that motivated the actual articles of impeachment invoked in the trial of Warren Hastings.

We now know how early it was that the company sought to take on the full apparatus of state function and authority, to claim sovereignty as well as the instruments of statecraft, long before the ambitions of Clive used the victories of Plassey and Buxar to justify the political triumph of the Diwani grant.[12] It is of course peculiar, in the context of this reminder of Burke's later sense of betrayal, how Burke was able to sustain the notion as late as the mid-1770s that the company was fundamentally a commercial enterprise, a pure expression of the trading firm that needed protection from the regulatory control of the (metropolitan) state. We know, too, that this was partly his political subservience to the Rockingham faction's own views as well as a logical consequence of his early belief that the conceits of Indian sovereignty—whether that of the Mughal, the nawab, or the raja—were not in conflict with the commercial interests and circumscribed nature of company activities in India. But I take Burke at his word: it would be unfair to him to assume that his ire at the company was only the result of feeling either hoodwinked or controlled by forces he had to exorcise in the tragic failure of the trial. After all, the success of company ideology and the sustainability of this ideology in the oft-repeated imperial claim that the company was only belatedly and against its will forced into assuming a political character was in large part the result of the fact that it seemed to be true to large sections of the British public, at least until the scandals of the east forced the reevaluations and reforms of the late eighteenth century. At the same time, the issue before us here is nothing less than one of the major conundrums of eighteenth-century political and economic theory.[13] Were commerce (especially global commerce) and sovereignty separable? Were the ascendant political defenses of trade and commercial enterprise driven by, compatible with, or justifications for the growing imperial interest of European powers? Was Adam Smith being disingenuous—especially given the imperial climate of his times—when he wrote that it was in the interest of sovereigns to "allow the most perfect freedom of commerce"?[14]

Smith's enduring embrace of the free market in fact was for him deeply tied to his critique of the East India Company, believing it likely to lead to disastrous consequences for India. Referring to the Regulating Act of 1773, he noted:

> It is a very singular government in which every member of the administration wishes to get out of the country, and consequently to have done with the government, as soon as he can, and to whose interest, the day after he has left it and carried his whole fortune with him, it is perfectly indifferent though the whole country was swallowed up by an earthquake.[15]

Sovereignty could only be genuinely exercised by people who were likely to stick around for the long haul, and in any case it was not to be used to govern decisions having to do with trade and production. As he famously asserted, monopolies and markets were in fundamental contradiction, and the East India Company was the worst kind of monopoly. But as regulation and reform began to bring the excesses of company servants under control, the company itself became even more like a state and less like a trading firm. Ironically, calls for free trade became the cover for the return and efflorescence of private trade, the success of reform the basis for the steady diminution of the company role in economic activity. The company survived the challenges of Burke and Smith, but as time went on the company was not so much taken over by the state as it was turned into the state. Whether in the hands of Cornwallis, Wellesley, Bentinck, or Dalhousie, the company negotiated issues around sovereignty, empire, and global trade in ways that hardly resolved the moral contradictions of eighteenth-century company rule. Ironically, all this led inexorably to the dissolution and demise of the company itself and the gradual slide into direct British rule. The company might have set the terms for the British state in India, but it could not survive its origins in the conceit of free trade, even under imperial conditions of monopoly capitalism.

By the time of the charter renewal debates of 1813—a time when the great moral issues around renewal were directed to the civilizing mission of the company and the moral degradation implied by customs such as sati—the argument for a continued monopoly was destined to fail. Meanwhile, the fiscal crises of the company, unresolved by the projected increases in revenue from new and improved land revenue settlements, only led to greater indebtedness and deficit financing. The company-state qua state could no longer control either the imperative toward militaristic expansion (and the escalating costs associated with this) or the proliferation of private trading that stretched across India, beyond the three presidencies, even as it secured ever greater global interdependence in regions well beyond direct imperial control. Strangely, as Philip Lawson has observed, the one trade monopoly retained by the company was that to China in tea, only a few years before "an addendum to the East India Company's main trading interest in India."[16] The big story of the nineteenth-century company-state was that it soon became a shadow state for Britain, no longer a potential competitor either to the sovereign interests of Parliament or to the commercial interests of British traders. The assumption of direct British rule by Victoria in 1858 resolved at least one great moral conundrum, one that Burke would have continued to be exercised about had he lived longer, but it was in the end almost anticlimactic. The trial of Bahadur Shah had none of the significance in Britain as did the trial of Warren Hastings; it was a hurriedly held military commission based on contradictory arguments about treason and fear-mongering assertions about an international Islamic conspiracy. The slumped and often slumbering figure of the last of the Mughals gave vivid testimony to the fact that the old regime was already over, despite the high symbolic importance of deposing the Mughal Emperor and assuming direct royal rule over India. It also made clear that the eighteenth-century critique of empire had been strangely resolved by the full embrace of empire by the British state.

The company-state thus became, slowly but surely as the eighteenth century gave way to the nineteenth, the colonial state par excellence. This transformation was far less a break than an evolutionary process in which the moral rebukes of Burke, Smith, and other eighteenth-century critics were accommodated but fundamentally unaddressed by a refashioning of the economic functions of the company. While the formal monopoly was once used both to curtail competition from outside (by restricting the India trade to the company) and inside (by extending company privileges to company traders engaged in private trade), as well as to organize the putative scope and responsibilities of the company bureaucracy, it was steadily whittled away by the needs of an expansionist state and an emerging global market. Economic monopoly was converted into imperial sovereignty in large part so that the excesses and scandals of eighteenth-century greed and peculation could be first controlled and then released from the controls of the monopoly form. Debates over monopoly gave way to debates over sovereignty, and as Indian nationalism was born in the years after the great rebellion, these debates took on a different life of their own. It is worth returning to those early debates, for they afford us an opportunity to rethink the history of the company, and all that it represented, in relation to our current predicament around the role and scale of states and markets in our contemporary political economy. All the ingredients were there— massive public indebtedness, escalating levels of deficit financing, incessant military overextension, moral crusades (many of them completely unrelated to the real issues of the day), market mechanisms that seemed to encourage private greed and malfeasance while evading any effort to fix accountability and responsibility on the guilty parties, even, in some of the revenue instruments traded in Madras and Tanjore, the equivalent of collateralized debt obligations around mortgages and loans that everyone knew would never actually end in private default.

It is always tempting to view the past far too much in relation to the present, but I do believe that at this juncture and in this place a new history of the East India Company will be of interest to a much broader public than many might at first think. Not that the lessons will all be encouraging, since we learn once again how halting and inadequate reforms have been and how easily the structures of scandal find other outlets and institutional avenues to reemerge and even on occasion to flourish, checked if never really abated. But the company-state is a salutary case for rethinking the history both of the state and of global capitalism, especially as it makes clear the fuzzy boundary between the two in the emergent global context of the long eighteenth century. If the company cast itself as a vital rival to the British and Indian state alike, it did so not only as a monopoly trading firm but as an umbrella for private trade that, before as well as after the reforms, neither welcomed nor produced anything resembling the genuine conditions of a free market. Even in its attenuated nineteenth-century form, the company was more important for providing the base on which the colonial state was designed than it was for detaching global enterprise from the political interests of imperial rule.

It is bracing to remember that Adam Smith, the appointed apostle of neoliberalism, was not only deeply skeptical about the monopolistic constitution of the company but actually held that the corruption of the company and its traders was endemic to imperial conditions. We can also take heart from the moral passion of a figure like Burke, who is too readily pigeonholed as a cranky and reactive political conservative for his contemporaneous writings on the French Revolution. Burke was able to overcome his early faith in the unregulated workings of both empire and the market and spend his final years mounting a campaign to protect the principles of sovereignty and commercial exchange in the larger context of a coherent, if in the end unrealizable, faith in the goals of political perfectibility and social progress. Burke's brilliant career was of course tempered by failure, first in his inability to press charges against Benfield and then in his failure to convert the spectacular theater of the trial of Warren Hastings into a successful prosecution. But Burke's failure is a salient reminder that the political, economic, and moral issues raised by the recent financial crisis should not be allowed simply to fade away in the face of the current assault on the state and the single issue of debt. We historians have an opportunity to bring the company back in, not just into older debates about expanding global markets and imperial rule but into the current debate around the state, the market, and the associated issues of corruption, debt, and moral responsibility. This, indeed, is Edmund Burke's enduring provocation.

9

The Idea of Empire

When Michael Hardt and Antonio Negri published their influential book, *Empire*, in 2000, it seemed unexceptional to many readers to assume that the term "empire" could be wrested away from its old meaning to apply to a new organizing principle for the global capitalist social order they described.[1] The age of empire had given way to the age of globalization, with the demise of the Cold War, dramatic changes in the European Union, the increasing spread and reach of international organizations, the economic rise of China and India, and clear indications of the potential power of new postnational social and political movements. As timely as the book first appeared to be, both for its critique of the sufficiency of national sovereignty as the basis for global rights, justice, and welfare, and for its utopian evocation of the prospect of new global political structures, it soon became clear that the older meaning of empire had hardly become irrelevant. The fallout from 9/11 and the panic about the political aspirations of some forms of Islamic fundamentalism had the ironic effect of recuperating the old idea of empire, at least for a time. The historian Niall Ferguson was quick to instruct U.S. policy makers that the British Empire, for all its problems, constituted a powerful historical model for goals that were still relevant: the spread of free trade and global prosperity as well as the cultivation of democracy. In naming America's presence in the world as "imperial," Ferguson sought both to rescue the idea of empire from its postcolonial stigma of shame and to remind Americans that if they were to understand the real lessons of history, they would not only become more imperial but more British.[2]

Although Ferguson's pious suggestion was consonant with the hopes and dreams of some in the Bush administration—especially Cheney, Wolfowitz, and Perle—and had the short-lived support of commentators such as Michael Ignatieff, it turned out there was little appetite either within the Beltway or on Main Street for reliving the glory days of the Raj and profound suspicion about the idea that empire should be overtly championed as a legitimate goal of U.S. foreign policy.[3] While imperial debates over nation building, extraterritoriality, warfare, and sovereignty had echoes in the years of conflict in Iraq and Afghanistan, the idea of empire never really caught on. It was still the case, as William Langer, a Harvard historian and a critical figure first in the Office of Strategic Services during World War II and then in the postwar CIA, wrote, that "the idea of empire is dead, and no one in this country, so far as I know, believes that the security of the United States can be strengthened by direct control of foreign peoples."[4]

If Ferguson's contemporaneous embrace of empire ultimately failed to provide a new charter for American foreign policy, it nevertheless signaled a shift in the historical judgment about empire among many academics who had increasingly lost interest in the full-bore critique that had begun in the wake of the protests around the war in Vietnam. Imperial historians in the United States started emphasizing the dialogic exchanges of imperial relationships more than the domination and hegemony that characterized these relationships, rescuing the "agency" of imperial subjects who had been suppressed less by empire than by critics of empire. Despite the fact that the American wars in the Middle East—and Ferguson's call to the imperial burden—reminded some historians of the need to call attention to the dangerous pitfalls of imperial history, the overwhelming reaction was to complicate empire by naturalizing it as an artifact of a particular moment in history, arguing not only that empire was a legitimate form of sovereignty in the eighteenth and nineteenth centuries but that in empire's earliest days it was less malignant than often thought, a force for progressive change and a prelude to modernization and democratization. Conrad's famous denunciation of Belgian colonialism in *Heart of Darkness* gave way to romantic stories of the connections, intimate and otherwise, between colonizers and colonized, when they didn't reverse the tables completely in the depiction of the colonized as captives.[5] Even E. M. Forster's sensitive critique of empire in *Passage to India*—he concluded his great novel by lamenting that true friendship between colonizers and colonized would be impossible as long as empire continued—seemed an extreme view belied by example after example of friendship and love.[6]

I began *The Scandal of Empire* with the claim that empire in India was a problem from the start, though I emphasized in that work (in marked contrast to earlier books where I focused on the view from India) that the problem was recognized in the metropole as much as—if not more than—it was in the colony.[7] I asserted in particular that empire in India was born in scandal for the colonizers as well as the colonized. I used the extraordinary drama of the impeachment trial of Warren Hastings (1786–1795) as the narrative fulcrum for a larger story about the origins and transformation of empire, exploring categories such as corruption, spectacle, economy, sovereignty, state, history, and tradition. The trial of Warren Hastings—prosecuted so valiantly by Edmund Burke—was a spectacular pretext for exploring a larger historical conundrum. How was it that when the trial opened in 1786 it was the greatest spectacle in late eighteenth-century Britain: an event that captured and crystallized decades of anxiety, envy, consternation, and scorn at the role of India, and the East India Company, in the generation of wealth and power for a new generation of returned Britons. That early imperial activity might have led to the consequent despoliation of India—whether seen in the massive famine in the rice bowl of Bengal (witnessed by many in Britain because of the global stock market crash caused by the bursting of a speculative bubble based on fantasies of the agricultural riches of India) or the destruction of circuits of trade that had sustained both the conspicuous wealth of the Mughal empire and the developing networks of global exchange across the Indian Ocean all the way to the port cities of China—might have been less important than the local effects of empire, but they were the stock in trade of local debate. How then was it that, when the trial closed in 1795, not only was Hastings acquitted but England snored through the final deliberations? How, in other words, and despite Burke's eloquent, ferocious, and much heralded assault on the East India Company, did empire become acceptable for the nineteenth, and indeed much of the twentieth, European centuries? And was it the case that, despite Burke's evident scorn for the actions of the men who became known as "Nabobs" in eighteenth-century Britain, his attack played an unintentional role in the cleansing of the imperial ideal for a new kind of imperial rule—with the metropolitan state explicitly taking over the previous role played by trading companies and commercial exchange? As I asked in my book, how did Burke's rage become so quickly absorbed by the historical logic of empire?

Burke was not always committed to the reform of Britain's imperial relationship with India. He began his political career as a member of the Rockingham faction, supporting the corrupt but victorious Robert Clive—self-appointed "founder" of the British empire in India, and also the richest man in England as a result—during the parliamentary hearings on the financial and political corruption of East India Company affairs in 1772. As a member of the opposition party, however, Burke became known as a critic of empire in his attitude toward the Americas, where he consistently supported the colonists, and became exercised in particular about the abrogation of civil rights and other punitive responses to rebellion in Britain's efforts to stem the tide of secessionist and then revolutionary fervor. He was also well known for his virulent critique of the Protestant Ascendancy in Ireland. Despite writing a long defense in 1777 of a Hindu kingdom in southern India against the predatory designs of a Muslim nawab—whose debts had proved such a lucrative basis for the enrichment of company officials in Madras—he did not turn systematically against the company until the early years of the 1780s. In those years he became increasingly focused on—some have said obsessed with—India. Burke spent the last decade of his life in the vain effort to impeach the governor-general of Bengal, Warren Hastings—when he wasn't, that is, writing tracts fulminating against the perversion of liberty in France and the ignominy of revolutionary violence in the attack on the French monarchy and all that was fundamental to its ancient constitution.

When Burke shifted his interests to India, he noted that

we find the greatest difficulties in the exclusive administration of that vast, heterogeneous, intricate Mass of Interests, which at this day forms the Body of the British Power. Under any form of government, this would be difficult; under ours, it comes to be a matter of the greatest complexity; because, in an hundred instances, the Interest of our Empire is scarcely to be reconciled to the Interest of our Constitution.[8]

For Burke, the ancient constitution represented what he considered to be a paramount value, both because it expressed the necessary traditions that had been forged through English history and because it was in manifest accord with universal principles to which he gave a natural or even divine justification.

Burke never attacked the idea of empire itself. In all of his impassioned assaults on the abuses and corruption of East India Company officials, he maintained his belief that England could rule India in conformance both to the dictates of its own ancient constitution and India's. Although he was very clear that India had an ancient constitution of its own, he was never precise about what it really was. Even as he began his writings about India with a certain degree of consternation about the possibility that Muslim rulers could establish political legitimacy with Hindu subjects, he never fully accepted that company officials could subordinate their commercial interests to the high standards of England's ancient constitution, let alone India's. This was part of his deep concern about the fundamental entailments of commerce itself, for Burke never fully succumbed to the enthusiasm of the Scottish Enlightenment for the positive (and even necessary) relationship of commercial exchange and cross-cultural sympathy. As he bitterly said in his speech on Mr. Fox's East India Bill in 1783:

In India, all the vices operate by which sudden fortune is acquired; . . . Arrived in England, the destroyers of the nobility and gentry of a whole kingdom will find the best company in this nation, at a board of elegance and hospitality. Here the manufacturer and the husbandman will bless the just and punctual hand, that in India has torn the cloth from the loom, or wrested the scanty portion of rice and salt from the peasants of Bengal, or wrung from him the very opium in which he forgot his oppressions and his oppressor.[9]

His greatest concern about commerce—both in Britain and in India—
emerged when it seemed able to make sovereignty itself an element of
exchange. As he put it in the same speech, the company had "sold" the
Mughal emperor:

> The first potentate sold by the Company for money was the Great Mo-
> gul,—the descendant of Tamerlane. This high personage, as high as hu-
> man veneration can look at, is by every account amiable in his manners,
> respectable for his piety, according to his mode, and accomplished in all
> the Oriental literature. All this, and the title derived under his charter to
> all that we hold in India, could not save him from the general sale. Money
> is coined in his name; in his name justice is administered; he is prayed
> for in every temple through the countries we possess;—but he was sold.[10]

And if the company demeaned Mughal sovereignty, it did worse for
Britain. He was irate that the East India Company's status was represented as being "merely a Company formed for the extension of the British Commerce" when it was, in reality, "a delegation of the whole power
and sovereignty of this kingdom sent into the East."[11] This for Burke was
unconscionable, and it was this sense of betrayal and deception regarding principles of sovereignty that led to Burke's devotion of the last decade of his life to a cause that seemed, in the eyes of many of his contemporaries, extraneous to his truest political convictions and ambitions.[12]

India was critical in eighteenth-century Britain for everything from
the emergence and development of financial markets—the second-
largest number of shares traded on Exchange Alley were attached to
company operations—to the major geopolitical blow represented by
the loss of the American colonies. It was a place, increasingly *the* place,
where individual careers could be sought and fortunes could be made.
It was also a growing source of public revenue for the British military-
fiscal state—at war repeatedly with the French over the long eighteenth
century—even as it was the principal site of global conflict over commerce as well as geopolitical advantage. It was also a site of conspicuous
corruption; the three most important parliamentary inquiries in England into public corruption throughout the entire century concerned the
company. The first two of these involved Lord Robert Clive; the third
was the impeachment trial of Warren Hastings. While it is arguable that

the widespread focus on company corruption was in part an elaborate displacement of the growing concern about old corruption at home onto the more distant and therefore less dangerous forms of corruption overseas, the sense of scandal was palpable. It was conveyed as much by the inability of the historian Robert Orme to complete his great history of India for fear that his heroic account would be sullied by the "money story" of the 1760s and 1770s as it was by the fact that Burke turned his attention almost single-mindedly to India for the last decade of his life.[13] If empire seemed a natural political form, there was a widespread perception in Britain that the East India Company was rotten to the core. Burke's persistent refrain that empire was in theory okay, a political ideal that could be realized in accord with universal political principles and moral precepts, was perhaps as much a reflection of the need to hold all politics to a higher standard as it was an effort to suggest that empire was in fact worth the risk of undermining the entire political fabric of Britain at home as well as abroad. While he clearly shared Gibbon's view that empire would inexorably lead to decline and fall if it continued the way it was going, ever since his plea for conciliation in America he had argued for a form of empire that seemed an impossible ideal.[14] His "idea of an Empire" was an "aggregate of many states, under one common head," in which "the subordinate parts have many local privileges and immunities" and in which "a claim of Liberty" would never be "tantamount to high treason."[15] And it was also a plea that political morality be accorded priority over abstract claims about economic virtue.

For Burke, the constitution encoded not just abstract laws but also the particular genealogies of history, tradition, and place. As he said, the nation itself is "not an idea only of local extent, and individual momentary aggregation; but it is an idea of continuity, which extends in time as well as in numbers and in space."[16] Each nation was therefore different according to its own history of development and accommodation, and while some were more evolved, as well as doubtless more in line with natural or divine principle, the insistence on the particularity of sovereign forms was part of what made him suspect that the commercial interest of the company could never be the proper basis of imperial rule in India. Hastings was far less a rogue imperialist than Clive—he was in many respects the official who crafted the foundations of a colonial state that long outlived the mercantilist origins of empire—but more than anything else he came to represent the British disregard for India's sovereignty. Burke might have worried most about the implications of this disregard on the English constitution itself—even as what worried him most about the French Revolution was what it might mean for emergent forms of democracy at home—but in the end his commitment to the ancient constitution made his conservatism on the subject of sovereignty seem almost radical in comparison to his contemporaries in England and Europe.

Burke was certainly not the only eighteenth-century thinker concerned with sovereignty, but as British political theory steadily provided a more capacious justification for the establishment of Parliament's authority, it also accommodated itself to a Westphalian commitment to international relations that could only apply to Europe (not unlike Churchill's Atlantic Charter two centuries later). Meanwhile, the great thinkers of the Scottish Enlightenment underwrote the expanding age of commerce through their liberal understanding of the relationship between sympathy and exchange. Not all was uncomplicated, as even Adam Smith was concerned to dismantle mercantilism in part because of a concern about the untidy conflation of sovereign and commercial interests in places like India. But Burke seemed far more exercised than his contemporaries with the way both public trade and private interest undermined clear commitments to sovereignty both at home and abroad. Claims for liberty must never be charged with treason.

If Burke was so exercised about the assault on Indian sovereignty by Hastings and the East India Company, we might predict that he would have been relieved when Queen Victoria announced direct rule over India in 1858. Finally, the British Crown dismantled the unwieldy structure of dual sovereignty, dispensing in one neat blow with the pathetic fiction that the East India Company was the legitimate arbiter of British control over the Indian subcontinent while nominally conceding ultimate sovereignty to the Mughal emperor, by then in any case only called the king of Delhi. Burke would doubtless have been deeply troubled by the violence of the attacks on British men and women in the events stemming from the Meerut Mutiny of 1857, and he would certainly have recognized the diminution in the political authority of the Mughal ruler. The British had progressively curbed the real power of the Mughals, withholding tribute, declaring Shah Alam a pensioner of the British when they rescued him in Delhi from Maratha assault, and restricting the movements and the influence of the last emperor, Bahadur Shah, from the time he assumed the throne in 1838. The Mughals may have been kept, but they were kept on thrones, for the very reason stated by the governor-general, Marquis Wellesley, shortly after the British stormed Delhi in 1803: "Notwithstanding His Majesty's total deprivation of real power, dominion, and authority, almost every state and every class of people in India continue to acknowledge his nominal sovereignty. The current coin of every established power is struck in the name of Shah Aulum."[17] Things had not changed in that respect from Burke's time. Bahadur Shah spent his declining days writing Urdu poetry rather than ruling India, but the fiction of dual sovereignty was allowed to continue both because it was convenient and, especially given the peculiar status of the company as the vehicle for British imperial rule, necessary.

Burke had been critical of Hastings's expansionist policy in India, his ill-fated efforts to contain the Marathas, and his disregard for sovereign treaties and understandings. But soon after Burke's disappearance from the scene—Burke died, exhausted and disappointed, soon after the great trial concluded in 1795—the policy of expansion and annexation picked up steam once again, especially under Lord Wellesley in the early years of the nineteenth century, and then a half-century later with Lord Dalhousie, who finally assumed control over the kingdom of Awadh in the heartland of Mughal power and Indian agricultural wealth in 1856. This final annexation was soon followed by a military mutiny, which itself led to a series of revolts across northern and western India. Delhi was the scene of the most dramatic moment in the great revolt, when the Meerut mutineers converged on the Red Fort to declare their fealty to Bahadur Shah. Soon after the British retook Delhi in October 1857, they put the last Mughal emperor on trial in the Red Fort, the last seat of Mughal authority. In January 1858, a British court held that the elderly, weak, and often dazed emperor was in fact the agent of a rebellion over which he appeared to have little real control—even as he had earlier been held to be the agent of company sovereignty in a parallel doubling of kingly authority and impotence under mid-nineteenth-century conditions of colonial occupation. Bahadur Shah dozed through much of the trial, which would have convicted him to death had he not been promised a reprieve from capital punishment when he gave himself up.

The charge was treason: "For that he, being a subject of the British Government in India, and not regarding the duty of his allegiance, did, at Delhi, on the 11th of May, 1857, or thereabouts, as a false traitor against the State, proclaim and declare himself the reigning king and sovereign of India."[18]

The trial itself was by any standard a mockery of British justice. While it was clear that the mutiny was sparked by the distress of (mostly) Hindu sepoys at the introduction of a new cartridge encased in animal fat, it was equally clear that this affront had only lubricated growing discontent over matters of military discipline and policy in a wider field of panic and outrage about the British presence in India, especially the growing level of proselytizing missionary activity and the annexation of Awadh. The trial summarily dispensed with these concerns as if they were unthinkably absurd. Instead of taking seriously significant evidence of widespread disaffection, the British charged Bahadur Shah with masterminding an Islamic revolt. Since no political rationality or cause could be conceded, the king was charged "rather as the head of the Mahommedan religion in India than as the descendant of a line of Kings."[19] In language that bears uncanny comparison to sentiments freely expressed in the last decade, Major Harriott asserted that

> the known restless spirit of Mahommedan fanaticism has been the first aggressor, the vindictive intolerance of that peculiar faith has been struggling for mastery, seditious conspiracy has been its means, the prisoner its active accomplice, and every possible crime the frightful result. . . . Thus the bitter zeal of Mahommedanism meets us everywhere. It is conspicuous in the papers, flagrant in the petitions, and perfectly demoniac in its actions.[20]

The trial was enabled by the atrocity stories of the Meerut Mutiny, the siege of the Residency in Lucknow, the massacre of British women and men in Kanpur, and in particular the deaths of forty-nine men, women, and children of European and mixed European descent in Delhi on May 16, 1857. But the real issue at stake was sovereignty, and accordingly Bahadur Shah had to be charged with masterminding both the mutiny and the massacre. Harriott, the British prosecutor, put it like this:

There was a previous preparation among the sepoys; and there was also a general unsettling of men's minds throughout the country, and among the Mahommedans in particular. . . . Coupling this with the prophecy among the Mahommedans that English sovereignty in India was to cease 100 years after its first establishment by the battle of Plassey in 1757, we are able to form something more than conjecture as to the causes which have given to Mahommedan fanaticism its delusive hope of recovering all its former prestige. . . . I have endeavoured to point out how intimately the prisoner, as the head of the Mahommedan faith in India, has been connected with the organization of that conspiracy either as its leader or its unscrupulous accomplice.[21]

Since the emperor had power and influence as a Muslim rather than as a sovereign ruler, there was no contradiction in the British charge of treason. The threat in India was fanaticism, a Mahommedan conspiracy, rather than a political revolt based on social, cultural, and economic issues that reflected on the nature of British rule, and certainly not based on any efforts on the part of the British to introduce Christianity by force (a claim that was debunked by noting that there could be no such thing as the forcible introduction of Christian beliefs).

Harriott referred to "this possessor of mere nominal royalty" as a religious head in language that seemed deliberately to refute any thought that there might be a larger political claim either against British rule or on behalf of Indian sovereignty.[22] The British held that after 1803, when they took then-emperor Shah Alam under their protection, the Mughals forfeited all real claims to sovereignty. Shah Alam had petitioned for protection at that fateful moment only eight years after the cessation of the Warren Hastings trial, and according to Harriott, protection

was accorded, and from that moment, the titular Kings of Delhi became pensioned subjects of the British. . . . The English, under Lord Lake, appeared as his deliverers, and with generous sympathy for his misfortunes, bestowed on him rank and pension which, continued to his successors, have maintained them in honour and in influence, till, like the snake in the fable, they have turned their fangs upon those to whom they owed the very means of their existence.[23]

The problem with that argument, of course, was that it ran up against what at the time had been a false front, a carefully kept deception. The British never proclaimed at the time what they later claimed, namely that the Mughal emperors had lost their sovereignty in the crisis of 1803 (nor would it have been unusual for a vassal to play a key role in restoring an emperor to the throne after such a grievous attack).

Nevertheless, by the time of the Meerut Mutiny, most Britons seem to have forgotten that they were dissembling, and although there were British observers of the trial who clearly knew the charges against Bahadur Shah to be trumped up, there was little sense of embarrassment when Victoria assumed direct rule after all this was over. Bahadur Shah was simultaneously declared to be a fiction of the Indian imaginary and an agent of "Mahommedan" insurgency. The trial transcript is an unsettling document to this day, and not just because of the charge of an international Islamic conspiracy. The document gives testimony to an explicit erasure of the political contradictions inhabiting the British occupation of India, the displacement of real political grievances and issues on to charges of religious fanaticism, and the seamless translation of economic interest and military might into political right. The trial worked first to transpose sovereign authority, however diminished, into treason, and then to transform commercial interest into the newly fashioned sovereign authority of empire. Burke would have rejected both.

Leaving Burke aside (for a moment), the explicit eighteenth-century concerns with sovereignty as a central issue in political theory and for European states largely vanished in the great imperial nineteenth century. Significantly, when the Cambridge imperial historian J. R. Seeley predicted in his lectures of the 1870s that European empires would soon give way to the much more effective empire nation-states of Russia and the United States—where contiguous space and sovereign claims would not present the political, economic, and social difficulties of overseas empires—there was a foreshadowing of how sovereignty might become an issue in an era of imperial overreach.[24] Sovereignty only really resurfaced as a major concern in the next century with the rise of colonial nationalism in Asia (and then Africa) and the European tensions that led to the First World War.

Sovereignty was, in fact, the key issue of the twentieth century, as it played itself out through the steady delegitimization of the idea of empire and the mapping of regional, ethnic, and religious struggles onto cartographic nationalisms. In India, it was hardly surprising that when there was another momentous trial in the Red Fort, in 1946, a clear case of treason turned out to be judged as about nationalism rather than merely a grievous breach of military discipline. Three members of the Indian National Army (INA)—soldiers in the British Army who had been taken prisoner by the Japanese after the fall of Singapore and then were released to fight the British under the leadership of Subhas Chandra Bose—were put on trial for waging war against the king-emperor of India. Defended by nationalist lawyers, including Jawaharlal Nehru, they were acquitted of charges of being responsible for murder, allowing them to be released from jail with nothing other than dishonorable discharges and proscriptions on collecting further military salary or pension. Whereas an imperial century before, Bahadur Shah was transported to Burma for the rest of his life for purported treason against the king, the soldiers of the INA were brought back from Burma and made into national heroes despite declaring that they had waged war against England.

Burke would assuredly not have approved of the INA, but I can't imagine that he would have objected to the nationalist claims of the colonized in India any more than he did in the case of America two centuries earlier. By then, of course, Burke's views were hardly relevant, except as a classic British figure whose fiery orations against British corruption and excess were read as inspirational by many Indian schoolchildren before and after independence. My point here, though, is somewhat different. As Burke has been invoked in subsequent political thought, it was of course his reflections on the French revolution that became increasingly significant, as he was seen as a voice of tradition and sometimes even reaction in the face of student movements, communist desire for revolution, guerilla warfare, and general social unrest. Burke's views on sovereignty ceased to be critical even to canonical histories of Western political thought, but so did most other concerns with sovereignty in a body of critical theory increasingly dominated from the 1960s and 1970s on the one side by Derridean poststructuralism and on the other by Althusser, Gramsci, Foucault, and other theorists of power, the state, and "governmentality." It was in this context that "postcolonial interventions" were chiefly responsible for keeping theoretical concerns with sovereignty alive, championing clear postcolonial desires to achieve the full promise of nationalism against the backdrop of increasing cynicism about the nation, which reminded Western readers of the traumatic and crippling legacies of colonial rule. The publication of Ranajit Guha's "Dominance Without Hegemony" in 1992 made clear that postcolonial perspectives were not about to let go of the concern to keep sovereignty as a key category for thinking through the legacies of empire at a time when general critiques both of nation-states and of liberal theories of sovereignty were achieving their own form of dominance.[25]

The fall of the Soviet Union and the demise of the Cold War provided a new backdrop for thinking about sovereignty, however, as the United States became a new kind of world power without the territorial extensions of empire. Postcolonial critiques of empire finally could be connected with global suspicion about the "new world order" aspirations of the United States. Hardt and Negri's critical proposals about a new idea of empire reflected a widespread desire to fashion new forms of sovereignty that would transcend the flawed nation-state, a judgment now increasingly seen as applying not just to the former imperial powers but also to the once colonized states. Benjamin had once been read for his critical sense of the modern, but he began to be seen more in terms of his role in generating the idea of the "state of exception," as Carl Schmitt's critique of liberal sovereignty was dusted off and recuperated via Benjamin and Agamben.[26] Schmitt's observations about sovereignty through his stark acceptance of the logic of friends and enemies (and his associated sense of the fundamental if hidden necessity for the transcendence of sovereign authority as well as his critique of Anglo-American legal imperialism) connected to Agamben's preoccupation with the growing population of subjects effaced from sovereign concern and protection. Out of this conjuncture, Negri's anarchist sensibilities (his sympathy with the "multitude," as he put it) and new forms of global social movements emerged as fundamental to the critical theoretical landscape of the new era of global capitalism launched in the 1990s.

As these new political and critical aspirations increasingly propelled new formulations about global sovereignty, the use of the tragic events of 9/11 to justify warfare on the part of the United States has made clear that political theory is lagging far behind economic theory in this, our global age. While there have been few measurable advances in imagining new transnational forms of sovereignty, there is growing fear in

Western circles that the hegemony of the West (and most recently the United States) will be replaced not by new structures and organizations but rather by newly powerful nation-states, most significantly China, that are on the rise economically, demographically, politically, and militarily. In the end, the full delegitimation of empire may await the transfer of imperial power from West to East, from former colonizer to former colonized. Ironically, the conservative Edmund Burke would have had no trouble accommodating such a massive world shift of power within his own theoretical vocabulary, however much he might have been horrified by any divergence from his ideal construction of the ancient English constitution. In the end, Burke's idea of empire was so elevated above the real conditions of imperial possibility that he would not explicitly tether empire to any particular nation, culture, or constitution.

What would it mean to live in a truly postimperial world? Are there elements of empire that might still, *pace* Hardt and Negri, be useful in imagining a new kind of global sovereignty, this time attached to international organizations that either are connected to the United Nations or, as many now would prefer, grow out of a different kind of multinational process or set of movements? More to my point here, what kind of history of empire should be written at a time when empire's end is genuinely imminent? At a moment when the memory of empire is dim and the immediate and most devastating consequences mediated by a growing expanse of postcolonial time, does the polemic of Burke—a polemic that strangely foreshadowed the most severe critics of empire in the postcolonial mode—have any residual utility or force? And do the distinctions made by historians such as Guha—who insisted on the clear divide between liberal nation and despotic empire—make sense any longer, now that we must negotiate new claims for postnational sovereignty that tend to blur distinctions and make the separation between hegemony and dominance ever more precarious? And given the wildly different scale of power and influence attached to different nations and economies of the world, should the critique of hegemony be in any event tempered, if only to make possible new forms of international consensus and cooperation, inevitably flawed though they might be?

I end this chapter as I began this book, by reflecting on the peculiar role of the United States in the post–World War II context and its importance for shaping not just my own scholarly perspectives but many of the conditions of current thought about states, nations, empires, and, now increasingly, global markets. It is well known that Roosevelt's decision to enter World War II—a decision forced upon him by the Japanese attack on Pearl Harbor but long anticipated as Roosevelt saw the threat to Great Britain posed by Hitler's imperial ambition—effectively ended the era of isolationism and general opposition to aggressive and expansionist foreign policy (despite tacit assumptions about the need to preserve American interests in parts of Latin America and the Philippines). What is less well known is that Roosevelt himself was nevertheless deeply opposed to Britain's imperial position in the world and wished to see it neither preserved after the war nor inherited by the United States in the postwar shuffle of world power. Roosevelt developed an especially critical view of Britain's empire in India, nurtured by growing concern on his part that the Japanese representations of their mission as anti-Western (and anti-imperial) would find a receptive audience in India as they developed their foothold in southeast Asia and marched across Malaya and then Burma on their way to take on Britain in Asia. Some historians have noted that the most serious disagreements between Churchill and Roosevelt—dwarfing their differences of opinion about direct engagement in Europe—concerned India, leading to one exchange in which Churchill threatened to resign as prime minister in response to Roosevelt's insistence on decolonization.

In the end, Roosevelt had to back away from his most virulent anti-imperial posture, first with Churchill and India, then with de Gaulle and the French relationship with Indochina. The Americans soon became far more focused on the postwar threat from the Soviet Union than on the postwar configuration of power across Asia, developing in any case their own concerns about the political struggle in China. As revealed, however, in the language quoted above from William Langer, few argued for any formal imperial position on the part of the United States, and years later even the arguably imperial actions of the United States in Vietnam were clothed in the language of self-determination and democratization. In arguing for a return to a British imperial model in response to the attacks of 9/11, Niall Ferguson failed not just to appreciate the extraordinary consensus among historians about the failed premises and broken promises of the imperial past but also the extent to which the views of the Bush administration on issues as various as preemptive war and its long-term goals in the Middle East were at deep odds with the formal rhetoric and customary commitment of both the foreign policy establishment and the broad public. American empire might continue on in its worldwide expanse of military bases, dependent regimes, and support for corporate hegemony in both oil and outsourcing, but it would never be explicitly acknowledged again. The idea of empire was dead.

The reality of empire, of course, was different. It is in this context, however, that our invocation of Edmund Burke might be most salutary. Burke would have railed against any effort to smuggle in imperial designs, policies, or actions in direct opposition to a formal commitment to a postimperial world. Burke would have given voice to a different postcolonial ideal, one that would necessarily be consistent with his abstract principles concerning ancient constitutions and enduring principles, even if the realities had in fact been newly fashioned in hastily written constitutions and political systems during the postwar decades of decolonization. And Burke's legacy might also serve as a useful guide for imagining postcolonial forms of transnational compact, forms that could provide new models for international cooperation and commitment to issues ranging from markets and climate to poverty and justice. As we debate the adequacy of sovereign forms to economic forces and environmental realities, it may be more important than ever to preserve a memory of Burke's great passion and its extraordinary resonance with the legacy of postcolonial aspirations for sovereignty that a critical history of empire records. The idea of empire may well be dead, but the lessons of its history should not be forgotten.

Part IV

The Politics of Knowledge

10

In Near Ruins

Cultural Theory at the End of the Century

The Villa San Girolamo, built to protect inhabitants from the flesh of the devil, had the look of a besieged fortress, the limbs of most of the statues blown off during the first days of shelling. There seemed little demarcation between house and landscape, between damaged building and the burned and shelled remnants of the earth. . . . Between the kitchen and the destroyed chapel a door led into an oval-shaped library. The space inside seemed safe except for a large hole at portrait level in the far wall, caused by mortar-shell attack on the villa two months earlier. The rest of the room had adapted itself to this wound, accepting the habits of weather, evening stars, the sound of birds. There was a sofa, a piano covered in a grey sheet, the head of a stuffed bear and high walls of books. The shelves nearest the torn wall bowed with the rain, which had doubled the weight of the books. Lightning came into the room too, again and again, falling across the covered piano and carpet.

—Michael Ondaatje, *The English Patient* (1993)

The English patient of Ondaatje's novel is a man burnt black beyond recognition, beyond identity. Cared for by a shell-shocked Canadian nurse, he lies in the Villa San Girolamo, a bombed-out ruin in the hills north of Florence, a structure that once housed a nunnery and then the Germans. They mined the place when they left, only to have it taken over by the Allies as a hospital and morgue. By the time the novel opens, the only patient left is a man who has forgotten his name and lost his history. His body, iconic in early passages of the body of Christ, reveals nothing in its charred flesh. His sense of self is anchored only in the fragmentary narratives of his life in the desert and his notes and diary entries inscribed on the margins and in the added pages of his one possession, a battered copy of *The Histories* by Herodotus. His stories fill the villa during the days just after the cessation of war in Europe, his life the vehicle for Ondaatje's extraordinary elegy on the decline and fall of Western civilization. If Herodotus and Florence together signify the best of the West, the great moments of Western self-invention and achievement, the rise of history and art, the triumph of beauty and reason, the English patient is the ideal subject of the Enlightenment. He is also the exemplar of colonial knowledge and the epitome of colonial adventure. An expert on the desert, he knows the Bedouin as only a colonial agent could:

> I am a man who can recognize an unnamed town by its skeletal shape on a map. . . . So I knew their place before I crashed among them, knew when Alexander had traversed it in an earlier age for this cause or that greed. I knew the customs of nomads besotted by silk or wells. When I was lost among them, unsure of where I was, all I needed was the name of a small ridge, a local custom, a cell of this historical animal, and the map of the world would slide into place.[1]

There was no uncertainty, no resistance, no self-doubt; the cartography of colonial knowledge was total and absolute, no fragment less than the sign of the whole.

Colonial knowledge was also, so the claim went, disinterested. The English patient went to the desert, with other English friends, because of his love of untamed spaces: "We seemed to be interested only in things that could not be bought or sold, of no interest to the outside world."[2] But if knowledge was pure, if only in its originary Enlightenment conceit, it was soon overtaken by war and the imperatives of nation-states. Madox, the patient's best friend through ten years of desert exploration, could not bear the onset of war, the way it divided him from his small circle of friends, the noise it brought to his quiet fantasy of the desert: "And Madox returned to the village of Marston Magna, Somerset, where he had been born, and a month later sat in the congregation of a church, heard the sermon in honor of the war, pulled out his revolver and shot himself. . . . Yes, Madox was a man who died because of nations."[3] Clifton, who had joined the desert party on a lark after Oxford and marriage, turned out to be an intelligence officer for the British, his accumulated knowledge of the desert an added advantage once war was declared. And the English patient, well, he wasn't really English, after all. His story, first told in fragments that gave nothing away, was finally extracted during a long session of morphine, administered by Caravaggio the thief, who had used his skills for the counterintelligence efforts of the British and then, in the aftermath of war, followed his old family friend Hana, the nurse, to the villa. The English patient, Almásy, was in fact Hungarian and had turned to help the Germans after the onset of war, guiding spies such as Rommel across the great North African desert. Caravaggio, with a thief's expertise in fragments, deduced his identity from the stories he first heard, having followed Almásy's case when he was posted in Cairo. But he could not have guessed the contingence of Almásy's betrayal.

Ondaatje's novel, at first seemingly seduced by the omniscience of colonial knowledge, traces its inexorable progression to the nuclear explosions over Hiroshima and Nagasaki. In the end, the novel—and this is where the true difference lies between fiction and history—is a romantic tale, writ small. Almásy had fallen in love with Clifton's wife when she seductively recited lines from Herodotus by a desert campfire. It was an ancient story of betrayal, first by a husband of his wife, and then in return by a wife who conspires with the man her husband had chosen to see her naked in order to appreciate the beauty of his wife. As Almásy said when he narrated this story of falling in love, "Words, Caravaggio. They have a power."[4] History turned into romance through the seduction of language. But desire folds back into history when the story continues, for Almásy chose to side with the Germans only because the English suspected him, refusing to help him when he crawled into a military camp from a ruined desert crying out for them to rescue Katharine, whom he names, wrongly, as his wife. Though her husband is now dead, victim of a suicide crash that sought to take his wife and her lover to the next world with him, Almásy is unable to speak the husband's name, a name resonant with English upper-class credentials and military significance. And so he cannot save the woman he adores, and in retreat joins the enemy. Madox and Clifton die from broken hearts, Katharine from the misrecognition of war, and Almásy fades away (his colonial knowledge of the desert the means of his escape), only to be burned black, beyond recognition. When Almásy finally tells his tale, he has moved beyond desire for either morphine or memory. Strangely, without memory all he can do is read the history of Herodotus. And he comes to his end, for his death is just a matter of time, a romantic who could not accept the inevitable appropriation of his knowledge and life:

> We die containing a richness of lovers and tribes, tastes we have swallowed, bodies we have plunged into and swum up as if rivers we have hidden in as if caves. I wish for all this to be marked on my body when I am dead. I believe in such cartography—to be marked by nature, not just to label ourselves on a map like the names of rich men and women on buildings. We are communal histories, communal books. We are not owned or monogamous in our taste and experience. All I desired was to walk upon such an earth that had no maps.[5]

He was, in the end, misguided. The irreducible condition for such romance was the colonial map that led directly to world war after world war, not to mention the daily oppressions of colonial rule. And in the final scene in the villa, the English patient has a gun directed at him by the Sikh sapper who had also taken refuge in the villa, a loyal soldier who had spent the war defusing unexploded bombs. He held his gun on the English patient after hearing about the explosion of the atomic bomb, a bomb he could never defuse. Holding the charred throat in the rifle's sight, he says,

> My brother told me. Never turn your back on Europe. The deal-makers. The contract makers. The map drawers. Never trust Europeans, he said. Never shake hands with them. But we, oh, we were easily impressed—by speeches and medals and your ceremonies. What have I been doing these

last few years? Cutting away, defusing, limbs of evil. For what? For this to happen.[6]

And when Caravaggio shouted out that the English patient was not English, it did not matter at all, though the sapper left him unharmed, returning home instead, though with his own troubling memories of Hana, his lover, to disturb the simple pleasures of his own national awakening.

The Florentine villa is still a ruin. The majestic mansion built by culture was hollowed out by the middle of the century, destroyed from within by the convulsions of world war, dismantled from without by the relentless historical logic of decolonization. Until the war it was still possible for many to believe the truth of Matthew Arnold's pronouncements on the relationship of culture and anarchy. For Arnold, culture was not just the irrelevant preoccupation of the pedant, of interest only to "a critic of new books or a professor of *belles lettres*."[7] Neither was culture of concern only to the upper classes. Culture was about the pursuit of perfection, about the contemplation of and devotion to sweetness and light: "It seeks to do away with classes; to make the best that has been thought and known in the world current everywhere; to make all men live in an atmosphere of sweetness and light, where they may use ideas, as it uses them itself, freely."[8] Culture was thus, for Arnold, a "social idea": "The men of culture are the true apostles of equality. The great men of culture are those who have had a passion for diffusing, for making prevail, for carrying from one end of society to the other, the best of knowledge, the best ideas of their time."[9] These men of culture must strip the discourse of culture of all jargon and cant, humanizing and diffusing the benefits of culture for all. But the more Arnold argues, the more it becomes clear how limited his notion of equality is: the masses should have culture disseminated to them by the "men" of culture in order to stem the inherent anarchy of the crowd. Culture, which is animated by religious impulses and the modern substitute for religion, "is the most resolute enemy of anarchy."[10] And culture combats anarchy not just through its celebration of the sublime but because it teaches us to nourish "great hopes and designs for the State."[11] If culture is religion, the state is the new citadel of the sacred: "Thus, in our eyes, the very framework and exterior order of the State, whoever may administer the

State, is sacred."[12] And so the state and culture conspire to check the unruly and uplift the public, to forbid both "despondency and violence."

Culture in Arnold's Victorian view of the world has thus not only been tamed but harnessed to the task of state control in the face of growing concern over the unruly mobs that threatened the pretensions and peace of a democratizing and secularizing England.[13] Arnold makes explicit the disciplining function of cultural value and the cultural elite; it is hardly surprising that Arnoldian phrases crop up time after time in the rhetoric of the conservative right in America (and Britain) today. William Bennett and Lynn Cheney both quoted Arnold in their attacks on the National Endowments for the Arts and the National Endowments for the Humanities, giving voice to the feeling of many on the right that culture is supposed to combat anarchy rather than promote it. But Arnold's gloss of culture—the best that has been thought and known—as "sweetness and light" in the service of the state and the "men of culture" seems not only to provide a target for the most reductionist materialist critique of the superstructure but to parody even the most benign celebrations of culture emerging out of Enlightenment discourse itself. Edmund Burke, whose writings on the sublime were of critical importance in the foundation of Enlightenment aesthetics, realized that the power of culture was more complicated; Burke privileged darkness over light, secrecy over clarity. He also saw terror as the true source of the sublime: "Whatever is fitted in any sort to excite the ideas of pain, and danger, that is to say, whatever is in any sort terrible, or is conversant about terrible objects, or operates in a manner analogous to terror, is a source of the sublime; that is, it is productive of the strongest emotion which the mind is capable of feeling." For Burke, the sublime has much more to do with pain than with pleasure.[14]

The sublime for Burke is not just about pain and terror but, anticipating Kant, about the incommensurability of experience, at least some kinds of experience, and reason. As Sara Suleri has written,

> Burke's famous catalog of the horrors of sublimity is thus strongly linked
> to a sense of temporal disarray, to a conviction that sequential derange-
> ment must necessarily attend the spectator's implication in the sublime.
> If a discourse of difficulty is the only idiom that will suffice to represent

such derangement, then it demands to be recognized as clarity on its own territory, and resists a translation into aesthetic luminosity.[15]

Suleri stresses the performative entailments of the sublime, the implication of any reading of the sublime in the yawning chasm between representation and event. The artifice of art calls attention to this gap; the power of representation is a conceit, predicated on the ultimate powerlessness of all representation. But the sublime is equally invested in the excess of all that is signified, the horrible truth that both representation and affect fall so far short of that which we seek to apprehend and understand. Culture in this view is not simple sweetness and light; art does not necessarily contain chaos.

Nevertheless, the sublime is hardly a revolutionary category; despite Burke's strong, even obsessional, critique of England's colonial relationship with India, his position on the French Revolution was entirely reactionary. What is temporal disarray in Suleri's analysis is more generally, in Hayden White's reading, the aestheticization of history.[16] As Thomas Weiskel has suggested, "The dissociation or dualism at the core of the eighteenth-century sublime had profoundly ideological implications, and the various forms of alienation reinforced by the sublime . . . could not be shaken until these ideological correlatives were questioned in the ferment of social revolution."[17] The sublime was calculated to escape history, even if, for a commentator such as Burke, the sublime could be produced by the extraordinary character of history.[18] The Enlightenment view of the sublime set the stage for the ideologies of romanticism, in which the exquisite aesthetics of experience and the quiet contemplation of beauty set art free from history at the same time that history became not just ignored but suppressed by the rise of romanticism more generally.[19] And Kant's linkage of the sublime to the transcendental properties of aesthetic judgment, in which the gap between signifier and signified calls attention to the very limits of nature itself, provides the basis for his understanding of the infinite: "The sublime is that, the mere capacity of thinking which evidences a faculty of mind transcending every standard of sense."[20] The sublime for Kant is "the disposition of soul evoked by a particular representation engaging the attention of reflective judgment, and not the Object."[21] In such a view, the sublime is about those glimpses, fragments, and perhaps even ruins that signify that which cannot be signified, providing mere shadows for the quiet contemplation of aesthetic categories. The sublime is thus about escape and transcendence, hardly the stuff of either history or critique.

Kant's transcendental escape from history and materiality thus provided the philosophical basis for a romantic view of the world; Kant exempted all feelings of pleasure and displeasure from the realm of objective truth, consigning them instead to the autonomous domain of the aesthetic, "one whose determining ground cannot be other than subjective."[22] In addition to rejecting the didactic function of art, Kant delineated an aesthetic that was divorced completely from the social. Jerome McGann has written that "Kant's aesthetic has dominated western attitudes toward art and poetry for more than a hundred and fifty years," providing the justification for Coleridge's discussion of the harmonizing powers of Imagination, and explaining the philosophical basis for poetry, such as Wordsworth's *Tintern Abbey*, that memorializes "certain private and intensely subjective moments of imaginative insight which he has known 'oft, in lonely rooms, and mid the din of towns and cities.' "[23] But if the romantic imagination took flight from the world not just of rational thought but also of materiality and history in poetry, it perhaps was lodged most extravagantly in the landscape where ruins, rather than lonely rooms, took pride of place; I refer here to the visual cartography of the picturesque. By the last years of the eighteenth century, the cult of the picturesque had attained primacy in England as a general attitude to art and nature. Associated at first both with the classical landscapes of Claude Lorraine, Gaspar Poussin, and Salvator Rosa and with the more naturalistic views of Ruysdael, Hobbema, Cuyp, and van Goyen, the picturesque became the site for considerable argument about the character of the relationship between art and nature. The picturesque tradition frequently combined rigorous Enlightenment attitudes about the need to depict the natural world scientifically and romantic convictions that art had to represent the experience of the beautiful and the sublime afforded by nature rather than nature itself. On the one hand, various protophotographic techniques and devices sought to capture nature on paper, with the use of artist's viewers, the Claude glass, the camera obscura, and the camera lucida. On the other hand, while these processes were advocated because of the transparency they established between the real and the representational, they were also thought to improve the picture, giving objects better perspective and more pleasing tinges and hues. Indeed, the mode of the picturesque increasingly sought to improve nature; the term itself could only be applied to certain kinds of natural settings, constituent features, and artistic compositions. Pictures often had to have mountains or hills as backdrops (even in lowland areas), lakes or rivers closer in, and gnarled trees, luxuriant vegetation, and ruined buildings closer still. Frequently, picturesque scenes seemed most readily obtainable in Hellenic or oriental settings.

In England, the picturesque also became the site of a reaction to the transformations of history represented most dramatically by the French Revolution. The craze to redesign garden landscapes along classical lines in the middle decades of the eighteenth century was soon followed by serious rethinking. The magnificent prospects advocated by Addison and "Capability" Brown were attacked for their radical resort to reason rather than tradition and nature. The gothic imaginary of gentlemen gardeners such as Uvedale Price and Richard Payne Knight gave visible form to the critical concerns of Burke, who wrote that "the science of constructing a commonwealth is not to be taught a priori. . . . The nature of man is intricate; the objects of society are of the greatest possible complexity: and therefore no simple disposition or direction of power can be suitable either to man's nature, or to the quality of his affairs."[24] Ann Bermingham argues that Burke's conservatism and his concomitant commitment to complexity can be seen in the new picturesque aesthetic, where old gardens are preserved, and new gardens are wildly overgrown, even derelict. The new picturesque was steeped in nostalgia for the wildness of nature and the haunting call of grandeur, signified best by towering mountains and stupendous buildings. As for buildings, nostalgia was best conveyed through the image of ruins.[25]

The ruin was a sign of loss, of absence. Crumbling rock, fragments, and shards stood for wholes that could never again be achieved, if even conceived. Ruins were approachable and representable, but only because they were but shadows of their former selves. Ruins made ancient truth both literal and literary. In ruins, the hollowed-out shells of ancient truth appeared majestic, approachable only through art—painting and poetry in particular. The science of archaeology was born in the attempt to recover the truth of the past concretely, but the allure of archaeology was always predicated on the impossibility of scientific fantasy (not to mention its inescapable relationship to plunder and the fantasy of instant wealth). Ruins also promised glory through recuperation rather than revolution, representing Burke's concern about the politics of the age as well as about the relationship between history and the sublime. Perhaps more than anything, ruins made palpable the chasm between reality and representation, between desire and dejection, between now and then, lodging temporal alterity resolutely within the past rather than in some utopian future. The ruin not only housed culture; it stood for it: like culture itself, the ruin was at once material and ethereal, simultaneously about history and memory, a sign of achievement and a signal of failure, an inspiration for life as well as an intimation of death.

If culture's cavernous lack is the site of its power as well as the basis on which it can be wielded as an instrument of power, the ruin helps us understand why culture must always be linked to the incommensurable. In Arnold, culture becomes both didactic and inspiring, containable but dangerous. For Burke, the danger is more palpable; the power of culture is in part its excess, the uncontainability of the sublime. And for the picturesque tradition, which sought to contain beauty by conventions of distancing, the experience was always on the verge of leaking beyond the borders of carefully composed canvases and gardens. Representation turned out to be as uncontrollable as the referential affects of romantic aspiration. The modern career of culture has always had to negotiate these tensions, requiring the convictions and investments of class power to sustain any confidence in the controlled and controlling uses of culture. But it is precisely these tensions—the quarrels over the empty spaces between representation and reality—that produce the terrific for Kant, the terrible for Burke, and the horrible for Benjamin. No matter where we rest our critical position, we find that culture is not quite itself, not nearly as comfortable as Arnold would have us believe. For us all, culture is a site of extreme ambivalence, whether we refer to the ruin in the garden, the nude in the museum, or the discordance in a work of modern music. Now we attempt to clothe ambivalence in a different kind of distance, and we shift from the effort to describe and contain the sublime to a critical consideration of the political implications of the power of culture. But we are still drawn to culture as if to a specter, the ghost of a past that still excites and the haunting possibility of a future we think we desire. Culture eclipses temporality itself even as we try to historicize it. Culture becomes a trace of its own representational artifacts that can be critiqued only when we are still compelled by the terrible pull of the sublime. As the impossible object of our critical conscience, culture either floats away into thin air as absence or takes the form and presence of the ruin.

In the Midrash story of the Tower of Babel, those who actually saw the ruins of the tower were doomed to forget the past, to lose sight of history altogether, to forfeit even their capacity to know themselves.[26] While ruins would seem to be about history, more often they are about the need to obliterate history, as well as signs of the death of history. Walter Benjamin distinguishes historical materialism from the history of Fustel de Coulanges, who "recommends . . . to historians who wish to relive an era . . . that they blot out everything they know about the later course of history."[27] Benjamin goes on to write, in his now famous passage, that

> without exception the cultural treasures he [the historical materialist] surveys have an origin which he cannot contemplate without horror. They owe their existence not only to the efforts of the great minds and talents who have created them, but also to the anonymous toil of their contemporaries. There is no document of civilization which is not at the same time a document of barbarism.[28]

The ruin is the document of civilization par excellence; it signifies the most onerous toil of the slaves and subalterns who executed the political and architectural ambitions of great civilizations, and the history of its contemplation generates nostalgia, which is the forgetting rather than the remembering of history, the forgetting of the conditions of possibility of history, not to mention its later course. But for those, unlike Benjamin, who have traditionally celebrated culture and civilization, the only horror attendant upon the contemplation of ruins is that of shock at the decline and fall of what once was great. The ruin is the only connection between the wonders of the past and the degradation of the present. The ruin puts us in awe of the mystifications that made civilization magnificent in the first place. The ruin is culture, both its reality and its representation.

If Benjamin teaches us more powerfully than perhaps any other modern critic that culture is a ruin, he betrays some measure of his own nostalgia when he defines the aura of traditional aesthetics. In Benjamin's early philosophy he had identified the aura, or uniqueness, of art as the source of its value; by the time he wrote his masterful essay "Art in the Age of Mechanical Reproduction," he had reversed his view.[29] Whether it is produced by "cult value" (the ritual attribution of magical value) or by the logic of exhibition (the public presentation of works of art), Benjamin now views the aura of art, that quality of authenticity and presence that produces the sublime, as an endangered species. Art changes fundamentally once the technical means of reproduction enter the modern world with photography in the nineteenth century. In a flashback to his earlier position, the moment when the aura appears lost produces a "melancholy, incomparable beauty."[30] Nevertheless, Benjamin argues strongly that the loss of the aura opens up new possibilities for a revolutionary aesthetic, for the politicization and radicalization of art. Film is exemplary of the new aesthetic regime: according to Benjamin, film promotes a "revolutionary criticism of traditional concepts of art."[31] By its substitution of the camera for the public, film loses the aura of performance; by its reproducibility and accessibility, it makes every viewer an expert. Film embodies the principle of the mechanical reproduction of art, thus irrevocably changing "the reaction of the masses toward art."[32] Benjamin had extraordinary confidence in the progressive implications of the new age of film.

But Benjamin's faith in the technologies of aesthetic reproduction and the critical capabilities of the masses (politically self-conscious if also absentminded) was strenuously opposed by Adorno, who was far more distrustful of the "laughter of the proletariat in the movie house" and far more impressed by the capacities of the fascist state and the capitalist elite to appropriate the technologies of production.[33] The argument between Benjamin and Adorno over popular and elite culture continued to haunt our understandings of culture in the final years of the twentieth century. Now the question is not whether culture, or the sublime, can be contained so much as whether the modern technologies of the sublime will render containment that much more secure. Adorno's critique of the culture industry, composed in its most complete and polemical form after his move to America, still provides the most eloquent critique of mass culture we have today.[34] Adorno lamented that "real life is becoming indistinguishable from the movies."[35] He argued that "the stunting of the mass-media consumer's powers of imagination and spontaneity does not have to be traced back to any psychological mechanisms; he must ascribe the loss of those attributes to the objective nature of the products themselves, especially to the most characteristic of them, the sound film."[36] Adorno wrote more generally that "the culture industry as a whole has molded men as a type unfailingly reproduced in every product."[37] Anticipating current theoretical preoccupations with cultural hegemony and discursive domination, Adorno carefully dissected the ways in which the modern subject was converted into a consumer, a consumer whose needs, interests, and beliefs could be controlled and manipulated by the apparatuses of a mass media that produced pleasure (and incited further consumption) by stifling the possibility of critical reflection. With polemical rhetoric still unrivaled by other denunciations of the conceits of bourgeois liberalism, Adorno noted at the end of his essay that the methods of the fascists had reached their final apotheosis in modern America, where the "freedom to choose an ideology . . . everywhere proves to be freedom to choose what is always the same."[38]

Using Benjaminian language, if to rather different ends, Adorno wrote, "Today aesthetic barbarity completes what has threatened the creations of the spirit since they were gathered together as culture and neutralized."[39] The culture industry has rendered culture nothing but style, in which the commoditization of all aesthetic value reveals itself in the reduction of art to imitation. Adorno held up older and more classical forms of culture in contrast, noting that "the great artists were never those who embodied a wholly flawless and perfect style, but those who used style as a way of hardening themselves against the chaotic expression of suffering, as a negative truth."[40] While recognizing that art is always ideology, Adorno saw the confrontation with tradition in classical forms as the contradictory space for the expression of suffering and for the necessary admission of failure through self-negation, the contradictions of any effort to transcend the particular limits of social existence. In this short aside, Adorno made reference to a lifetime of critical efforts to engage in ideology critique through great works of art, in particular the modernist musical experiments of composers such as Schoenberg.

Adorno's commitment to the critical potential of high modernist aesthetics and his despair about mass culture were functions of his experience of the normalization and appropriation of a classical tradition under the Nazi regime as well as of the apparent utility of mass culture for totalitarian state systems and American capitalist market forces alike. Benjamin's belief in the potential of mass media was forged through his fascination with early film, as was his political and cultural affiliation with Brecht. Benjamin was convinced that the loss of aura represented by filmic media would render culture both more accessible and more political, but even if his commitment to Marxist doctrine and revolutionary praxis was far firmer than that of Adorno, it seems likely he would have worried along with Adorno about the production of new consumer subjectivities under the postwar American regime of capital. The war itself, despite Adorno, left traditional European culture as a ruin, both architecturally—many of its most conspicuous symbols were literally ruined—and spiritually; it was clear to many that the heart of European culture had in some ways led to fascism and the Holocaust. Ideology critique seemed woefully insufficient. At the same time, the ruins of Europe paved the way for the emergence of American hegemony over world culture, ruining cultural sensibilities in precisely the terms laid out so eloquently by Adorno. Culture under the new regime became always already a ruin in the face of programmed obsolescence and the relentless advance of the new. After the war, culture was taken over by Eisenhower's military-industrial complex and Hollywood's fantasy factories. And the Cold War deployment of modernization, appropriating all the other uses of the modern to the world order of American power, affiliated the new with economic power, technological superiority, progress, and pleasure. The lure of the modern was more powerful than ever, and once again the modern came as a sign of Western power.

And so we return to the Villa San Girolamo. The Florentine shrine of culture was a ruin, its inhabitants shell-shocked. The image recapitulates the modernist critique of the sublime, forcefully set in motion by Nietzsche when, arguing that both the Apollonian and the Dionysian principles were conjoined in aesthetic production and experience, he took the Kantian tradition to task for failing to recognize that "the sublime is the artistic taming of the horrible."[41] Nietzsche's insistence on the Dionysian side of the sublime anticipated the later writings of

Georges Bataille, who viewed cultural value and meaning as necessarily implicated in violence and excess. Focusing on rites of sacrifice and the close relations between ritual and war, Bataille interrogated the horror at the heart of culture, celebrating transgression as the fundamental modality of the sacred. For Bataille, as for Nietzsche, the moment of excess was about both sexuality and about death.[42] And even here, surveying the theoretical genealogies of our current condition, Ondaatje captures this sad sense of the sullied sublime. We see in his novel the necessary affiliation of love and violence; Almásy's love is obliterated by war, even as Hana and the Sikh sapper are torn apart by the nuclear explosion thousands of miles away. Violence is what predicates love (in the colonial terrain of the desert or in the ruined villa), and violence is the force that ultimately disrupts it.

In the end, the English patient, the man who used Herodotus as his guide through the deserts of life, lay waiting for death, burned black beyond identity. He was a man who embodied the best of colonial knowledge yet turned out to be not quite what he seemed; he belonged to all of Europe, erasing the distinctions between Allies and Axis by revealing the common heritage and fundamental flaws of both sides. The tragic elegy of his life provided the pretext for the ultimate intention of the novel, the devolution of cultural capital from Almásy and his Oxford education to the likes of Caravaggio and Hana, the one a streetwise though chastened thief, the other a young and beautiful woman who had already seen the empty deception of the domestic dream. And perhaps even more significantly, the position of critique is appropriated in the end by the silent sapper, the Sikh from India who recognizes the ultimate deception, the terrible tyranny of the West, the translation of European colonial power into American English. The ruin that haunts the final pages of the novel is that of Hiroshima and Nagasaki, cities instantaneously converted to rubble by the unprecedented power of nuclear explosion. When the sapper returns home, he does so to join in the final struggle of the nationalist movement, to attempt to free himself, for good, of the ruination of the West.

I have sought to capture, or at least evoke, the predicament of cultural theory today, fifty years after the end of the war; during these intervening years, American power has waxed and waned, popular culture has exploded across the globe, decolonization has transformed the cartography of colonial power, and the death of communism has led to the demise of the Cold War and the epiphany of global capitalism. Ondaatje wrote his allegory from the perspective of these transformations; in an earlier novel set in Toronto he had written about the historical production of subjects such as Caravaggio and Hana (*In the Skin of a Lion*), and in a personal memoir he had evoked the lush colonial past that had generated his own mediated relationship with his home, Sri Lanka (*Running in the Family*). In particular, Ondaatje tells his tale from the position of one who celebrates an escape from the West at the same time that he is irrevocably trapped in its embrace. Decidedly not a postcolonial theorist, Ondaatje has reflected deeply on the entailments of the history and genealogy of the West for cultural migrants such as himself; he has immersed himself in the poetic possibilities of a colonial language at the same time that he dreams of the authentic heat and passion of his youth; he has identified the hybrid formations that relentlessly enclose his own capacity for history and utopia. Without any explicit reference to Adorno, he exemplifies Adorno's own reflection about the dislocations of his life and times: "for a man who no longer has a homeland, writing becomes a place to live."[43]

Writing itself is not a neutral space. In the last fifty years we have learned how much it matters from where we write, to whom we write, and more generally how writing is positioned in geopolitical, sociohistorical, and institutional terms. If Ondaatje's *English Patient* can signify the monumental shifts in our cultural and intellectual landscape that have been brought about by decolonization and resurgent nationalism, it can also remind us that in cultural theory, postcolonial critiques are necessary features of all the new landscapes we inhabit or survey. Postcoloniality, in other words, is not just something out there; neither is it (nor should it be) simply a new name for a token inclusionism in our cultural business as usual. Rather, the postcolonial condition is the historical precipitate of centuries of Western political and economic domination, itself enabling, even as it was enabled by, centuries of cultural and intellectual colonization. Postcoloniality signifies those places and peoples that resist the universalization of positionality and perspective, even as it underscores the extraordinary power of the forces of universalization. Postcoloniality reminds us of the fact that culture and modernity were always flawed, always predicated on violence and domination even as they were the terms of seduction for colonization itself.[44] When the critique of the Enlightenment comes out of colonial history, we remember that Burke's eloquent defense of good government and disinterested despotism was in the service of imperial ideals even as it was posed against imperial realities. We remember that culture has always been a specter, haunting any attempt to reconstruct cultural authenticities untouched by colonial power even as it leaves a trace of violence, along with the promise of utopia, in every moment of historical imagination and political desire. The angel of history speaks with sadness not just about the atrocities of the past but the atrocity of history itself, propelled as he is into the future by the terrible storm called progress.[45]

If such critiques, whether formally postcolonial or not, have subjected traditional notions of Western culture to serious scrutiny, they have also challenged the disciplinary integrity of another field born out of the historical need of the West to understand the world beyond: anthropology. Should a field so seemingly tainted by its origins within the violence of colonialism continue as a privileged site of cultural critique in the postcolonial world? We are now well acquainted with reflexive positions within anthropology that adumbrate the horrors of the colonial past and the extent to which both the subjects and the imperatives of anthropological knowledge participate in those horrors. The nuclear calculus of Hiroshima was but a sign of the legacies of colonial history; the sapper's alienation from the normalizing technologies of Western warfare a token of nationalist resistance. But the anthropological concept of culture has survived both the implosion of the atom and the decolonization of empire; indeed, now anthropological imaginaries are serving other purposes, inserting difference into the social scientific canon, justifying a wide variety of identity politics and political claims, animating critique from multiple perspectives. Increasingly, culture can be used to critique the West at the same time that it can be deployed to deflect any interrogation of local cultural politics.

None of this is resolved, and anthropology may be consigned to a state of perpetual crisis. It has certainly not resolved the argument between Benjamin and Adorno nor fixed upon new ways to engage the field of culture that entirely escape the problematic legacies of class hegemony, colonial domination, and capitalist exploitation. Anthropologists are still uncertain about their place as intellectuals, and wherever they are positioned, or position themselves, they are not completely sure what these places signify in relation to concerns of constituency and representation, let alone the politics of criticism. The argument between Benjamin and Adorno continues to haunt all of us; we are not sure whether to find resistance in culture (whether "low" or "high"), to attempt to provoke subversion in culture through ideology critique, or to feel embarrassment about the choice of culture as the field of criticism and interpretation in the first place.

But we keep coming back to the ruins of culture. We may feel horrified, but we also feel inspired; we may feel dispirited, as did Adorno, but we cannot escape the rhetorical echoes of Benjamin's utopian aspiration. When we confront the overdetermination of logics of cultural production and consumption, we may nowadays think more of Foucault than of Marx; when we experience the excess of cultural meaning and signification, we may refer more to Bataille than to Burke. But we keep coming back. We stroll across the dilapidated ramparts, we climb the devastated staircase, we sift through the sandy shards, we back up on a grassy knoll until we can see the grandeur and the beauty of the prospect. But there we are, and we cannot just stand back, despite the fact, perhaps because of the fact, that we now know the ruin is littered with unexploded mines. When we walk in the library, we know, as did Hana, that one wrong step may detonate a deadly bomb. We pull books down from shelves knowing not what we may find, nor how old books might read again, now after the war. We plant flowers in the garden, never sure if the weeds we pull or the sharp blade of our trowel will trigger an explosion. We seem always to live in near ruins.

11

G. S. Ghurye and the Politics of Sociological Knowledge

It is a great honor to be asked to deliver the first Ghurye Memorial Lecture in the Department of Sociology at Bombay University. Dr. Ghurye not only played the signal role in establishing this department as one of the leading departments of sociology in India; he was the most influential Indian academic to write about Indian sociology during the colonial period. The basic facts of Professor Ghurye's life and work are well known here: his academic training in Bombay and Cambridge; his long service as head of the Department of Sociology at Bombay University from 1924 until his retirement in 1959; his extraordinary contributions to our understanding of caste, race, and tribal identities; and his relentless commitment to building the research capacity and relevance of Indian social science. And for those who think that retirement means the end of intellectual influence—and I am getting to the stage of life where I have begun to worry about such things—it is reassuring to note that Ghurye wrote seventeen books after his retirement. Many of these books addressed current and critical issues in India—on topics ranging from social and political tensions to regionalist tendencies—revealing the extent to which Ghurye always thought about the contemporaneous present in his sociological work, however historical that work was. While upholding the highest standards of empirical method and theoretical rigor, Ghurye also made clear how important it was to use the insights of social science to advance social and political causes. He was a fervent nationalist and a great champion not just of Indian social science but also of Indian intellectual autonomy and self-sufficiency, so much so that he might be labeled, along with so many other laudatory titles, one of India's first postcolonial intellectuals.

It is an especially meaningful honor for me to give this lecture because of the extent to which Ghurye has influenced my own work on caste and Indian society. He was the first anthropologist to turn his attention to the dangerous effects of colonial discourse and colonial institutions on the fundamental institutions of Indian society. Indeed, much of the critical thrust of my own work concerning caste in Indian society can be found in his early work's careful dissection of the ways in which colonial preoccupations with caste and race contributed to the reification of caste as a form of social stratification characterized by separate identities and competing political agendas. His critique of colonialism was both prescient and profound, for he understood the hidden and dispersed effects of colonial policy on Indian society in the grips of nationalist mobilization. In his canonic work, *Caste and Race in India*—a text that was revised five times as questions of caste and race moved across a changing political and sociological terrain—Ghurye was especially concerned to evaluate the claims of the colonial state's canonic anthropologist, H. H. Risley, about the racial origins of caste.[1] As the chief ethnographic officer of the colonial government in the early twentieth century, Risley had written that the centrifugal forces of caste would retard the development of nationalism (even after the swadeshi movement)— an argument made on the basis of extensive anthropometric research that caste was largely based on racial groups and differences. Ghurye challenged Risley directly and ultimately determined that only in the Punjab and parts of the United Provinces was there anything like a correlation between race and caste, in which Brahmans betrayed physiognomic indications of their hereditary connection to the Aryan invaders of the subcontinent. Everywhere else, and for all other groups, general miscegenation had eroded any racial distinctness to caste. Ghurye emphasized the mixing of castes particularly in Maharashtra and Madras— an observation that had particularly stark political implications since the anti-Brahman movement had become the most potent and, at least according to Ghurye, threatening challenge to the nationalist cause.

I encountered some of the writings of Ghurye while writing my first research paper on the rise of the anti-Brahman movement in southern India, some forty years ago. I was struck by how Ghurye used the dispassionate tone and method of social science to suggest that the stark caste divisions in the south were in fact based on faulty assumption and partial data. His confidence in the assimilative power of Indian civilization seemed at odds with what I saw as I was conducting research in 1971 Madras: the new electoral success of the DMK, first under Annadurai and then Karunanidhi, and the powerful rhetoric of E. V. Ramaswamy Naicker (known more commonly as Periyar). I was struck that there seemed to be a parallel civil rights movement taking place in Tamil Nadu, on the other side of the world from the civil rights movement that defined American politics during the decades after India's own independence. Given this background, I was fascinated with the parallels between caste and race, not to mention, especially over the years since, the comparisons between debates around affirmative action in the United States and reservations in India.

But it was only years later, when I had begun to think about the relationship between British colonial anthropology and the conduct of colonial occupation of India, that I became intrigued by Ghurye's critique of colonial anthropology and the racial theories of H. H. Risley. I learned that Ghurye was especially critical of Risley's role in politicizing caste, particularly in relation to the census. Risley was not the first to use the decennial census for collecting and presenting material about caste.[2] Ghurye felt, however, that the apparatus of the census, along with various decisions of government, had encouraged the anti-Brahman movement. In particular, he criticized the use of quotas to restrict government employment for Brahmans in Maharashtra and Madras. Ghurye, a Brahman and a staunch nationalist, was skeptical from the start about the rhetoric of the maharaja of Kolhapur, who spearheaded the Maharastrian non-Brahman movement and was given to requesting "the protection and guidance of the British Government until the evil of caste-system becomes ineffective" in connection with the early implementations of home rule.[3] Ghurye acknowledged Brahman dominance in administrative positions but noted that the initial complaints of non-Brahman activists had been addressed by non-Brahman political mobilization alone: "An analysis of the membership of the various local bodies in the presidencies of Bombay and Madras clearly proves that the non-Brahmans know their rights and are generally keen to conduct a strong campaign against any measure which they feel unjust to them."[4] Ghurye argued very strongly against the policy of reservations, which he viewed as "opposed to the accepted criteria of nationality and the guiding principles of social justice."[5] And he accepted that the non-Brahmans might have legitimate grievances and exist as a single class in structural terms, in relation to social matters, "because the attitude of the Brahmins as regards food and social intercourse, and religious instruction and ministration towards them, has been uniform."[6] But he strongly opposed the notion that legislative sanctions or reserved posts would address this issue: "Whatever liberalizing of the Brahmin attitude in this respect has taken place during the last forty years is mainly due to education and social reform campaign and not to the very recent reserved or communal representation."[7] Indeed, Ghurye argued that the "restriction on the numbers of the able members of the Brahmin and the allied castes, imposed by this resolution of the Government, penalizes some able persons simply because they happen to belong to particular castes," at the same time clearly abandoning "the accepted standard of qualifications and efficiency."[8] Ghurye not only believed that reserved representation was not necessary, but harmful "in so far as it tends to perpetuate the distinction based on birth," something he felt was both counterproductive and antinational: "to harp on the caste differences and to allow special representation is to set at naught the fundamental condition for the rise of community feeling."[9] Given the early collaboration between the non-Brahman movement and the British, Ghurye's argument was not altogether far-fetched, even if in retrospect we might view his confidence in the political system to redress caste inequality and his view of caste as fundamentally nonpolitical as problematic, and not just because of the possible challenge to a unified nationalist movement.

Now I will confess that as ready as I was to blame the British for using the old imperial technique of divide and rule, this is where I began to have my doubts about Ghurye's motives. As I noted before, I came to the questions around caste in India from the twin vantage point of anti-Brahmanism in Madras and a concern with race in the United States, but while I was instructed by Ghurye's challenge to Risley's racial thinking (finding in it useful parallels as well with Franz Boas's debunking of some of the biological assumptions in U.S. racial thinking), I read the debate over reservations both through the lens of the non-Brahman movement in southern India and the civil rights struggle in the United States. And while I had become aware, for example, that the Justice Party in Madras had become a problematic vehicle for elite non-Brahman political mobilization, not only exclusive of lower caste non-Brahmans but also of Dalits, and clearly antinational, I believed that some form of affirmative action was necessary to counter historical oppression and create new opportunities for social mobility.

Ghurye, nevertheless, made for powerful reading. He may not have been the first to argue against the policy of reservations and the effects of politicizing caste, but he made the most eloquent, and academically compelling, critique of the relationship of caste and politics in the decades immediately preceding independence. Further, Ghurye was perhaps the first real scholar to suggest that the politicization of caste was not merely a natural outgrowth of the traditional institution but a conscious design of British colonial policy. The principal colonial lesson of the great rebellion of 1857, according to Ghurye, was that the "safety of the British domination in India was very closely connected with keeping the Indian people divided on the lines of caste."[10] Ghurye quoted James Kerr, the principal of the Hindu College of Calcutta, as having written that the spirit of caste "is opposed to national union" and argued more generally that a policy of divide and rule on caste grounds influenced the policy and conduct of many British officials.[11] He further suggested that the British were so receptive to the arguments on the part of leaders of the non-Brahman movement in favor of reservations and caste quotas precisely because "as a logical development of the attitude of the Government [reservations] nursed, rather than ignored, the spirit of caste."[12] And so, when writing against the non-Brahman movement in his own Bombay Presidency, Ghurye used an anticolonial argument to support his concern that national life, because of the rise of caste enmity and conflict, could "be reduced to an absurdity."[13]

He concluded his chapter on the effects of British rule on caste by noting that "Even the apex of the ancient scheme, the priesthood of the Brahmin, which has been . . . the great bond of social solidarity in this finely divided society, is being loosened by caste after caste. At about the end of the British rule in India, caste-society presented the spectacle of self-centred groups more or less in conflict with one another."[14] His arguments against colonial policies of divide and rule, eloquent and persuasive though there were, stood side by side with his nostalgia for an age in which the otherworldly prestige of the Brahman could be acknowledged for its innocent capacity to hold Indian society together. This is not to say that Ghurye was completely naïve about the realities of the caste system. Even though he lamented the decline of the "priesthood" and was particularly worried about the rise of prejudice against Brahmans, he clearly supported Gandhi's attempts to ameliorate the conditions of the untouchables (even as he disapproved of Ambedkar's attempt to politicize caste to that end). But he was resolutely opposed to the politicization of caste, whether by the British or by forces in the anti-Brahman movement. And his greatest concern in the politicization of caste seemed to be the generation of bad faith around both Brahmans and Brahmanism, the latter being for him the font of principles that were fundamental to Indian civilization.

In an important sense, Ghurye's effort to recuperate Brahmanism and to disparage some of the claims of the non- or anti-Brahman movement must be situated in terms of his larger critique of colonial anthropology, especially his important interventions in the debate over tribes (and his famous rivalry with Verrier Elwin, the architect of tribal policy under Nehru). In 1943 Ghurye published *The Aboriginals—So Called—and Their Future* (republished after independence as *The Scheduled Tribes*).[15] This book, in part a response to Elwin's pamphlet, "Loss of Nerve," directly refuted the caste-tribe distinction, seeing it as a result of colonial policy and classification rather than as fundamental either in Indian history or sociology.[16] His evaluation of tribal worship led him to see significant similarities with lower caste rituals even as he drew parallels between tribal dialects and Dravidian languages. At the same time, he made clear how dangerous it was for the national cause to draw attention to these kinds of differences, or as we might say today, to reify and essentialize them.

Although Ghurye led with a political commitment to national unity, his principal argument was historical, much of it based on the colonial archive itself. And it was the combination of his historical framework with his critical sensibility regarding the colonial that connected my own scholarly interests most directly with those of Ghurye. My Ph.D. advisor was Bernard Cohn, an anthropologist who went back to the colonial archive to trace the origins of contemporary political and social formations and who developed a deeply cynical understanding of the way the British used even the most benign forms of colonial knowledge to rule and control India. For Cohn, grammars were as much an instrument of policy as land revenue and military control, and in a pathbreaking essay from 1969 he argued—with clear influence from Ghurye—that the decennial census had played a constitutive role in the development of modern caste forms and identities.[17] I carried Cohn's interests to my ethnohistorical work on a princely state in southern India, where colonialism had operated only through indirect means, hollowing out kingly power but hardly reshaping caste relations to the same extent as seemed to have happened in the core areas and cities of the principal colonial presidencies. Indeed, I discovered that the princely states were convenient vehicles of colonial policy too.

Ghurye's own argument about the development of nonregulation tribal areas under colonial rule, in which he showed how these areas were devised by the British for their own reasons, struck a chord to say the least. Scheduled districts—the precursors of excluded areas—were not artifacts of precolonial isolation so much as the products of deliberate colonial policies of sequestration and division. Ghurye believed that tribal groups should be incorporated within new parliamentary institutions—using reservations for members of backward tribes—and that tribal groups more generally should be allowed to continue the process of absorption, assimilation, and progressive social change that had characterized them before the British conquest of India.

As Ghurye noted in the preface to his book, India had been formed over its long history by many "ethnic stocks and cultures," "the process of assimilation of smaller groups of different cultures into larger ones or of less homogeneous cultures . . . steadily going on."[18] But when the British arrived on the scene, "the old process of assimilation was upset [and] new problems arose."[19] Ghurye wished now to return to an earlier, precolonial, dynamic, to a process that had a marked resemblance to the kind of argument subsequently made by his student, M. N. Srinivas, about "sanskritization." But in his work on tribals, he stressed the connections between tribal groups and lower castes rather than the role of Brahmans as either trustees (to use a Gandhian idiom) or as the priesthood (to use his own). It was only in his writing on caste, where he focused more on the non-Brahman movement, that he stipulated the role of Brahmans, and indeed of early textual constructions of caste, as fundamental.

Ghurye's framework was more unitary than that of Srinivas, whose rubric of sanskritization was modulated to include different kinds of Indic models for social mobility and change. But Ghurye's sense of the assimilative character of Indian civilization not only anticipated Srinivas's argument, but it also predated, and undoubtedly influenced, the modernization theories of much American anthropology, including the work of Oscar Lewis, Robert Redfield, McKim Marriott, and Milton Singer. When anthropologists had described social forms and village customs in India in the 1950s, they wrote about the twin processes of universalization and particularization, about the mimetic logic of caste and hierarchy more generally, and about the harmonious relationship between great and little traditions. Although U.S. writing in the 1950s was less evolutionary than Ghurye's, it is clear that the general models of civilizational unity and social differentiation shared a great deal in common. And Ghurye's work allows us to tease out parallels between anticolonial nationalism and Cold War modernization theory as well as to ask some new and more comparative questions about the inherently traditionalist emphasis on religious values and ritual expressions.

In particular, while Ghurye delineated the segmental division of society, focusing on issues around marriage, occupation, and commensality, he maintained the necessity of the Brahman. Major groups, he wrote, were invariably, "held together by the possession . . . of a common priesthood."[20] Because of this, the system of hierarchy was characterized throughout by harmony:

> Common service to the civic life, prescriptive rights of monopolist service, and specific occasions for enjoying superiority for some of the castes, considered very low, made the village community more or less a harmonious civic unit. Complete acceptance of the system in its broad outlines by the groups making up that system and their social and economic interdepen-

dence in the village not only prevented the autonomous organization of the groups from splitting up the system into independent units, it created a harmony in civic life. Of course, this harmony was not the harmony of parts that are equally valued, but of units which are rigorously subordinated to one another.[21]

Ghurye's emphasis on harmony was predicated on his reading of textual accounts from the Vedas to the Manu Dharma Shastras. These were the ultimate sources for his emphasis on the role of the priesthood, the sacred dimensions of caste differentiation, and the values that underlay the social compact of Hindu society.

Ghurye's complex position reveals more than the specific conjunctures of his own time and place. Influenced by Chiplunkar as well as other major figures in early twentieth-century Maharashtra, he was, in the words of A. R. Momin, "steeped in ultra-nationalism and revivalism."[22] Additionally, his specific scholarly investment in Sanskritic texts and learning sustained his understanding of the ideal of caste harmony. As Momin has put it, "Ghurye's early background in the classics and his life-long preoccupation with textual and scriptural sources led him to adopt the Brahmanical model of Indian society, which is too idealistic and over-arching."[23] To put this in proper context, Ghurye had come of age as an academic at a time when the anti-Brahman movement in Maharashtra appeared to many to be collaborationist with British rule and organized around antinationalist principles and alliances. Yet his path-breaking analyses of caste and tribe anticipate other conjunctures as well, between anticolonial nationalism and social conservatism, between a critical relationship to colonial transformations of caste and tribe and a newly revitalized commitment to an idea of the Indian social as fundamentally harmonic, between a critical reaction to the colonial denunciation of Indian society and the idea of Indian civilization as essentially Hindu. His nationalist agenda, therefore, reveals some of the significant tensions of nationalism itself; he belittled the political aspirations of non-Brahmans while making very little mention of Muslims in Indian society.[24] To many at the time, and many more in retrospect, he seemed to be arguing against the political mobilization of cultural and social identities for the redress of historical oppression and stigmatization. From some perspectives, his greatest concern seemed to be the loss of Hindu community in the face of attacks on the sacred charter of Brahmans and Brahmanism.

Ghurye was a particularly important figure in these growing conjunctures, as he both made such an early, and forceful, argument against the social effects of British rule and correlated his sociological theories with contemporary political predicaments. But his work invites us to consider more generally the question of the politics of sociological knowledge in India. Even as Ghurye kept adjusting his sociological research and insights to address contemporary issues, his work demands critical analysis in the context not just of changes since his death but also of the kinds of contemporary pressures, implications, and entailments of sociological work in India on questions concerning caste, race, and tribe: the primary preoccupations of Ghurye's academic work and for twentieth-century sociology/anthropology in and about India.

In Ghurye's latter-day writings about caste, he made clear that he in fact disagreed with Gandhi's sense that caste could be recuperated through the ideal sense of the *varna* system, the fourfold division of Indian society into classically conceived social groups. And Ghurye was well aware that modernization was not in fact leading to the demise of caste predicted by Weber and others. But he was not an advocate of the idea of the modernity of tradition, to take the phrase of Lloyd and Susanne Rudolph.[25] He was adamantly opposed to the belief that the "slow consolidation of the smaller groups into larger ones" would lead to the end of caste. Indeed, he felt that the non-Brahman movement of Maharashtra (and, although in different respects, the movement in Tamil Nadu as well) had extremely dangerous effects. "The sub-castes that join together to create a super-organization retain their internal feelings of exclusiveness in fair vigour. The new organization takes up a rather militant attitude against other castes, especially those which are popularly regarded as immediately higher or lower than the caste which it represents."[26] The problem, for Ghurye—and this was the very problem that had been so egregiously exacerbated by British colonial rule—was "caste-patriotism, which creates an unhealthy atmosphere for the full growth of national consciousness."[27] Indeed, "acute conflict" would be the only result. Ghurye was worried that this conflict would lead to social tensions that would hinder both nationalism and indeed national unity. He was also concerned about the politicization of anti-Brahman sentiment, since it would block the development (or in his view the re-instantiation) of the proper separation between religion and politics and potentially lead to a wanton attack on Hindu ideas and institutions.

Ghurye recognized throughout his career that the scheduled castes were in many respects a special case. He noted that Ambedkar was a primary drafter and sponsor of the Indian Constitution, which solemnly asserted that the People of India had "constituted themselves into a Sovereign Democratic Republic," with general claims on behalf of all its citizens for justice, liberty, equality, and fraternity.[28] Yet he also noted with growing concern that the Constitution, and, even worse, amendments to the Constitution, had introduced fundamental contradictions around the relationship between justice and equality. When Article 16 asserts that "nothing in this article shall prevent the State from making any provision for the reservation of appointments or posts in favour of any backward class of citizens which, in the opinion of the State, is not adequately represented in the services under the State," Ghurye sees an open door for the erosion of his dream for a casteless society.[29] While he understood the need for reservations for the scheduled castes and tribes, he was deeply concerned about the likelihood that any initial time limits would be extended indefinitely. He was far more concerned about the slippery language around backward castes, defined in Article 360 as the "weaker sections of the people." As he went on to observe, "To a student of Indian society as to any politician who has judiciously and without preconception tried to understand the social climate that had come to settle down during the last stages of the British rule in India, the need to ponder over the rather inharmonious provisions mentioned above in a Constitution that was to usher in a casteless society should have been clear."[30]

Ghurye accordingly lamented both the ambiguity of the Constitution and the degree to which political concerns seemed to propel a proliferation of provisions even as the category of backward caste would relentlessly expand. Decisions to allow states to draw up their own lists of backward castes and to repeatedly extend provisions meant originally to be temporary only made matters worse. Though Nehru had opposed extensions and decried the creation of vested interests through these provisions, Ghurye was not wrong to anticipate the further, and indefinite, politicization of caste, if not the fundamental reasons leading to it. And while Ghurye had welcomed the Hindu Marriage Act of 1955 for its rational embrace and state licensing of intercaste marriages, he was deeply concerned when Tamil Nadu enacted "self-respect" marriages, for the rhetoric around these marriages rendered caste as the major sign of Hindu beliefs and rituals rather than as something that could be overcome while still holding to what he felt to be fundamental about Hinduism itself. To be sure, Ghurye understood that Tamil Nadu had a far more distinctive non-Sanskritic linguistic and literary tradition than North India, and a history less characterized by Brahman influence. But Tamil politics was moving in precisely the wrong direction, providing all the necessary warning signals for why India should become casteless rather than plural.

I had commenced my own study of caste through attempting to understand the reasons why caste politics became so dominant in the Tamil-speaking region of southern India. The literary history of the region offers few clues about the rise of caste politics—Tamil had an ancient classical tradition, to be sure, but Sanskrit and Tamil had coexisted happily for centuries, along with a host of other languages, including Telugu, Kannada, Marathi, and Persian. It was only when the missionary philologist Robert Caldwell began to charge that Brahmans were outsiders, and Sanskrit the vehicle of their colonization of Tamil culture, that caste—coded here as anti-Brahmanism—and literature began to be linked. But even the rise of the cult of Tamilttay, the mother goddess of Tamil, did not exacerbate the role of caste in political discourse and mobilization. Those who were deeply invested in Tamil itself, from the literary collector of Sangam poetry, U. V. Swaminathan, to the great poet Subrahmanian Bharati, were often Brahmans and rarely xenophobic. Anti-Brahmanism itself formally began with the Justice Party and the early efforts on the part of elite non-Brahmans to gain access first to government employment and then to university admission. It was E. V. Ramaswamy Naicker who most insistently linked anti-Brahmanism with a host of other oppositional stances, against North India, against Sanskrit and Hindi, against Hindu practice and precept, and indeed against the forms of Indian nationalism more generally that either refused to take on caste politics directly or sought either to use or placate religious sentiment on behalf of political causes.

Early on in my academic work I became fascinated with E. V. R., or Periyar, as he became known, and it was through seeking to understand Periyar's own quixotic political life, as well as following his enormous if also contradictory political influence, that I initially sought to understand the nature of caste relations in southern India. For Periyar, as indeed for Gandhi, religion and politics could not be separated, but—and of course the political quarrel began with Gandhi—in Periyar's case this meant that religion had to be rejected entirely, a plea that, despite the role of secularism in the Dravidian movement, has had fair less consequence than his critique of caste. But the more I learned about Periyar, the more I realized that he hardly unlocked the key to understanding the significance of caste in southern India.

When I began my graduate study of India in the early 1970s, social scientists and historians in North America were seeking to understand caste by stripping away the weight of colonial anthropology (and the colonial archive), even as they were reading the work of Ghurye, Srinivas, and Karve, among many others, to understand the effects of colonial history as well as of modern change on the traditional features of Indian society, caste and kinship especially. There was a great deal of attention to the work of Indologists, since the most authentic meanings of caste were assumed to predate colonial rule. It was in this context that the publication of Louis Dumont's *Homo Hierarchicus* was so important.[31] When I first read this extraordinary tome I was struck not just by the elegant reversal of Tocqueville's reflections on America and the ingenious critique of the American conceit of social stratification but also by the fact that Dumont seemed to have ignored his own extended fieldwork, in a Kallar village in Tamil Nadu. The Pramalai Kallar of Tirumangalam presented a picture of an Indian social world in which Brahmans, and principles around purity and pollution, seemed about as far away as anywhere in South Asia. Yet there was no doubt that the rich cultural world conveyed by Dumont's careful ethnographic sensibility was also a world that had been consigned by conventional opinion, both societal and academic, to the lowest reaches of social prestige. So perhaps it made sense after all that Dumont interpreted his fieldwork as grist for the mill of a totalizing theory that accorded encompassing significance to a grand Indological conception of sacred, and indeed sacerdotal, values.

It was only some years later, however, when I had become seriously immersed in my own archival and field research on the Pudukkottai Kallar, that I began to focus on the need to critique Dumont as a general theorist of the social, as well as in relation to his overarching views of Indian civilization. Even as I was intrigued by his critique of the mystifications involved in American understandings of equality, I was also suspicious of the idealism of his account. But when I realized in my own fieldwork that the Pudukkottai Kallar were at the top of the social hierarchy—indeed that the princely state had allowed the survival of customs and beliefs that even relegated Brahmans to a position below kings in the ritual displays of hierarchy both in court and in temple ceremony, I believed that I had encountered a signal exemplification of the extent to which the political and the religious were in fact part of a single continuum, and how Dumont's Brahmanic view of the world was at odds with the actual anthropological history of the Kallars. And it was then that I began to think about the effects of colonial rule in a much more comprehensive way, drawing inspiration from Ghurye and from Cohn and ultimately writing a book in which I tried to demonstrate not just the nature of social change under colonialism but the way a Dumontian view could in some ways only be possible after colonial rule.[32]

Where did this leave the politics of my own scholarly intervention? In the context of academic discussions in the West, it seemed clear. Assumptions and assertions about the timeless hold of the caste system, and indeed of religious preoccupations that legitimated inequality and oppression, were not just false but deeply implicated in the West's own colonial subjugation of the East. Caste (and its relationship to religion), as it had developed over the course of the last two hundred years, was in part the product of explicit efforts to justify, and then sustain, colonial control and occupation. And in a postcolonial context, conventional Western beliefs that poverty and backwardness were the inevitable by-products of culture rather than of colonial rule could be directly critiqued. From my standpoint, I could also engage in a critical way the epistemological formations of my own education, cultivated as it had been by Cold War preoccupations, and heavily influenced by its classical (aka orientalist) origins. In short, I was in agreement with Ghurye about the impact of British colonialism on caste, but I shared neither his sense of what caste had been before the colonial nor his alarm over the ways in which caste might be the necessary vehicle of social and political mobilization in postindependence India. At the same time, I could prove Dumont wrong but also recuperate his critique not only of the epistemological problems of Western social science but of how value systems concealed, whether through direct embrace or denial, contradictions that either inserted inequality in place of equality or oppression in place of hierarchy.

In Tamil Nadu, however, my interlocutors were quick to worry that by focusing on the role of the British, I was running the risk of letting Brahmans off the hook. In the context of Dalit politics, I soon realized that this concern was even more intense, a fear that criticism of colonialism would both ignore the useful role that some colonial reforms played in addressing untouchable issues and indeed blame the British for the millennial sins of Brahmans and other upper caste groups. At first I wasn't sure if the disinterest in colonialism was because of its historical distance and the predictable fading of historical memory or because the stark opposition between colonialism and nationalism never really made any sense in an environment in which nationalism seemed so clearly casteist—a kind of alibi for deferring serious attention to social injustice. Whether this was so or not, the stakes and meanings that attend current-day writing about caste are perhaps more vexing today than ever before. And while the role of the state, and in the case of India the role of the state in regard to reservation policy especially, continues to be the key site of debate about caste, increasingly the real questions that confront us have to do with the relationship between the new economic regime of liberalization and the social. What difference has liberalization made to caste as either the marker or the medium for social differentiation? Has liberalization in fact made state reservations less important? Is the marketplace socially blind? Or, rather, is the global marketplace an opportunity for privilege to be recoded as about money rather than social identity? What kind of pressure can be exerted on the corporate sector? And what kinds of extranational means of pressure, justice, etc. might actually be possible given the limited political structures for international or global governance?

No politics can exist without history, to be sure, and there are lessons aplenty to be learned from reading and engaging the extraordinary corpus of G. S. Ghurye. It is fascinating to use the present moment, for example, to consider the historical relationship between anticolonialism and the idea of civilization, or the historical parallels between Cold War social science in the West and nationalist anthropology in India. But Ghurye's own relentless engagement with the present surely suggests that the time is right to launch a new set of political questions about how to engage in the sociological analysis of caste in India today. Whether we confront issues of reservations, caste politics, or globalization, the task of sociology will be to anticipate the questions of the future as much as rehearse the questions of the past. And for this task, whatever the problems of Ghurye's legacy, his insistence on the relevance of social science for contemporary social and political debates will continue to serve us very well indeed.

12

South Asian Studies

Futures Past

Origins

South Asian studies in the United States began in the conjuncture between Sanskritic scholarship and the strategic concerns and contexts of
World War II.[1] This conjuncture has had vast importance in the shaping
of South Asian area studies, which in its early years was dominated by
a fascination on the one hand with ancient Indic civilization and on the
other with contemporary society, politics, and economy. Only in recent
years (the 1990s) have the fields of colonial and postcolonial studies,
modern history, and contemporary cultural studies emerged as a new
kind of foundation for the study of South Asia. It is the aim of this chapter to tell the story of this transition and to speculate in preliminary
ways about the larger implications of this transition as we look toward
the next century.

The person at the heart of the original conjuncture was W. Norman
Brown, the founder of the University of Pennsylvania's Department of
South Asia Regional Studies and professor of Sanskrit at Penn between
1926, when Franklin Edgerton vacated the Sanskrit Chair and moved
to Yale, and 1966, when Brown retired.[2] Along with several specialists
of the Near East, Brown founded the Oriental Studies Department in
1931, and he played a key role in initial discussions in the 1930s, some

of them sponsored by the Committee on Indic and Iranian Studies of the American Council of Learned Societies. But it was the war and the dearth of personnel trained to deal with issues in contemporary Asia that crystallized these discussions, both for South Asia and other area studies initiatives. Brown was recruited by William Donovan to work for the Research and Analysis Branch of the Office of Strategic Services, and many of the scholars he recruited to help him staff the South Asia desk returned with him to the University of Pennsylvania at the end of the war. The University of Pennsylvania was the only university conducting any courses of intensive language and area study during the war, and it was at the University of Pennsylvania that South Asian studies was to be born soon after the war was over.

In 1944 Brown advocated the serious development and funding of Oriental Studies in a draft document in which he wrote: "During the course of the war the US govt. agencies have needed information about the Orient to a degree far beyond anticipation. . . . Our nation must never again be caught so ill-equipped with knowledge and specialists on the Orient as it was at the end of 1941."[3] It was with this intellectual argument and rhetorical justification that Brown advocated Asian studies. The context for interdisciplinary regional studies was in large part the result of a broad-based sense of world civilizational areas in which the present—however embedded in the historical experience of colonialism and no matter how quickly drawn into the spiral of modernization and technological transformation—could not be understood without taking into account the great sweep of the civilizational past.

Soon after the war, Brown abandoned the idea of regional oriental studies and argued instead for the development of a more bounded version of South Asian regional studies. No doubt this decision was influenced by the announcement of India's independence in the summer of 1947, the very summer that the University of Pennsylvania offered a summer school in Indian studies for the first time. This summer session, funded by the ACLS among other sources, served as the basis for the establishment of the Department of South Asia Regional Studies in 1948, an institutional development that was funded by the Carnegie, Rockefeller, and Ford Foundations.[4] Brown recruited a number of scholars who had worked with him first during the war in Washington, where they furnished South Asian expertise for military and strategic purposes:

by the academic year 1949–1950, a complete program for South Asia Regional Studies, both at the undergraduate and graduate levels, had been established under Brown's leadership, and an affiliated faculty of twenty-one scholars, covering such fields as geography, linguistics, sociology, language instruction in Hindi, and other affiliated fields in Asian studies, were listed in the catalog.

The Department of South Asian Studies (and the area center that subsequently developed out of this initiative once federal funding was established for area studies in the 1950s) at Penn both trained many of the first generation of U.S. South Asianists and provided a model for and a set of institutional and intellectual concerns critical to the development of South Asian studies across the United States. Additionally, graduate students interested in South Asia but working at other universities often went to the summer sessions at Penn and established ideas and contacts that carried Penn's influence far and wide. In the summer of 1948, according to the reminiscences of Robert Crane, four scholars who went on to play major roles in South Asian studies all attended the summer session and began close professional and personal associations that were to last for some thirty years and affect developments at universities as various as Chicago, Michigan, and Duke, as well as at Penn.[5] One of these was Richard Lambert, a prominent sociologist who later succeeded Brown as chair of the Penn Department in 1966 and who was one of the chief advocates for South Asian studies in the 1960s and 1970s. Also in Philadelphia that summer was Richard Park, a political scientist who earned a Ph.D. from Harvard in 1951 for work on India before joining the faculty at Berkeley that same year, later becoming the first director of the Berkeley South Asia Program and also creating the Modern India Project, which was sponsored by the Ford Foundation and ran between 1954 and 1957. In 1959 Park moved to the University of Michigan, where Crane had begun teaching Indian history in 1956. According to Crane, the South Asia Program at Michigan was

> designed as a multi-disciplinary program, a format already well established . . . in the Center for Japanese Studies. The Asian Studies Committee of the University was creating a new, multidisciplinary undergraduate core course in comparative Asian civilizations. This new core course received Foundation and University support and this enhanced our need

for qualified South Asianists on the faculty. That facilitated a challenging offer to Richard Park who, in 1959, became an Associate Professor of Political Science and Director of the new Center for Southern Asian Studies.[6]

Park not only continued to play a major role in the development of South Asian studies at Michigan and elsewhere (ultimately becoming President of the Association for Asian Studies in 1978); he also soon became one of Norman Brown's key collaborators in the establishment of the American Institute for Indian Studies in 1961.

In many ways, then, W. Norman Brown set the tone and the most prominent institutional context and agenda for the early development of South Asian studies in the United States, both through his intellectual vision and his institutional investments. His legacy continues to be seen at Penn and perhaps even more importantly in the American Institute of Indian Studies, which, since its origins, has been the primary funding agent for U.S. doctoral and postdoctoral research on South Asia. Given his preeminent importance in the establishment of South Asian studies, it is worth dwelling for a moment on Brown's own scholarly interests and commitments. Brown was classically trained as a Sanskritist, earning his Ph.D. in 1916 under Maurice Bloomfield at Johns Hopkins (six years after his father, who had been a missionary in India, also attained a Ph.D. in Sanskrit under Bloomfield at Hopkins for a thesis on the human body in the Upanishads).[7] Norman's thesis had been on the relationship between the Panchatantra and modern Indian folklore, and it was part of a broader collaboration that included Franklin Edgerton's more philologically based work on the classical text. Brown's own work bridged philological and contemporary issues, demonstrating, according to Rosane Rocher, "a basic interest in studying the Indian tradition from its most ancient sources to its most recent manifestations."[8] Rocher also notes that this mix of interests seemed based in part on the fact that Brown had spent a number of years in India as a young boy with his missionary father and could never completely adapt to the European-based philological classicism of Sanskrit studies as it existed in the United States at the time. Although he established a formidable reputation as a classical scholar, he was interested in addressing contemporary issues from an early stage in his career. During the 1930s he wrote a manuscript entitled "Why Conflict in India," which described political developments in the Indian subcontinent and, according to Rocher, "evinced strong sympathies for the nationalist movement." It was in part because of this interest that he was called to Washington during the war.

It was on the basis both of the unpublished manuscript prepared before the war and his wartime experience in Washington that Brown ultimately wrote a book entitled *The United States and India and Pakistan*, published in 1953 in the American Foreign Policy Library by Harvard University Press. In 1954 it was awarded the Watamull Prize, given by the American Historical Association, for the best book in the history of India. The book provides a basic summary of Indian history from the Indus Valley, through British colonial history, to partition, and it presents a great deal of material about contemporary politics, economic development, and relations between the United States and both India and Pakistan. However, Brown's scholarly background and interests emerge at various points in the narrative. For example, he writes early on in the book, "The greatest achievements of characteristic Indian civilization are in religion and philosophy."[9] And for him, these achievements are not only Hindu; they refer in particular to an abstract form of monistic philosophy associated with the term *advaita* and the thinker Shankara. Brown's orientalist perspective also shows through when he discusses language groups in India. He calls Sanskrit the "cement that bound together diverse linguistic groups in a cultural unity, and though the Aryan language complex is an immigrant in India, we commonly call the country's culture Aryan."[10] He goes on to say that "the preeminence of Sanskrit as a medium of educated communication throughout India was impaired by the Muslims as they spread over the country. . . . In the period of their power the position of Sanskrit declined."[11] In the wake of partition and within the context of major tensions both between India and Pakistan and between Muslims and Hindus within India, such scholarly statements were unexceptional. Nevertheless, it was wrong to claim that Sanskrit was ever a cement of the kind adumbrated by Brown, nor that "Muslims" as a community "impaired" the preeminence of Sanskrit.[12] And although Brown was sympathetic with the cause of Indian nationalism, his fundamental lack of suspicion about the role played by colonial rule in the prelude to partition allows him to follow up his pronouncements about the role of Muslims in disrupting the cultural unity of India with the following problematic statement: "By far the most effective force in separating Indian communities from one another and so producing national disunity has been religion. At the same time religion, at least in the case of Hinduism, contributed to the formation, growth, and power of nationalism."[13]

While Brown's intentions were framed within his own larger goals to increase understanding and exchange between India (and Pakistan) and the United States, it was also the case that his sense of modern Indian history was profoundly shaped by his disciplinary concern with issues of religion and classical Sanskritic (and in his terms "Hindu") civilization. Given his founding role in South Asian studies as well as his own popular writings about South Asia, these views both established their authority on the weight of colonial and Indological knowledge and worked further to establish, within the context of postwar/Cold War American liberalism, a whole set of conventional understandings about the essential nature of religious identity and ontology in the Indian subcontinent. In his book, Brown explains the partition of India as

> a direct result of communalism. . . . The Muslims in pre-partition India disliked the beliefs and ways of the Hindus, distrusted them, and as a minority feared for their treatment if they should have to live in a state where the Hindu majority had power. The Hindus in their turn disliked the ways of the Muslims, and, though a majority, feared the rise to power of the Muslims under whom they had experienced centuries of oppression. . . . The basis of Hindu-Muslim communalism lies in cultural differences.[14]

Brown goes on to give summary versions of Islam and Hinduism, in which Islam is represented as requiring a strident form of monotheistic uniformity whereas Hinduism is open to an endlessly proliferating array of diverse possibilities.

In promulgating these views of religion and of the implications of religious life for political and cultural outcomes and convictions, Brown, with the greatest of authority, naturalizes the partition of India even as he recognizes it as a source of perilous insecurity for the subcontinent. Brown further avers that Hindus have no theory of the state and precious little in the way of history, that caste is an ironclad social fact destined to dominate politics, and that women are horribly backward.[15] All this serves as the frame for Brown's review of the depressing condition of agricultural production, oppressive poverty both in the countryside and the cities, and the many problems confronting the establishment of democratic politics across the subcontinent.

Nevertheless, Brown was convinced that greater knowledge about the subcontinent, as well as cultural exchange between its nations and the United States, would lead to a happier and more prosperous world. He was tireless in his criticisms of those Americans who out of ignorance or malice (or both) had contributed to negative images of the subcontinent, and he was convinced that the deep, if frequently difficult, friendship between the United States and India would be furthered significantly by educational and cultural developments. Thus he saw his work with university programs, as well as in the solicitation of foundation support for the development of South Asia (and other) area studies, the constant lobbying for government support for programs in education and culture, as a life work that was simultaneously political and academic. And in this endeavor, the establishment of the American Institute of Indian Studies, financed principally by Indian rupee repayment for loans to India from the United States and by a startup grant from the Ford Foundation, and dedicated to the support of American academic research in South Asian studies, was his crowning achievement.[16]

Norman Brown's life not only documents many of the most important aspects of the early formation of South Asian studies in the United States; it also helps to explain why area studies at the University of Pennsylvania and elsewhere privileged a combination of classical Indological scholarship and modern political and economic concern in the early history of the field. Penn was soon joined by a number of other institutions that sought to introduce the serious study of South Asia into their programs of research and teaching during the postwar academic boom years, among them Berkeley, Michigan, Chicago, Columbia, and Wisconsin. In the early years, the most important institutional developments outside Penn took place at the University of Chicago, where the study of South Asia emerged principally out of the efforts of Robert Redfield and Milton Singer to introduce a comprehensive program in the comparative study of civilizations. Singer, who began teaching core social science core courses to undergraduates at the University of Chicago after completing his Ph.D. under Rudolph Carnap in philosophy, became a close associate of Robert Redfield's in the late 1940s, just as

Redfield was attempting to develop an integrated plan for the study of culture and civilization. At that time, Redfield was a major figure in social science and in anthropology at Chicago, having served as dean and principal advisor to Robert Maynard Hutchins for many years and having written important work on folk cultures, the folk-urban continuum, and the civilizational contexts for understanding local communities.[17] In the late 1940s, Redfield drafted a plan for an Institute in Cultural Studies that he saw as the basis for a comprehensive and "comparative study of the principal systems of values of the societies that have mattered most in history."[18] Upon hearing that the Ford Foundation would support his project in 1951, he recruited a number of colleagues to help him run the program; most important among these was Singer.[19]

Milton Singer had first become a close intellectual colleague of Redfield's when he wrote a paper on the study of American civilization in 1949 titled "How the American Got His Character," and, by the fall of 1951, he was co-teaching courses with him in cultural anthropology.[20] In large part through this association, Singer came to see himself as an anthropologist and in 1955 accepted a formal position within the department of anthropology at Chicago. In the early 1950s, Redfield and Singer used their grant money to sponsor a series of conferences in "civilizational studies," collecting the proceedings in a book series entitled "Comparative Studies of Cultures and Civilizations," published by the University of Chicago Press. During this time Redfield worked out many of his earlier ideas about great and little traditions, civilizational process, and the role of anthropology in investigating folk cultures within a larger civilizational context. Singer worked with Redfield in the preparation of a methodological treatise, never finally published, that began to chart out a set of disciplinary procedures privileging context-based anthropological fieldwork and local study of little traditions and the text-based study of language, literature, philosophy, cultural history, and the history of civilizations for understanding great traditions. In the early phase, they were especially influential in the field of Chinese studies. But soon Singer turned his attention to the study of India, and he became primarily interested in the development of South Asian civilizational studies.

In the academic year 1953–1954, Singer engaged in a year-long postdoctoral study of India, spending the fall term at Penn studying with

Brown and the winter term at Berkeley working with the anthropologist David Mandelbaum.[21] While at Berkeley, Singer was especially influenced by the work of M. N. Srinivas, an Oxford-trained anthropologist who had published his *Religion and Society Among the Coorgs of South India* in 1952.[22] Singer quickly grasped that Srinivas's idea of sanskritization, in which notions of Brahmanic Hinduism spread in part through a process of status emulation, could be seen as an illustration of Redfield's ideas about the interactions of great and little traditions. Inspired by Redfield and Srinivas, Singer committed himself to a plan for field studies in India that led to many years of sustained research and publication on India. At Chicago he began immediately to orient the Chicago civilizations project toward the study of India. Singer and Redfield planned a symposium on the Indian village that brought eight social anthropologists to work with graduate students in Chicago, leading to the volume edited by McKim Marriott entitled *Village India*.[23] The papers all argued that villages in India were not self-sufficient units, isolated in conventional anthropological terms from larger civilizational forms and processes, and the papers established India as a primary site for the working out of Redfield's and Singer's programmatic agenda. Marriott's paper argued that classical and folk forms, and by implication civilizational and village sites, were vitally connected through processes he labeled particularization and universalization. Shortly after the volume's publication, Marriott was recruited from Berkeley back to Chicago, where he had done his Ph.D., and once there he went on to advocate the importance of empirically based long-term fieldwork studies in India.

If the University of Pennsylvania was dominated by Brown's combination of Indological scholarship and current events, and Berkeley's South Asia initiatives were activated principally through the work of the anthropologist David Mandelbaum, Chicago's history reveals a combination of these two tendencies in the working out of Redfield's and Singer's civilizational agenda for the study of South Asia.[24] Anthropological concerns and fieldwork methods were linked to the textual concerns first of Sanskritists and then, increasingly, specialists in modern languages, to provide a particular disciplinary framing for South Asian studies.[25] As for other areas, political science played an important role in the first postwar decades (before methodological concerns in the discipline began to challenge the importance of comparative politics).

Indeed, among Asianists in the United States, anthropology played a more significant role for South Asian studies than any other subarea with the exception of Southeast Asia. And it is noteworthy that when the University of Chicago decided to hire a tenured historian of South Asia to develop a serious graduate program in this field, it recruited an anthropologist with historical interests rather than a historian who would have been, as was the case with Holden Furber at Penn, initially trained in the history of the British empire. Bernard Cohn, an anthropologist trained at Cornell and later the chair of the department at University of Rochester, was invited to Chicago in 1963, and he soon became the pioneer for the development of the social history of India in the United States.[26] Although Cohn introduced a powerful note of critique to the position of anthropology in area studies, he has also maintained a close interdisciplinary relationship throughout the years between the fields of history and anthropology.

This review of historical and disciplinary origins has suggested ways in which South Asian studies has been produced in the United States out of a curious conjuncture between Indology and anthropology, in the context of a recognition of the strategic importance of South Asia and the growing need to educate Americans, academics and others alike, about a place that was populous but poor, largely democratic but politically fragile, and likely to be of growing military and political significance in a postcolonial Cold War world system. These conjunctures both reflect and were in large part responsible for installing a set of dominant themes for the representation of South Asia, perpetuating some colonial and orientalist forms of knowledge and producing other new American ones. Specifically, serious academic study in the United States of the contemporary political, social, and economic predicament of the new postcolonial nations of South Asia was initially mediated by forms of knowledge focusing either on India's antiquity or its most remote hinterlands. Current political and economic dilemmas were accordingly approached in part through assumptions about India predicated principally on readings of classic texts and backwater contexts. Thus it was that essential statements about the nature of Hinduism and Islam could be accepted as both true and relevant in regard to understanding contemporary South Asia, and thus it was that questions about the political stability of a nation and the economic viability of a society could be evaluated in relation to timeless truths about Indian culture. Further, this history reveals how many components of colonial knowledge about India could be appropriated with only minor modifications in the formation of a new postcolonial academic orthodoxy.

The Middle Period

The establishment of federal funding for area studies programs in 1959 (the National Defense Education Act, Title VI allocation, was passed in late 1958) and the steady increase in support for the study of foreign area languages and cultures (in the late 1950s and 1960s the Ford Foundation played a critical role in providing this support) provided a great boon to the development of South Asian studies during the 1960s and 1970s.[27] The University of Pennsylvania continued to be an important center for South Asian studies and expanded in a number of disciplinary directions, though like other universities with separate departments for South Asian studies (e.g., Chicago and Berkeley) it was able to hire an unusual concentration of language and literature specialists. Penn became known for its powerful group of Sanskritists (including linguists and philologists) at the same time that it continued to be strong in social science fields such as history, sociology, and economics. Berkeley became an important player in fields ranging from history and economics to anthropology and linguistics. Wisconsin emerged as another center for South Asian studies, with faculty appointed in fields such as political science, sociology, and history, as well as across the humanities. Programs of various sizes developed during these decades in places as various as the universities of Michigan, Washington, Minnesota, Virginia, and Texas. Columbia had a small but well-placed group of South Asianists led by figures such as Ainslee Embree in history and Howard Wriggins in political science. And Chicago grew rapidly to become one of the most active centers during these years, certainly in the social sciences. As can be noted even in this incomplete inventory, these were years when social science disciplines across the board discovered the importance of South Asian studies; although today it is difficult to locate South Asianists in disciplines such as sociology and economics and indeed even, increasingly, in political science, these were years when figures such as Richard Lambert, Richard Park, Joseph Elder, and Leo Rose played central roles.

Perhaps the most important contribution of the NDEA funding of South Asian studies was the growing stress on language study during this period, in large part because of the direct linking of graduate funding to serious language learning. Many of the great early figures of South Asian studies, with the exception of the Sanskritists, had little if any knowledge of South Asian languages and engaged in research on South Asia using either English or local interpreters. Often this was because these scholars had been "retooled" as South Asianists after initial training in other fields as well as because research in areas such as election analysis involved a combination of statistical methods and interviews with high-level officials, usually in English. Increasingly a new generation of scholars was trained specifically in South Asian studies with language skills and cultural expertise. At universities such as Penn, Chicago, and Berkeley, faculty were hired during these years to teach Hindi and other Indian languages, sometimes in conjunction with other disciplinary interests. While language skills were not in those early years as important for South Asian studies as they were for East Asian studies, the sense of South Asia as a region that could be approached solely through English (and occasionally Sanskritist) changed dramatically during these years.

The 1960s witnessed the growing seriousness and quality of work on South Asia in a number of different regards. Amateurish prognostications about India's democratic viability were increasingly supplanted by serious analyses of political and social change. Lloyd and Susanne Rudolph, who had been hired by Chicago to teach political science, published an important study in 1967 entitled *The Modernity of Tradition* that complicated social scientific conceptions of "modernization" as well as of the constituent categories of modernity and tradition. It built powerfully on the work of other scholars (some completing their doctoral work on South Asia under the Rudolphs, as for example Robert Hardgrave) on subjects as various as caste politics and legal change.[28] Bernard Cohn developed a history program at Chicago rooted in interdisciplinary methods and serious attention to language and culture. In 1970 he published an essay reviewing the state of the art in South Asian history, and noted that the historian's contribution has largely been a negative one. The historian sensitive to social components in South Asian history has contributed to a questioning of the timeless view which social scientists have used in their discussion of modern South Asia. The historian has pointed to the complexity of the process of political change, especially in the study of the nationalist movement, by pointing to regional and caste differences in participation in the movement.[29]

However, he suggested a bright and powerful future for South Asian history, based both on his assumption of fruitful interchange among social science disciplines and on the recent and promising work of younger scholars in the field, including J. H. Broomfield, Eugene Irschick, S. N. Mukherjee, John Leonard, Peter Marshall, David Kopf, Ronald Inden, and Tom Kessinger (some of whom were or had been his students).[30] Cohn was as excited by the discovery of new kinds of sources for the writing of Indian history as he was by the new historical writing itself.

Bernard Cohn's work and influence on the field more generally was innovative and highly significant not only because of his enterprising rethinking and dramatic expansion of the sources, methods, and questions of historical work but for two other, though related, reasons. First, as mentioned before, he had been trained as an anthropologist and thus brought to his historical sensibility a lively sense of social theory as well as direct experience of village fieldwork. Indeed, many of his writings over the years had argued for new collaborations between history and anthropology, with the aim of making history more adventurous in theoretical as well as empirical terms and of making anthropology grapple with the essential change*fulness* of South Asian society. Second, Cohn early on developed a critical sense of British colonial rule. In a set of early papers he wrote about the history of Western knowledge about India and began to subject Western social science to epistemological criticism. He noted in 1970 that not only was the idea of an autonomous village world in India a myth, but that it was a myth specifically created by the British.[31] In his early writing he focused more on the creation of new institutions by innovations in areas such as land policy; in later writing he focused increasingly on British colonialism and its forms of knowledge. Indeed, long before the critical work of Edward Said and the new field of postcolonial studies, Bernard Cohn had suggested ways in which colonial rule would not have been possible without the development of certain forms of colonial knowledge, at the same time that he critiqued the implication of Western social scientific knowledge about India in the maintenance of basic colonial categories and assumptions.

Cohn's inventive sense of how to study different aspects of colonial history not only anticipated many recent theoretical developments well outside South Asian studies; it also directly inspired a great deal of historical and anthropological work on the character of the colonial state. In Cohn's own writing, colonialism was no longer a historical irruption that had to be stripped away to get down to the real subject of anthropology but rather the focus of the study of social transformation in all societies touched by world systems of colonial rule. For Cohn, colonialism played a critical role in the constitution of the metropole—in the formation of the state and in the development of its basic forms of knowledge—even as it shaped, through its cultural technologies of domination, much of the modern history of colonized places and peoples. Cohn wrote a steady stream of innovative and influential articles on various aspects of his research, ranging in focus from the imperial *darbars* (political functions and processions) in Delhi to the enumerative technologies of power deployed by the census, from the specific careers of terms like "village," "tribe," and "caste" to the anthropology of the colonizers as well as the colonized. Beyond his writing, Cohn also exerted important influence on the shaping of South Asian studies through his students, his role in teaching and research at the University of Chicago, as well as through professional networks and scholarly collaboration, as for example in his early recognition of and participation in the Subaltern Studies history project. Cohn also participated in the 1983 Subaltern Studies Conference in Canberra, subsequently publishing his paper "The Command of Grammar and the Grammar of Command" in the fourth volume of the publications of the Subaltern Studies Collective.[32]

If Cohn's critique of Western social science led both to wide-ranging critiques and an intense interrogation of colonial genealogies of knowledge, it for a time seemed to be also part of an allied movement based principally in Chicago that attained a great deal of influence, particularly in anthropology, during the decade of the 1970s. I refer here to a new set of proposals made under the banner of an "ethnosociology of India." The principal architects of these new ideas were McKim Marriott and Ronald Inden. Marriott's work brought together new scholarship on village India and expanded the insights of Redfield, Singer, and Srinivas in relation to his own intensive fieldwork experience, first in Uttar Pradesh and later in Maharashtra. He became interested in particular in the question of how to understand the nature of hierarchy in caste society. After focusing on the question of caste ranking and the relationship of attributional statements concerning status to empirical practices in the domain of food exchange, Marriott became increasingly intrigued by cultural questions around the meaning of caste. In one sense, he built on the generally accepted understanding of the goal of social anthropological research, at least at Chicago, that Singer articulated in the following passage:

> The understanding of another culture or civilization, as social and cultural anthropology rightly teaches, requires that the foreign traveler rid himself of ethnocentrism and look at another culture in its own terms. Malinowski's axiom that a major aim of ethnology is to understand the "native" from his point of view, his relation to his world, has been accepted by anthropology since the 1920's.[33]

Marriott worried with unusual intensity about how this might be accomplished. Influenced in part by his colleague David Schneider's view that cultural domains had to be identified and described in terms consistent with the cultural object of study, Marriott began to collaborate with the historian Ronald Inden, whose 1972 Chicago dissertation had established an innovative model for the cultural analysis of early Indian texts.[34] Deriving "native" terms and categories from classical sources such as the Manu Dharma Shastras (Hindu prescriptive texts about social duties and orders), Inden and Marriott wrote a series of papers in the early 1970s that argued that Indian society could only be properly understood in relation to a monistic worldview. Their papers combined a rigorous critique of prevailing social scientific theories and procedures—ranging from American empiricism to French idealism—with a programmatic set of recommendations for a new kind of cultural analysis to be pursued both in textual analysis and contextual fieldwork. The primary emphasis was to be on "native" terms and categories. Ethnosociology was to mean "Indian" sociology rather than Western.

The ethnosociology project was in ascendency for quite some time, propelling many a graduate dissertation at Chicago and elsewhere and defining a number of important conferences organized by the Social Science Research Council and other research organizations.[35] Ethnosociology was certainly an outgrowth, at least in part, of serious language study, and it was a consequence of serious frustration with a social scientific inheritance—from Weber to Durkheim, and from colonial ethnography to comparative social stratification studies—that offered little genuine guidance in the quest to understand the complex social and cultural realities of a much mystified subcontinent. However, as it soon became clear that Cohn's initial support gave way to greater and greater qualification, that the Rudolphs among many others had residual commitments to comparative social science that they did not wish to relinquish, and that scholars outside of Chicago, even in nearby Michigan, failed to accept the "Indianness" of this new endeavor, ethnosociology began to lose influence. In a review of a book on Bengali kinship by Ronald Inden and Ralph Nicholas, Tom Trautmann, a historian of ancient India at the University of Michigan, asked whether anyone outside of Chicago believed any of this.[36] And although some scholars in India were intrigued by this new work, including T. N. Madan and Veena Das, most "Indian" social scientists were unclear why these Chicago anthropologists claimed "insider" knowledge of the realities of Indian social science. In retrospect, ethnosociology was a peculiar product of a certain strand of American liberal social theory (which stressed cultural relativism as the antidote to comparative social science) that was in some ways a continuation of earlier trends in South Asian studies: a heady stew made of equal parts Indology and cultural anthropology. And while ethnosociology took advantage of, and further encouraged, serious language study, encouraging full immersion in classical texts and ethnographic contexts, it represented a retreat from some other key components of area studies. For example, there was no room within ethnosociology for a critical engagement with "modernity," since modern forms were signs of the contamination of the West; likewise, there was little interest within the project in contemporary politics or social-economic dilemmas. And ethnosociology entailed characterizations of India that rendered Indian cultural truth both timeless (i.e., ancient) and religious (i.e., Hindu). Viewed today, ethnosociology appears, despite

its many virtues and claims, not only as another mainstream manifesta-
tion of Western social science but as an academic movement that continued to build on older civilizational models that had little interest in the
present predicament and problems of the subcontinent.

At the same time that ethnosociology played such an important role
in Chicago, a number of scholars in the United States were engaged in
serious study of Islamic history, institutions, and identities in South
Asia. Among many other examples, Barbara Metcalf, who taught at Penn
for much of the decade before moving to UC Davis, wrote a study of the
Deoband revival movement; John Richards, who taught at Wisconsin
before moving to Duke, wrote on Mughal rule in Golkonda in southern
India; Richard Eaton of the University of Arizona published an account
of Sufism in Bijapur; Richard Barnett published his work on the history
of Awadh in the seventeenth and early eighteenth centuries; and David
Lelyveld of the University of Minnesota finished his own study of Sir
Sayyid Ahmad Khan and the making of Aligarh Muslim University.[37]

There were other scholarly voices engaged in very different kinds of
research and teaching during these years. Burton Stein, a historian of
ancient southern India who taught at the University of Hawaii but was a
visiting professor at places such as Penn and Chicago, inspired a group
of students who worked on different aspects of the social, cultural, and
economic history of southern India, especially in the Tamil country.[38]
Stein, who like Cohn had interests that bridged history and anthropology, never completely shed his interest in material determinations (even
when he failed to identify them in much of his own work on medieval
South Indian peasant state and society). Stein shared with Chris Bayly
a Braudelian interest in long-term change and with David Washbrook
a concern to chart the history of capitalism in India. He was more in
tune with the "Cambridge school" suspicion of Indian nationalist ideology than most other American historians of India, most notably Leonard
Gordon, Eugene Irschick, and Stanley Wolpert. Stein's interest in the
longue durée and his fascination with the connection of cultural questions and material conditions exercised an important corrective for a
number of scholars given the dominance of abstract cultural analysis
brought about by the institutional centrality of certain people at the
University of Chicago and the continued weight of Indological interest.
He provided the basis for important connections between American and

British scholarship after moving from Hawaii to London, while playing a continuously innovative role in the development of workshop ideas and research projects. He also inspired a great deal of work on southern India, the Tamil country in particular, and gave rise to a number of studies that attempted to link premodern and modern questions. Not only did Stein influence my own attempt to write about political authority in Tamil Nadu between the seventh and the nineteenth centuries; he also influenced the work of David Ludden, a Penn-trained historian who focused on agrarian issues and wrote a powerful study of peasant society and institutions in the southern Tamil region.[39] Stein also encouraged the economic historian Sanjay Subrahmanyam—who later collaborated with the religious and literary scholars David Shulman and V. Narayana Rao in a study of Nayaka cultural history—to think about cultural issues.[40]

South Asian studies in the United States in its first thirty years was for the most part a very American affair. There were multiple relations with England, not only because of the close relationship of academic institutions and disciplines between the two nations but because South Asian studies was more firmly rooted in British history than it was in the United States, where Asia typically means East Asia. However, in the early decades, very few scholars from South Asia were actually hired to teach in North American universities. The Indian scholars who were most influential in the West (e.g., M. N. Srinivas in anthropology, Rajni Kothari in political science, Romila Thapar in history, and Amartya Sen in economics) stayed in India for the most part, at the same time that increasing levels of exchange, collaboration, and institutional participation led to closer and closer intellectual and social ties among academics in India and the United States. Many of the debates held by American academics—over the significance and impact of green revolution technologies, over questions about the relationship of agricultural and industrial development, about social redistributive policies, about levels of state control over economic growth, over the stability of the Indian state and the future of democracy, and over the perdurance of caste, untouchability, and communal tensions in Indian society and political life—were also held with and in close relationship to debates within India itself. But these debates were frequently characterized by various tensions: over the relationship of American academics to U.S. state policies (e.g., at the time of the Bangladesh war); over the relationship of academics in India and the United States to the emergency called by Prime Minister Indira Gandhi between 1975 and 1977; in relation to the place of Marxism in the Indian academy and the resilient concern about the role of U.S. cultural, political, and economic imperialism; and over the role of development and its perceived connections to U.S. interests, international markets, and the continued commitments of Indian state socialism.

I have so far said little about some of the fields that played extremely important roles in the history of South Asian studies in the United States. The largest percentage of active academics, according to statistics compiled by the Association for Asian Studies in 1991, were in religion and philosophy. In earlier years, these fields were dominated by missionary connections and backgrounds. The Divinity School at the University of Chicago, for example, regularly trained missionaries about to go off to do church work in India, at least up to the point that missionary activity in India began to be controlled and then curtailed after Indian independence. But in later years the fields of religion and philosophy maintained a strong interest in things Indian, and many departments of religion considered it necessary to have scholars of Hinduism and/or Buddhism on staff.

While much important scholarship and teaching had been done in areas defined in one way or another by religion, there were obvious problems with the disproportionate attention paid to religion rather than, say, contemporary politics. And given that contemporary politics in South Asia problematized and politicized the study of religion to an unprecedented extent, the disciplinary concentrations and divisions too often reflected basic problems and preoccupations of the U.S. relationship with India.

Despite the classicism of much South Asianist scholarship, there was widespread recognition from the start that academics had to address questions of modernity. W. Norman Brown's recruitment to South Asian studies was mediated in important ways by the security considerations of the U.S. state during the war and in the Cold War era. But it is also the case that nationalism in India, and the long heroic struggle against British colonial rule, fell on sympathetic ears in the United States, from the reporting of William Shirer for the *Chicago Tribune*, to W. Norman

Brown's own predilections, to Martin Luther King's admiration for and use of the nonviolent methods of Mahatma Gandhi. Historians in the United States for many years focused on issues around the nationalist movement and tended to take serious issue with British academic trends that worked to disparage the integrity of nationalist mobilization. And academics from a variety of disciplines took particular interest in the lives and works of Gandhi and Nehru. An inventory of works on Gandhi over the last fifty years would touch every discipline and betray a steady fascination with the man who still appears to many as emblematic of the best of modern India.

Modern Times

From the perspective of the waning years of the twentieth century, when this essay was first written and later revised for publication, the modern era of South Asian studies could be said (by some at least) to have been propelled by the publication of Edward Said's *Orientalism* in 1978.[41] Although Said wrote principally about the Middle East and from the disciplinary position of literary studies, his critique could be and often was directly transposed onto South Asian studies, both in relation to the colonial past and the scholarly present (and the myriad relations between the two). In the early years after the publication of this work, a number of South Asianists reacted sharply against Said's critique, but it soon became clear that there was no going back to an age of pre-*Orientalism* innocence.[42] Although there were many contentious arguments about the status of the Saidian critique and its relevance for South Asian studies, as for example at the year-long seminar held at the University of Pennsylvania in 1988–1989 entitled "Orientalism and Beyond: Perspectives from South Asia," Said's intervention represented a substantial shift in the way area studies began to be perceived across the humanities and social sciences.[43]

If orientalism put the area studies paradigm into critical perspective, it only delivered the first major blow. The fall of the Soviet Union and the end of the Cold War led many social scientists, long concerned about the methodological weakness of area studies scholarship, to charge that the era of area studies was over. Social scientists such as Robert Bates had long called for a disciplinary turn in fields such as his own, namely African studies, but toward the end of the century, the growing prestige of core social science disciplines meant, among many other things, that there was a growing rift between the interests of area studies scholars and the kind of work supported and rewarded in departments of political science, sociology, and economics.[44]

These assaults on area studies came from many places and had growing impact both on disciplinary practices and university life, but excellent work continued to be done within the area studies paradigm, and efforts to reconstitute area studies in more comprehensive and comparative institutional settings—as for example in the creation of the International Institute at the University of Michigan in the early 1990s—continued to reflect the importance of this work. One index of the vitality of South Asian studies during the last two decades of the twentieth century—an index as well of the shifting interests of scholars in the field—could be traced by a cursory look at the workshops and conferences sponsored by the South Asia joint committee of the Social Science Research Council (SSRC) during this period. The South Asia Political Economy Project (SAPE), organized by scholars such as Michelle McAlpin, an economic historian; Veena Das, an anthropologist from Delhi University; and Paul Brass, a political scientist, among others, attempted to link critical political economy concerns with cultural analysis.[45] A similar venture on agricultural terminology was organized by Arjun Appadurai, an anthropologist then at Penn, and Pranab Bardhan, an economist at Berkeley. Barbara Stoler Miller, a Sanskritist, organized a conference on patronage with art historians, historians, and anthropologists. Susan Wadley, an anthropologist, collaborated with Pranab Bardhan on a workshop concerning "Differential Mortality and Female Healthcare in South Asia." Appadurai, along with fellow scholar Carol Breckenridge, a historian and founding editor of the journal *Public Culture*, organized a series of conferences in the late 1980s and early 1990s around questions concerning the transformations of modernity in South Asia in relation to global developments and influences.[46] A series of conferences linking feminist scholarship and activism began to introduce serious feminist concerns into areas as diverse as anthropological research on violence to historical research on migration and political change to women's political participation in and recruitment to Hindu fundamentalist movements.

Humanist scholars (among them, the Sanskritist Sheldon Pollock of the University of Chicago) concerned with South Asian languages, classical as well as modern, organized workshops that attempted to stimulate new forms of research in literary history, the sociology of literature, and the implications of critical theory in the humanities for the study of South Asian literatures. Historians, anthropologists, art historians, political scientists, and others collaborated in efforts to understand the transformations affecting debates over and sentiments relating to the history and future of nationalist ideology and institutions. Other leading scholars arranged for collaborations between medical practitioners and a range of social scientists to investigate questions concerning disease, epidemics, health care, and international medical crises. In the mid-1990s, the committee began to organize an ambitious project on the study of industrialization and its social effects; at the same time it inaugurated a project on the oral history of partition and war in Bangladesh. The committee also initiated a long-term project on the question of governance in South Asia.

Part of the success and excitement of SSRC-sponsored workshops and research initiatives had been their necessarily interdisciplinary character. The joint committee, which aimed to represent different disciplines as well as different regions related to the study of South Asia, typically approved no project that had not had interdisciplinary framing and ambition. The interdisciplinary character of area studies had much to do with the history of social science funding, from Ford interest in interdisciplinary program development in the 1950s and 1960s to SSRC commitments ever since the joint committee was formed in the 1970s. This interdisciplinary context had more often than not been responsible for the innovative and exciting work done in areas such as South Asian studies. While this investment in interdisciplinary studies led in part to the disciplinary blowback against area studies, it was also the case that the social science disciplines became more committed to new kinds of sophisticated methodological and theoretical work, making some work in area studies appear both methodologically crude and insufficiently comparative. By the end of the decade, despite both the continuing importance of regions and of scholarship focused on these regions, it became almost impossible to persuade most departments to hire scholars credentialed in area studies unless they were fundamentally comparativists and also on the cutting edge of disciplinary theory and method. Reflecting these changes, Kenneth Prewitt, president of the Social Science Research Council, dissolved the area subcommittees in the mid-1990s and replaced them with more thematic comparative committees. While Title VI support kept area studies alive, increasingly area centers became charged with little more than organizing language instruction and community outreach. And as the social sciences disengaged from area studies, fields such as history and a number of humanistic disciplines became more global and more engaged with area studies scholars. History in particular benefitted from the extraordinary interest and excitement generated by the collective convened by the brilliant historian, Ranajit Guha, under the name of "Subaltern Studies."

Perhaps the single most important development on U.S. campuses in South Asian studies, however, was not the growing intellectual exchange and collaboration among scholars but rather the growing numbers of students in language, civilization, and area studies courses who came from South Asian backgrounds, most of them children of immigrants who moved to the United States from India after the change in the immigration act of 1965. The success of most South Asia programs in ensuring regular funding for the teaching of Hindi and Urdu was the direct result not of pressure from graduate programs but rather from a growing population of undergraduates, many of South Asian backgrounds, who took these classes. The experience I had of teaching South Asian Civilization at the University of Michigan in the early 1990s, where close to 80 percent of the students who took this course came from immigrant backgrounds, was no longer exceptional. As South Asian students were both more numerous and more active on campuses across the country, regularly claiming significant proportions of student activity funds for South Asia–related programming, and increasingly advocating South Asia courses for reasons of heritage and community organization, colleges and universities began to pay a different kind of attention to South Asian studies. Where once arguments for courses and faculty were made for strategic reasons combined with the goal of international understanding, arguments were now often made through constituency representation on the part of a vocal and talented community. And funding for South Asia–related activities increasingly came from community gifts and endowment projects. In the last few years of the twentieth century, new programs began to spring up on campuses such as the University of California at Santa Cruz, Rutgers, and the State University of New York at Stony Brook; funds were raised for chairs in Sikh and Tamil studies as well as Indian studies more generally; and the politics of nation, community, and culture began to erupt at universities such as the University of British Columbia, Berkeley, Michigan, and Columbia.

The growing relationship between South Asian Studies and South Asian Americans was a great boon to the field and provided both a new constituency and urgency to a field that had previously been restricted for the most part to graduate studies and undergraduate courses in religion and philosophy. While South Asian Americans typically maintained close relations with South Asia itself, reflecting a new kind of immigration and a very different situation than has applied, for example, in the relations between African and African American studies, the American experience was not merely a continuation of the middle-class experience in South Asia. Indeed, one of the consequences of these new collaborations had been a tendency to focus even more on some of the cultural questions noted above than on economic ones, leave alone questions concerning the poor in South Asia, whether in the cities or the countryside. And the politics of middle-class India, for example in the domain of rising communalist tensions and the strong role played by organizations such as the VHP in the United States, began to play themselves out in the American context, where the immediate stakes of these tensions—as in proximity to riot situations or palpable communal conflict—were largely invisible. Additionally, disagreements emerged between donor communities and universities, as happened at the University of Michigan when the first occupant of the chair in Sikh studies was declared by many devout Sikhs as blasphemous because of his doctoral dissertation work, in which he subjected the Sikh scripture to hermeneutical exegesis.

Because of its political instability, Pakistan had attracted particular interest among political scientists, and because of its poverty, Bangladesh had been a special province for development economists.[47] Sri Lanka has been entirely left out of my discussion above, despite deep ties between southern India and the island, through both Buddhism and the Tamil migrations. Sri Lanka produced four of the finest anthropologists then teaching in U.S. universities and has occasioned more interest within anthropology generally than has been the case for other disciplines, tied as many of them are to the importance of the nation-state as an object of study.[48] Nepal has also been a site for important anthropological work, though increasingly it attracted interest on the part of development economics and applied social scientists in areas such as forestry and water management.[49] Once again, smaller nations tended to attract more attention from anthropology than from history.

These problems notwithstanding, South Asian studies in the United States was in some ways in better shape by the end of the century than it had ever been before. Thanks to subaltern studies and trends in comparative history, South Asian history was thriving, and thanks to postcolonial studies, South Asia became important in the humanities well outside the traditional Indological niches of earlier years. While South Asia did not fare very well in the hard social sciences, neither did other areas outside North America and Europe. Although the growing population and interest of South Asian Americans led to new issues and problems in the field, there was little doubt that this new constituency would continue to grow and demand greater representation for South Asia in university life. South Asian cultural studies—in areas such as film, music, the arts, and popular culture—seemed likely to grow in part because of this kind of connection.

Despite the loss of commitment to area studies in disciplines such as economics and political science, it seemed increasingly urgent to ensure serious research interests in areas around political theory and political institutions, the effects of economic liberalization on political, social, as well as local economic phenomena, and the implications of new state forms and ideologies for other aspects of contemporary life in the subcontinent. Areas of increasing interest included questions having to do with governance, with rethinking the relationship of state and society, state and nation, nation and internation. At the same time, it seemed clear that no study of contemporary politics could be done without looking as well at global forces such as the IMF and the World Bank, U.S. foreign policy, the United Nations and issues on the flip side of world legitimacy that have to do with the role of international "mafia" groups in the underworld economy of currency smuggling, illegal weapons trades, drugs, etc. Unfortunately, the hard social science disciplines that would seem particularly relevant here were largely impervious to foundation attempts to encourage "area" study through special grant initiatives. Ironically, some of the first signs of a sea change in the importance of South Asia began to be seen in schools of business and public policy. This trend only got stronger as India's economy began to grow at rates close to 10 percent a year in the final years of the 1990s. Now, in the early years of the twenty-first century, India has become of interest in an entirely new way to scholars across many disciplines and arenas of professional study. In the rush to study about, invest in, and collaborate with India in particular, the greatest concern for area studies becomes once again how to ensure the highest levels of research and teaching in traditional fields, especially language study, but also the study of history—both ancient and modern—and culture. We can only hope that new wealth in South Asia will help support the humanities as well as the many new initiatives in the world of business, technology, and global markets.

Part V

University

13

Franz Boas and the American University:
A Personal Account

I begin with a confession. Strictly speaking, I had no business being asked to be the Franz Boas Professor of Anthropology at Columbia. I knew very little about Boas from my graduate education at the University of Chicago and, even while teaching courses on the history of anthropology, had included only short sections of Boas on the syllabus. Partly this was because of my focus on Asia and Africa, the sites of British colonial history, and my interest in the relationship of anthropology to all that. And partly this was because of the disciplinary formation of anthropology at Chicago, which in any event I inhaled indirectly since I did my Ph.D. in the history department. I always cited Boas as especially useful as an illustration of the necessity of the connection between anthropology and history, but I must say that I never found Boas as useful in thinking through the issues confronting me in my own work as other classical figures in the field, ranging from Marcel Mauss to Louis Dumont and from E. E. Evans-Pritchard to Edmund Leach. Morgan, Maine, and Weber seemed of more relevance to the Indian case.

I had also been critical of the insistence on the four-field approach, an approach associated by many with Boas, for all students interested in being certified in anthropology. When I co-founded an interdepartmental Ph.D. program in anthropology and history at the University of Michigan, I had specifically fashioned the program to combine cultural or social anthropology with the kind of historical training done in history departments (rather than insisting, for example, that archaeology be the only form of historical practice prescribed for an anthropologist). I had thought of linguistics as less important than learning languages; it seemed necessary to stress the textual and archival skills of a historian more than the importance of analyzing grammar or linguistic structure. And I had felt that physical anthropology in particular should be a separate field of biological research and teaching, hardly necessary—let alone genuinely attainable—for the training of a historical anthropologist in the late twentieth century. So when I got the call to come to Columbia to chair and rebuild the anthropology department and assume the Boas Professorship, I thought—though I fear many others thought this, too—why me? In fact, I soon came to see the ways in which fate had done me a great honor by bringing me into Boas's shadow and how fortunate I had been to be given that historical opportunity in the larger context both of the discipline of anthropology and of the development of the arts and sciences at Columbia University. Here I will give several examples of how I came to understand that this was so.

Boas came to anthropology from a background in physics and natural science, though he had a serious interest in Kantian philosophy as a graduate student and was deeply influenced by the revolution in historicist thinking in Germany during the middle years of the nineteenth century, especially thanks to the work of thinkers such as Ranke and Dilthey. His growing sense of the importance of empirical research, the problems with the tendency to seek general laws for all questions concerning human history, and his developing understanding of the differences between the natural and the human sciences in the years after he completed his Ph.D. in physics and began to shift to anthropological research were neatly captured in his 1887 essay "The Study of Geography."[1] He insisted on a separation between natural science, where general laws were fundamental, and historical science, based on a specific understanding of phenomena on their own terms. After his Baffin Island expedition, he noted further that "ethnological phenomena are the result of the physical and psychical character of men, and of its development under the influence of the surroundings."[2] By surroundings he meant both geography and sociology, the relation of man to environment and of man to man. And history was critical to the understanding of both geographical and sociological context. Boas's commitment to particularity and empirical research was deeply influential, especially in the establishment of fieldwork as the fundamental method of American anthropology, though it has been noted that many of his most illustrious students came to depart from him in their subsequent interests in developing more general theoretical approaches in anthropology. But it is fair to say that Boas provided a critical pedigree for the emergence of historical anthropology in the United States, both for researchers working in areas where archives were of less value than material collections of art, artifacts, and archaeological records and for anthropologists deeply committed to archival research, including such figures as Eric Wolf, Marshall Sahlins, Bernard Cohn, and Clifford Geertz.

Accordingly, it seemed perfectly consistent—even Boasian—to contemplate rebuilding the Columbia anthropology department around a general commitment to historical anthropology. It also seemed consistent to think of rebuilding the department in aggressively interdisciplinary ways. I became increasingly skeptical about the claim on the part of some that Boas's principal legacy was that of four-field anthropology. First, he never gave the same weight to each of the fields; much of the work in archaeology during his time did not impress him at all, and Columbia came to have a strong reputation in the field only after Boas had retired. And, as is well known, his interest in biological anthropology came out of a very specific concern to counter racial thinking, which through his life and career was most authoritatively anchored in biological theories of racial difference. Boas worked systematically to undermine these theories, showing conclusively, in numerous studies, the extent to which the traits that were seen as effects of racial difference were in fact cultural—and that culture itself was the product of human surroundings that changed over time and space in ways that accorded determinative authority to history rather than biology. Given the context of his times, Boas correctly felt that anthropologists needed to conduct studies ranging from human evolution to anthropometry in order to demonstrate conclusively the limits of racial thinking. He would doubtless have continued to be interested in the uses and misuses of genetic theories in more recent years as well as invested in combating the perdurable character of biological determinism in much American social thought. His alliance with W. E. B. Du Bois and his lifelong commitment to championing the rights of African Americans were as important to his interest in biological anthropology as his engagement with Darwinian thought and evolutionary theory more generally. If Boas had ever been called upon to adjudicate the debate between cultural and biological determination, there is no doubt which side he would have been on, and I can't help but wonder how he would think about the organization of anthropological research and teaching at the dawn of the twenty-first rather than the twentieth century. Indeed, I suspect that as a disciplinary path-breaker he would have fully understood why it was that some biological anthropologists at Columbia decided to found a new department in evolutionary, environmental, and ecological biology to develop new areas of teaching and research distinct from (yet complementary to) cultural and social anthropology.

I believe instead that Boas would have agreed with Maitland's canonic contention (cited by Evans-Pritchard) that anthropology must choose between being history and being nothing.[3] And I have sought inspiration, if not always outright license, from Boas in working to bring a new kind of interdisciplinary compact to the field of anthropology. In addition to justifying the hiring of historians, political scientists, and others in an anthropology department (Boas himself didn't have a Ph.D. in anthropology), this has been a means of expanding the international reach of the department. Specifically, I sought to hire anthropologists from the parts of the world where anthropology has not always been strong or even legitimate. And I have assumed that a critical relationship to the field could be the basis for its reimagination and reinvigoration rather than its desecration and demise. In reading back over the writings of Boas, I believe that I have made too little of the Boasian mandate for what I tried to do in his department. At the same time, however, now that I am dean of the faculty of Arts and Sciences, I have come to realize that there is still much for me to learn from Boas's own example and thoughts about the educational mission of the American university more than a hundred years ago. Clearly way ahead of his time, he understood the need for, as well as the problems in, the effort to bring the arts and sciences together, training his students in the methods and epistemologies of both the natural and the human sciences. Boas had prescient, not to mention controversial, views about the problems with imperialism and nationalism. He was committed to the role of advocacy in academic life; at the same time he was passionately opposed to the use of anthropology by state interests, especially when done in covert ways that undermined the very premise of anthropological fieldwork and scientific autonomy. Boas was acutely conscious of the need to protect academic freedom, in the face of the forces controlling and governing university life, from boards of trustees to university administrators, to what may be merely the effect of the limited imaginations of students and faculty. He was committed to expanding the global reach of the curriculum and understood the importance of Asia and Africa to the changing world. And Boas understood that the ultimate influence of any scholar is most significantly secured through the work of students, who in his case ranged from Kroeber, Herskovitz, and Sapir to Benedict, Hurston, and Mead, to all of whom he explicitly gave the freedom to adapt and respond to an ever-changing world.

I have already commented on Boas's sense of the distinction between the natural and the human sciences, even as I would further note that his inclusion of biological investigations in the multiple fields of the anthropological sciences was only in part motivated by specific concerns with racial thought. Boas was ambitious for anthropology, wishing to make it a genuinely holistic discipline, one that self-consciously and deliberately brought together the cultural interests and historical perspectives of the humanities, the contemporary concerns of social science, and the scientific rigor of his own early studies in physics, psychology, and geography. But he also thought about the university well beyond the department. He knew that the teaching of physical anthropology required significant cooperation with the department of zoology as well as with the medical school. He did not differentiate between the importance of studying linguistics and the need to study the actual languages relevant to the fieldwork to be conducted. In his annual letter to the president of Columbia University of 1902, he wrote that

anthropological teaching may be made very useful in the undergraduate course, and particularly in connection with the teaching of history and social science. It is perhaps the best means of opening the eyes of students to what is valuable in foreign cultures, and thus to develop a juster appreciation of foreign nations and to bring out those elements in our own civilization which are common to all mankind.[4]

He was especially excited by the developments at Columbia around the study of China. He had been extremely supportive of efforts in the American Museum of Natural History to develop collections from eastern Asia and had hoped that these collections "would give an impetus which might lead the universities of our city, particularly Columbia University, to take up the establishment of an East Asiatic Department."[5] He was elated when the Department of Chinese was established in 1901, upon the appointment of Professor Friedrich Hirth, though he was aware that the establishment of a single professorship in Chinese was hardly adequate for what he had in mind. As he had written to President Butler earlier that year, he was most enthusiastic about the establishment of the department but also noted that "the whole domain of Chinese culture is so enormous that a single scientist can master this subject just as little as a single man can master the whole of the culture, language and literature of Europe."[6] And two years later, in a report to the American Museum of Natural History, he wrote that "it would rather seem that what we have to aim at is the gradual establishment of a department in which all the different cultures of Eastern Asia are represented, and in which information on the products, commercial possibilities and social status of these countries can be imparted."[7]

Boas was interested in politics outside the academy as well as within. George Stocking has noted that he had left Germany at least in part because "he could not accept in silence the Bismarckian turn to imperialism nor the intolerance that accompanied it." He later left Clark University several years after being appointed there in protest against the infringement on his research by the president and his associated concerns (shared by others on the faculty) regarding academic freedom. Boas began writing on matters concerning race in the early years of the twentieth century in journals associated with the social welfare movement, something many of his Columbia colleagues were involved in as well, though his statements about racial equality became increasingly progressive and assertive over time, as has been wonderfully discussed and analyzed by Lee Baker.[8] Boas became especially politicized vis-à-vis the problems of American political life because of World War I and the attacks upon German Americans. In his famous letter of 1916 to the *New York Times*, he wrote about his gradual disillusionment with America. He had believed that the United States was unique among powerful

Western nations in disavowing imperial ambition and international meddling. However,

> a rude awakening came in 1898, when the aggressive imperialism of that period showed that the ideal had been a dream. Well I remember the heated discussions which I had that year with my German friends when I maintained that the control of colonies was opposed to the fundamental ideas of right held by the American people, and the profound disappointment that I felt when, at the end of the Spanish war, these ideals lay shattered.[9]

Boas went on to note that he had grown up with an aversion to a one-sided nationalism and had felt that America had been not only the most tolerant nation in the West but one in which nationalism had not been positioned in opposition to other nations, cultures, and ways of looking at the world. "As a matter of fact," he wrote,

> the number of people in our country who are willing and able to enter into the modes of thought of other nations is altogether too small. . . . He [the average American] claims that the form of his Government is the best, not for himself only, but also for the rest of mankind; that his interpretation of ethics, of religion, of standards of living, is right. Therefore he is inclined to assume the role of a dispenser of happiness to mankind. We do not find often an appreciation of the fact that others may abhor where we worship. I have always been of the opinion that we have no right to impose our ideals upon other nations, no matter how strange it may seem to us that they enjoy the kind of life they lead, how slow they may be in utilizing the resources of their countries, or how much opposed their ideals may be to ours.[10]

And he went on to note the irony that "our intolerant attitude is most pronounced in regard to what we like to call 'our free institutions.' "[11]

Boas's anthropological commitment to cultural relativism was also a political commitment to tolerance for national difference in political as well as cultural matters. And his anthropological insistence on science as a universal method found its political parallel in his understanding of international law, which he felt Americans tended to treat as absolute only when it served American interests. He detected a kind of arrogance that would lose America its rightful place as a model nation and friend to all other nations. "If we were neutral in spirit as well as in letter, if we did not meddle with the affairs of other continents, if we had no unfair racial discrimination against certain immigrants, the United States would have only friends among the nations."[12] As a German and as a Jew—an identity that he came to rediscover through anti-Semitism experienced in the United States—he was fiercely committed to a kind of American nationalism that would abandon the narrow provincial xenophobia that was part of his sense of Europe. At the same time, he was deeply sympathetic to the aspiring nationalism of colonized countries. Along with W. E. B. Du Bois and the social reformer Upton Sinclair, he was a member of the national council of the Friends of Freedom for India. And he became an increasingly vocal advocate for the rights of African Americans, supporting Du Bois and the NAACP, as well as collaborating with scholars such as Carter Woodson and Elsie Clews Parsons, and recruiting graduate students, most notably Zora Neale Hurston, to work on questions ranging from folklore to physical anthropology, to demonstrate both the cultural richness and the racial equality of African Americans. Boas's support for "Negro Folklore," however, became steadily less significant in part because of concern among some that he was more interested in the question of what had survived from African culture than in investigating the independent vitality of African American culture, especially in the U.S. South. But in the 1920s and 1930s, Boas and some of his Columbia students became active participants in the Harlem Renaissance, a movement that took place next door to a university that was too often in those years (and famously for many years thereafter) seen as self-consciously segregated from its own Harlem neighborhood.

This short survey of some of Boas's educational and political concerns makes clear the extent to which they were integrally linked and how they were fundamental to his role in conceptualizing and launching modern American anthropology. Boas saw anthropology as a means to establish the ubiquity and the integrity of the concept of cultural difference, to show that cultural difference is about history and geography rather than race and biology, and to declare the importance of global literacy and awareness. He was concerned about how American undergraduates were to be trained as citizens in the twentieth century; at the same time he was committed to training new generations of graduate students to take on in their scholarship the new global realities and challenges of the twentieth century. He understood that anthropology must include and foster scientific studies of human evolution on the one hand and nascent area studies on the other, to combat the racial and national provincialism that grew in an America formed by a history of tolerance but increasingly driven by imperial ambition. And he was deeply critical of any direct complicity between anthropological knowledge and the national state project, as made manifest in his famous letter of 1919 to the *Nation*, under the heading "Scientists as Spies," in which he lambasted the prostituting of science, and of democracy, when anthropologists were employed by the U.S. government to engage in military espionage.[13] For this he was censured by the American Anthropological Association, a move driven by some of the Harvard Peabody anthropologists who had been involved in the effort. He also came under criticism from the trustees of Columbia. Francis Bangs, a trustee and alumnus of the law school, joined with his fellow alumnus John Pine to try to make Columbia seem a more patriotic institution. Bangs, who was also implicated in Charles A. Beard's decision to resign from Columbia after the war, had criticized Boas in 1918 for teaching "Anthropology, as construed from a German standpoint." As a result, Boas moved his principal teaching and administrative activities to Barnard, where he stayed for a decade until Butler wooed him back to Columbia in 1929.

It will therefore come as no surprise that Boas was deeply committed to the principle of academic freedom. Boas was very clear—and his time at Columbia with the sometimes headstrong Butler as president provided him with many opportunities to make his case—about the need for faculties of universities to cling hard to their academic freedom and to resist efforts to control them either by administrators or by trustees. But he was also concerned about the extent to which the professional guilds of disciplines and departments would limit the freedom to teach and learn in new and interesting ways. He wrote that "universities can not be the home of the *universitas literarum*, of the world of knowledge, if their faculties are closed corporations, and if university research and instruction are a monopoly of those who have secured recognition by appointment by the board of trustees of an established university."[14] He believed in the importance of bringing public intellectuals and other public figures to the university to help leaven convention and bring new ideas to the classroom. He also believed that students should be involved in the organization of their own curriculum and the introduction of new perspectives in the structures of knowledge. He wrote that the "restriction of the freedom of the student is brought about, in part at least, by the rigid administrative organization of departments of instruction. Although in theory these are conceived of as purely administrative divisions, they very often work out in reality as so many schools which prevent the student from looking beyond the narrow walls that are built up around him."[15] Although he did not wish to blame the stultification of university learning on either faculty or students, he nevertheless held that "the departmental organization of faculties is a hindrance to the freedom of the student."[16] He consistently opposed the hyperprofessionalism of the university, in order to preserve his sense of the shifting needs of research and indeed of society itself. He was accordingly one of the great defenders of the liberal arts.

This is not the Boas I worried about when I first came to Columbia, and he continues to be an inspiration. Had I known what I now know about Boas and his thoughts about politics and education, I would have felt even more comfortable than I did in asserting Boas's example for expanding the undergraduate program, taking regional studies seriously, becoming more interdisciplinary, and challenging conventional wisdom about the borders between the university and the society at large. And now that I am charged with managing departments across the arts and sciences (albeit as one of those administrators Boas warned his colleagues about), I am often inspired by Boas's influence well beyond the specific discipline of anthropology. Indeed, Boas's compelling legacy— his dynamic building of a discipline, his concerns about matters ranging from global imperialism to race relations, his progressive educational vision, his commitment to the importance of all three divisions of the arts and sciences, his championing of an enlightened and global understanding of cultural difference, and his sense of the need to keep innovating and changing the way faculty and students teach and learn—is an extraordinary reminder of the need for the university to continue to change in order best to protect what we hold most dear about its past.

14

Scholars and Spies

Worldly Knowledge and the Predicament of the University

F ranz Boas was without debate the most important anthropologist in the United States during his long career, most of which he spent at Columbia University. He founded the first American department of anthropology in 1896 and trained some of America's most important anthropologists before retiring after forty years of chairing his department. Many of his students went off to other major universities to establish departments of anthropology that carried on his work and academic mission, including Alfred Kroeber of Berkeley and Melville Herskovitz of Northwestern. Boas famously trained Zora Neale Hurston, Margaret Mead, and Ruth Benedict and collaborated directly with W. E. B. DuBois in the establishment of the NAACP, all while formulating a rich historical concept of culture that enabled him to reconstitute the basis on which cultural differences could be understood and analyzed; Boas used his anthropological work for many purposes, both to attempt to unite the social and human sciences with the natural sciences and to refute evolutionary understandings that naturalized ideas of racial inferiority.

Boas was an important and influential theorist as well as fieldworker, an institution builder, and an active public intellectual. In this last capacity he not only championed the rights and civilizational claims of African Americans but also criticized American foreign policy, especially in connection with his dissent over Wilson's decision to enter World War

I. His opposition to the war led him to make public attacks on a group of Harvard anthropologists for collaborating with the war in a way he thought fundamentally compromised the conduct of science. In a letter to the editor of the *Nation* in 1919, under the title of "Scientists as Spies," Boas not only called Wilson a hypocrite and American democracy a fiction; he also decried the "prostitution" of science by anthropologists who had worked as government spies in Mexico during the war under cover of anthropological fieldwork:

> Sir: In his war address to Congress, President Wilson dwelt at great length on the theory that only autocracies maintain spies; that these are not needed in democracies. At the time that the President made this statement, the Government of the United States had in its employ spies of unknown number. I am not concerned here with the familiar discrepancy between the President's words and the actual facts, although we may perhaps have to accept his statement as meaning correctly that we live under an autocracy; that our democracy is a fiction. The point against which I wish to enter a vigorous protest is that a number of men who follow science as their profession, men whom I refuse to designate any longer as scientists, have prostituted science by using it as a cover for their activities as spies.

What he means by this is explained slightly later in his letter:

> We all know scientists who in private life do not come up to the standard of truthfulness, but who, nevertheless, would not consciously falsify the results of their researches. . . . A person, however, who uses science as a cover for political spying, who demeans himself to pose before a foreign government as an investigator and asks for assistance in his alleged researches in order to carry on, under this cloak, his political machinations, prostitutes science in an unpardonable way and forfeits the right to be classed as a scientist.[1]

The anthropologists whom Boas railed against had been recruited by the U.S. Office of Naval Intelligence in some of the first fledgling efforts of espionage sponsored by the U.S. government, working in Central America to report on German U-boats and submarine bases along the Gulf of Mexico. Boas's attack led to his being censured by the American

Anthropological Association, which also charged that he was conducting vicious academic politics—Columbia versus Harvard—by other means, but it was most importantly a reflection of his conviction that anthropology had to follow the highest scientific standards. It was on the basis of scientific authority and method that he made his claims about fundamental issues concerning the nature and meaning of race, culture, human biology, civilization, and history. It was therefore not without irony that many of his closest students and colleagues worked in intelligence and as spies for the U.S. war effort in World War II, in what seemed at the time—a time when there was little dissent among academics about the war—a natural extension of Boas's fundamental belief in the public calling of science.

Indeed, Boas was hardly against using anthropology for public and even political purposes, and it was precisely his influence that led some of his most illustrious students, perhaps most conspicuously Margaret Mead and Ruth Benedict, to use anthropology for the war effort during World War II. The use of scholars was only in part an effort to find plausible covers for spies, since in the early years of developing an intelligence service they were the most obvious subjects to tap. In fact, at the dawn of World War II, the United States was the only "great power" without a formal and central institution charged with the collection and production of global "intelligence." Both the Army and the Navy had intelligence units, among them the ones for which the Harvard anthropologists had spied in the earlier war, but for the most part they were staffed by military officers with no particular expertise in intelligence or, for that matter, in world affairs, and the FBI was limited by statute (if not always by practice) to domestic activities. The economic crises of the 1930s had exacerbated isolationism, a tendency that took on particular force in various political movements conceived to keep the United States out of World War II. Roosevelt, however, was not only under growing pressure from Churchill to provide logistical, economic, and soon military support for Britain's war effort; he was aware early on of the need for the United States to play a more active role on the world stage to consolidate its own power and prosperity. As he contemplated the likely entry of the United States into the new war, he became keenly aware of the need for a new kind of brain trust, one organized to provide strategic as well as military intelligence.

In 1940 FDR, who increasingly anticipated the likely need for direct American involvement, called on William J. ("Wild Bill") Donovan, a prominent New York lawyer who had been a likely, though Republican, candidate for secretary of state, to conduct a series of overseas missions as his personal representative. Donovan traveled to England during the summer of 1940 to assess Britain's capacity to resist a possible German invasion, consulted extensively with British intelligence officials, and then spent several months visiting the Balkans and other countries in the Mediterranean basin. He returned to Washington convinced that the United States was in urgent need of strategic information as well as of more general political and psychological knowledge, to prepare for what he felt to be the coming "total" war. When he submitted his memo to Roosevelt, he recommended that the president assemble a team of "carefully selected trained minds." On July 11, 1941, Roosevelt created a new civilian position—the coordinator of information (COI)—reporting directly to him. He asked Donovan to serve in this role.

Donovan commenced his work by establishing what he called the "Research and Analysis Branch" (R&A), convinced as he was that the fundamental challenge was that the United States lacked basic knowledge about the world. He developed a highly academic notion of strategic intelligence, predicated in large part on his admiration for the intelligence services of the British empire.[2] He was not wrong, either about the capabilities of existing military intelligence agencies or about the virtually nonexistent reservoir of knowledge about the world available outside these agencies in government and elsewhere. Universities were especially deficient in scholarly expertise about the world outside Europe and North America. There were historians of Germany and Russia, but contemporary social science was barely developed, and the few scholars who worked on regions outside the West were mostly anthropologists working on tribal and primitive societies or classicists working on ancient civilizations. Donovan decided to engage in a massive effort to recruit leading academics to serve as civilian researchers with the goal of generating detailed empirical reports that were then to be analyzed by a board of analysts responsible for making policy recommendations. Consulting with Archibald MacLeish, who as librarian of Congress convened representatives of the Social Science Research Council and the American Council of Learned Societies to recommend scholars appropriate for such a project, Donovan asked James Phinney Baxter III, the president of Williams College and a respected U.S. diplomatic and military historian, to head the board. Baxter in turn recruited William L. Langer, a diplomatic historian at Harvard, who set out to recruit the best and the brightest, often irrespective of their particular expertise. Almost all the scholars who were called served, despite difficult conditions and some misgivings. Most of them shared the belief that scholars were obliged to come out of their ivory tower and serve the national interest, compelled by the circumstances of the war and their advocacy for American intervention to make their training and learning relevant.[3]

Pearl Harbor not only put paid to American reluctance to join the war; it also led Roosevelt to create the Office of Strategic Services (OSS), a much more ambitious enterprise that was to be established and directed by none other than Donovan, who brought the Research and Analysis Branch directly into his newly formed OSS in early 1942. A year into the experiment, he decided to scrap the functional subdivisions—mostly organized around the constituent disciplines—and reorganized the groups to reflect "the regional theaters of operation rather than the inherited academic division of labor."[4] While economists in particular resisted this regional reorganization, they eventually fell into line on the basis of the arguments made regarding the need for strategic knowledge.

The new regional and interdisciplinary groups focused first on Europe, the Soviet Union, Asia, and later Latin America (and then became even more regionally specific over time). Baxter recruited Sherman Kent, a historian of early nineteenth-century France from Yale, first to organize the political group and then to establish the European division. Conyers Read, a historian of Tudor England, was brought in from the history department at Penn to direct research on the British Empire. Gerold T. Robinson, a historian of Russia with a Ph.D. from Columbia, was recruited from Cornell to set up the USSR division. Ralph Bunche was recruited from Howard University to deal with "the subjects of colonial policy and administration, native problems, and race relations" within the British empire.[5] A cohort of historians, some already eminent and most on their way to becoming so, were brought to Washington, forty professional historians in all, including seven future presidents of the American Historical Association.

While the Washington campus grew, the OSS also placed academics in overseas missions, to collect and analyze information. London was the largest of these "branch" campuses, but there were missions in other parts of Europe, North Africa, the Middle East, and Asia. Academics were posted not just to these missions but as "agents" to gather intelligence outside the mission bases as well. The anthropologists Cora Du-Bois and Gregory Bateson were installed as undercover agents in Kandy, Sri Lanka, where they coordinated the work of agents across both India and Southeast Asia. Joseph Spencer and John K. Fairbank were among some fifty China specialists who were sent to bases in the wartime capital at Chungking and later Kunming. Other analysts were moved into newly "liberated" areas as soon as they had been secured, as for example in Algiers, and some OSS operatives, including Perry Miller, Franz Neumann, John Clive, Carl Kaysen, Carl Schorske, H. Stuart Hughes, and Felix Gilbert, were sent to Germany at the end of the war to evaluate conditions and adjudicate the future of the universities there.

Under the OSS, the Research and Analysis Branch had prepared reports on a wide range of issues, from the political views of Charles de Gaulle to the supply of oil in the eastern front, from the looting, damaging, and possible removal of valuable artworks in Germany to the condition of food rations across Europe. Regional specialists produced reports on the history and status of the Communist Party of India and on the puppet regime in Nanking. Historians looked back on the way experiences in the First World War might help predict possible outcomes in the new war, while economists attempted to measure the productive capacity and economic resilience of Germany under increasingly desperate wartime conditions. Anthropologists famously studied whether Japanese soldiers would ever surrender or whether the assassination of the emperor would lead to victory, while psychologists evaluated German predilections to follow authority figures and analyzed German political speeches for clues about military operations.

Even if it was the case—as many in the Truman administration argued—that the OSS had limited influence on the outcome of the war itself, these wartime efforts did have a profound effect on the intellectual landscape of postwar American university life, muffled though it was by the lifetime vow of secrecy OSS operatives took. Many OSS scholars were profoundly affected by their wartime experience, including Herbert Marcuse, who worked throughout the war in the OSS writing long tracts delineating the fascist state's manipulation of crude populist politics. Ruth Benedict, one of Boas's most accomplished students, wrote her classic study, *The Chrysanthemum and the Sword*, based on the study she did on Japanese behavioral patterns for the Office of War Information.[6]

The most significant legacy of the Research and Analysis Branch was significantly not in European studies, despite the important role of Europeanists, but in the postwar development of area studies. McGeorge Bundy, the former dean of the Faculty of Arts and Sciences at Harvard who had gone on to work for the Kennedy administration and then head the Ford Foundation, wrote in 1964 that:

> The first great center of area studies in the United States was not located in any university, but in Washington . . . in the Office of Strategic Services. In very large measure the area study programs developed in American universities in the years after the war were manned, directed, or stimulated by graduates of the OSS—a remarkable institution, half cops-and-robbers and half faculty meeting.

The Ford Foundation had been one of the great funders of area studies, along with Carnegie and Rockefeller, and Bundy was well aware of the direct line from the OSS to the postwar emergence of area studies in major U.S. universities.

Philip Mosely, a longtime professor of Russian studies at Columbia, wrote that during the time of the R&A,

> the field of inquiry was, if anything, wider-ranging, more recalcitrant, and more poignant in its meaning for human lives than even the broadest academic program of today. The R & A experience showed that analysts of many different skills not only could but must work in harness to accomplish many types of research. . . . Thus the determination to establish graduate programs of interdisciplinary teaching and research on Russia and the U.S.S.R. grew out of both prewar hopes and war-time urgencies.[7]

OSS alumni were to be found in all major area studies programs, often becoming the founders of new programs in the postwar years. Gerold Robinson went from his role as head of the R&A Russia desk to move from Cornell to Columbia as professor of History, where he became the first head of the Russian Institute at Columbia before passing it on to Mosely. John K. Fairbank returned to Harvard from his time in China with the OSS to set up the largest postwar program in East Asian studies. David Mandelbaum, who had spent some war years in India doing field-work and writing reports, was hired by Berkeley in large part to set up a program of South Asian studies there. W. Norman Brown, professor of Sanskrit at Penn, founded the first South Asia regional studies program and the American Institute of Indian Studies. He is a signal example of the influence of the OSS on area studies and for me the most compelling given his founding role in my own field of South Asian studies.

Brown had been recruited to the University of Pennsylvania in 1929 as the only India specialist. Despite his scholarly specialization, he did in fact develop an interest in contemporary India and spoke Hindi as a result of his missionary upbringing. That was enough for his colleague, Conyers Read, to recruit him to head the India desk for the OSS. When Brown moved to Washington in mid-1942, he recruited a miscellaneous group of students and young academics to work with him on the India desk, also working closely with Ralph Bunche in the British Empire section and with Dean Rusk, who worked in the Pentagon. Brown presided over his interdisciplinary team of scholars, overseeing the preparation of a number of manuscripts that, whether written by him or not, all bear his influence. The papers document a growing American critique of British imperial rule in South Asia and a developing consensus about the importance of supporting the Indian nationalist movement, espe-cially the goal of Gandhi to lead India to political independence without either a violent struggle against the British or the setting of caste or class interests against each other. Gandhi's noble vision and his embrace of nonviolence appealed to Brown, even as U.S. academics and policy mak-ers were largely unsympathetic to British empire and Churchill's impe-rialist jingoism in particular. The United States also saw the empire and Churchill's adamant refusal to give nationalist sentiment any quarter as a great potential threat to the war effort against Japan. The major mis-sion of the India desk in Washington, and increasingly of U.S. operatives in India, was to monitor the extent and character of Indian disaffection with British rule and to evaluate whether this disaffection would lead either to noncooperation with the allied effort or, even worse, active collaboration with Japan. FDR himself had been on record for some years for his general disapproval of British colonial rule in India, and some of his sharpest exchanges with Churchill concerned the empire.

While Churchill famously declared that the empire would not end on his watch, Roosevelt became increasingly disturbed by the failure of the British to engage Indian leaders in serious negotiations about self-rule.

Roosevelt never pushed the diplomatic disagreement to the breaking point, deferring instead to wartime exigencies and Churchill's strenuous insistence on American neutrality on India. But it is striking how different the developing world view of U.S. political leaders and scholars was from the prevailing view among the British, who saw their empire as critical to their survival, both during the war and afterward. FDR's two wartime emissaries to New Delhi, Louis Johnson and William Phillips, had been welcomed initially by the British because of their proempire views but soon became deeply supportive of Indian nationalism, fearing as they did the possible support for a Japanese invasion across the Burma border, and in the end genuinely embracing the cause of self-determination in India (a conviction that was significantly aided by their respect for Gandhi and Nehru). Both Johnson and Phillips were sent back to the United States after falling afoul of the British Raj; Phillips was the source of a major diplomatic crisis when his report to FDR, containing serious criticisms of the British policy of divide and rule, was leaked to the press and emerged in Drew Pearson's column in the *Washington Star*.

Phillips, who had been the head of the OSS office in Britain before being sent to India, had in fact established an office in Delhi that engaged in far more active intelligence activities than merely using British compilations of political information. He initiated clandestine information gathering through a network of Americans installed in various posts in India and Ceylon, ostensibly on other missions, including Olive Reddick, who went on to run the Fulbright Program in India; Maureen Patterson, who became the South Asia Bibliographer at the University of Chicago; and Cora DuBois, who became the first tenured woman in anthropology at Harvard. DuBois, an anthropologist who had initially studied Southeast Asia before turning to South Asia, was soon moved to Kandy to work with Gregory Bateson, where—before she revolutionized American cuisine—they were ably assisted by Julia Child.

In 1944, W. Norman Brown advocated the serious development and funding of Oriental Studies in a draft document in which he wrote: "During the course of the war the US govt. agencies have needed information about the Orient to a degree far beyond anticipation. . . . Our nation must never again be caught so ill-equipped with knowledge and specialists on the Orient as it was at the end of 1941." He also noted, giving voice to another area of growing U.S. interest, "The postwar Orient will also probably be freer than before to engage in trade with the Occident. . . . To meet this new situation America will need to acquire information and develop personnel able to handle the increased political, business, and cultural relations."[8] In 1947 he revised this draft and expanded his vision of Oriental Studies in a document that led to the creation of the first department of South Asian Regional Studies at Penn, securing major funding from the Carnegie, Rockefeller, and Ford Foundations.[9] To do so, he recruited all the scholars who had worked with him during the war in Washington in the Research and Analysis Division. By the academic year 1949–1950, a complete program for South Asia regional studies had been established under Brown's leadership, and an affiliated faculty of twenty-one scholars, covering such fields as geography, linguistics, Hindustani, sociology, and other affiliated fields in Asian studies, was listed in the catalog. The Penn Department of South Asian Studies and the area center that subsequently developed once federal funding was established for area studies in the 1950s both trained many of the first generation of U.S. South Asianists and provided a model for and a set of institutional and intellectual concerns critical to the development of South Asian studies across the United States during the postwar years.

South Asian area studies thus was born almost fully formed in the immediate postwar years, reflecting both the work that had been associated with the strategic concerns of the OSS in World War II and the peculiar intellectual orientation and perspective of Brown: his missionary roots, his Sanskrit scholarship, and his sense that Indian nationalism would be fully compatible with the role he envisioned for the United States in the postwar period. He was a textbook orientalist: as he wrote in his major work, published in 1954, *The United States and India and Pakistan* (in the same series as books with similar names written by Fairbank and Reischauer about the United States and China and Japan respectively): "The greatest achievements of characteristic Indian civilization are in religion and philosophy."[10] Brown's intentions were framed within his larger intention to increase understanding and exchange between India (and Pakistan) and the United States, and his political sensibility was not just anticolonial but liberal, though he believed that change would come slowly to a civilization that had remained fundamentally the same across five thousand years, save for the introduction of Islam, something he saw as deeply destabilizing given the communal conflict it brought in its wake.

This is the historical background that provided the context for my own academic socialization into South Asian studies, from the Indian office of the Fulbright program (which funded my father to go to India to teach at a southern Indian college and thus began my entry as a twelve-year-old into a relationship with India that led to my academic career) to the creation and funding of area studies at universities such as Chicago where I did my graduate work, courtesy in part of the National Defense Education Act, Title VI. While uniting the humanities and the social sciences in a partnership that carried on Langer's vision of useful knowledge, area studies was itself committed to a new kind of relationship between the United States and the developing world, assured that American global interests had little in common with those of previous European empires, that modernization was an inexorable process that would lead to political and economic development along with mutual understanding, shared interests, and commercial exchange with the United States, and that U.S. universities had to provide training in regional languages, cultures, politics, and histories to create a new cadre of intellectuals and academics prepared to guide U.S. attitudes toward a new world order.

These convictions were soon both enhanced and colored by the growing sense of a world struggle with the Soviet Union, as the Cold War became a central justification for area studies, even as many area studies academics, including many former OSS operatives, found themselves targeted by McCarthy, HUAC, and an aggressively partisan CIA and FBI. Area studies became further polarized and politicized by the growing opposition to the war in Vietnam in the 1960s and later in the political and epistemological critiques of the 1970s and 1980s. The final critique of area studies, however, was enabled, perhaps even caused, by the geopolitical transformations that began with the fall of the Berlin Wall and the demise of the Soviet Union, the end of the Cold War as we knew it. Area studies continued in U.S. universities after 1989, but they lost considerable prestige and became increasingly directed by scholars in the humanities rather than the social sciences. Since then the social sciences have largely rejected the preoccupations of area studies as insufficiently rigorous, comparative, and relevant to the new phenomena labeled under the term "globalization." While 9/11 rekindled the same kinds of concerns expressed by Brown about how ill-prepared the United States was in 1941, propelling funding support for Arabic language and regional study (while also precipitating new political conflict over the nature of Middle Eastern area studies), the tide of globalization was too strong to turn back. Ironically, much of the support for area studies over the past two decades has come from immigrant and international communities that have understood the importance of supporting curricular and scholarly commitments to specific regions and nations to celebrate their achievements and take advantage of the power of endowments to gain greater recognition and attention.

Despite the multiple agendas and sometimes fractious history of area studies, there was remarkable agreement about its fundamental goals and purposes. There is far less agreement today about what "global studies" should be, perhaps in part because of the less cohesive nature of its origins. Most observers, both inside and outside the academy, acknowledge the need to understand the structure and function of global economic markets, financial systems, and issues around global sovereignty that emerge both in relation to the role of markets and various geopolitical issues. While there is general recognition of the importance of understanding the resilience of cultural, religious, and social differences in the globalizing world, there is little agreement about how to do this. And there is even less agreement about how to chart new institutional mechanisms for global governance given challenges ranging from climate change to international law, global inequality, and the need to regulate global markets and financial institutions. Given the scale of these challenges and the extent to which they simply do not map on to any available constitutional and theoretical models for sovereignty, the lack of consensus may be inevitable, but it is also a symptom of the extent to which globalization does not pose the same kind of discrete strategic challenge as the opening of the world for the U.S. government in the years during World War II and its immediate aftermath.

The belated recognition that American universities had little in the way of expertise in the histories, cultures, literatures, languages, societies, and politics of discrete world regions might have been the inevitable consequence of a newly dominant nation entering a world war and assuming a new set of global geopolitical and economic interests, but in retrospect I believe it had an extraordinarily salutary effect on our academic institutions well beyond those interests. Whole new worlds of academic inquiry opened up, creating new programs, centers, institutes, and departments while expanding the horizons of all civilizational, historical, political, literary, and social study. Perhaps most important of all, the teaching of languages from Indonesian to Wolof, and Vietnamese to Tamil, was supported on a massive scale for the first time. The rapidly expanding scale of the American university at least into the mid-1970s allowed for innovation rather than conflicts over scarce resources. Anthropology and geography had initiated the study of the wider world, though with an emphasis on the primitive and the peripheral, so it was for the first time that core departments of history, political science, economics, and sociology included world specialists, even as anthropology embraced the study of "complex societies" and as new humanistic disciplines were added through departments of regional languages and literatures. While area studies were often confined to graduate training and faculty research, they constituted some of the most significant investments on the part of major foundations, new governmental programs, and university administrations in the decades after the war, leaving their imprint in new schools and institutes of international affairs as well as in new programs and departments.

There is both personal irony and a more general theoretical alert in recounting this history. My own academic concerns featured an early concern not just with the historical problematic of empire but with the strategic distortions of proper knowledge about India emerging out of colonial history, yet these very issues are written everywhere into the opportunities and conjunctures of my academic life. I had begun my formal interest in India by tracing the contradictions encountered by Gandhi in battling both British rule and Indian customs around caste privilege. Later, as I struggled to identify and isolate the specific conditions of the early modern state and society in southern India, I became aware of the extent to which contemporary preoccupations, debates, and source materials, in anthropology and Indian studies more generally, were deeply embedded in a history of colonial knowledge. As I came to understand the extent to which the nature and status of anthropological knowledge had emerged out of colonial institutions and interests, I turned much of my scholarly work to tracing and then critiquing the genealogies of my own disciplines, assuming all the while that historicist critique could predicate a more neutral, objective, enlightened, and enlightening framework for understanding objects of study like the "caste system." Yet here I am, suggesting that the direct roots of my academic interests reside in espionage, even if they also resonate with the early American reaction to the conceits of British empire in India.

The reflexive turn of my own work was naturally part of a much wider set of conjunctures in the academy during the post-Vietnam years. This was a time of rampant historicism, during which many colleagues began to excavate the very ground on which we all stood and which we had all taken for granted, to show how complicit we were—whether we knew it or not—in the rise of capitalism, empire, modernity, Europe, America, and so on. All disciplines and fields had been "invented," and usually not for good reasons. Using sound and often ingenious historical research, colleagues demonstrated, in one of my favorite examples, that Shakespeare first became canonical in the curricula of English studies in Indian rather than British universities because of the imperial need to have an English genius celebrated in the canon rather than a long list of Greek and Roman authors. But then we learned that the canonic importance of the Greeks had in any event been part of a longer history of philhellenism in which Greek texts, many of them rescued from the ravages of the Dark Ages by Arabic scholars, had been appropriated in order to establish the civilizational pedigree of northern and western Europe over the claims of others in Europe and beyond (e.g., the Arab world) to cultural dominance. Even science, as we began to learn from Thomas Kuhn and Paul Feyerabend (as well, of course, from the revelations about and consequences flowing from the Manhattan project), had social and political histories that required our critical attention. Indeed, it was instrumental (and mostly invidious) invention—to paraphrase the old story about the world resting on a succession of turtles—all the way down.

Just to be clear, I recant nothing. Nor do I forget the reasons why this period of reflexive historicism was so central to the engagement of many in the post-Vietnam period with the verities of the knowledge we sought to critique in the face of revelations about the role of academic institutions in the political events we found so disturbing. It is noteworthy, however, that many of us who engaged in critiquing the foundational histories of our disciplines not only stayed inside the university but sought to reshape these disciplines in ways that responded productively to the provocation of knowing our selves better through knowing more about our histories. Meanwhile, the new histories we wrote revealed not just the implication of knowledge in the rise of modernity but also the creative potential of critical thought (and of the university itself). In his cogent critique of Allan Bloom's *Closing of the American Mind*, for example, Lawrence Levine demonstrated that the curriculum in American colleges had changed continuously over the past two hundred years, reflecting not just the interest of some early educators in promoting classical studies to secure their status as elite but also the ways new and progressive social and political movements exerted their influence as well. And I have noted here the salutary effects of drafting academics as spies, and then spies to be academics, for the rise of area studies. The histories of invention were not all bad.

In a way, however, Bloom still hovers over us as a disturbing reminder of the perils of critical historicist preoccupation. Bloom had been especially scathing about the rise of historicist thinking, even though his actual call to a fixed idea of "nature" (which is why, he wrote, that "philosophy, not history or anthropology, is the most important human science") was historically flawed, to say the least. Those who knew Bloom, or for that matter even those who read Saul Bellow's peculiarly honest novel about him, remember how odd a figure he was to mobilize populist reaction against the so-called politicization of the American university. Yet the success of his screed was not just an academic extension of the Reaganite reaction to the campus wars of the Vietnam era but a symptom of two allied but contradictory intellectual problems. The first was that the epistemological grounds of critique were usually far from clear. I mean by this that we rarely specified whether there was some underlying sense that knowledge could be "uncontaminated" by history and, if so, what that might look like, whether at root there was an implied commitment to neo-Rankean objectivism or a Foucauldian allegiance to Nietzsche's relentless critique of Enlightenment knowledge. The second was that historicism had seemed to become an end in itself.

Small wonder perhaps that Bloom's interest in teaching about morality resonated with a larger concern about the moral (and for that matter political) lessons we were conveying in our scholarship and especially in our classrooms. If the decades of the sixties, seventies, and eighties were when the humanities went into real crisis, we all know that we have never fully recovered.

We also know, however, that we will not recover our earlier centrality, leave alone innocence, by returning to a state of denial either about the historical entailments of our most fundamental commitments or about the urgency of engaging with the most pressing issues of our day. To conclude, I return to the problematic of globalization, acknowledging that for all their ills and all their benefits, neither area studies nor the disciplines we have in place are fully equipped for this contemporary challenge. In the face of massive global transformations that now connect each part of the world, we need to find better ways to understand global flows and processes; the cost of labor and commodities; the circulation of desires, pleasures, ideas, and movements; the international character of information and media; and the unprecedented connectivity and pace of the world in which we live as borders and the Iron Curtain have broken down, markets opened up, air travel increased, and the Internet developed, all while new digital technology and global commerce determine the fundamental dimensions of economic life. Globalization requires different disciplinary, theoretical, methodological, and conceptual frameworks to grasp what many of us see as not just new but radically transforming the relationship of discrete places to a world without place.

Yet, as if to dramatize the loss of cartographic anchors and disciplinary moorings, we confront unprecedented levels of disagreement about fundamental questions, from ideas and constitutional provisions about academic and political freedom to basic assumptions about virtually every global issue, whether cultural, political, social, intellectual, environmental, or economic. Not only are there radically differing global contexts for, say, freedom of speech, the press, or academic work; there are also extravagantly different ways of reading almost every global issue. Examples abound, from the recent controversy at Yale regarding the opening of a liberal arts college in Singapore to the swirl of questions around freedom of speech in China or the Gulf, to debates over censorship in India and Europe, to the wide range of views over the costs and benefits of the new global financial system. On the one hand, we know that studies of domestic economies, cultural movements, technological innovation, and climate change must all be cast in a global context. On the other hand, we also know that global studies—if they are genuinely to be global—cannot be done without situating them, intellectually as well as institutionally, dialogically as well as practically, in specific global places (and definitely outside the metropolitan centers of the West).

What we need, perhaps, is to embrace a new kind of worldly knowledge, a term I use both to get around the limitations of the terms global, local, area, regional, etc. and to avoid some of the moral pitfalls in debates over similar kinds of terms such as cosmopolitanism. Cosmopolitanism, a worthy ideal to be sure, not only begs a set of questions about centers and peripheries, elites and nonelites, inequality and dominance, the subsidiary status of certain kinds of communities and identities, but it also implies acceptance of the stubborn incommensurability of many global phenomena. Worldly forms of knowing must engage the contextual protocols of knowledge making and teaching in a global setting precisely because the internal and external boundaries of an older area studies model have been redrawn and reconstituted. This means asking not just about the nature of the global but about global knowledge itself: about, that is, the global implications of our most distinctive identities and commitments, not just about where we are from, but about the fundamental locations inherent in the selves we make and the publics we serve.

In this account, historicism is always necessary to maintain both a sense of contingency and a faith in the possibility of change, even if I also believe that it must be offset by an acknowledgment of the power of the past and a resolute commitment to truth and positive knowledge. To return to the example with which I began this lecture, Boas was in fact more outraged by the misuses of science than he was motivated by the uses of scientific authority for social justice. His faith in science was absolute, even though there is no doubt from the record of his life about the way that faith had been molded by his passion about such public issues as racial equality and anti-imperialism. We can in fact celebrate the historicist embedding of knowledge in the world while also insisting on the priority of moral questions in guiding our engagement with the world. We should, in other words, be able to learn from the time when many of our scholars were spies without becoming spies all over again.

15

The Opening of the American Mind

When Allan Bloom's infamous book, *The Closing of the American Mind*, was published in 1987, it was, as Camille Paglia later declared, the "first shot of the culture wars."[1] Bloom's book—by any account an odd amalgam of polemical denunciation, philosophical argument, and autobiographical memoir—quickly generated a spirited debate about college life, the place of the liberal arts, and as Bloom put it, "the state of our soul." The book sold close to half a million copies in hardback and was number one on the *New York Times* bestseller list for four months. Roger Kimball, who went on to write his own blast at the current state of the American university, declared, in his *New York Times* review, that Bloom's book was "essential reading for anyone concerned with the state of liberal education in this society," praising its "pathos, erudition, and penetrating insight."[2] For the most part, however, the book was received by fellow academics either with scorn or anger, both because of the direct and caricatured attack on the professoriate and because the argument itself was based less on reason—the term that Bloom used as his highest goal—than on passion, as Alexander Nehamas asserted in a thoughtful and devastating review in the *London Review of Books*.[3]

Nehamas found Bloom far from convincing about the Greeks and noted that the reactionary political agenda that lurked throughout the pages of the book was "uncanny" in its consistency. But he was most critical about Bloom's eulogy for the aristocracy not just in his uncritical invocation of a classical world as utopian but in his lament for the disappearance of a space for elite students to imbibe the eternal wisdom of philosophy. Martha Nussbaum was even more scathing in her review in the *New York Review of Books*, sharing Nehamas's consternation at Bloom's unabashed elitism while disputing even his right to claim the mantle of "philosopher."[4] Lawrence Levine, an American historian, responded by writing a book under the same title as this chapter, demonstrating that Bloom's evocation of a nineteenth-century world in which college students developed moral fiber and philosophical erudition through a classical education was historically false, arguing instead that while change in the academy has always been contested and slow, it was the inexorable consequence of changing historical circumstances throughout the nineteenth and twentieth centuries.[5] Curiously, even some conservative critics bridled at Bloom's evident distaste for some American values. Thomas G. West, writing under the mantle of the Claremont Institute, noted that

> instead of debunking the founding, Bloom should be celebrating it as a fund of wisdom to be recovered for the sake of the very enterprise he wishes to foster. Instead of confusing the issue by speaking of today's left as an extreme version of the Founder's principles, he should be vigorously denouncing the leftist hatred of political liberty, liberal education, and religion, the bulwarks of American constitutionalism.[6]

West went on to observe that the problem stemmed from Leo Strauss, whose love for ancient Greece led him never fully to embrace American-style modernity.

If Bloom became the poster child for a neoconservative onslaught against the university, he was an odd one, to say the least. Leaving aside his early death from AIDS and Saul Bellow's full-throated depiction of Bloom in his thinly disguised "memoir novel" *Ravelstein*, Bloom's book would hardly be embraced by most who attack the university at the current moment, whatever their political perspective.[7] Twenty-five years on, it is hard to avoid a feeling of nostalgia for the virulent days of the "culture wars," given that many participants on different sides of the debate shared a common conviction about the importance of a humanist education. Yet while Bloom took aim at the students and faculty of 1968 and after for their flaccid moral and intellectual proclivity to openness and relativism, his specific target within the university was hard for me not to take personally, since he very clearly targeted the kind of disciplinary portfolio that has made up my own academic life and that underwrites all of the chapters in this book. As he wrote early in *Closing*, "Nature should be the standard by which we judge our own lives and the lives of peoples. That is why philosophy, not history or anthropology, is the most important human science."[8] He equated history and anthropology with the doctrine of cultural relativism, charging that this doctrine "succeeds in destroying the West's universal or intellectually imperialistic claims, leaving it to be just another culture."[9] He claimed that the "recent education of openness . . . pays no attention to natural rights" and that it was sullied by a form of historicism that only showed how "the beginnings were flawed."[10] History should provide moral examples for emulation; the study of culture should affirm the transcendence of certain principles over others. Small wonder that history and anthropology were dangerous disciplines.

Bloom celebrated reason, but he did so in part by asserting that "prejudices" were no less important than a commitment to truth. He wrote that "prejudices . . . are divinations of the order of the whole of things" even as "error . . . alone points to the truth and therefore deserves our respectful treatment."[11] He seemed more intrigued by belief than by argument, more hailed by principles that could claim universal authority than by the distracting details and data that inevitably undermined conviction. Bloom was desirous of the certainty and power of the sacred, impatient with the scholarly investment in disagreement, revisionism, and complication. He accepted that the "dogmatic skeptic" might view nature itself as a prejudice, only to respond by suggesting that it might be "our first task to resuscitate those phenomena [the lush profusion of expressions of nature] so that we may again have a world to which we can put our questions and be able to philosophize."[12] History—which he saw as a version of historicism that situated events, values, and decisions in their specific historical context—and anthropology—which he viewed as insisting on convictions of cultural relativism—were to Bloom "a means to avoid testing our own prejudices."[13] And despite his critique of the influence of Nietzsche on latter-day academics, he shared Nietzsche's scorn for the small-minded historians (and by implication anthropologists) who could not understand the larger stakes and goals of philosophical inquiry. In such a philosophical project, self-understanding takes place at the expense of any other kind of understanding (of different selves, places, events, and so on) and in the end becomes an agonistic exercise for the expression not so much of nature but of prejudice itself. It is a theoretical aspiration that not only takes umbrage at the whole history of modernity (whether in America or elsewhere) but also disparages the very curiosity that has been fundamental to the advancement of knowledge as well as to our educational mission for many years.

Bloom expressed sympathy for old-fashioned religious beliefs, traditional social and cultural prejudices, and conventional practices not because he held or followed them. He used the anchors of tradition to provide the basis for what in his book became a critique of the present, a way of highlighting the unspoken prejudices that were part of what to him was the bland equanimity and moral decline that pervaded the university after 1968. He believed that the suspension of disbelief was the basic requirement for a genuinely open education. The problem, however, was that he was able to suspend disbelief around only those areas for which he already expressed sympathy. He claimed a real openness—to other histories and cultures, to other traditions and texts, to other perspectives and prejudices—yet he used partial readings and understandings to dismiss them in comparison to his ideal image of Socratic Greece. If his idea of "college" was really so narrow, even his defense of the idea of a shared classical education—hedged by his own ironic awareness of the possible misuse of canons—seemed an impossible ideal for the present age, an aspiration that was inexorably bound to be frustrated by any realistic effort to define and defend the liberal arts for our time. If the culture wars provided fuel for a growing public antipathy to the humanities—and while Bloom played an unfortunate role in raising the ante, he had little trouble caricaturing some of the excesses of humanistic work—the "wars" did reflect the fundamental importance of humanist education in the last decades of the twentieth century. There is in fact considerable pathos in going back to this text, since a teacher like Allan Bloom could have mobilized his extraordinary passion and knowledge to promote the kind of self-discovery that is part of the wonderful legacy and promise of the liberal arts without giving in to angry polemic. At a time when students are abandoning the humanistic liberal arts in favor of majors and programs that promise—or at least seem to them more likely to produce—immediate financial reward, the polemics of and around Bloom seem at best a distraction and at worst a major impediment to the kind of coherent defense of the liberal arts that we so desperately need.

I grew up with the kind of religious faith that Bloom would appear to have endorsed or at least admired. My father was raised on a farm in Iowa, the descendent of a family of German immigrants who had two generations earlier taken the boat to America to escape the Prussian draft. When it became clear that his congenitally bad heart would make it impossible for him to live the physically demanding life of a farmer, he went off to a local college with the idea that he would become a Presbyterian minister in an Iowa parish. Although he followed the general plan, he moved from a seminary in Chicago to New York, where he began to study with the liberal theologians Paul Tillich and Reinhard Neibuhr, ultimately earning a Ph.D. in philosophy at Columbia for writing a dissertation on the theology of the American Transcendentalists (Theodore Parker in particular). When he returned to the Holland (Iowa) German Presbyterian Church for his ordination, he was cross-examined by the church elders to discern whether the "taint of the east"—by which they meant the East Coast of America—had made him unsuitable. Although he passed the test and was ordained, he never followed the pastoral route, joining the professoriate instead. My mother was a school teacher and a dietician who followed my father from the Midwest to New York, where she completed a master's degree at Columbia's Teacher's College and worked for a time at *Good Housekeeping*. A few years later, after my father took up a teaching position at the Yale Divinity School, my mother strayed from Presbyterianism and joined a local assembly of Plymouth Brethren in a suburb of New Haven. I grew up cognizant of, and occasionally caught between, the differences—and occasional tensions—of two disparate (and even opposing) strands of Protestant belief and practice. I was baptized twice, once as an infant in a Presbyterian church, later as a young adult, fully immersed not just in the water of a small pool under the pulpit but also in the heady atmosphere of fundamentalist Christianity.

I grew up preoccupied, in other words, by questions of faith. Long before I understood the full implications of doctrinal debates over the relative priority of faith or works, or about the relationship of individual decisions regarding belief to the community of believers, or about the status of scripture, I had a palpable sense of the importance of certain theological distinctions. On rare though memorable occasions my parents would betray the passions that could attach themselves to these questions—usually leading to a period of silence on the part of my mother that would in turn lead to profuse apologies on the part of my father. There were times when my fundamentalist Sunday School teachers would question whether some of those professors of religion at Yale—my father excepted, of course—were really Christians. I was hailed by the immediacy of the fundamentalist message, convinced that my personal relationship with God was of greater importance than any other relationship, troubled by the fact that I had no special conversion narrative to which I could give witness. I was unable to shed the sense that because my parents had me baptized as an infant I could not claim some dramatic moment on my own road to Damascus when I became a Christian. This "personal" failure led to a peculiar form of self-doubt, a sense that exacerbated my discontent with certain doctrines, not to mention the lectures in summer Bible camp about the folly of scientific assertions concerning evolution that were at first unconvincing and later on embarrassing. And after I went to India as a twelve-year-old I could no longer believe that my own brand of Christian belief was the only path to God. Even as I set out on our year abroad aboard a Greek ocean liner in June 1963, I sensed that the world I had known was opening up dramatically and, as it did so, that my convictions about religion and belief were to be fundamentally challenged.

I wrote in the introduction about how my year in India was transformative, making India the touchstone, or counterpoint, for understanding both my own circumstances and the assumptions as well as the habitus of my life, in the end installing India as the object of a lifetime of scholarship and engagement. But the year in India also played a critical role in changing my relationship to belief, to certainty, to my childhood sense of the vastness of the world. And even as I encountered difference, I also came to sense a broader kind of universality, in which the acknowledgment of—and the effort to comprehend—differences might be the basis for a richer kind of life. I realized that the doctrinal differences of my own upbringing were small in the great scheme of things. Far from losing my belief, the year helped me broaden significantly my understanding of belief itself.

As I returned to an America that was about to be launched into the full meaning of its new decade, I could not yet know that my experience in India would be critical for my own coming of age during the years of growing controversy over U.S. involvement in Vietnam. I did, however, soon become aware of the influence of Mahatma Gandhi on Martin Luther King, and as I began to ask my father to take me to the Yale Chapel to hear the sermons of William Sloane Coffin after he returned from Selma, Alabama, I was struck by the openness of a more ecumenical church to social and political engagement and advocacy. I joined many others of my generation in being swept up by the civil rights movement and the growing concern about Vietnam (not insignificantly inflected by the role of the draft in the lives of young men), while seeking both to get into a good college and figure out the relationship between those turbulent times and my own hopes and dreams (and fears). I wrote papers in high school about Hinduism and comparative ideas of religion. I also began to read some of the books on my father's shelves—including Bertrand Russell's *A History of Western Philosophy*, the writings of Dietrich Bonhoeffer—a courageous theologian who was executed by the Nazis for his active involvement in the resistance—and Thomas Altizer's provocative works on "Christian" atheism and the "Death of God," works famously featured in a *Time* cover story on the death of God in 1966.[14] Theology, religion, politics, and my experience of the world through the year in India all conspired to make my own encounter with the sixties both unique and, in a way, typical for the times. This ferment was only enhanced by the intellectual intensity of my undergraduate liberal arts education. Ideas had more rather than less power because they had such powerful stakes for individuals trying to make sense of the world—a world that posed existential issues at the same it seemed to require critical and meaningful engagement. By the time I went to college in 1968, I had given up all traces of a fundamentalist faith, though I was more engaged than ever in religious questions in my intellectual endeavors.

As befit the times, I went to a college that had abandoned all but the most rudimentary of distribution requirements. I could choose my courses and my course of study as I wished, the only real obstructions to full freedom of choice being one "Freshman Humanities" course that was mandated and another course in "behavioral psychology" that fulfilled a science requirement. I took the psychology course because of the instructor, who had taught a freshman seminar on "free will and necessity" jointly with a professor of religion, in a riveting display of intellectual debate between a Skinnerian and a Hegelian. We were told on the one hand about the experiments of B. F. Skinner with pigeons, all suggesting the extent to which human experience was dictated by biology and conditioning, and on the other about the autonomy of human judgment and experience through reading Ernst Cassirer, Reinhold Neibuhr, and Herbert Marcuse. The questions raised during the course stayed with me, reverberating in literature courses whether I read Dante or Flannery O'Connor, in philosophy and religion classes where I studied phenomenology and world religions, and eventually in the interdisciplinary major I adopted in politics, economics, and history.

The interdisciplinary major was modeled on the famous Oxford PPE course (philosophy, politics, and economics) in both content and form (with very small classes called tutorials). It was, however, fundamentally different, since it concerned Asia and Africa and experimented with a form of area studies that was embedded within a program in "Western" studies rather than isolated from it. This program provided me with the best of a liberal arts education, with all the intellectual intensity Bloom could have desired, and though I read a great deal of Western thought both through literature and philosophy (and for that matter social science, from Marx and Weber to modernization theory), my moral education hardly suffered because I spent a great deal of time studying those parts of the world that extended beyond the classical West. My move to history (and anthropology) was governed by my continued preoccupation with India as well as with my sense of the need to embed myself in the civilizational history and cultural context of a specific place that defied easy characterization. Yet my sense of "cultural" difference, and my instinctive modes of comparative analysis, were inevitably dictated by my coming of age in late twentieth-century America and of being from the West, even as my sense of the moral issues at stake were only heightened by engagement with other traditions, perspectives, and histories. As the pace of globalization has only quickened and intensified in the years since, the certainties of cultural lineage and identity have been inevitably questioned and increasingly seen as hybrid, contingent, and connected across a world stage. Unfortunately, however, at the very time when questions raised by the kind of moral and political education I had seem more compelling than ever before, the liberal arts is under siege, charged as irrelevant, wasteful, and unnecessary.

It is frequently said, and not just by supporters of Bloom's distinctive polemic, that the politicization of the humanities is what created the conditions for its loss of standing and support. The culture wars were started, in some of these views, by those professors who imposed their own politics on philosophy, literature, history, art, and even music. The politics around Vietnam became steadily corrosive of the study of culture, especially the great and transcendent record of Western accomplishment and genius, while the special achievements of Western traditions were undermined and distinctions between high and low culture blurred. It is true that there was a growing tendency to historicize works of culture, to situate cultural production in its time and focus much more on context than had been the usual tendency in forms of study that privileged the text (whether literature, art, architecture, or whatever) in its own terms. Some of the great works of cultural criticism and analysis in the past decades have come precisely from linking historical and sociological study to cultural texts, which inevitably has meant examining the politics of those involved in the production, consumption, and use of culture. While on occasion there have been assumptions about politics that have been too unreflective about multiple political perspectives and possibilities—as also perhaps the reductive potential of some versions of historicism—these extremes have been no more egregious than occasions when historical and sociological considerations have been deliberately banished from view for fear they would sully the transcendent effects of culture. Yet any commitment to full inquiry and the dictates of both reason and truth requires teaching students, in the words of Walter Benjamin, that "there is no document of civilization which is not at the same time a document of barbarism."[15] Even the famously conservative political theorist Edmund Burke said something similar when he wrote about the origins of British imperial rule in India, as we saw in chapter 7. He proclaimed—about government rather than civilization, though he saw the two as mutually interdependent—"there is a secret veil to be drawn over the beginnings of all governments. They had their origin, as the beginning of all such things have had, in some matters that had as good be covered by obscurity."[16] Burke and Benjamin would only rarely be brought into conversation on this subject, for while Burke understood the need to respect the veil, Benjamin was keen to uncover the story of origins. Both of these great critics, however, agreed not just about the origin story but also about the absolute importance of preserving civilization despite its seamy beginnings and entailments.

Some, like Bloom, who have maintained that the disappearance of a classical core curriculum of Western texts was responsible for the decline in the standing of the liberal arts in general and the humanities in particular, might in fact believe that these texts can, indeed should, be read without calling attention to contradictions, failures, and any mention of barbarism (except, of course, on the "other" side). The loss of a sense of common purpose in education, the diminution and then, in many cases, abandonment of distribution requirements, the attacks on canons, the infighting over identity politics and modes of representing different kinds of histories and selves in the humanities and humanistic social sciences have all accordingly been affiliated to and in some cases blamed directly on the so-called culture wars of the post-1968 decades. The culture wars were in part symptoms of changes in American society that were seen by these critics as distasteful and, in some cases, dangerous. It is important, however, to remember not just, as Lawrence Levine reminded us, that today's core was yesterday's avant-garde but that the culture wars were also symptoms of the centrality of the liberal arts. Many who have dismissed the liberal arts in their newly inclusive forms were, or would have been, impatient with the older liberal arts as well. Bloom was only tapping into populist sensibilities in his denunciation of the frivolity of the academy, not in his defense of abstruse philosophy in the context of Socratic Greece. During my years at Columbia I strongly advocated for the importance of a core curriculum since it constituted the major part of the liberal arts component of an undergraduate education there and, most importantly, provided a local vehicle for the articulation of questions, traditions, and debates that become, through the pedagogy of a faculty engaged with myriad disciplinary questions well outside the scope of the core itself, the basis for collective discussion of moral, social, economic, political, and philosophical issues of signal contemporary significance. It is clear to me, however, that these goals can be achieved through any number of means, as long as the collective mission of teaching is taken seriously by faculty who have more often than not been hired, reviewed, and promoted primarily because of their accomplishments in their own disciplines and because of their specific research.

We must not, therefore, succumb to Bloom's stark divide between his idea of transcendent truth and the immanent realities that have played so critical a role in my own engagement with the history and anthropology of India (and empire). By the same token, I resist the separation between teaching and research, between general and professional education, between the goals of a college and the aspirations of a university. The American university system has become so successful precisely because it combines these features rather than insulating them from one another. Indeed, this is why I argue that the kinds of intellectual challenges that are part of undergraduate education in both the liberal arts and sciences are critical to the formulation and defense of the idea of the research university. Without in any way detracting from the critical importance we place on the university for fostering research that will produce better knowledge, policies, medicines, products, and ideas, I would also suggest that it is this core commitment that provides the most secure ground on which to predicate a response to the prevailing loss of public confidence in the basic value of education itself.

Hanna Holborn Gray, a historian and former president of the University of Chicago, has also written in favor of the fundamental value of the liberal arts for the idea of the university. In a series of lectures she gave at the University of California in 2009, she used the competing—if more often than not also complementary—ideas of Clark Kerr, the former chancellor of Berkeley and president of the University of California, and Robert Maynard Hutchins, the legendary president of the University of Chicago from 1929 to 1951, to make her argument.[17] Kerr became seen as a visionary leader as he formulated and helped secure the acceptance of the "Master Plan" of 1960, in which the three different systems of colleges and universities in California were classified along a grid from educating all high school graduates to producing the highest levels of research but with the promise that merit would be rewarded and opportunities would be made available for all students to rise to their highest possible level. The plan legitimated the concentration of research in its flagship institutions while making the system of education—from community colleges across the state to the Berkeley campus that was by then Harvard's peer—integrated in an unprecedented way: in Kerr's distinctive words, a "multi-versity." Hutchins had become famous for advocating the foundational importance of undergraduate education, promoting a focus on "great books" and stressing the "collegiate" idea for a university that was also known for its interdisciplinary graduate programs.

Gray shows that both Kerr and Hutchins played powerful roles in making the university what it is today, with Hutchins maintaining its core values concerning general education—educating young people to become genuine citizens—while Kerr crafted the institutional conditions for its embrace of the American ideal of educating as many of its citizens as possible. Gray notes that they were both "utopians," following in the footsteps of others who believed that the university was the one institution that could aspire toward utopian ideals and at the same time find actual ways to implement them. She is more sensible than this, and indeed she warns against seeking to transform the university into a real "social utopia," suggesting instead that the "unique purposes of education, scholarly learning, and the preservation and creation of knowledge within the conditions of the greatest possible freedom" are "utopian enough."[18] But she too conveys concerns about the realities of university life, in her own way echoing not just Hutchins but more recent critics, from Mark Taylor to Andrew Delbanco, who continue to argue for versions of Hutchins's collegiate ideal, if in different registers.[19] She is concerned that faculty "live increasingly within their departments—and now also in the mounting number of semiautonomous institutes and centers that have become the coin of the academic realm," with the result not just of lessening the vigor of "faculty participation or interest in general university affairs" but also of enabling "styles of free agency and independent entrepreneurship."[20] And she recognizes that the "prestige of [undergraduate] teaching has continued to decline," noting that this prestige "is not even wholly secure in the smaller colleges that pride themselves on being teaching institutions."[21] She argues instead for the importance of the liberal arts, "both to provide some core of a general education and of a broad cultural perspective valuable in themselves and for the capacities of mind they help develop" and because in the end they add immeasurably to the specialized research to which students and faculty ultimately turn their attention.[22]

Despite his signal role in inventing the modern American university system, Kerr was in fact, as Gray points out, always troubled by the institutional juggernaut American education was becoming. He shared much of Hutchins's sense of the significance of the collegiate ideal, while embracing the institutional and political needs of the state of California (and by implication the nation) in promoting a more diverse and differentiated reality. While he was an unapologetic advocate of mass education as part of a genuinely meritocratic system, of advanced research, and of much-needed specialization, he too worried about the decline of the prestige of the humanities, the exclusive focus of some faculty on research and graduate rather than undergraduate education, and the loss of common knowledge and values. He had been as shaped by his own liberal arts education in a small and distinguished eastern college as he was by his experience leading the preeminent system of public higher education in the nation. His writings (and speeches) both while in office and afterward reveal the steady refrain of one committed to the same kind of utopia as that held onto by Hutchins and many others, including Gray. Yet, as Gray also implies, Kerr left a much greater legacy for the idea of the American university than did Hutchins, not least because he attempted to balance Hutchins's concerns in the context of institutions that could serve a much broader public in the late twentieth century.

As we inherit these debates—and in some respects the debates have changed little over the past century—we confront the demands of a new century and the growing public concern about not just the goals of higher education but even more critically its cost. Kerr's Master Plan is no longer adequately funded by the state, and it is unfortunate but likely that in an age of massive government debt, public disenchantment with higher education, and growing privatization, it never will be again. As the burden for funding education shifts from governments to students (and former students, as alumni philanthropy has been a major source of funding for elite private colleges and increasingly for public colleges too), the idea of the university has come under greater public scrutiny than ever before. And as the scrutiny has intensified, not only has access to a college degree become more difficult, but so too has the expectation that the value of college be measured by the literal value of a degree in the form of jobs and earnings. The liberal arts now often seem to be a luxury that only the elite can afford, and even they—to the dismay of many educators in top schools—seem increasingly skeptical. Some have attributed this decline to the economic downturn, others to the ever-growing need for technological and entrepreneurial innovation, though for some this is yet another example of the pervasive anti-intellectualism of American life, a version of American pragmatism that has no interest in the liberal arts in any form. But, as Richard Hofstadter—who wrote the most influential book on this subject—has shown, the real problem may be the ambivalence of the intelligentsia about playing its full public role.[23] It is urgent that the professoriate come forward to make coherent and powerful arguments on behalf of the kind of liberal education that has now been recognized around the world as our signature brand, rather than either dissolving into internecine rancor or losing our resolve for the pedagogical mission.

The liberal arts have been fundamental not just to the constitution of the American middle class but also to the creativity of mind and spirit that flowers in areas ranging from the arts to the sciences, from engineering to entrepreneurship. It is often the case that business educators and scientists—as well as employers in many professions—find themselves in agreement that their best students need not just math and statistics but also philosophy and literature to thrive. The professoriate should be able to argue for the importance of a rigorous moral and political education in the most general of terms without either relying solely on such measures as the continuing percentage of "English majors" or instrumentalizing the value of a liberal arts degree. The most successful site for rethinking some of the fundamental structures of the university is likely to be undergraduate teaching, the utopian space of the college as imagined by Hutchins, yet lodged at the heart of all genuinely great research universities, as envisioned by Kerr.

Utopia will always be more an aspiration than a reality for the university, but it is critical for us to keep in mind our collective commitments even at a time of unprecedented change and challenge for the institutional realities we confront. We must ensure that our passion for the power of the classroom is still palpable even when using new technological means to help us teach (and learn) or when pursuing ever more specialized research. We know that the very specialization so distrusted by Hutchins has been fundamental to the advances in knowledge and discovery that have been especially critical in the age of technology and information, but we are reminded from Kerr's ambivalence, and Gray's reflection, that many of those who have taken on the burdens of managing the realities of the university research infrastructure that is more complicated and costly than ever before also do so in large part because they share some of Hutchins's abiding belief in the transformative necessity of knowledge for its (and our) own sake.

Bloom notwithstanding, it has become increasingly clear to educators from almost all backgrounds that any liberal arts education in the twenty-first century must include significant attention to the global contexts that not just inform but now constitute the world in which we live. My passage to India might have opened up a world along lines that were already set by the American aftermath of World War II, with Fulbright's major program to facilitate cultural exchange as the catalyst, and the development of university area studies as the conduit that linked an interest in India to a scholarly career. But as walls fell, markets opened, people moved, and so-called developing economies began to grow at a record pace, the world changed. Like all great transitions, these changes have been more gradual and continuous than we often think, yet there is no doubt that the rate of change has accelerated in significant respects.

Whereas universities began to introduce general education courses in fields such as "Asian civilization" in the postwar period as part of a recognition of the need to introduce students to the existence of great and vibrant civilizations alongside the West, it seemed clear at the time that only "Western civilization" had been able to propel a full embrace of change, from the Renaissance to the onset and advance of modernity. Max Weber was read to show not only the inextricable, if in part counterintuitive, relationship between Protestantism and the rise of capitalism but also, in concert with assertions from Hegel, Marx, and modernization theory, that for reasons lodged deep in the history of civilizations only the West was dynamic and progressive in political, cultural, social, and economic registers. All this now has to be rethought.

In my own scholarly work, as the pages of the book reveal, I was never persuaded that the regnant social and political theoretical frameworks that had positioned the relationships (and differences) between "West" and "East" were independent of the historical disparities in world political and economic power. And over the years I came to be much more interested in the history of imperialism than with essential civilizational differences. As a "cultural," or "anthropological," historian, I was less intrigued by the history of warfare and trade that led to imperial outcomes than in the intellectual and cultural consequences of these shifts in world history. Although I began my formal scholarly career studying kingship, I soon came to see the institution of "caste" as emblematic of this epistemological realignment: a fundamental and evocative way of illustrating the way cultural representations and institutions came to embody the larger narrative of political and economic history. In the end, however, the crux of the issue was always history itself, the way history was written by victors rather than victims, the extent to which the stories we enshrined in official narratives of the past could be used to justify and legitimate rather than question and critique the present. Nevertheless, history is too important, and too contradictory, to allow for a simple rewriting; neither power nor culture worked in mechanical ways (to say the least). Each rewriting of history revealed other victors, new victims, and unanticipated complexities. This is why the critical apparatus of historical method and thought has always to be directed first on itself, why the endless revisionism of historical writing is as much an

expression of a fundamental commitment to truth as it is an acknowledgment that this truth is always greater than we are.

Truth, however, cannot reside in the abstract and transcendental
alone; it must be constantly tested not just by historical context but also
by the demands of the present. Given the long history of imperial rule
and global trade that has been foundational for the rise of the West,
those demands should have included global perspectives well before
the recent emergence of globalization as such a powerful force. I hope,
therefore, that the essays in this book provide far more than just a refu-
tation of Bloom's own conviction that only an exemplary and triumpha-
list history of the West can predicate a fundamental engagement with
the debates surrounding the role of the liberal arts and sciences. I also
hope that this book does more than simply provide an account of the
relationship of the disciplines of history and anthropology in the case
of South Asian studies, or even more broadly an idiosyncratic genealogy
of the transition from area studies to global studies. In reviewing, and
in some cases rewriting, essays dating across the same twenty-five years
that spanned my own first encounter with Bloom through to my taking
on Kerr's mantle as chancellor of the University of California at Berkeley, I have, to be sure, traced an intellectual career that has been firmly
situated in these issues and transitions even as it has been profoundly
rooted in the university. Yet I have included a series of reflections on
questions that are both greater than their immediate focus and, perhaps,
applicable to other more enduring dilemmas separated by time as well
as place. In recounting the opening of one American mind in the passage
I took to India fifty years ago, I have thought again about religious difference, intellectual doubt, cultural diversity, moral conviction, economic
structure, and political failure in ways that I suspect are shared by many
who have different autobiographies and, for that matter, different archives. Those of us who reflect back on the archives of our own lives
all share in common a belief in the possibility of knowledge about the
world, and about ourselves, that may indeed seem naïve and mistakenly
utopian. But that is what keeps making us return to those archives of
old, to tell us something new we never could have known before.

Notes

Introduction: Passage to India

1. A. L. Basham, *The Wonder That Was India: A Survey of the Culture of the Indian Sub-Continent Before the Coming of the Muslims* (New York: Grove, 1959).
2. Colin Turnbull, *The Forest People* (New York: Simon and Schuster, 1961); Colin Turnbull, *The Mountain People* (New York: Simon and Schuster, 1972).
3. Nicholas B. Dirks, *Castes of Mind: Colonialism and the Making of Modern India* (Princeton, N.J.: Princeton University Press, 2001).
4. Louis Dumont, *Homo Hierarchicus: An Essay on the Caste System* (Chicago: University of Chicago Press, 1970).
5. McKim Marriott, "Interactional and Attributional Theories of Caste Rank," *Man in India* 39 (1959): 92–107; McKim Marriott, "Hindu Transactions: Diversity Without Dualism," in *Transaction and Meaning: Directions in the Anthropology of Exchange and Symbolic Behavior*, ed. Bruce Kapferer (Philadelphia: ISHI, 1976), 109–142; McKim Marriott, "Constructing an Indian Ethnosociology," in *India Through Hindu Categories*, ed. McKim Marriott (New Delhi: Sage, 1990), 1–39.
6. White had delivered lectures at my undergraduate college during my senior year; the book itself was only published in 1973. See Hayden White, *Metahistory: The Historical Imagination in Nineteenth-Century Europe* (Baltimore, Md.: Johns Hopkins University Press, 1973).
7. Nicholas B. Dirks, *The Hollow Crown: Ethnohistory of an Indian Kingdom* (Cambridge: Cambridge University Press, 1987).
8. Louis Dumont, *Une sous-caste de l'Inde du sud. Organisation sociale et religion*

des Pramalai Kallar (Paris: Mouton, 1957); translated as *A South Indian Sub-caste: Social Organization and Religion of the Pramalai Kallar* (Delhi: Oxford University Press, 1986).

9. Despite many convergent assumptions, ethnosociological work frequently took Dumont as the target par excellence of anthropological critique.

10. Bernard S. Cohn, *India: The Social Anthropology of a Civilization* (Englewood Cliffs, NJ: Prentice-Hall, 1971); Bernard S. Cohn, *An Anthropologist Among the Historians and Other Essays* (Delhi: Oxford University Press, 1987); Bernard S. Cohn, *Colonialism and Its Forms of Knowledge: The British in India* (Princeton, N.J.: Princeton University Press, 1996). See also Nicholas B. Dirks, "Bernard S. Cohn (1928–2003)," *American Anthropologist* 107, no. 4 (2005): 751–753.

11. Michel Foucault, *The Order of Things: An Archaeology of the Human Sciences* (New York: Pantheon, 1971); Michel Foucault, *Discipline and Punish: The Birth of the Prison* (New York: Vintage, 1979); Michel Foucault, *The History of Sexuality*, vol. 1: *An Introduction* (New York: Pantheon, 1986).

12. Edward Said, *Orientalism* (New York: Vintage, 1979).

13. Ranajit Guha, *Elementary Aspects of Peasant Insurgency in Colonial India* (Delhi: Oxford University Press, 1983); Ranajit Guha, *Dominance Without Hegemony: History and Power in Colonial India* (Cambridge, Mass.: Harvard University Press, 1997).

14. See my discussion of this in the introduction to Nicholas B. Dirks, ed., *Colonialism and Culture* (Ann Arbor: University of Michigan Press, 1992).

15. Clifford Geertz, *The Interpretation of Cultures: Selected Essays* (New York: Basic Books, 1973).

16. Immanuel Wallerstein, *Open the Social Sciences: Report of the Gulbenkian Commission on the Restructuring of the Social Sciences* (Palo Alto, Calif.: Stanford University Press, 1996).

17. Nicholas B. Dirks, "Is Vice Versa? Historical Anthropologies and Anthropological Histories," in *The Historic Turn in the Human Sciences*, ed. Terrence McDonald (Ann Arbor: University of Michigan Press, 1996), 17–51; Nicholas B. Dirks, "Slouching Towards Ambivalence: History, Anthropology, and Postcolonial Critique," lecture, University of Rochester, March 2000.

18. Norman O. Brown, *Life Against Death: The Psychoanalytical Meaning of History* (Middletown, Conn.: Wesleyan University Press, 1959); Huston Smith, *The Religions of Man* (New York: Harper & Row, 1958); Herman Melville, *Moby-Dick; Or, The Whale* (New York, 1851).

1. Annals of the Archive:
Ethnographic Notes on the Sources of History

This paper was originally prepared for a conference entitled "Early Modern History and the Social Sciences: Braudel's Mediterranean Fifty Years After," which took place in Bellagio, June 23–27, 1997.

1. Anthony Grafton, *The Footnote: A Curious History* (Cambridge, Mass.: Harvard University Press, 1997). Grafton's fine book both traces the history of the footnote in modern historical writing and treats the complex and contested history of the documentary source for historical research. Grafton also notes that while Leopold Ranke proclaimed and propounded the place of the archive for history, he was neither the first to do so, nor by any means solely, if even principally, reliant on archival sources. See Grafton, *The Footnote*, 4.

2. This chapter is mostly personal reflection about my own research based in the history of South Asia, hardly an adequate basis for the historicizing of the archive. Indeed, such a project would entail, at the very least, comprehensive and comparative historical research on different national archives, combined with reflection and critique, drawing from recent debates in the philosophy of history as well as methodological concerns of practicing historians. Unfortunately, historians often betray a serious reticence to combine these registers. I will comment on preliminary efforts in this direction in the final section of this paper.

3. Although I did my Ph.D. in a department of history, my adviser, Bernard S. Cohn, had originally been trained as an anthropologist and thus introduced his history students to both anthropology and its adherents.

4. I took my inspiration from Bernard Cohn, not only because of his witty and perceptive account of his fieldwork among historians but because he questioned the nature and history of the colonial archive in terms of what he called a "colonial sociology of knowledge." See Bernard S. Cohn, "An Anthropologist Among the Historians: A Field Study," *South Atlantic Quarterly* 61, no. 1 (1962): 13–28; Bernard S. Cohn, *Colonialism and Its Forms of Knowledge: The British in India* (Princeton, N.J.: Princeton University Press, 1996).

5. Nicholas B. Dirks, "Colonial Histories and Native Informants: Biography of an Archive," in *Orientalism and the Postcolonial Predicament*, ed. Carol Breckenridge and Peter van der Veer (Philadelphia: University of Pennsylvania Press, 1993), 279–313.

6. H. H. Wilson, *Mackenzie Collection: A Descriptive Catalogue of the Oriental Manuscripts . . . Collected by the Late Lieut. Col. Colin Mackenzie* (Calcutta, 1828).

7. Nicholas B. Dirks, *The Hollow Crown: Ethnohistory of an Indian Kingdom* (Cambridge: Cambridge University Press, 1987).

8. Ranajit Guha, *A Rule of Property for Bengal: An Essay on the Idea of Permanent Settlement* (Paris: Mouton, 1963); Eric Stokes, *The English Utilitarians and India* (Oxford: Clarendon, 1959).

9. Nicholas B. Dirks, *Castes of Mind: Colonialism and the Making of Modern India* (Princeton, N.J.: Princeton University Press, 2001).

10. This approach can be seen clearly in H. H. Risley's famous (and influential) ethnographic observation that caste would assuredly be an impediment to national mobilization. H. H. Risley, *The People of India* (Calcutta: Thacker, Spink & Co., 1908), 282. See Dirks, *Castes of Mind*, chap. 3.

11. Uday Singh Mehta, *Liberalism and Empire: A Study in Nineteenth-Century British Liberal Thought* (Chicago: University of Chicago Press, 1999).

12. Nicholas B. Dirks, "The Policing of Tradition: Colonialism and Anthropology in Southern India," *Comparative Studies in Society and History* 39, no. 1 (1997): 182–212.

13. Foucault's original lecture on governmentality was delivered at the Collège de France on February 1, 1978. See Michel Foucault, *Security, Territory, Population: Lectures at the Collège de France, 1977–78* (New York: Picador/Palgrave Macmillan, 2007), 87–114.

14. Dirks, *The Hollow Crown.*

15. Karl Marx, *The Eighteenth Brumaire of Louis Bonaparte* (Chicago: Charles H. Kerr, 1913), 9.

16. Reinhart Koselleck, *Futures Past: On the Semantics of Historical Time* (Cambridge, Mass.: MIT Press, 1985).

17. Archival science has been born out of the generally accepted mandate that the modern archive maintain records that satisfy two conditions, first that they were records of state administration, and second that they can be demonstrated to serve historical and administrative purposes distinct from the original one. See Hilary Jenkinson, "Reflections of an Archivist," in *A Modern Archives Reader: Basic Readings on Archival Theory and Practice*, ed. M. Daniels and Timothy Walch (Washington, D.C.: National Archives and Records Services, 1984).

18. G. W. F. Hegel, *Phenomenology of Spirit* (Oxford: Clarendon, 1977); Koselleck, *Futures Past.*

19. Ernst Posner, "Some Aspects of Archival Development Since the French Revolution," in *A Modern Archives Reader: Basic Readings on Archival Theory and Practice*, ed. M. Daniels and Timothy Walch (Washington, D.C.: National Archives and Records Services, 1984).

20. Judith Panitch, "Liberty, Equality, Posterity? Some Archival Lessons from the Case of the French Revolution," *American Archivist* 59, no. 1 (1996).

21. Philippe Sagnac, *La legislation civile de la revolution française (1789–1804)* (New York: AMS, 1973), 85.

22. Panitch, "Liberty, Equality, Posterity," 34.

23. Jennifer Milligan, " 'What Is an Archive?' in the History of Modern France," in *Archive Stories: Fact, Fictions, and the Writing of History*, ed. Antoinette Burton (Durham, N.C.: Duke University Press, 2005).

24. As a result of the Public Records Act of 1838. F. S. Thomas, *Hand-Book to the Public Records* (London, 1853).

25. T. Schellenberg, *Modern Archives: Principles and Techniques* (Chicago: University of Chicago Press, 1964).

26. Nicholas B. Dirks, "History as a Sign of the Modern," *Public Culture* 2, no. 2 (1990): 25–32; Ranajit Guha, *Dominance Without Hegemony: History and Power in Colonial India* (Cambridge, Mass.: Harvard University Press, 1997).

2. Autobiography of an Archive

1. T. V. Mahalingam, *Mackenzie Manuscripts: Summaries of the Historical Manuscripts in the Mackenzie Collection*, 2 vols. (Madras: University of Madras, 1972–1976).
2. Bronislaw Malinowski, *Myth in Primitive Psychology* (New York: Norton, 1926).
3. Nicholas B. Dirks, "Political Authority and Structural Change in Early South Indian History," *Indian Social and Economic History Review* 13, no. 2 (1976): 125–157.
4. Burton Stein, *Peasant State and Society in Medieval South India* (Delhi: Oxford University Press, 1980).
5. H. H. Wilson, *Mackenzie Collection: A Descriptive Catalogue of the Oriental Manuscripts . . . Collected by the Late Lieut. Col. Colin Mackenzie* (Calcutta, 1828).
6. From his letter written to the Board of Revenue, Madras, December 24, 1800, Tamil Nadu Archives (catalogue number unavailable).
7. Thomas Trautmann, *Aryans and British India* (Berkeley: University of California Press, 1997); Paul B. Courtright, "Wilson, Horace Hayman (1786–1860)," *Oxford Dictionary of National Biography* (Oxford: Oxford University Press, 2004).
8. "Letters and Reports from Native Agents Employed to Collect Books, Traditions, etc., in the Various Parts of the Peninsula," British Library (BL), India Office Records, Mackenzie Collection, Unbound Translations, Class XII, vol. 1, no. 3.
9. "Biographical Sketch of the Literary Career of the Late Colonel Colin Mackenzie . . . Contained in a Letter Addressed by Him to the Right Hon. Sir Alexander Johnston . . . ," *Madras Journal of Literature and Science* 2 (1835): 262–290.
10. BL, India Office Records, Mackenzie Collection, Uncatalogued Miscellaneous Papers, Box 3, nos. 83, 84, 85.
11. National Archives of India, Survey of India Records, vol. 41, letter to Col. Close, May 29, 1801.
12. National Archives of India, letter to Clive, in "Second General Report on the Mysore Survey," July 12, 1803.
13. "Biographical Sketch of . . . Colin Mackenzie," 265–266.
14. National Archives of India, "Memoir of the Civil Administration, Police, Commerce, and Revenue Management of the Balla Ghaat Carnatic," from "Enquiries Instituted in 1800 and 1801 and Information Collected for Captain Mackenzie on the Mysore Survey, by Cavelly Venkata Boria, Interpreter to the Survey."
15. Ibid.
16. This and the following quotations on these matters are all from the Survey of India Records, National Archives of India.

17. James Prinsep, "Report of the Committee on Papers on Cavelly Venkata Lach-mia's Proposed Renewal of Colonel Mackenzie's Investigations," *Journal of the Royal Asiatic Society* 5 (1836): 512.
18. W. C. Mackenzie, *Colonel Colin Mackenzie: First Surveyor-General of India* (Ed-inburgh: W. & R. Chambers, 1952).

3. Preface to the Second Edition of *The Hollow Crown*

1. David Ludden's review of *The Hollow Crown* in the *Journal of Interdisciplinary History* 20, no. 2 (1989): 338–340.
2. The terms here are Homi Bhabha's; see, for example, his "Of Mimicry and Man: The Ambivalence of Colonial Discourse," *October* 28 (1984): 125–133. In my own work I use these terms to refer to the ways in which Mackenzie's "native informants" engaged in both mimicry and menace. See my "Colonial Histories and Native Informants: Biography of an Archive," in *Orientalism and the Postcolonial Predicament: Perspectives on South Asia*, ed. Carol Breck-enridge and Peter van der Veer (Philadelphia: University of Pennsylvania Press, 1993), 279–313.
3. *Journal of the Royal Society of Arts* 57, no. 2,942 (April 9, 1909): 417.
4. Frederick Mullaly, *Notes on Criminal Classes of the Madras Presidency* (Ma-dras, 1892).
5. Mullaly, *Criminal Classes*, v.
6. Ranajit Guha is the brilliant founder of the Subaltern Studies collective and author of *Elementary Aspects of Peasant Insurgency in Colonial India* (Delhi: Oxford University Press, 1983).
7. Gyan Prakash, "Writing Post-Orientalist Histories of the Third World: Indian Historiography Is Good to Think," in *Colonialism and Culture*, ed. Nicholas B. Dirks (Ann Arbor: University of Michigan Press, 1992), 353–388.
8. My advisors were initially impatient with my reliance on the other texts and insistent that I foreground the Kattapomman text because of its clear textual enunciation of the culture of kingship in premodern southern India.
9. Dumont does refer to the Tondaiman kings of Pudukkottai and writes bril-liantly about the relationship between kingship and kinship in former *palai-yakkarar*—both Kallar and Maravar—domains; what I mean is that this dis-cussion never becomes relevant for his more general characterization of the place of Kallars in South Indian society, let alone his understanding of the caste system in India writ large. See Louis Dumont, *Hierarchy and Marriage Alliance in South Indian Kinship* (London: Royal Anthropological Institute of Great Britain and Ireland, 1957).
10. As is pointed out firmly, though charitably, by Ian Copland in his magnificent review of my book: "The Historian as Anthropologist and the Study of South Asia: 'Ethnohistory' and the Study of South Asia," *South Asia* 11, no. 2 (1998), 101–116.

4. Castes of Mind: The Original Caste

1. Abbé Jean Antoine Dubois, *Description of the Character, Manners, and Customs of the People of India; and of their Institutions, Religious and Civil*, trans. Henry K. Beauchamp (London, 1817), 29.
2. John Wilson, *Indian Caste* (1877; New Delhi: Deep Publications, 1976), 11.
3. Louis Dumont, *Homo Hierarchicus: The Caste System and Its Implications*, trans. Mark Sainsbury et al. (1966; Chicago: University of Chicago Press, 1980).
4. Ibid., 232.
5. Ibid., 234.
6. Ibid., 235.
7. Jan Heesterman, *The Inner Conflict of Tradition: Essays in Indian Ritual, Kingship, and Society* (Chicago: University of Chicago Press, 1985), 193.
8. Ibid., 8.
9. Nicholas B. Dirks, *The Hollow Crown: Ethnohistory of an Indian Kingdom* (Cambridge: Cambridge University Press, 1987).
10. Alexander Dow, *The History of Hindustan* (London, 1768–1771).
11. Monstuart Elphinstone, *The History of India*, 2 vols. (London, 1842).
12. James Mill, *The History of British India* (London, 1820).
13. H. H. Wilson, *Mackenzie Collection: A Descriptive Catalogue of the Oriental Manuscripts . . . Collected by the Late Lieut. Col. Colin Mackenzie* (Calcutta, 1828); W. C. Mackenzie, *Colonel Colin Mackenzie: First Surveyor-General of India* (Edinburgh: W. & R. Chambers, 1952).
14. The Mackenzie Collection is housed in the British Library, London; and the Government Oriental Manuscripts Library, Chennai.
15. Jorge Luis Borges, "The Analytical Language of John Wilkins," in *Other Inquisitions, 1937–1952*, trans. Ruth Simms (Austin: University of Texas Press, 1964), 101–105.
16. The Mysore Survey Documents, National Archives of India, New Delhi.
17. Mackenzie's drawings are held in the Prints, Drawings, and Photographs Section of the British Library's Asia, Pacific, and Africa Collections and are catalogued in Mildred Archer, *British Drawings in the India Office Library*, 2 vols. (London: Her Majesty's Stationery Office, 1969).
18. Ibid., 534–538.
19. BL, India Office Records, Board of Control collections, no. 541 (1816).
20. Quoted in Dubois, *Description*, vii.
21. Cavelly Venkata Ramaswamie, *A Digest of the Different Castes of the Southern Division of Southern India, with Descriptions of their Habits, Customs, Etc.* (Madras, 1847).
22. See, for example, the extensive manuscript collections of Walter Elliott (British Library, London), which drew heavily on the Mackenzie Collection.
23. See Anand Yang, ed., *Crime and Criminality in British India* (Tucson: University of Arizona Press, 1985); David Washbrook, "Law, State, and Agrarian

Society in Colonial India," *Modern Asian Studies* 15, no. 3 (1981): 649–721; Alfred Horsford Bingley and Arthur Nicholls, *Brahmans: Caste Handbook for the Indian Army* (Simla, 1897).

24. M. A. Sherring, *Hindu Tribes and Castes* (1871–1881; New Delhi: Cosmo, 1974).

25. James Tod, *Annals and Antiquities of Rajasthan; or, The Central and Western Rajpoot States of India*, 2 vols. (1829–1832; London: Routledge & Kegan Paul, 1950).

26. Sherring, *Hindu Tribes*, 274–296.

27. *Man* 1 (1901): 138. Such interpretation often rested in a peculiar set of notions about origins, which themselves had less to do with history than with a set of functional correlates assumed to be demonstrated by the particular origins of any given group and its derivative occupational and social status. These preoccupations were reflected in the kinds of information (texts, traditions, statistics) the colonial state collected, stored, and published.

28. This paragraph summarizes the pathbreaking work of Bernard S. Cohn in *An Anthropologist Among the Historians and Other Essays* (New Delhi: Oxford University Press, 1987).

29. H. H. Risley, *The People of India* (London: W. Thacker & Co., 1908).

30. H. H. Risley, *The Tribes and Castes of Bengal: Ethnographic Glossary* (Calcutta, 1892).

31. William Crooke, *Tribes and Castes of the North-Western Provinces and Oudh*, 4 vols. (Calcutta, 1896).

32. Risley, *Tribes and Castes*, 278.

33. *Journal of the Royal Society of Arts* 52 (April 9, 1909).

34. Tamil Nadu Archives, Public Department, Madras, Government Order (GO) no. 647, June 26, 1901.

35. Ibid.

36. Edgar Thurston, *Ethnographic Notes in Southern India* (Madras, 1906).

37. Edgar Thurston, *Castes and Tribes of Southern India* (Madras: Madras Government Press, 1909).

38. Risley, *The People of India*, 282.

39. Ibid., 291.

40. Ibid., 293.

41. Ibid., 300.

42. S. V. Ketkar, *History of Caste in India: Evidence of the Laws of Manu on the Social Conditions in India During the Third Century AD, Interpreted and Examined; with an Appendix on Radical Defects of Ethnology* (1909; Jaipur: Rawat, 1979).

43. Ibid., 1.

44. Ibid., 53–54.

45. Ibid., 78–82.

46. G. S. Ghurye, *Caste and Race in India* (New York: Knopf, 1932).

47. Ibid., 157.

48. Ibid., 160.

49. Ibid., 164.

50. Partha Chatterjee, *Nationalist Thought and the Colonial World: A Derivative Discourse?* (London: Zed, 1986).

51. For an excellent example, see Henry Louis Gates Jr. ed., *"Race," Writing, and Difference* (Chicago: University of Chicago Press, 1986); for a recent sympathetic assessment of this field of study, see Robert Young, *White Mythologies: Writing History and the West* (London: Routledge, 1990).

52. Edward Said, *Orientalism* (New York: Vintage, 1979).

53. See Fredric Jameson, "Third-World Literature in the Era of Multinational Capital," *Social Text* 15 (1986), 65–88; and the response by Aijaz Ahmad, "Jameson's Rhetoric of Otherness and the 'National Allegory,'" *Social Text* 17 (1987): 3–25. For more recent criticisms of postorientalist writing, see Henry Louis Gates Jr., "Critical Fanonism," *Critical Inquiry* 17, no. 8 (1991): 457–470; Aijaz Ahmad, "Between Orientalism and Historicism: Anthropological Knowledge of India," *Studies in History* 7, no. 1 (1991): 135–163.

54. See my *The Hollow Crown*.

55. This is neither to argue against the discipline of anthropology itself nor to suggest that the simple reallocation of history either to India or to anthropology will solve all the problems I have identified. I have elsewhere suggested that one of the principal tasks of a postcolonial anthropology is to challenge current certainties about the universal character of history and the meaning of historicism. History too can be reified and essentialized. See Nicholas B. Dirks, "Is Vice Versa? Historical Anthropologies and Anthropological Histories," in *The Historic Turn in the Human Sciences*, ed. Terrence McDonald (Ann Arbor: University of Michigan Press, 1996), 17–51.

56. Benedict Anderson, *Imagined Communities: Reflections on the Origin and Spread of Nationalism* (London: Verso, 1983).

5. Ritual and Resistance: Subversion as a Social Fact

1. Clifford Geertz, *The Interpretation of Cultures: Selected Essays* (New York: Basic Books, 1973), 142.

2. Sherry Ortner, *Sherpas Through Their Rituals* (Cambridge: Cambridge University Press, 1978), 1.

3. Ibid., 2.

4. Sherry Ortner, *High Religion: A Cultural and Political History of Sherpa Buddhism* (Princeton, N.J.: Princeton University Press, 1989).

5. Sherry Ortner, "Theory in Anthropology Since the Sixties," *Comparative Studies in Society and History* 26, no. 1 (1984): 126–166.

6. See Pierre Bourdieu, *Outline of a Theory of Practice*, trans. Richard Nice (Cambridge: Cambridge University Press, 1977).

7. See William Sewell, *Work and Revolution in France: The Language of Labor from the Old Regime to 1848* (Cambridge: Cambridge University Press, 1980).

8. Stuart Clark, "French Historians and Early Modern Popular Culture," *Past and Present* 100, no. 1 (1983): 62–99; Hans Medick, "Missionaries in the Row Boat? Ethnological Ways of Knowing as a Challenge to Social History," *Comparative Studies in Society and History* 29, no. 1 (1987): 76–98.

9. Max Gluckman, *Custom and Conflict in Africa* (Oxford: Blackwell, 1956), 109.

10. Natalie Davis, *Society and Culture in Early Modern France: Eight Essays* (Palo Alto, Calif.: Stanford University Press, 1965), 130.

11. Stephen Greenblatt, *Shakespearean Negotiations: The Circulation of Social Energy in Renaissance England* (Berkeley: University of California Press, 1989), 42.

12. Mikhail Bakhtin, *Rabelais and His World*, trans. Hélène Iswolsky (Cambridge, Mass.: The MIT Press, 1968).

13. Terry Eagleton, *Walter Benjamin; Or, Towards a Revolutionary Criticism* (London: Verso, 1981), 148.

14. Peter Stallybrass and Allon White, *The Politics and Poetics of Transgression* (Ithaca, N.Y.: Cornell University Press, 1986).

15. Rosalind O'Hanlon, "Recovering the Subject: Subaltern Studies and Histories of Resistance in Colonial South Asia," *Modern Asian Studies* 22, no. 1 (1988): 189–224.

16. Jean Comaroff, *Body of Power, Spirit of Resistance: The Culture and History of a South African People* (Chicago: University of Chicago Press, 1985), 196.

17. Alf Lüdtke, "Organisational Order or *Eigensinn*? Workers' Privacy and Workers' Politics in Imperial Germany," in *Rites of Power: Symbolism, Ritual, and Politics Since the Middle Ages*, ed. Sean Wilentz (Philadelphia: University of Pennsylvania Press, 1985), 304.

18. Alf Lüdtke, "Everyday Life: The Articulation of Needs and 'Proletarian Consciousness'—Some Remarks on Concepts" (unpublished ms., n.d.), 4.

19. See Stuart Hall and Tony Jefferson, eds., *Resistance Through Rituals: Youth Subcultures in Postwar Britain* (London: Hutchinson, 1976); Dick Hebdige, *Subculture: The Meaning of Style* (New York: Methuen, 1979).

20. See Michel de Certeau, *The Practice of Everyday Life*, trans. Steven Rendall (Berkeley: University of California Press, 1984).

21. James Scott, *Weapons of the Weak: Everyday Forms of Peasant Resistance* (New Haven, Conn.: Yale University Press, 1985).

22. Comaroff, *Body of Power, Spirit of Resistance*.

23. Nicholas B. Dirks, *The Hollow Crown: Ethnohistory of an Indian Kingdom* (Cambridge: Cambridge University Press, 1987).

24. Louis Dumont, "A Structural Definition of a Folk Deity of Tamil Nad: Aiyanar, the Lord," *Contributions to Indian Sociology* 3 (1959): 75–87.

25. Puddukottai Record Office, R.D. no. 1587 of 1923, March 30, 1925.

26. See also Arjun Appadurai and Carol Breckenridge, "The South Indian Temple:

Authority, Honour, and Redistribution," *Contributions to Indian Sociology* n.s. 10, no. 2 (1976): 187–211.

27. Kathleen Gough, "The Social Structure of a Tanjore Village," in *Village India: Studies in the Little Community*, ed. McKim Marriott (Chicago: University of Chicago Press, 1955), 36–52.

28. See Dirks, *Hollow Crown*.

29. Appadurai and Breckenridge, "South Indian Temple."

30. Arnold van Gennep, *The Rites of Passage* (Chicago: University of Chicago Press, 1960).

31. Victor Turner, *The Ritual Process: Structure and Antistructure* (Chicago: Aldine, 1969).

32. See Greenblatt, *Shakespearean Negotiations*.

33. Ibid.

6. The Policing of Tradition: Colonialism and Anthropology in Southern India

1. October 23, 1891. The *Madras Mail* was the largest English daily in Madras at the time.

2. Lata Mani, *Contentious Traditions: The Debate on Sati in Colonial India, 1780–1833* (Berkeley: University of California Press, 1998).

3. Gayatri Chakravorty Spivak, "Can the Subaltern Speak?" in *Marxism and the Interpretation of Culture*, ed. Cary Nelson and Lawrence Grossberg (Urbana: University of Illinois Press, 1988), 271–313.

4. Individual vows, such as those that involved the piercing of the body in fulfillment of various pledges, were never subjected to administrative concern; however, when vows led to activities such as firewalking in public, collective, ritual events, some of the same concerns that we find in regard to hookswinging were also raised. For a superb anthropological account of different rites in Sri Lanka, see Gananath Obeyesekere, *Medusa's Hair: An Essay on Personal Symbols and Religious Experience* (Chicago: University of Chicago Press, 1981).

5. For an important account of the development of colonial contradictions around public space in northern India, see Sandria Freitag, *Collective Action and Community: Public Arenas in the Emergence of Communalism in North India* (Berkeley: University of California Press, 1989).

6. For a suggestive analysis of left- and right-hand castes in southern India and contests over space, see Arjun Appadurai, "Right- and Left-Hand Castes in South India," *Indian Economic and Social History Review*, 14, no. 1 (1974): 47–73.

7. For an account of missionary responses to hookswinging, see the recent book by Geoffrey Oddie, *Popular Religion, Elites, and Reform: Hook-Swinging and Its Prohibition in Colonial India, 1800–1894* (Delhi: Manohar, 1995).

8. Tamil Nadu Archives (TNA), Judicial Department, Madras, GO no. 83, January 14, 1892.

9. See British Library (BL), India Office Records, V/23/139 ("Selections from the Records of the Madras Government, Reports on the Swinging Festival and the Ceremony of Walking through Fire, Madras: 1854").

10. TNA, Judicial Department, Madras, GO no. 1257, July 7, 1892.

11. Letter from J. H. Wynne, acting district magistrate, to J. F. Price, chief secretary to government, Judicial Department. TNA, Judicial Department, Madras, GO no. 856, May 5, 1892.

12. Kallan is the singular form of Kallar, a caste group of some colonial notoriety in the southern region of the Tamil country because it is associated with thievery on what was at times considered a professional basis. Kallars were in fact a major landed group that tended to reside in mixed or dry agricultural zones and had been associated in intimate ways with precolonial chiefs and their military systems. Their association with criminality had both to do with their military prowess, amply displayed in early wars with, or involving, the British, and their forms of land control and local authority, based as they were in protection systems. See my book, *The Hollow Crown: Ethnohistory of an Indian Kingdom* (Cambridge: Cambridge University Press, 1987).

13. TNA, Judicial Department, Madras, GO no. 856, May 5, 1892.

14. See Oddie, *Popular Religion*, 47–68; also Edgar Thurston, *Ethnographic Notes in Southern India* (Madras: Government Press, 1907), 487–501, 510–519.

15. TNA, Judicial Department, Madras, GO no. 856, May 5, 1892.

16. TNA, Judicial Department, Madras, GO no. 1321, July 22, 1892.

17. TNA, Judicial Department, Madras, GO nos. 2662 and 2663, December 21, 1893.

18. TNA, Public Consultations, vol. IV, nos. 35–37, December 21, 1858.

19. Letter dated September 27, 1858, in ibid.

20. See Nicholas B. Dirks, "The Conversion of Caste: Location, Translation, and Appropriation," in Peter van der Veer, *Conversion to Modernities: The Globalization of Christianity* (New York: Routledge, 1996).

21. Quoted in Oddie, *Popular Religion*, 175–184.

22. TNA, Public Department, Madras, Minutes of Consultation, February 18, 1854.

23. TNA, Judicial Department, Madras, GO nos. 2662 and 2663, December 21, 1893.

24. TNA, Judicial Department, Madras, GO no. 1418, August 27, 1890.

25. TNA, Judicial Department, Madras, GO no. 990, May 25, 1892.

26. TNA, Judicial Department, Madras, GO nos. 2662 and 2663, December 21, 1893.

27. This is a view that is echoed in large part by Oddie. After dismissing those critics of colonialism who merely focus on colonial sources rather than the truths available in them, he emerges with an analysis that could have been

developed without any of the sources. His book, which I came across just in the final stages of preparing this essay, provides some useful, mostly London-based, sources for the analysis of hookswinging but exemplifies the historiographical problems suggested throughout this study.

28. TNA, Judicial Department, Madras, GO nos. 2662 and 2663, December 21, 1893.

29. Ibid.

30. All quotes in this paragraph and the next are from ibid.

31. For a helpful account of the rise of bourgeois morality in nineteenth-century Britain, see Peter Stallybrass and Allon White, *The Politics and Poetics of Transgression* (London: Methuen, 1986).

32. TNA, GO nos. 2662 and 2663, December 21, 1893.

33. Ibid.

34. Quoted in ibid.

35. This petition is enclosed and translated in TNA, Judicial Department, Madras, GO no. 1284, May 27, 1894.

36. TNA, Judicial Department, Madras, GO no. 2627, November 2, 1894.

37. See my argument in "From Little King to Landlord: Colonial Discourse and Colonial Rule," in *Colonialism and Culture*, ed. Nicholas B. Dirks (Ann Arbor: University of Michigan Press, 1992).

38. For an example of this view, see Oddie, *Popular Religion*.

39. Dirks, *The Hollow Crown*.

40. BL, India Office Records, P/4621, Madras Judicial Proceedings, September 24, 1894.

41. See M. N. Srinivas, *Social Change in Modern India* (Berkeley: University of California Press, 1968).

42. The particular example comes from Pudukkottai; see Dirks, *Hollow Crown*. For other examples, see Franklin Presler, *Religion Under Bureaucracy: Policy and Administration for Hindu Temples in South India* (Cambridge: Cambridge University Press, 1987); and Arjun Appadurai, *Worship and Conflict Under Colonial Rule: A South Indian Case* (Cambridge: Cambridge University Press, 1981).

43. See the argument in Eric Hobsbawm and Terence Ranger, eds., *The Invention of Tradition* (Cambridge: Cambridge University Press, 1983). See my longer critique of this position in "Is Vice Versa? Historical Anthropologies and Anthropological Histories," in *The Historic Turn in the Human Sciences*, ed. Terrence McDonald (Ann Arbor: University of Michigan Press, 1996).

44. See Nicholas B. Dirks, "Reading Culture: Anthropology and the Textualization of India," in *Culture/Contexture: Explorations in Anthropology and Literary Studies*, ed. Jeffrey Peck and E. Valentine Daniel (Berkeley: University of California Press, 1996).

45. TNA, Public Department, Madras, GO no. 6/6A, January 10, 1893.

46. Frederick S. Mullaly, *Notes on Criminal Classes of the Madras Presidency* (Madras, 1892).

47. Ibid., v.

48. TNA, Public Department, India, GO no. 647, June 26, 1901.

49. In the early 1890s the Bertillon system of using anthropometric measurements had been adopted first in Bengal, then in Madras. The idea was to identify habitual criminals who moved from place to place and shifted their identities. In India, the Bertillon system was applied according to conventions set out by the colonial sociology of criminal castes. The basic operational principle was that "only members of criminal tribes and persons convicted of certain definite crimes" should be so measured (TNA, Judicial Department, Madras, GO 1838, September 9, 1893). Since most crimes were committed by circumscribed groups of people, anthropometry seemed to be the perfect means to apprehend the principal suspects. As E. R. Henry, the inspector general of police in Bengal put it, "With anthropometry on a sound basis, professional criminals of this type will cease to flourish, as under the rules all persons not identified must be measured, and reference concerning them made to the Central Bureau." Nevertheless, there was residual concern that measurements varied not only from measurer to measurer but from measurement to measurement. The instruments were costly, the course of instruction was lengthy, the statistics were hard to classify, and the measurement process itself was time consuming.

50. Fingerprinting was considered error free, cheap, quick, and simple, and the results were more easily classified. By 1898, Henry wrote that "it may now be claimed that the great value of finger impressions as a means of fixing identity has been fully established" (TNA, Judicial Department, Madras, GO no. 1014, July 1, 1898).

51. Edgar Thurston, *The Castes and Tribes of Southern India*, 7 vols. (Madras: Government Press, 1907). The entries on each caste range in length from one sentence to seventy-five pages and include such salient ethnographic facts as origin stories, occupational profiles, descriptions of kinship structure, marriage and funerary rituals, manner of dress and decoration, as well as assorted stories, observations, and accounts about each group. Naturally, Thurston also included the results of his anthropometric researches, which he said were "all the result of measurements taken by myself, in order to eliminate the varying error resulting from the employment of a plurality of observers" (1:xii).

52. The fourth chapter is entitled "Deformity and Mutilation"; the next, "Torture in Bygone Days," is followed by such other chapters as "Slavery," "Firewalking," "Hookswinging," "Infanticide," and "Meriah Sacrifice." If the caste-by-caste entries in the volumes of Thurston's ethnographic survey focus on the social (which for the British in India was synonymous with caste), these essays instead focus on the body. See chapter 3.

53. Thurston, *Castes and Tribes*, 1:xi.

54. Ibid., 75, 310.

55. See "Castes of Mind," in this volume.

56. See Ashis Nandy, *The Savage Freud and Other Essays on Possible and Retrievable Selves* (Princeton, N.J.: Princeton University Press, 1995), 32–52; Veena Das, "Strange Response," *Illustrated Weekly of India* (February 28, 1988): 30–32.

57. See Jomo Kenyatta, *Facing Mount Kenya: The Tribal Life of the Gikuyu* (New York: Vintage, 1962).

58. Susan Pederson, "National Bodies, Unspeakable Acts: The Sexual Politics of Colonial Policy-making," *Journal of Modern History* 63, no. 4 (1991): 647–680.

59. See Alice Walker and Pratibha Parmar, *Warrior Marks: Female Genital Mutilation and the Sexual Blinding of Women* (New York: Harcourt Brace, 1993).

60. For example, while I understand why Nandy points out the colonial character of postcolonial condemnations of sati, I do not accept that this should constitute the primary basis for a critique of the positions taken by the secular intellectuals (see Nandy, *The Savage Freud*).

7. Imperial Sovereignty

1. Benedict Anderson, *Imagined Communities: Reflections on the Origin and Spread of Nationalism* (London: Verso, 1983).

2. This was not only true in the early years, when modern nations emerged, but also in the late nineteenth and early twentieth centuries, when the European nations congealed around even more narrowly defined cultural identities; see, for example, Ann Stoler, *Race and the Education of Desire: Foucault's History of Sexuality and the Colonial Order of Things* (Durham, N.C.: Duke University Press, 1995).

3. See Richard Helgerson, *Forms of Nationhood: The Elizabethan Writing of England* (Chicago: University of Chicago Press, 1992).

4. David Armitage, *The Ideological Origins of the British Empire* (Cambridge: Cambridge University Press, 2000).

5. J. G. A. Pocock, *The Ancient Constitution and the Feudal Law: A Study of English Historical Thought in the Seventeenth Century* (Cambridge: Cambridge University Press, 1957).

6. John Brewer, *The Sinews of Power: War, Money, and the English State, 1688–1783* (New York: Knopf, 1989).

7. *The Nabob*, Samuel Foote's popular Haymarket play, exemplified the public image of these returned India men. Reprinted in *Plays by Samuel Foote and Arthur Murphy*, ed. George Taylor (Cambridge: Cambridge University Press, 1984).

8. Pocock, *The Ancient Constitution*; Sankar Muthu, *Enlightenment Against Empire* (Princeton, N.J.: Princeton University Press, 2003); Jennifer Pitts, *A Turn to Empire: The Rise of Imperial Liberalism in Britain and France* (Princeton, N.J.: Princeton University Press, 2005).

9. Philip Stern, *The Company-State: Corporate Sovereignty and the Early Modern Foundations of the British Empire in India* (Oxford: Oxford University Press, 2011).

10. See the discussion of this in H. V. Bowen, *Revenue and Reform: The Indian Problem in British Politics, 1757–1773* (Cambridge: Cambridge University Press, 1991), 64–66.

11. Ibid., 76–77.

12. Holden Furber, *John Company at Work: A Study of European Expansion in India in the Late Eighteenth Century* (Cambridge, Mass.: Harvard University Press, 1948); Peter James Marshall, *East Indian Fortunes: The British in Bengal in the Eighteenth Century* (Oxford: Clarendon, 1976).

13. British Library (BL), India Office Records, Despatch Book, vol. 91, June 9, 1686, 142, 145; cited in K. N. Chaudhuri, *The Trading World of Asia and the English East India Company, 1660–1760* (Cambridge: Cambridge University Press, 1978), 454.

14. C. A. Bayly, "The British Military-Fiscal State and Indigenous Resistance: India 1750–1820," in *An Imperial State at War: Britain from 1689 to 1815*, ed. Lawrence Stone (London: Routledge, 1994), 205.

15. H. H. Dodwell, *The Cambridge History of India, British India, 1497–1858* (Delhi: S. Chand & Co., 1968), 5:591.

16. For my own analysis of shared sovereignty and notions of proprietary rights in precolonial India, see my *The Hollow Crown: Ethnohistory of an Indian Kingdom* (Cambridge: Cambridge University Press, 1987).

17. Bayly, "British Military-Fiscal State and Indigenous Resistance," 206.

18. BL, India Office Records, Home Miscellaneous, vol. 211, speech dated November 24, 1772.

19. Letter from Robert Clive to William Pitt, principal secretary of state, January 7, 1759, quoted in George Forrest, *The Life of Lord Clive* (London: Cassell, 1918), 413.

20. Quoted in Percival Spear, *Master of Bengal: Clive and His India* (London: Thames and Hudson, 1975), 145.

21. Quoted in Forrest, *Life of Lord Clive*, 256–258.

22. As Percival Spear approvingly put it, "the dominion of Bengal was not desired in itself, but only as a safeguard for peaceful commercial operations. . . . Rule by legal fiction and by deputy was both safer and cheaper in the conditions of the time." *Master of Bengal*, 156.

23. Quoted in Bernard S. Cohn, *Colonialism and Its Forms of Knowledge* (Princeton, N.J.: Princeton University Press, 1996), 59.

24. Quoted in Bowen, *Revenue and Reform*, 10.

25. BL, Eg. Mss. 218, ff. 149–151.

26. Quoted in Bowen, *Revenue and Reform*, 9–10.

27. Thomas Pownall, *The Right, Interest, and Duty of Government, as Concerned in the Affairs of the East Indies* (London: 1781), 3.

28. Bowen, *Revenue and Reform*, 12.
29. Quoted in Bowen, *Revenue and Reform*, 173. George III was upset at the about-face, writing to North, "I own I am amazed that private interest could make so many forget what they owe to their country." Quoted in Lucy Sutherland, *The East India Company in Eighteenth-Century Politics* (Oxford: Clarendon, 1952), 258.
30. Quoted in Bowen, *Revenue and Reform*, 113.
31. G. R. Gleig, *Memoirs of the Life of the Right Hon. Warren Hastings, First Governor-General of Bengal* (London: R. Bentley, 1841), 534–544.
32. Quoted in Philip Lawson, *The East India Company: A History* (London: Longman, 1993), 128.
33. Edmund Burke, "Speech on Fox's Indian Bill," in *The Writings and Speeches of Edmund Burke*, ed. Peter J. Marshall (Oxford: Clarendon, 1981), 5:425.
34. Bernard S. Cohn, "Representing Authority in Victorian India," in *The Invention of Tradition*, ed. Eric Hobsbawm and Terence Ranger (Cambridge: Cambridge University Press, 1983), 165–209.
35. Edmund Burke, "Speech on a motion made in the House of Commons, May 7, 1782, for a committee to inquire into the state of the representation of the Commons in Parliament," in *The Writings and Speeches of Edmund Burke*, ed. Peter J. Marshall (Oxford: Clarendon, 2000), 7:94–95.
36. Ibid., 95.
37. See J. G. A. Pocock, "Burke and the Ancient Constitution," in *Politics, Language, and Time: Essays on Political Thought and History* (New York: Atheneum, 1971), 202–232.
38. Burke's speech of February 16, 1788, quoted in Marshall, ed., *Writings and Speeches of Edmund Burke*, 6:341.
39. Ibid., 6:345–346.
40. Ibid., 6:346.
41. Ibid., 6:350–351.
42. Carl Schmitt, *Political Theology: Four Chapters on the Concept of Sovereignty*, trans. George Schwab (1922; Chicago: University of Chicago Press, 2005), 5, 12–13.
43. Quoted in Pocock, "Burke and the Ancient Constitution," 227.
44. Nathaniel Halhed was a noted orientalist and compiler of Hindu law codes. See Rosane Rocher, *Orientalism, Poetry, and the Millennium: The Checkered Life of Nathaniel Brassey Halhed, 1751–1830* (Delhi: Motilal Banarsidass, 1983), 48.
45. Marshall, ed., *Writings and Speeches of Edmund Burke*, 6:348–349.
46. Burke, "Policy of Making Conquests for the Mahometans," in *The Writings and Speeches of Edmund Burke*, ed. Peter J. Marshall (Oxford: Clarendon, 1981), 5:41–124.
47. Marshall, ed., *Writings and Speeches of Edmund Burke*, 6:348.
48. Quoted in Pocock, "Burke and the Ancient Constitution," 227.

49. Marshall, ed., *Writings and Speeches of Edmund Burke*, 6:351.

50. Ibid., 6:367.

51. Uday Singh Mehta, *Liberalism and Empire: A Study in Nineteenth-Century British Liberal Thought* (Chicago: University of Chicago Press, 1999), 149.

52. Ibid., 186.

53. Ibid., 189.

54. Mehta writes that "this neglect is evident in both historical political theory and contemporary normative scholarship. Historically, the fact that most British political theorists of the eighteenth and nineteenth centuries were deeply involved with the empire in their writings and often in its administration is seldom given any significance or even mentioned in the framing of this intellectual tradition." Mehta, *Liberalism and Empire*, 6.

55. Armitage, *Ideological Origins of the British Empire*, 3.

56. Linda Colley, *Britons: Forging the Nation, 1707–1837* (New Haven, Conn.: Yale University Press, 1992).

57. I do not mean to exonerate the liberal political tradition, for Mehta and other critics are clearly correct to note the ways in which liberal theory depends on exclusions to its universal claims. But this does not mean that Burke's peculiar commitments to universalism and particularity escape the very same anthropological conundrum.

58. Burke, of course, would have preferred a successful prosecution, and he was deeply embittered by the failure of the trial. Yet he had made his argument in such a way that even though Hastings was let off, his passion became redundant after Lord Cornwallis had succeeded Hastings and begun the reforms of the 1784 Pitt Act. In this sense, despite his own intentions, Burke's fevered rhetoric served as a brilliant means to exorcise the past of corrupt and despotic nabobs.

8. Bringing the Company Back In: The Scandal of Early Global Capitalism

1. Nicholas B. Dirks, *The Scandal of Empire: India and the Creation of Imperial Britain* (Cambridge, Mass.: Belknap Press of Harvard University Press, 2006).

2. Clive defended himself against charges of corruption by exclaiming, "Mr. Chairman, at this moment I stand astonished at my own moderation!" Ibid., 17.

3. *The Correspondence of Edmund Burke* (Cambridge: Cambridge University Press, 1960), 2:434.

4. Edmund and William Burke, "Policy of Making Conquests for the Mahometans," in *The Writings and Speeches of Edmund Burke*, ed. Peter Marshall (Oxford: Clarendon, 1981), 5:41–124.

5. Ibid., 5:117–118.
6. Edmund Burke, *The Works of Edmund Burke* (London: George Bell and Sons, 1906), 3:134.
7. Ibid., 3:134–135.
8. Ibid., 3:187.
9. Ibid., 3:187.
10. Ibid., 3:188–189.
11. Ibid., 3:192.
12. Philip Stern, *The Company-State: Corporate Sovereignty and the Early Modern Foundation of the British Empire in India* (Oxford: Oxford University Press, 2011).
13. H. V. Bowen, *The Business of Empire: The East India Company and Imperial Britain, 1756–1833* (Cambridge: Cambridge University Press, 2006); Robert Travers, *Ideology and Empire in Eighteenth-Century India: The British in Bengal* (Cambridge: Cambridge University Press, 2007).
14. Adam Smith, *An Inquiry Into the Nature and Causes of the Wealth of Nations* (1776; Chicago: University of Chicago Press, 1976), 2:154.
15. Ibid., 2:157.
16. Philip Lawson, *The East India Company: A History* (London: Longman, 1993), 142.

9. The Idea of Empire

1. Michael Hardt and Antonio Negri, *Empire* (Cambridge, Mass.: Harvard University Press, 2000).
2. Niall Ferguson, *Empire: The Rise and Demise of the British World Order and the Lessons for Global Power* (New York: Basic Books, 2002).
3. Michael Ignatieff, "The Burden," *New York Times Magazine* (January 5, 2003).
4. William Langer, "The United States as a World Power," in *The Challenge to Isolation, 1937–1940* (New York: Harper, 1952), 337.
5. Joseph Conrad, *Heart of Darkness* (1899; London: Penguin, 2007).
6. E. M. Forster, *A Passage to India* (1924; New York: Knopf, 1992).
7. Nicholas B. Dirks, *The Scandal of Empire: India and the Creation of Imperial Britain* (Cambridge, Mass.: Belknap Press of Harvard University Press, 2008).
8. See David Bromwich, *A Choice of Inheritance: Self and Community from Edmund Burke to Robert Frost* (Cambridge, Mass.: Harvard University Press, 1989), 15.
9. Edmund Burke, "Speech on Fox's Indian Bill," in *The Writings and Speeches of Edmund Burke*, ed. Peter J. Marshall (Oxford: Clarendon, 1981), 5:403.
10. Ibid., 5:448.

11. Edmund Burke, *The Works of the Right Honorable Edmund Burke* (Boston, 1866), 9:349.
12. See Frederick Whelan, *Edmund Burke and India: Political Morality and Empire* (Pittsburgh, Penn.: University of Pittsburgh Press, 1996).
13. See Dirks, *Scandal of Empire*, 246–248.
14. Edward Gibbon, *The Decline and Fall of the Roman Empire* (1776–1789; New York: Modern Library, 1995).
15. Edmund Burke, "Speech on Conciliation with America," in *The Works of Edmund Burke* (London: George Bell & Sons, 1901), 1:477.
16. Edmund Burke, "Speech on a Motion Made in the House of Commons, May 7, 1782, for a Committee to Inquire into the State of the Representation of the Commons in Parliament," in *The Works of the Right Honorable Edmund Burke* (Boston, 1884), 7:95.
17. Arthur Wellesley, *The Despatches, Minutes, and Correspondence, of the Marquess Wellesley, K.G., during his Administration in India* (London, 1837), 153.
18. *Accounts and Papers of the House of Commons* (London, 1859), 18:141.
19. Ibid., 18:152.
20. Ibid.
21. Ibid., 18:147–48.
22. Ibid., 18:134.
23. Ibid., 18:139.
24. J. R. Seeley, *The Expansion of England* (1883; Chicago: University of Chicago Press, 1971).
25. Ranajit Guha, "Dominance Without Hegemony and Its Historiography," in *Dominance Without Hegemony: History and Power in Colonial India* (Cambridge, Mass.: Harvard University Press, 1997).
26. Giorgio Agamben, *Homo Sacer: Sovereign Power and Bare Life* (Stanford, Calif.: Stanford University Press, 1998); Walter Benjamin, "Theses on the Philosophy of History," in *Illuminations* (1955; New York: Harcourt, Brace, Jovanovich, 1968).

10. In Near Ruins:
Cultural Theory at the End of the Century

1. Michael Ondaatje, *The English Patient* (New York: Vintage, 1993), 18–19.
2. Ibid., 143.
3. Ibid., 240–242.
4. Ibid., 234.
5. Ibid., 261.
6. Ibid., 284–285.
7. Matthew Arnold, *Culture and Anarchy* (1869; New York: Cambridge University Press, 1990), 68.

8. Ibid., 70.

9. Ibid.

10. Ibid., 204.

11. Ibid.

12. Ibid.

13. For a social history of the uses of culture in nineteenth-century Britain, see Tony Bennett, "The Exhibitionary Complex," in *Culture/Power/History: A Reader in Contemporary Social Theory*, ed. Nicholas B. Dirks, Geoff Eley, and Sherry Ortner (Princeton, N.J.: Princeton University Press, 1994), 123–154.

14. Edmund Burke, *A Philosophical Enquiry Into the Origin of Our Ideas of the Sublime and Beautiful* (1757; New York: Oxford University Press, 1990), 36.

15. Sara Suleri, *The Rhetoric of English India* (Chicago: University of Chicago Press, 1992), 39.

16. See Hayden White, *The Content of the Form: Narrative Discourse and Historical Representation* (Baltimore, Md.: Johns Hopkins University Press, 1987), 68.

17. Thomas Weiskel, *The Romantic Sublime: Studies in the Structure and Psychology of Transcendence* (Baltimore, Md.: Johns Hopkins University Press, 1976), 19.

18. This is Suleri's argument about Burke, that his notion of the sublime was in part a confrontation with the excessive recalcitrance and difference of Indian particularities; see Suleri, *The Rhetoric of English India*.

19. See Jerome McGann, *The Romantic Ideology: A Critical Investigation* (Chicago: University of Chicago Press, 1982).

20. Immanuel Kant, *Critique of Aesthetic Judgment*, cited in Ernst Cassirer, *Kant's Life and Thought* (New Haven, Conn.: Yale University Press, 1981), 328.

21. Ibid.

22. Jerome McGann, *Social Values and Poetic Acts: The Historical Judgment of Literary Works* (Cambridge, Mass.: Harvard University Press, 1988), 36.

23. Ibid., 39–40.

24. Edmund Burke, "Reflections on the Revolution in France," in *The Writings and Speeches of Edmund Burke*, ed. L. G. Mitchell (Oxford: Oxford University Press, 1990), 8:111–112.

25. Ann Bermingham, "System, Order, and Abstraction: The Politics of English Landscape Drawing Around 1795," in *Landscape and Power*, ed. W. J. T. Mitchell (Chicago: University of Chicago Press, 1994), 78.

26. "The ruins of the Tower can be seen to this day. But he who sees them is cursed with the loss of memory. All the people on earth who go around saying, 'Who am I, Who am I,' are ones who have seen the ruins of the Tower of Babel" (*Midrash Rabbah*).

27. Walter Benjamin, *Illuminations* (New York: Schocken, 1988), 256.

28. Ibid.

29. Susan Buck-Morss, *The Origin of Negative Dialectics: Theodor W. Adorno, Walter Benjamin, and the Frankfurt Institute* (New York: Free Press, 1977), 147.

30. Benjamin, *Illuminations*, 226.

31. Ibid., 231.

32. Ibid., 234.

33. Buck-Morss, *Origin of Negative Dialectics*, 149.

34. See Max Horkheimer and Theodor Adorno, *Dialectic of Enlightenment* (New York: Herder and Herder, 1972), 120–167.

35. Ibid., 126.

36. Ibid.

37. Ibid., 127.

38. Ibid., 166–167.

39. Ibid., 131.

40. Ibid., 130.

41. Friedrich Nietzsche, *The Birth of Tragedy* (New York: Vintage, 1964), 60.

42. See Georges Bataille, *The Accursed Share: An Essay on General Economy* (New York: Zone, 1991).

43. Buck-Morss, *Origin of Negative Dialectics*, 190.

44. I refer here, of course, to the field that has been established in the wake of Edward Said's *Orientalism* (New York: Vintage, 1979); for Said's most recent treatment of the relation of imperialism to Western cultural legacies, see his *Culture and Imperialism* (New York: Knopf, 1993).

45. Benjamin writes, "The angel would like to stay, awaken the dead, and make whole what has been smashed. But a storm is blowing from paradise; it has got caught in his wings with such violence that the angel can no longer close them. This storm irresistibly propels him into the future to which his back is turned, while the pile of debris before him grows skyward. This storm is what we call progress." See *Illuminations*, 259–260.

11. G. S. Ghurye and the Politics of Sociological Knowledge

1. Govind Sadashiv Ghurye, *Caste and Race in India* (New York: Knopf, 1932).

2. See chapter 4.

3. Ibid., 166.

4. Ibid., 167.

5. Ibid, 168.

6. Ibid.

7. Ibid., 169.

8. Ibid., 162; he went even further to suggest that "perhaps, in the name of justice and efficiency, the time has come when the interests of the Brahmins have to be protected against the majority party" (291), though ultimately he dismissed this idea as well, arguing that special representation was unnecessary and harmful.

9. Ibid., 169.

10. Ibid., 163.

11. Ibid., 164.

12. Ibid., 162.

13. Ibid., 170.

14. G. S. Ghurye, *Caste and Race in India* (Bombay: Popular Prakashan, 1969), 303.

15. G. S. Ghurye, *The Scheduled Tribes* (1943; Bombay: Popular Book Depot, 1959).

16. Verrier Elwin, *The Loss of Nerve: A Comparative Study of the Contact of Peoples in the Aboriginal Areas of the Bastar State and the Central Provinces of India* (Bombay: Wagle, 1941).

17. Bernard Cohn, "The Census, Social Structure, and Objectification in South Asia," reprinted in *An Anthropologist Among the Historians and Other Essays* (Delhi: Oxford University Press, 1987).

18. G. S. Ghurye, *The Aborigines—So Called—and Their Future*, 3rd ed., *The Scheduled Tribes* (1943; Bombay: Popular Prakashan, 1963), xii.

19. Ibid.

20. Ghurye, *Caste and Race in India*, 27.

21. Ibid.

22. A. R. Momin, ed., *The Legacy of G. S. Ghurye: A Centennial Festschrift* (Bombay: Popular Prakashan, 1996), vii.

23. Ibid.

24. For example, in *Caste and Race in India*, he never raises the question of whether Muslims have caste.

25. Lloyd and Susanne Rudolph, *The Modernity of Tradition: Political Development in India* (Chicago: University of Chicago Press, 1967).

26. Ghurye, *Caste and Race in India*, 406.

27. Ibid., 407.

28. The Constitution of India, preamble.

29. The Constitution of India, art. XVI, § 4.

30. Ghurye, *Caste and Race in India*, 416.

31. Louis Dumont, *Homo Hierarchicus: An Essay on the Caste System* (Chicago: University of Chicago Press, 1970).

32. Nicholas B. Dirks, *The Hollow Crown: Ethnohistory of an Indian Kingdom* (Cambridge: Cambridge University Press, 1987).

12. South Asian Studies: Futures Past

The subject of this paper is South Asian Studies in the United States, and thus the story told here is incomplete. The paper was written for a conference on "Rethinking Area Studies," organized by David Szanton and funded by the Ford Foundation, held at New York University on April 24–26, 1998.

1. Any review of dominant trends in a field as complex and differentiated as South Asian studies is bound to be partial, to focus on certain players at the expense

of others, to critique certain configurations of knowledge while leaving others out of the picture altogether. Besides, this review is intended to highlight certain moments in the formation and working out of the field and not to provide a complete account. Nevertheless, I apologize in advance both to those who feel their work is unfairly singled out and subjected to symptomatic critique and to those who feel neglected by this highly personal and specific review.

2. For information about Brown, see Rosane Rocher's introductory essay in W. Norman Brown, *India and Indology: Selected Articles*, ed. Rosane Rocher (Delhi: Motilal Banarsidass, 1978); see also Richard J. Cohen, "Historical Notes: W. Norman Brown," in *South Asia News*, the bulletin of the South Asia Center at the University of Pennsylvania (Spring 1992): 16–18; and Jerome Bauer and Richard Cohen, "Historical Notes: Insight into the Origin of 'South Asia Regional Studies' at the University of Pennsylvania," in *South Asia News* (Autumn 1991): 14.

3. Jerome Bauer and Richard Cohen, "Historical Notes," 14.

4. See the *University of Pennsylvania Bulletin*, South Asia Regional Studies, Announcement for the Academic Year 1949–50 and Summer Session, 1949.

5. Although he also notes that this was the first summer session, so perhaps he was thinking of the summer of 1947. See Robert Crane, "Preface on Richard L. Park," in *Region and Nation in India*, ed. Paul Wallace (New Delhi: Oxford and IBH Publishing Co., 1985).

6. Ibid., 7.

7. See Rocher, "Biographical Sketch," in Rocher, ed., *India and Indology*, xviii.

8. Ibid.

9. W. Norman Brown, *The United States and India and Pakistan* (Cambridge, Mass.: Harvard University Press, 1953), 24.

10. Ibid.

11. Ibid.

12. See Sheldon Pollock, "The Death of Sanskrit," *Comparative Studies in Society and History* 43, no. 2 (2001): 392–426.

13. Brown, *United States and India and Pakistan*, 30.

14. Ibid., 130.

15. Ibid., 316.

16. The reference here is to Public Law 480, which even more significantly used loan repayment in the nonconvertible rupee currency for the development of library resources on South Asia in twelve participating U.S. libraries, including ten university libraries, the New York Public Library, and the Library of Congress.

17. Redfield had done his Ph.D. under Robert Park, the great Chicago sociologist, and had taught in the anthropology department since 1928. For a thorough study of Redfield's life and career, see Clifford D. Wilcox, "Encounters with Modernity: Robert Redfield and the Problem of Social Change," Ph.D. diss., University of Michigan, 1997.

18. Cited in ibid., 210.

19. Largely because Hutchins left the University of Chicago at that point and became associate director of the Ford Foundation.

20. Robert Redfield, "How the American Got His Character," *Ethics* 60 (October 1949).

21. Mandelbaum was the first American social scientist to do field research in India. For an account of his career, see Milton Singer, "David Mandelbaum and the Rise of South Asian Studies: A Reminiscence," in *Dimensions of Social Life: Essays in Honor of David G. Mandelbaum*, ed. Paul Hockings (Amsterdam: Mouton de Gruyter, 1987), 1–9.

22. M. N. Srinivas, *Religion and Society Among the Coorgs of South India* (Oxford: Clarendon, 1952).

23. McKim Marriott, ed., *Village India: Studies in the Little Community* (Chicago: Chicago University Press, 1955).

24. As at Penn, Yale, Columbia, Hopkins, and Chicago, Sanskritists arrived long before South Asian Area Studies. Arthur W. Ryder was appointed to a chair in Sanskrit at Berkeley in 1905 in the classics department. Murray Emeneau succeeded him as Sanskritist in 1940, and went on to become the key person in the establishment of the Linguistics Department at Berkeley in 1953. Emeneau, who did fieldwork in the Nilgiris of southern India and studied Dravidian philology, collaborated with Mandelbaum in the establishment of a Center for South Asian Studies in 1957, along with Richard Park, as mentioned above.

25. While in 1991, the average percentage of anthropologists among all disciplinary specialists in Asian studies was only 9.6 (and only 5.0 for China and inner Asia and 6.5 for Northeastern Asia), the percentage of anthropologists for South Asia was 14, surpassed only by Southeast Asianists, where anthropology was even more dominant, at 25 percent. For Eastern Asian studies overall, history was the dominant discipline; for South Asia, religion and philosophy claimed greater proportions of scholars than anywhere else, followed closely by history, political science, and anthropology.

26. Where he studied under Morris Opler, who ran a village studies project and trained a number of the early postwar anthropologists in the United States, including Pauline Kolenda, John Hitchcock, and Michael Mahar.

27. The Ford Foundation gave the University of Chicago 5.4 million dollars for area studies in the 1960s, including $1,786,000 specifically earmarked for South Asia.

28. Lloyd and Susanne Rudolph, *The Modernity of Tradition: Political Development in India* (Chicago: University of Chicago Press, 1967).

29. Bernard S. Cohn, "Society and Social Change Under the Raj," in *An Anthropologist Among the Historians and Other Essays* (Delhi and New York: Oxford University Press, 1987), 195.

30. See for example J. H. Broomfield, *Elite Conflict in a Plural Society: Twentieth-*

Century Bengal (Berkeley: University of California Press, 1968); Eugene Irschick, *Politics and Social Conflict in South India: The Non-Brahmin Movement and Tamil Separatism, 1916–1929* (Berkeley: University of California Press, 1969); S. N. Mukherjee, *Calcutta: Essays in Urban History* (Cambridge: Cambridge University Press, 1970); John Greenfield Leonard, "Kandukuri Viresalingam, 1848–1919: A Biography of an Indian Social Reformer," Ph.D. diss., University of Wisconsin-Madison, 1970; Peter J. Marshall, *Problems of Empire: Britain and India, 1757–1813* (London: Allen and Unwin, 1968); David Kopf, *British Orientalism and the Bengal Renaissance: The Dynamics of Indian Modernization, 1773–1835* (Calcutta: Firma K. L. Mukhopadhyay, 1969); Ronald Inden, *Marriage and Rank in Bengali Culture: A History of Caste and Clan in Middle Period Bengal* (Berkeley: University of California Press, 1976); Tom Kessinger, *Vilyatpur, 1848–1968: Social and Economic Change in a North Indian Village* (Berkeley: University of California Press, 1974).

31. Cohn, "Society and Social Change Under the Raj," 195.
32. Cohn's major works include *An Anthropologist Among the Historians and Other Essays* (Delhi: Oxford University Press, 1987) and his more recent *Colonialism and Its Forms of Knowledge: The British in India* (Princeton, N.J.: Princeton University Press, 1996); see also "The Command of Grammar and the Grammar of Command," in *Subaltern Studies*, ed. Ranajit Guha (Delhi: Oxford University Press, 1985), 4:276–329.
33. Milton Singer, "Introduction," in *When a Great Tradition Modernizes* (Chicago: University of Chicago, 1972), 3.
34. David Schneider, *American Kinship: A Cultural Account* (Englewood Cliffs, N.J.: Prentice Hall, 1968); Ronald Inden, "Marriage and Rank in Bengali Culture: A Social History of the Brahmans and Kayasthas in Middle-Period Bengal," Ph.D. diss., University of Chicago, 1972.
35. Four of the first workshops to be sponsored by the Social Science Research Council, beginning a long tradition of conferences, seminars, and workshops, were organized around Marriott's ethnosociology project. On the one hand, Marriott worked to diagram the major dimensions of a Hindu ethnosociology; on the other, philosophers such as Karl Potter sought to explore the philosophical dimensions of major Hindu themes, for example the question of Karma.
36. Thomas Trautmann, "Marriage and Rank in Bengali Culture [review of *Kinship in Bengali Culture*, by Ronald Inden and Ralph Nicholas]," *Journal of Asian Studies* 39, no. 3 (1980): 519–521.
37. Barbara Metcalf, *Islamic Revival in British India, Deoband, 1860–1900* (Princeton, N.J.: Princeton University Press, 1982); John Richards, *Mughal Administration in Golconda* (Oxford: Clarendon, 1975); Richard Eaton, *Sufis of Bijapur, 1300–1700: Social Roles of Sufis in Medieval India* (Princeton, N.J.: Princeton University Press, 1978); Richard Barnett, *North India Between Empires: Awadh, the Mughals, and the British, 1720–1801* (Berkeley: University

of California Press, 1980); David Lelyveld, *Aligarh's First Generation: Muslim Solidarity in British India* (Princeton, N.J.: Princeton University Press, 1978).

38. Among Stein's own works see, for example, *Peasant State and Society in Medieval South India* (Delhi: Oxford University Press, 1980); *Thomas Munro: The Origins of the Colonial State and His Vision of Empire* (Delhi and New York: Oxford University Press, 1985); and *Vijayanagara* (Cambridge: Cambridge University Press, 1989).

39. Ludden's advisor was Tom Kessinger, an anthropological historian who had been trained by Bernard Cohn at Chicago and who had written an ethnohistorical study of social relations within a North Indian village between the mid-nineteenth and mid-twentieth centuries, titled *Vilyatpur, 1848–1968: Social and Economic Change in a North Indian Village.*

40. Sanjay Subrahmanyam, *Symbols of Substance: Court and State in Nāyaka-Period Tamilnadu* (Delhi: Oxford University Press, 1992).

41. Edward Said, *Orientalism* (New York: Pantheon, 1978).

42. See, for example, David Kopf, "Hermeneutics Versus History," *Journal of Asian Studies* 89, no. 3 (1980): 495–506.

43. The volume that ultimately came out of this seminar was Carol Breckenridge and Peter van der Veer, eds., *Orientalism and the Postcolonial Predicament: Perspectives on South Asia* (Philadelphia: University of Pennsylvania Press, 1993).

44. Paul Kennedy, *Preparing for the Twenty-first Century* (New York: Random House, 1993); Robert Bates, "Area Studies and the Discipline: A Useful Controversy?" *PS: Political Science and Politics* 30, no. 2 (1997): 166–169.

45. Between 1979 and 1986 SAPE held fourteen conferences, some co-sponsored by the Indian Council of Social Science Research and the Ford Foundation with additional support from NSF. According to Maureen Patterson, "With its focus on development in post-Independent India, the SAPE planners wanted to go beyond a purely economic approach and 'envisioned a research alliance' to 'approximate a more contextual understanding of economic processes' (S. Rudolph, 2). They looked for 'anthropologically oriented scholars attuned to 'indigenous conceptual systems as bases for understanding, explaining, and interpreting South Asian institutions and behavior' . . . And the planners looked for economists. . . . Thus the project assembled anthropologists, economists and political scientists plus a few historians and proceeded to delineate three major areas to work on: . . . relationships between local power structures and agricultural productivity; . . . problems of health and nutrition at the household and family levels; societal responses to crises, or order and anomie in South Asian history and culture." Maureen Patterson, "South Asian Studies: Our Increasing Knowledge and Understanding," mimeographed manuscript (January 1988), 21.

46. Appadurai's early work was on the history of temples in southern India, but in recent years he made important and enormously influential arguments—

basing many of them in relation to South Asia—for the globalization of academic inquiry. See his *Modernity at Large: Cultural Dimensions of Globalization* (Minneapolis: University of Minnesota Press, 1996).

47. There are, however, significant exceptions. Perhaps the most important historian of Pakistan is Ayesha Jalal, whose book *The Sole Spokesman: Jinnah, the Muslim League, and the Demand for Pakistan* (Cambridge: Cambridge University Press, 1985), is a major contribution to the rewriting of the history of partition.

48. Stanley Tambiah at Harvard, Gananath Obeyesekere at Princeton, Valentine Daniel at Columbia, and H. L. Seneviratne at Virginia. All of these figures have been known not just for their excellent empirical studies in Sri Lanka, among other places, but also for their theoretical power and influence. For example, Tambiah has made important contributions to political anthropology, the anthropology of Buddhism, and the study of ethnic violence. See his *Sri Lanka: Ethnic Fratricide and the Dismantling of Democracy* (Chicago: University of Chicago Press, 1986); *Buddhism Betrayed? Religion, Politics, and Violence in Sri Lanka* (Chicago: University of Chicago Press, 1992); and *Leveling Crowds: Ethnonationalist Conflicts and Collective Violence in South Asia* (Berkeley: University of California Press, 1996). Obeyeskere is one of the most creative psychological anthropologists practicing today and raised many eyebrows when he bested Marshall Sahlins in a debate over Captain Cook in *The Apotheosis of Captain Cook: European Mythmaking in the Pacific* (Princeton, N.J.: Princeton University Press, 1992). Valentine Daniel, in addition to his early ethnosociological work and current work on the anthropology of violence, among many other things, is a specialist in the philosophy of Charles Saunders Pierce. See in particular his *Charred Lullabies: Chapters in the Anthropology of Violence* (Princeton, N.J.: Princeton University, 1996).

49. Cornell is a major center for Nepal studies, though students have worked in a number of other institutions, among them Michigan, Washington, Columbia, and Virginia.

13. Franz Boas and the American University: A Personal Account

Read April 25, 2008, as part of the symposium "Cultural Subjects and Objects: The Legacy of Franz Boas and Its Futures in Anthropology, Academe, and Human Rights," for the annual meeting of the American Philosophical Society in Philadelphia. In preparing this lecture, I drew especially from the following works: George W. Stocking Jr., ed., *A Franz Boas Reader: The Shaping of American Anthropology, 1883–1911* (Chicago: University of Chicago Press, 1974); George W. Stocking Jr., *Race, Culture, and Evolution: Essays in the History of Anthropology* (New York: The Free Press, 1968); Lee D. Baker, *From Savage to Negro: Anthropology and the Construction of Race, 1896–1954* (Berkeley: University of California Press, 1998); Douglas Cole, "'The Value of a Person Lies in His *Herzensbildung*': Franz Boas' Baffin Island Letter-Diary, 1883–1884," in *Observers Observed: Essays on Ethnographic Fieldwork*, ed. George W. Stocking Jr. (Madison: University of Wisconsin Press, 1983); and Regna Darnell, "The Development of American Anthropology, 1879–1920," Ph.D. diss., University of Pennsylvania, 1969.

1. Franz Boas, "The Study of Geography," *Science* n.s. 9, no. 210 (1887): 137–141.
2. Franz Boas, letter to the editor, *Science* n.s. 9, no. 228 (1887): 588.
3. E. E. Evans-Pritchard, *Anthropology and History: A Lecture Delivered in the University of Manchester* (Manchester: Manchester University Press, 1961), 20–21.
4. Stocking, ed., *Franz Boas Reader*, 291.
5. Ibid., 295.
6. Ibid., 296.
7. Ibid., 295.
8. Baker, *From Savage to Negro*.
9. Stocking, ed., *Franz Boas Reader*, 331–332.
10. Franz Boas, *Race and Democratic Society* (1945; New York: Biblo and Tannen, 1969), 169–170.
11. Ibid., 170.
12. Stocking, ed., *Franz Boas Reader*, 334.
13. Stocking, ed., *Franz Boas Reader*, 336–337.
14. Boas, *Race and Democratic Society*, 204.
15. Ibid., 207.
16. Ibid.

14. Scholars and Spies: Worldly Knowledge and the Predicament of the University

1. Franz Boas, "Scientists as Spies," letter to the editor, *Nation* (October 10, 1919): 797; reprinted in George W. Stocking Jr., ed., *A Franz Boas Reader: The Shaping of American Anthropology, 1883–1911* (Chicago: University of Chicago Press, 1974), 336.
2. Barry Katz, *Foreign Intelligence: Research and Analysis in the Office of Strategic Services, 1942–1945* (Cambridge, Mass.: Harvard University Press, 1989), 3.
3. Ibid., 7.
4. Ibid., 22.
5. Ibid., 8.
6. Ruth Benedict, *The Chrysanthemum and the Sword: Patterns of Japanese Culture* (Boston: Houghton Mifflin, 1946).
7. Philip Mosely, "The Growth of Russian Studies," in *American Research on Russia*, ed. Harold Fisher (Bloomington: Indiana University Press, 1959), 8.

8. Cited in Jerome Bauer and Richard Cohen, "Historical Notes: Insight Into the Origin of 'South Asia Regional Studies' at the University of Pennsylvania," in *South Asia News* (Autumn 1991): 14.

9. See the *University of Pennsylvania Bulletin*, South Asia Regional Studies, Announcement for the Academic Year 1949–50 and Summer Session, 1949.

10. W. Norman Brown, *The United States and India and Pakistan* (Cambridge, Mass.: Harvard University Press, 1953), 24.

15. The Opening of the American Mind

1. Allan Bloom, *The Closing of the American Mind: How Higher Education Has Failed Democracy and Impoverished the Souls of Today's Students* (New York: Simon and Schuster, 1987); Camille Paglia, "Ask Camille," *Salon.com* (July 22, 1997), http://web.archive.org/web/http://www.salon.com/july97/columnists/paglia2970722.html.

2. Roger Kimball, "The Groves of Ignorance [review of *The Closing of the American Mind*, by Allan Bloom]," *New York Times* (April 5, 1987).

3. Alexander Nehamas, "Swallowing Goldfish [review of *The Closing of the American Mind*, by Allan Bloom]," *London Review of Books* 9, no. 22 (December 10, 1987).

4. Martha Nussbaum, "Undemocratic Vistas [review of *The Closing of the American Mind*, by Allan Bloom]," *New York Review of Books* (November 5, 1987).

5. Lawrence Levine, *The Opening of the American Mind: Canons, Culture, and History* (Boston: Beacon, 1996).

6. Thomas G. West, "Allan Bloom and America," *Claremont Institute* (November 19, 2007), http://www.claremont.org/basicPageArticles/allan-bloom-and-america/.

7. Saul Bellow, *Ravelstein* (New York: Viking, 2000).

8. Bloom, *Closing of the American Mind*, 38.

9. Ibid., 39.

10. Ibid., 28–29.

11. Ibid., 43.

12. Ibid.

13. Ibid., 40.

14. "Toward a Hidden God," *Time* (April 8, 1966).

15. Walter Benjamin, *Illuminations* (New York: Schocken, 1988), 256.

16. Edmund Burke, "Speech on the Opening of the Impeachment," in *The Writings and Speeches of Edmund Burke*, ed. Peter J. Marshall (Oxford: Clarendon, 1991), 6:316–317.

17. Reprinted in Hanna Holborn Gray, *Searching for Utopia: Universities and Their Histories* (Berkeley: University of California Press, 2012).

18. Ibid., 91.

19. Mark Taylor, *Crisis on Campus: A Bold Plan for Reforming Our Colleges and Universities* (New York: Knopf, 2010); Andrew Delbanco, *College: What It Was, Is, and Should Be* (Princeton, N.J.: Princeton University Press, 2012).
20. Gray, *Searching for Utopia*, 85.
21. Ibid., 84.
22. Ibid., 60.
23. Richard Hofstadter, *Anti-Intellectualism in American Life* (New York: Knopf, 1963).

Permissions

"Annals of the Archive: Ethnographic Notes on the Sources of History." In *From the Margins: Historical Anthropology and Its Futures*, ed. Brian Axel, 47–65. Durham, N.C.: Duke University Press, 2002.

"Colin Mackenzie: Autobiography of an Archive." In *The Madras School of Orientalism: Producing Knowledge in Colonial South Asia*, ed. Thomas R. Trautmann, 29–47. New Delhi: Oxford University Press, 2009.

Preface to the second edition of *The Hollow Crown: Ethnohistory of an Indian Kingdom*, xxix–xxxiii. Ann Arbor: University of Michigan Press, 1993.

"Castes of Mind." *Representations* no. 37 (Winter 1992): 56–78.

"Ritual and Resistance: Subversion as a Social Fact." In *Contesting Power: Resistance and Everyday Social Relations in South Asia*, ed. Douglas Haynes and Gyan Prakash, 213–238. Delhi: Oxford University Press, 1991; Berkeley: University of California Press, 1992.

"The Policing of Tradition: Colonialism and Anthropology in Southern India." In *Comparative Studies in Society and History* 39, no. 1 (January 1997): 182–212.

"Imperial Sovereignty." In *Imperial Formations*, ed. Carole McGranahan, Peter Perdue, and Ann Stoler, 311–340. Santa Fe: School for Advanced Research Press; Oxford: James Currey, 2007.

"In Near Ruins: Cultural Theory at the End of the Century." Introductory essay to *In Near Ruins: Cultural Theory at the End of the Century*, ed. Nicholas Dirks, 1–18. Minneapolis: University of Minnesota Press, 1998.

"G. S. Ghurye and the Politics of Sociological Knowledge." First G. S. Ghurye Memorial Lecture, University of Mumbai, January 2010.

"South Asian Studies: Futures Past." In *The Politics of Knowledge: Area Studies and the Disciplines*, ed. David Szanton, 341–385. Berkeley and Los Angeles: University of California Press, 2004.

"Franz Boas and the American University: A Personal Account." *Proceedings of the American Philosophical Society* 154, no. 1 (March 2010): 31–39.

Index

GPSR Authorized Representative: Easy Access System Europe, Mustamäe tee
50, 10621 Tallinn, Estonia, gpsr.requests@easproject.com

www.ingramcontent.com/pod-product-compliance
Lightning Source LLC
Chambersburg PA
CBHW021845020426
42334CB00013B/189

9 780231 169677